Platonism and Naturalism

Platonism and Naturalism

The Possibility of Philosophy

Lloyd P. Gerson

Cornell University Press

Ithaca and London

Copyright © 2020 by Cornell University

All rights reserved. Except for brief quotations in a review, this book, or parts thereof, must not be reproduced in any form without permission in writing from the publisher. For information, address Cornell University Press, Sage House, 512 East State Street, Ithaca, New York 14850. Visit our website at cornellpress.cornell.edu.

First published 2020 by Cornell University Press

Library of Congress Cataloging-in-Publication Data

Names: Gerson, Lloyd P., author.
Title: Platonism and naturalism : the possibility of philosophy / Lloyd P. Gerson.
Description: 1st edition. | Ithaca [New York] : Cornell University Press, 2020. | Includes bibliographical references and index.
Identifiers: LCCN 2019018748 (print) | LCCN 2019019427 (ebook) | ISBN 9781501747267 (pdf) | ISBN 9781501747274 (epub/mobi) | ISBN 9781501747250 | ISBN 9781501747250 (cloth)
Subjects: LCSH: Plato—Influence. | Platonists. | Naturalism.
Classification: LCC B395 (ebook) | LCC B395 .G47 2019 (print) | DDC 184—dc23
LC record available at https://lccn.loc.gov/2019018748

Aslı
אשת חיל

Contents

ACKNOWLEDGMENTS ix

PART 1. PLATO'S REJECTION OF NATURALISM

1. INTRODUCTION 3
2. PLATONISM VS. NATURALISM 15
   2.1. *What Is Platonism?* 15
   2.2. *What Is Naturalism?* 22
   2.3. *Methodological, Philosophical Naturalism* 29
   2.4. *A Rapprochement?* 32
3. PLATO'S CRITIQUE OF NATURALISM 38
   3.1. *Some Hermeneutical Assumptions* 38
   3.2. *The Turn from Naturalism to Metaphysics* 43
   3.3. *Socrates's "Autobiography" in* Phaedo 48
   3.4. Republic *on the Subject Matter of Philosophy* 65
   3.5. Theaetetus *and* Sophist *on the Subject Matter of Philosophy* 71
4. PLATO ON BEING AND KNOWING 76
   4.1. *Forms as Explanatory Entities* 76
   4.2. *Eternity and Time* 88
   4.3. *Nominalism and Its Connection to Relativism* 99
   4.4. *The Nature and the Possibility of Knowledge* 108
   4.5. *Some Exigencies of Knowledge and Belief* 116

5. The Centrality of the Idea of the Good in the Platonic System (1) — 120
  5.1. The Idea of the Good, Unhypothetical First Principle of All   120
  5.2. First Principles in Parmenides   127
  5.3. First Principles in Sophist   135
  5.4. First Principles in Philebus   147
  5.5. First Principles in Timaeus   152
  5.6. Aristotle's Account of First Principles in Plato   155

6. The Centrality of the Idea of the Good in the Platonic System (2) — 163
  6.1. The Form of the Good and the Idea of the Good   163
  6.2. Virtue, Knowledge, and the Good   173
  6.3. Platonic Ethics without the Idea of the Good   179
  6.4. The Good, Ethical Prescriptions, and Integrative Unity   183
  6.5. Eros and the Good   187

Part 2. The Platonic Project

7. Aristotle the Platonist — 197
  7.1. Introduction   197
  7.2. Aristotle on the Subject Matter of Philosophy   198
  7.3. The Immateriality of Thought   209
  7.4. The Causality of the First Principle   220

8. Plotinus the Platonist — 224
  8.1. The Platonic System   224
  8.2. Critique of Stoicism   235
  8.3. Platonic and Stoic Wisdom   240

9. Proclus and Trouble in Paradise — 247
  9.1. The Dynamics of the Platonic System   247
  9.2. A Crack in the System?   250
  9.3. Damascius   254

10. Concluding Reflections — 261

Bibliography — 267

General Index — 285

Index Locorum — 293

Acknowledgments

Versions of some of the material in this book were delivered as lectures and conference presentations at Bar-Ilan University; Hameline University; University of California at Berkeley; Temple University; Durham University; the International Plato Society meeting in Brasilia, Brazil; Cambridge University; UNAM, Mexico City; Universidad Panamericana, Mexico City; Duquesne University; and the University of Chicago. I am grateful to the audiences at these presentations for their spirited engagement with my arguments.

Among my colleagues and friends who have read all or parts of drafts of this book are Francesco Fronterotta, Franco Ferrari, Brad Inwood, and Eric Perl. Their thoughtful and collegial disagreement with some of my ideas were as welcome as their warm encouragement. I am especially grateful to Nicholas D. Smith, who read the entire book and made extensive critical comments, all of which prompted me to make changes and additions (and a few tactical subtractions). I am grateful to an anonymous reader for Cornell University Press who prompted me to clarify some highly compressed and allusive arguments.

In this book, all translations are my own except where noted.

The work was completed with the generous support of the Social Sciences and Humanities Research Council of Canada.

Platonism and Naturalism

PART 1

Plato's Rejection of Naturalism

CHAPTER 1

Introduction

Some forty years ago, the late Richard Rorty wrote a provocative book titled *Philosophy and the Mirror of Nature*.[1] In that book, and in many subsequent books and essays, Rorty advanced the astonishing thesis that Platonism and philosophy are more or less identical. The point of insisting on this identification is the edifying inference Rorty thinks is to be drawn from it: If you find Platonism unacceptable, then you ought to abandon philosophy or, to put it slightly less starkly, you ought to abandon philosophy as it has been practiced for some 2,500 years. This is not, of course, to say that those trained in philosophy have nothing to contribute to our culture or society. It is just that they have no specific knowledge to contribute, knowledge of a distinct subject matter. What I and many others initially found to be incredible about the thesis that Platonism and philosophy are identical is that almost all critics of Plato and Platonism, from Aristotle onward, made their criticisms from a philosophical perspective. For example, to reject Plato's Forms was to do so on the basis of another, putatively superior, account of predication. How, then, could Rorty maintain that the rejection of Platonism is necessarily at the same time the rejection of philosophy? Rorty's insightful response to this question is that those who rejected Platonism did so from what we ought to recognize as a fundamentally Platonic perspective. That is, they shared with Plato basic assumptions or principles, the questioning of which was never the starting point of any objection. According to Rorty's approach, Platonism should not, therefore, be identified

---

1. See Rorty 1979, esp. pt. 3.

with a particular philosophical position that is taken to follow from these principles, but more generally with the principles themselves. Hence, a rejection of Platonism is really a rejection of the principles shared by most philosophers up to the present. It is from these principles, Rorty thought, that numerous pernicious distinctions arose. As he puts it in the introduction to his collection of essays entitled *Philosophy and Social Hope* (published in 2000), "Most of what I have written in the last decade consists of attempts to tie my social hopes—hopes for a global, cosmopolitan, democratic, egalitarian, classless, casteless society—with my antagonism towards Platonism." By "Platonism" Rorty means the "set of philosophical distinctions (appearance/reality, matter/mind, made/found, sensible/intellectual, etc.)" that he thinks continue to bedevil the thinking of philosophers as well as those who look to philosophy for some proprietary knowledge. Other important Platonic dualisms elsewhere rejected by Rorty are knowledge/belief, cognitional/volitional, and subject/object. These distinctions (among others) are the consequences inferred from the principles that together constitute Platonism.

Rorty maintained that the fundamental divide between Platonists (whether self-declared or not) and anti-Platonists is that the former believe that it is possible to represent truth in language and thought whereas the latter do not.[2] Rorty's antirepresentationalism thus extends far beyond a putative subject matter for philosophy. It leads him to reject the possibility of achieving the goal of truthful representations in the natural and social sciences generally.[3] Hence, his argument is basically an epistemological one, or anti-epistemological, if you will. The manner in which Rorty has posed the problem facing any anti-antirepresentationalist makes its solution impossible—for Plato or for anyone else. If all our encounters with the

---

2. See Rorty 2001, 2.

3. Cf. ibid, 8, "anti-representationalists [of which Rorty is one] see no sense in which physics is more independent of our human peculiarities than astrology or literary criticism." See also Price (2011, 12–16), whose antirepresentationalism is mainly a refinement of Rorty's view, although Price has a more optimistic view of philosophy than does Rorty. In chap. 9, Price distinguishes "object naturalism" and "subject naturalism," the former (mistakenly) committed to representationalism and the latter not. Price's wish to detach Naturalism from representationalism is ultimately a consequence of his adherence to the Humean claim that human beings are part of the natural world, in which case our capacity for (accurate) representations is at least compromised or endangered by advances in integrating human beings into the natural world scientifically. The position for which he argues he dubs "global expressivism." Price wants to treat claims to representation as a subject for "linguistic anthropology" which I take it is very close to what he regards as the sole subject matter of philosophy. As for natural science, Price wants to cast this in a rigorously nonrepresentationalist framework, meaning roughly that the deliverances of natural science can aspire to be nothing more than accounts of a linguistic community's engagement with our environment nonrepresentationally speaking. He calls his Naturalism "subject naturalism" as opposed to "object naturalism," which is in one way or another committed to a criterion for distinguishing better and worse representations of nature. See also Price 2008.

putative external reality are representational—whether these representations be conceptual or linguistic—then there is no neutral, nonrelativistic conceptual or linguistic perspective from which to ascertain the accuracy of our original representations. Rorty is so confident that the entire history of epistemology is wedded to some form of representationalism thus construed that he thinks that the unsolvable problem for representationalism can provide an inscription for epistemology's tombstone.[4] On Rorty's account, the differences among philosophers (and scientists) are far less significant than their shared commitment to representationalism. Hence, to identify Platonism and philosophy is not to fail to acknowledge that there are people who have called themselves philosophers and anti- or non-Platonists. It is, rather, to claim that what binds them together is a shared error in principle, an error that is most egregiously and fundamentally found in Plato and all those who follow in his path. Overcoming this error is tantamount to overcoming the enchantment of Platonism, that is, of philosophy.

Rorty's rejection of all types of representationalism does not permit him to distinguish the sciences from philosophy in any clear way. But his insistence on the dualisms that bedevil Platonism does suggest a subject matter for philosophy, broadly speaking. By "philosophy" Rorty means "systematic" thought as opposed to what he calls "edifying" thought.[5] The manner in which Rorty uses the word "systematic" is broader than the use according to which one might say that Hegel is a systematic philosopher and Hume is not. By "systematic" he means "having a distinct content or subject matter." Thus, anyone who thinks that it is possible for a philosopher to discover a single truth about the world requiring one or more of the above dualisms is embracing a distinctive or special type of error. She is entrapped by the lure of the systematic, that is, of a distinctive content or subject matter for philosophy.

Most of those who would reject a distinct subject matter for philosophy do not share Rorty's disdain for the sciences as a locus of truth about the world. The terms "Naturalist" and "Naturalism" are today embraced mainly

---

4. See Rorty 1979, esp. pt. 2. Many critics of Rorty, generally sympathetic to his approach, have struggled mightily to express Rorty's insights in a way that does not blatantly and unequivocally make the extramental world drop out of the epistemological equation. See, e.g., McDowell 2000, 109–124; M. Williams 2000, 191–213; Putnam 2000, 81–87; and Gutting 2003, 41–60.

5. See Rorty 1979, 5, 365–372, on the distinction between "systematic" and "edifying" philosophy. It is the former that Rorty wants to reject. Insofar as virtually all systematic philosophy has had recourse to some or all of the above dualisms, they can be said to be inheritors of Platonism or collaborators in a hopelessly corrupt intellectual project. For Rorty, natural science since the seventeenth century has been the largely misguided inheritor of the fundamental Greek philosophical error of thinking that accurate representations of the world are possible or even that meaningful content can even be given to the concept of "accurate representation."

by those who in general have no compunctions or guilt feelings about their promotion of certain representations over others, especially in the natural sciences. But self-declared Naturalists divide over whether philosophy has a distinct subject matter. Nevertheless, even among those Naturalists who insist that philosophy is not replaceable by the natural sciences, there is no one who thinks that this subject matter is as Plato conceives of it.[6] Plato tells us in his *Republic* in a clear and unambiguous way that the subject matter of philosophy is "that which is perfectly or completely real (τὸ παντελῶς ὄν)," that is, the intelligible world and all that it contains, namely, immaterial Forms or essences, souls, intellect, and a superordinate first principle of all, the Idea of the Good.[7] If Rorty is right, then the denial of the existence of this content is the rejection of philosophy.[8] Any form of Naturalism that does not endorse Rorty's strictures against representationalism is still going to insist that if there is, indeed, a subject matter for philosophy, it cannot be Plato's. In fact, the most consistent form of Naturalism in my opinion will hold that with the abandonment of the Platonic subject matter must go the abandonment of a distinct subject matter for philosophy. Indicative of what

---

6. Quine (1981, 21) takes philosophy as continuous with science, by which I take him to mean that the subject matter of philosophy is not different from that of science. For Quine, this is the result of the rejection of the analytic/synthetic distinction. See Morris 2018, 403–411. See also the famous gnomic utterance of Sellars (1963, 173): "Science is the measure of all things, of what is that it is, and of what is not that it is not." Sellars thought that making science the measure inverted Protagoras's point about humans being the measure. But, of course, it does no such thing since science is no less of a human product than are the ethical and political ideas that Protagoras had in mind. Sellars's Naturalism is rooted in what he calls "psychological nominalism," the view that all awareness of "abstract entities" is "a linguistic affair." See 1997, §29.

7. See *Rep.* 476A–480B. Cf. *Soph.* 254A8–10. I shall have much more to say about the *Republic* passage in chap. 3. My use of the loaded word "world" here is not intended to prejudge the contested matters regarding the separation of Forms. It is, however, intended to denote a distinct subject matter as is indicated by the use of the word "world" in "the musical world" or "the business world" or "the football world." See *Phd.* 79A6: δύο εἴδη τῶν ὄντων (two kinds of beings); *Rep.* 508C1, 517B3: νοητὸς τόπος (intelligible place), 509D1–3. I am glad to echo the caution of Reale (1997, 130) that "two worlds" should not be taken to suggest that the intelligible world contains "superthings" that are somehow physically separate from the sensible world. The primary meaning of "separate" for the intelligible world is "ontological independence." That is, the intelligible world could exist without the sensible world, but not vice versa. Here, "separate" is synonymous with prior in "nature or substance (φύσιν καὶ οὐσίαν)." See Aristotle, *Meta.* Δ 11, 1019a1–4.

8. See Rorty 1979, introduction, where he distinguishes Philosophy (with a capital "P") from philosophy, the former indicating a distinctive subject matter and the latter having several uses, including probably work on the theoretical foundations of a science. But Rorty is skeptical even about "philosophy" used in this way on the grounds that it presumes an illicit notion of representationalism according to which "good" or "correct" science achieves good or correct representations of reality. For Rorty, what is left is the philosopher as cultural critic or "all-purpose intellectual." Is it churlish to point out that this criticism logically entails objective standards, without which such criticism is indistinguishable from personal taste? Why is the "casteless society, etc." for which Rorty hopes superior to a totalitarian class society?

is at least the unclear putative non-Platonic subject matter for philosophy is the fact that there is virtually no agreement about its identity. How can there be a real subject matter for philosophy if no one agrees on exactly what it is? Even if, for example, one maintains that metaphysics—Naturalistically conceived—has a subject matter, it is doubtful that, say, any moral or political philosopher would identify philosophy with that. The disunity of subject matters among those who believe that philosophy has a subject matter but that it is not Plato's is, as I will try to show below, one reason for thinking, with Rorty, that there is no real non-Platonic subject matter for philosophy and so no subject about which philosophers strive to acquire knowledge.

The inclination to dismiss this view is, one might suppose, easily supported by adducing, for example, the philosophy of physics or of biology. There is, it will be said, nothing necessarily Platonic about their content, though the content is distinctly philosophical. The use of the word "philosophy" for the theoretical foundation of a natural science in fact goes back to Aristotle. He distinguishes "first philosophy (πρωτὴ φιλοσοφία)" and (implicitly) "second philosophy." The former is in line with Plato's position regarding knowledge of the intelligible world, the latter with the theoretical foundation of natural science.[9] Aristotle argues that the science of immovable being is the science of being qua being, that is, the science of all being. How exactly this is so remains a fundamental crux in Aristotelian scholarship. Here, I only wish to emphasize that Aristotle does not seem to suppose that the distinctness of the subject matter of first philosophy, namely, immobile being, means that the science of immobile being will have nothing to say about mobile being, among other things. In this, Aristotle is following Plato in his sketch of what philosophy is. Plato says that not only is the philosopher devoted to the intelligible world or to perfect being, but he is also able to see the things that participate in it for what they are.[10] I take it that this is just an application of the general principle ubiquitous throughout the dialogues that philosophy is relevant to our understanding of the sensible world, even though it is a different sort of study (μάθησις) with a different subject matter.

Stoicism provides an illuminating perspective on the Aristotelian claim. Since Stoics deny in principle the existence of anything not composed by physical nature, they would have to face the Aristotelian challenge that, for them, physics must be first philosophy. And though Stoics conceive of the principles of physics differently from Aristotle, it is indeed the case that they do not recognize a science distinct from the science of nature. Stoic

---

9. See Aristotle, *Meta.* E 1, 1026a15–32, and chap. 7, sec. 7.1.
10. See *Rep.* 476C7–D2. The point is that he knows sensibles as participants in the intelligible world in contrast to the lovers of sights and sounds who do not know this, rather taking sensibles as if they were the locus of true being.

metaphysics is just Stoic physics; they do not recognize a science of being qua being or of the intelligible as opposed to natural world. Is Stoicism, then, merely edifying philosophy? I would say that the history of Stoicism divides between those who, like the early Stoics, examined the principles of nature and those who, like the Roman Stoics, aimed to be edifying. The former were in principle doing nothing different from the theoreticians of early natural science like Aristoxenus and Eratosthenes and the latter were doing nothing different from psychotherapy. These are not intended to be pejorative comparisons. I aim only to offer some confirmation for Rorty's hypothesis that Platonism is philosophy and anti-Platonism is antiphilosophy. This ultrasharp division will have its most interesting results, I think, when, keeping it in mind, we consider various attempts by half-hearted Platonists to make strategic concessions to Naturalism and, mostly in our times, attempts by half-hearted Naturalists to make strategic concessions to Platonism.

Rorty's division of philosophy into the systematic and the edifying is, accordingly, a useful one so long as we understand that only the former claims to have a distinct subject matter. Edifying philosophy as methodological or substantive criticism refers to something entirely different both from what Plato and Platonists had in mind and from what Naturalists who reject Platonism have in mind, too.

Rorty's rejection of Platonism, identified with systematic philosophy, rests firmly upon his antirepresentationalist stance. He takes the contrast between antirepresentationalism and representationalism as even more fundamental than that between antirealism and realism, a contrast, he adds, that only arises for the representationalist.[11] What the antirepresentationalist "denies is that it is explanatorily useful to pick out and choose among the contents of our minds or our language and say that this or that item 'corresponds to' or 'represents' the environment in a way that some other item does not."[12] The reason for insisting on the uselessness or explanatory irrelevance of such supposed representations is evidently that, in order for representations to be of any help, we must be able to understand what it means for them to be good, accurate, or true representations. For a putatively useful representation is not just *any* representation, but one that successfully represents. Yet, as Rorty argues, there is "no way of formulating an *independent* test of the accuracy of representation—of reference or correspondence to an 'antecedently determinant' reality—no test distinct from the success which is supposedly explained by this accuracy."[13] Once the futility of laying down criteria for accurate representation is recognized, the tendency to postulate a form of antirealism as an antidote to the

---

11. See Rorty 2001, 2.
12. Ibid., 5.
13. Ibid., 6. Cf. Rorty, 1979, 170.

pseudo-problems of realism is rendered nugatory. Antirepresentationalism is thus not to be thought of as a form of antirealism or idealism in disguise but as a way of seeing why the whole debate between realism and antirealism has been utterly fruitless.

It would be facile in the extreme to maintain that Plato's epistemology is *non*representationalist and that therefore Rorty's criticisms do not touch it. Linguistic and conceptual representations in fact play a central role in Plato's thinking about cognition in general. Indeed, it is not too far off the mark to say that not only is Plato's epistemology in some sense representationalist but that his metaphysics is representationalist as well. What I aim to show, however, is that his metaphysical representationalism rests upon a nonrepresentational encounter with the external world. To put this claim another way, we could say that, for Plato, mental content is not *primarily* representational; representations themselves arise from nonrepresentational mental content. Thus, the tertium quid between representations and external reality that Rorty refuses to recognize is nonrepresentational mental content. This mental content is nonrepresentational, but its content is the content of reality. Representations, whether to someone else or to oneself, are expressions of that mental content. Thus, the supposed divide between epistemology and metaphysics, making the latter unattainable and the former useless, does not even arise.

Rorty's attack on representationalism encompasses the natural and social sciences, too. Most Naturalists or anti-Platonists throughout history do not share Rorty's antipathy to representationalism. Whether it be the Naturalism of Democritus or Hume or any from among dozens of contemporaries, the representational capacity of modern science is more or less unquestioned. It is, of course, possible for anti-Platonists to try to reconcile a consistent antirepresentationalism that does not see any difference in principle between astronomy and astrology and a representationalism that insists on the difference but not in realistic terms. Rorty's pragmatism or the nuanced antirealism of, say, Bas van Fraassen are only two from among many possibilities. It seems to me, however, that the Platonic response to antirepresentationalist and representationalist Naturalists is different in each case. Thus, Plato's response to Protagoras is strategically different from his response to Anaxagoras. I shall in the course of this book address both types of response in various places. But despite the different strategies, the responses share the attempt to vindicate a distinct subject matter for philosophy, namely, the intelligible world.

Rorty is in a way right to make his attack on epistemology the epitome of his attack on philosophy. Part of my task is to show that an effective response to this attack amounts not merely to a defense of the possibility of philosophy but of Platonism as well. Or, to put the point tendentiously, the defense of philosophy and of Platonism is one complex defense, with a number of interrelated parts. Philosophy, understood as having a distinct subject matter, begins with a distinction between appearance and reality, one of Rorty's fundamental rejected dualisms. Stated otherwise, this is the distinction between epistemic and nonepistemic appearances. For if reality is just as it appears, or if things do not appear otherwise than as they are, a distinct subject matter *dis*appears. At this elementary stage, philosophy is indistinguishable from any other explanatory discipline. And, indeed, the indistinctness of philosophy and natural science among the pre-Socratics has always been remarked upon by historians of ancient philosophy.[14] Rorty is correct that if the grounds for a distinction between appearance and reality are not established or are undercut, then natural science can fare no better than philosophy. As we shall see in the third chapter, Plato in his *Phaedo* takes the decisive step of separating the subject matter of philosophy from natural science by critically examining the explanatory model prevalent among his most illustrious Naturalist predecessors.

The initial reply to Rorty is, accordingly, one to be made both by philosophy and by natural science prior to their division. It is a reply that seeks to defend the cogency of explanation in general and whatever form of representationalism is required for explanation. Suppose that someone offers an explanation for a natural phenomenon, say, a volcanic eruption. Apart from the acceptance of this explanation, one may reject it in favor of another explanation or, like Rorty, reject it on the grounds that any explanation requires an illicit representationalism. Rorty is obviously in no position to reject any explanation on the basis of a better one; he must reject all explanations, whether the explanans falls within the realm of natural science or the realm of philosophy. His rejection, springing from his critique of representationalism, leads him at various times into quietism, relativism, skepticism, or pragmatism. I take it that the quietism is equivalent to disengagement from all philosophical and scientific discussion, which simply places him among the vast majority of people in the world for whom this book and any other even remotely like it is not written. As for the relativism and skepticism, I shall have much more to say in later chapters. That leaves the pragmatism to be dealt with here.

Many critics of Rorty, ultimately sympathetic to his overall approach, have struggled to express his insights in a way that does not blatantly and unequivocally make the extramental world drop out of the epistemological equation. Their convolutions in trying to do this while at the same time acknowledging Rorty's Davidsonian and Quinean insights into language and thought are a consequence of their sharing with Rorty the assumption that all that the extramental world could be is that which is representable by language and thought. These representations do not bear the marks of reality and reality does not bear the marks of representations. Thus, pragmatism becomes the mode of commensuration, the only means by which *any*

---

14. See, e.g., Cornford 1912, chap. 4; 1952, chap. 1.

linguistic or conceptual interaction with the world is possible.¹⁵ Pragmatism is, for Rorty, essentially like an animal's response to changes in the environment.¹⁶ Adaptability and "coping" replace representation.

The Platonic response to the affirmation of pragmatism on the basis of a rejection of representationalism is that the criteria for evaluating practical solutions require a mode of cognition unavailable to the antirepresentationalist. It is a mode of cognition that is not representational, because it is presumed by all representation. Plato's response to Rorty's pragmatism will deny his assertion that there is no difference between "it works because it is true" and "it is true because it works." As I have formulated this response, it is open to the charge of being far too hasty. I will, though, try to show that this mode of cognition is both ubiquitous and is, in fact, only possible if there is an intelligible world really distinct from the sensible world. In other words, the Platonic response to pragmatic Naturalism is to be sharply distinguished from any response rooted in representational Empiricism. The Platonic response to Rorty's version of Naturalism will also be the lever for the distinction of philosophy from the natural sciences.

I have argued in a previous book that Plato was a Platonist.¹⁷ By this I mean that, according to our best evidence taken from the dialogues, the testimony of Aristotle, and the indirect tradition, Plato had a distinctive systematic philosophical position. The position was built on the foundation of his rejection or correction of the philosophical positions of most of his predecessors. On the basis of this rejection, Plato argued, broadly speaking, for radically different answers to the questions that constituted his philosophical inheritance. First and foremost, this required the postulation of and argument for a distinct subject matter for philosophy, one that all his Naturalist predecessors either did not recognize or incorrectly conceptualized. Second, this required a systematization of the postulated subject matter.¹⁸ At the apex of the system is a superordinate first principle of all, the Idea of the Good, whose essential explanatory role in philosophy is explicitly affirmed by Plato.¹⁹ The explanatory function of this principle and the difficulties encountered in expressing this are one of the central themes of this book. Third, although the system did not need a rationale other than that knowledge of it was intrinsically desirable, still indispensable support for the truth of the system had to be sought in its explanatory role in solving this-worldly problems. It goes without saying, I think, that much of the

---

15. Cf. Davidson (1984, xviii), who denies that mind or language can be made to "correspond" to the world. Such correspondence would entail commensuration.

16. See Rorty 1982, 1995. By contrast, Quine ([1951] 1980, 44), sets his explicit pragmatism within a representationalist scientific viewpoint.

17. See Gerson 2013a. My claim that Plato had a philosophical system is not intended to deny the distinctive systematic efforts of, among others, the so-called Middle Platonists.

18. In the next chapter, I shall have more to say about what I mean by "systematization."

19. See, e.g., *Rep.* 511B2–C2.

material in the dialogues is concerned with human problems the solutions to which do not necessarily or obviously require recourse to the above system. So much would any honest Naturalist hold. It is a commonplace in both Plato and Aristotle that in practical affairs what is of primary concern is getting the right answer. Understanding why the right answer is so is secondary. But as Plato so vividly shows in book 10 of *Republic*, getting the right answer without knowing why it is the right answer, that is, being virtuous without philosophy, is likely ultimately to be disastrous. Even if most cannot ever attain to knowledge of why the right answers are so, there must exist such knowledge, and a well-ordered society must contain someone or other who has it.

The project of constructing Platonism, which Plato probably thought was identical to the project of doing philosophy, was an immense task. I suppose that the dialogues are records of the state of the art of the ongoing collaborative project initiated in the Academy. The history of Platonism in antiquity is the history of the contributions to this ongoing project. Unquestionably, that history includes deep disagreements among self-declared Platonists as well as fellow travelers. One simple reason for this—and the reason why these disagreements sometimes appear more serious than they actually are—is that the principles of Platonism are underdetermining for the solution to may specific philosophical problems. To take one simple example, the proof for the immortality of the soul, which is a proof that the soul in some way inhabits the intelligible world, does not yield a clear answer to the question of whether the soul when inhabiting that world has or does not have parts. Or if it does have parts, in what sense does it do so. Indeed, embracing Platonic principles does not entail anything about the identity of a person and his soul. In this book, I am not going to be much concerned with these disagreements. I do not intend to write a history of Platonism in antiquity. I am much more concerned with the disagreements insofar as they reflect on the principles themselves, that is, on how to conceive the architecture of the intelligible world and on the basic inventory of its inhabitants. In this regard, I am more than happy to call upon members of the Old Academy and all those Platonists up to Damascius to reap the benefits of their reflection upon Platonic principles. But I am going to focus especially on the contributions of Aristotle and Plotinus simply because their contributions to the project are immense and indispensable. Along the way, several others, in particular Proclus, will make what I hope will be timely guest appearances.

At the beginning of this introduction, I posed the opposition between Platonism and Naturalism as the opposition between philosophy and antiphilosophy. The latter opposition is obviously more contentious than the former since most Naturalists believe that there is room for philosophy within a Naturalist framework. I emphasize again that I am using the term "philosophy" as Plato uses it in *Republic* and am taking that as equivalent to what Rorty calls "systematic philosophy" and Aristotle calls "first philosophy." It is the existence of this that all Naturalists deny. Those who wish to preserve a subject matter for philosophy without identifying that with the intelligible world may want to argue that there is distinct work for, say, metaphysics or epistemology or ethics, without necessarily committing to anti-Naturalism. That is exactly what the Platonist denies is possible. In a number of places in the dialogues, Plato produces reductio arguments against relativists and materialists who take such an approach. His strategy, as we shall see, is to show that it is their implicit Naturalism that makes their position unsustainable.

In this book, I shall frequently make ancient Naturalists serve as proxies for contemporary Naturalists. I recognize that this approach is contentious because, among other things, it does not allow the Naturalist recourse to the spectacular achievements of modern science. It will be said that particularly with regard to human beings, quantum mechanics, evolution, microbiology, genetics, and neuroscience, to say the least, are necessary for the Naturalist to make the most forceful possible case against the putative Platonic alternative. A contemporary Naturalist no longer needs to rely on ancient, outdated science. This would seem to be undeniable. And to the extent that it is true, this book could only be part of a larger project. Nevertheless, I have discovered that time and again the anti-Naturalist arguments of Platonists are made at a sufficiently high level of generality so as to preclude dismissal based solely upon the scientific discoveries that they could not have anticipated. In any case, it is my hope that the account of Platonism that emerges from these pages will serve to sharpen the debate among contemporary proponents of Platonism and Naturalism.[20]

Contemporary Naturalists are legion; contemporary Platonists are somewhat fewer in number. The often stellar work of members of both these groups frequently suffer, I think, from a piecemeal approach to the issues addressed here. For example, many contemporary Naturalists argue in various ways that materialism or nominalism is false, but seldom try to show that antimaterialism and antinominalism are connected to each other and to antiskepticism. Conversely, an argument for materialism is only rarely connected to a defense of some positive epistemological doctrine. Rorty's legitimate complaint that Naturalists do not appreciate the consequence of their Naturalism needs to be recognized and addressed. Similarly, a benign appeal to antinominalism is seldom acknowledged to entail some form of

---

20. Rorty himself liked to say that in the dispute between Plato and Protagoras he, Rorty, was on Protagoras's side. I would expect that in this spirit contemporary Naturalists would, in the dispute between Plato and Anaxagoras, gladly take the latter's side, always with the proviso that it is a very long way indeed from *homoiomeres* to electrons. Cf. Fodor 2002, 21: "Lots of us think that, details aside, Lucretius had things about right. What there *really is* is atoms-and-the-void and there's really nothing else."

antimaterialism.[21] I think Platonism is a comprehensive worldview as is Naturalism and each should be treated as such. Of course, the Naturalist only needs to embrace a methodological Naturalism, thus turning over the entire intellectual enterprise to natural science. For the self-proclaimed Naturalist philosopher who thinks that there are real philosophical questions and answers to be asked and answered within a methodological Naturalist framework, success or failure of comprehensiveness is probably going to track plausibility in their conclusions.[22] For example, a defense of nominalism needs to be not just a defense of the claim that things do not really have properties, but it must also include a defense of how the thinking that appears to have universals as objects can occur. That is, not only does materialism entail nominalism, but materialism needs to be part and parcel of the defense of nominalism.

In this book, I aim to show that *the* fundamental question in philosophy today is whether or not there is a legitimate and distinct subject matter that can be usefully called philosophy. This fundamental question is not most perspicuously posed for the select group of thinkers who share the assumption that the existence of the subject matter is a foregone conclusion, and that only the details need to be addressed. It is best posed for those who dispute the very existence of the subject matter, that is, for Naturalists and for those who reject Naturalism, all of whom, I shall argue, are Platonists in one form or another. Those who want just enough Platonism or just enough Naturalism to defend a particular account of some phenomenon while at the same time remaining for the most part in the other camp are the main targets of this book. If I am unable to succeed in persuading anyone that Platonism is true or at least more plausible than they had hitherto thought, perhaps I can persuade some that to abandon Platonism is to abandon what Rorty calls "systematic philosophy" and what Aristotle calls "first philosophy" and what Plato calls simply "philosophy." Just as the possibility of a science of parapsychology hinges upon the question of the reality of parapsychological phenomena, so the possibility of philosophy rests upon the question of the reality of the intelligible world.

---

21. See Armstrong 1979 for an effort to join materialism and antinominalism. This effort, as I shall try to show, has very little chance of being successful.

22. See, e.g., Strawson 2012 on the rationale for panpsychism.

Chapter 2

Platonism vs. Naturalism

2.1. What Is Platonism?

"'Platonism' is said in many ways." Aristotle certainly did not say these words. Nevertheless, judging from his extensive criticisms of Plato and other members of the "Old" Academy, he might well have done so. Of course, Aristotle does not use the words "Platonism" or "Platonist," terms belonging to a time considerably far removed from the middle of the fourth century BCE.[1] He does, though, identify and attribute to Plato a philosophical position that, as I shall try to show, is in an important sense a systematic one. He also attributes, at least to Speusippus and Xenocrates, variations on this philosophical position. These facts alone justify us in asking whether we can find in the dialogues its lineaments. My reason for raising this historical question is frankly nonhistorical. That is, many contemporary philosophers embrace an opposing position, widely labeled "Naturalism." Strikingly, many of the arguments for this position are in fact arguments against elements of Platonism. Perhaps even more strikingly, these arguments are typically taken to lead to the conclusion that philosophy as traditionally understood is more or less a dead letter.[2] That is, philosophy does not rule over a subject matter that is distinct from the natural sciences, broadly speaking. I do not find anything ironic much less self-contradictory in a philosophical position that maintains the impossibility of philosophy. Ludwig

---

1. See Gerson 2013a, 4, on the (Roman) origin of the term *Platonicus*.
2. See http://www.telegraph.co.uk/technology/google/8520033/Stephen-Hawking-tells-Google-philosophy-is-dead.html.

Wittgenstein provided one rationale for the use of philosophy for its ultimate self-eradication. Similarly, it is not prima facie absurd to offer a political argument for the illegitimacy of the state, and hence for the illegitimacy of political doctrines as they are usually understood, that is, assuming the state's legitimacy.

If, in fact, we see Platonism and Naturalism as contradictory positions, we can deploy the analysis of arguments on each side in order to better understand the other. It is here, I believe, that the best argument for the relevance of the history of philosophy to philosophy itself can be found. For understanding Platonism is impossible without historical investigation. This claim seems easy to support on the basis of the staggeringly large number of manifestly false statements that are made about Plato's doctrines especially by those who seem to make it a personal principle to treat the history of philosophy cavalierly. It is a sobering thought that even among many who are very far from being disdainful of the history of philosophy, Platonism is often written about in such a way that the opposition between Platonism and Naturalism cannot but seem to be analogous to the opposition between astrology and astronomy.

A historical investigation of Platonism will typically focus largely on the variety of doctrines of soi-disant Platonists.[3] That these Platonists say contradictory things about what Plato believed is hardly a modern discovery.[4] As Sextus Empiricus tells us, one of the delightful tasks of Pyrrhonian Skepticism is to point out the contradictions found among the dogmatists, including, of course, Platonists.[5] It is possible, however, as I shall try to show, that the divisions among Platonists occur under the umbrella of shared principles, that these principles are found in the dialogues, and that these principles, not the putative inferences from them, are the elements of true Platonism. It seems to me that these principles taken together are underdetermining for the solution to many problems, problems that at least used to be thought of as philosophical in nature.[6] I do not think, for example, that the embrace of Platonism entails that one be committed to a particular answer to the question of how an immaterial mind can be related to a material body. More broadly, I do not think that Platonism has any specific religious

---

3. See, e.g., Bonazzi 2015, for an excellent and concise survey of the history of Platonism which, however, spends very little time on the arguments found in the dialogues.

4. See, e.g., Proclus (*In Parm.* 1.630–645), who records a number of radically different interpretations of Plato's *Parmenides* by Platonists.

5. See Sextus Empiricus, *PH* 1.79–91, for the trope based upon differences among people, including their beliefs.

6. The cosmology of Plato's *Timaeus*, "a likely story," provides the stellar example of underdetermination from primary principles. Plato's detailed cosmological explanations are never presented as entailed by first principles. On the contrary, given the strictly unintelligible Receptacle, underdetermination is endemic to any application of Platonic principles to the sensible world.

or even political implications. In saying this I do not mean to suggest that Plato did not have views about religion and politics. I mean only that these views do not follow from a commitment to Platonism. Thus, I think that the answers to contemporary political problems follow from principles that stand outside of Platonism.

Just as historical Platonism can be articulated in such a way that its opposition to contemporary Naturalism is clear, so contemporary Naturalism has its historical roots in the philosophical positions that Plato explicitly rejects in the dialogues. I believe that if we reconstruct Platonism at the requisite level of generality, we are in a far better position to see its historical scope. And as a result, we can see why, for example, Aristotle is most definitely a Platonist despite his rejection of Plato's positions on many matters.[7] Accordingly, I feel justified in helping myself to corrections Aristotle makes to Plato, not the least of which is the introduction of new technical terms.[8]

As for Plotinus, it certainly does not need emphasizing that he wished to be nothing but an accurate exegete of Plato. Many, however, including scholars of late Platonism, would vigorously dispute the claim that Plotinus is a reliable guide to *Plato's* Platonism. In a previous book, I hope to have shown that this charge is very much exaggerated, especially if Platonism is properly understood.[9] In any case, I am going to use Plotinus selectively as a source for crucial arguments that are, at least, only implicit in Plato. Indeed, Platonism properly understood makes possible the constructive use of genuinely Platonic material found in Plotinus's successors. In particular, Proclus, Damascius, and others have important roles to play as supporting characters. I forbear from going beyond pagan antiquity in this regard, not because I do not think there are important contributions to be made to Platonism there, but because I aim to stay within a strictly philosophical ambit, leaving to others the question of whether or to what extent Jewish, Christian, and Islamic theological ideas are compatible with Platonism. I should add, however, that I think that, for example, Thomas Aquinas is as obviously a Platonist as is Aristotle, even though I see his theological position as quite independent of that fact.[10]

I have elsewhere argued for the position that Plato's Platonism rests upon the foundation of his rejection of many, though not all, of the doctrines of

---

7. See Gerson 2005b.

8. Rorty (2000, 1) insisted, rightly in my view, that his rejection of Platonism must be understood equally as a rejection of Aristotelianism.

9. See Gerson 2013a. Also Yount 2014.

10. See O'Rourke 1992. Craig (2016) argues that Platonism is *incompatible* with Christianity. His reason is that Platonism posits multiple necessary and eternal entities, the Forms, whereas Christianity must maintain the uniqueness of the necessity and eternity of God. This is mistaken as an account of Platonism in many ways, as we shall see.

his major predecessors.[11] These include materialism, mechanism, nominalism, relativism, and skepticism. In subsequent chapters, I shall go into some detail regarding the particular arguments found in the dialogues against those who were thought by Plato to hold these positions. Here, I want to stress that Plato's rejections of these positions—making him, for example, an antimaterialist—are offered only as the foundational considerations for Plato's systematic construct. I have no idea if there was a specific moment in time when Plato moved from being a critic of philosophers in his own history to being a constructive metaphysician in his own right. Indeed, it is possible that his intellectual movement went the other way. Although it is not an essential part of my argument, I suspect that by the time Plato wrote any dialogues, he was settled both in his criticisms and at least in the outlines of his positive construct. In short, I see no evidence that there is any dialogue in which Plato held views other than those that make up what I and the later ancient tradition call "Platonism." In saying this, I definitely mean to include those so-called Socratic dialogues that are supposedly innocent of metaphysical pretensions.

Let me briefly offer operational definitions of the five "antis" just mentioned. Although the terminology (with the exception of materialism) is modern, all of these pertain to identifiable and distinct philosophical positions maintained by certain interlocutors in the dialogues. These are positions that are decisively rejected on the basis of explicit arguments. Those who think that these arguments are not ones which Plato himself endorses may suppose that I must be referring to "Plato" not Plato, and to "Platonism" not Platonism. I do not believe that this baseless conceit serves philosophy or its history. But there it is.

By "nominalism" I mean the view that if two or more things are the same, then they must be identical. In other words, there is no conceptual space for sameness that is not identity. Thus, two or more things, just because they are numerically distinct, cannot be the same. Alternatively, nominalism may be understood to be the view that there is no grounding for true predicative judgments, since such judgments suppose—incoherently—that predicates are and are not identical with their subjects.

By "materialism" I mean the view that the only things that exist are bodies, that is, three-dimensional solids, and whatever supervenes on or is epiphenomenal to these bodies. Alternately, materialism may be understood as the view that there do not exist any immaterial entities, that is, entities that are not ontologically dependent on bodies in some way. Materialists, beginning with Plato's predecessors, attempt to finesse the apparent relevance of the immaterial to our ordinary discourse in a variety of ways. All of these share the view that the putatively immaterial can have no explanatory

---

11. See Gerson 2013a, chap.1.

relevance. Given this, it is not surprising that Plato will attack materialism for its inadequate notion of explanation.

By "mechanism" I mean adherence to the principle of causal closure. That is, the view that all causal explanations available to us are found within a Naturalistic framework. Roughly, for an adherent of mechanism, natural science is the sole locus of causal explanations.

By "relativism" I mean the view that there exists no normativity independent of the interests or beliefs or desires of one or more human beings. Nothing can be said to be good or bad, right or wrong independently of individual or collective human perspectives.

By "skepticism" I mean the view that there exists no infallible cognition. Accordingly, the ne plus ultra of cognition, whatever it may turn out to be, is fallible. This is so because all cognition is representational and there can be no guarantee that representations are accurate. Indeed, a skeptic of this sort may deny the possibility of accurate representation altogether. This approach generally leads to a pragmatic criterion for determining the ne plus ultra of cognition. Among contemporary philosophers, the rejection of the possibility of infallible cognition usually does not entail an explicit embrace of skepticism. For example, varieties of reliabilism maintain that fidelity to a reliable process of knowledge acquisition usually does result in knowledge, but not always or necessarily. The very idea of reliability as a criterion of knowledge is essentially pragmatic.[12] According to Plato, however, such an approach commits one to the deeply obscure notion of nonentailing evidence and to a conflation of knowledge and rational belief.

Plato rejects all these views with arguments, sometimes very elaborate and sometimes quite concise. As we shall see, the arguments for the rejection of one view often support and are supported by arguments for the rejection of another view. These arguments are the regular business of the quotidian world of Platonism as found in the dialogues and as reported in the oral tradition. All these negative arguments make up the foundation of Platonism.

The central pillar of the positive construct on the basis of this foundation is clear and unambiguous. It is an "unhypothetical first principle of all" called in *Republic* "the Idea of the Good" and, according to Aristotle's testimony, identified by Plato with "the One."[13] I devote separate chapters

---

12. A hallmark of a criterion of knowledge is that employment of the criterion yields truth. But the use of the criterion of reliability does not guarantee truth. Once a criterion is disengaged from truth, the result is pragmatism of some ilk.

13. See *Rep.* 509B; Aristotle, *Meta.* A 6, 987a29–988a17, and N 4, 1091b13–15. Aristotle's identification of the Good with the One is supported by a wealth of evidence in the indirect tradition. See Krämer 1990, 203–217, and Richard 1986, 250–355, for texts and translations of the evidence. The indirect tradition refers to all the testimony about Plato's philosophy that does not come from those in personal contact with Plato, roughly the members of the Old Academy. But the indirect tradition is important because it is based on those members of the

to the Idea of the Good in the dialogues and to its central place in Plato's philosophy. Here, it suffices to point out that the claim for the systematic nature of Plato's philosophy rests principally on the very idea of there being a first principle of all. This can most easily be seen in Plato's *Phaedo* taken together with several specific points in Aristotle's testimony. Briefly, in *Phaedo* Plato provides Socrates with an autobiography, one that is very likely in fact his own.[14] In it, we see Socrates turning away from the sorts of explanations—materialist and mechanistic, as I shall call them—offered by Anaxagoras in favor of his own "simple hypothesis," namely, the positing of a Form or Forms to explain the teleological dimension of natural phenomena. The positing of a Form may if necessary be superseded by the positing of a higher, presumably more comprehensive Form until one reaches "something adequate (τι ἱκανόν)." For a variety of textual and philosophical reasons, it is in all likelihood the *unhypothetical* first principle of all that Plato has in mind here.[15] If this is so, the explanatory path that the philosopher is supposed to follow, while acknowledging material or mechanistic conditions, and while passing through hypothesized Forms, always ends in the identical unique place, namely, the Idea of the Good or the One.

The centrality of this "explanatory reductivism," as I shall call it, is reinforced by Aristotle's testimony to the effect that Plato derived Forms from the One, via their initial reduction to Numbers.[16] The possibility of reduction on the basis of the unity of the explananda is the basis for the systematic nature of explanation.[17] That is, the "something" that is "adequate," the unhypothetical first principle of all, serves the identical function in *all*

Old Academy who had this personal contact. Some of it includes, for example, direct quotations from Speusippus.

14. Aristotle, *Meta*. A 6, 987a32–b10, says that (a) Socrates was not interested in natural philosophy, that (b) Plato, not he, separated the Forms, and that (c) Plato's philosophy was Pythagorean in shape. The autobiography has "Socrates" interested in both (a) and (b) and (c) friends with Pythagoreans, Cebes, and Simmias. We should compare *Parmenides* 129Eff., where the "young Socrates" is represented as having a "theory of separate Forms." This is patently a self-reference by Plato. It is implausible that in one dialogue Plato is representing the real historical Socrates in his youth but that in another he is using Socrates to represent his own youth. See Sedley 1995, 3–26, for detailed evidence from the dialogue indicating that the autobiography is really that of Plato himself.

15. See chap. 5, sec. 5.1, on the meaning of "unhypothetical" here.

16. See *Meta*. A 6, 978b18–22. Cf. A 5, 987a13–19; A 8, 990a29–32; Z 11, 1036b13–25; Λ 8, 1073a18–19; M 6, 1080b11–14; M 7, 1081a5–7; M 8, 1083a18, 1084a7–8; M 9, 1086a11–13; N 2, 1090a4–6; and N 3, 1090a16. At M 4, 1078b9–12, Aristotle distinguishes a mathematical and a nonmathematical version of the theory of Forms. It is perhaps the case that at some point in time, ascertainment of which is unavailable to us, members of the Academy hypothesized the reduction of nonmathematical Forms to Numbers. If this is so, this fact in itself is evidence of the systematizing tendency of Platonism.

17. See Plato, *Men*. 81C9–D1: ἅτε γὰρ τῆς φύσεως ἁπάσης συγγενοῦς οὔσης, καὶ μεμαθηκυίας τῆς ψυχῆς ἅπαντα (inasmuch as all nature is genetically connected and the soul has learned everything [prior to embodiment]).

philosophical explanations. The hallmark of a system is its complex unity or, stated otherwise, the unificatory process of explaining any complex. The sharp divide between those who insist on the systematic nature of Plato's philosophy and those who eschew any systematization of the multivoiced dialogues rests almost entirely on whether or not one takes seriously what is said in *Phaedo* and *Republic* and elsewhere about first principles and what Aristotle reports about Plato's philosophy, as that appears in the dialogues and as it was apparently orally transmitted to Aristotle and others.

As will become increasingly clear throughout this book, my setting Platonism and Naturalism in stark opposition follows from the exegetical position I take regarding the Platonic system. For if Platonism is not a systematic unity, the foundational elements of that system as mentioned above begin to fall apart. Each of Plato's arguments against his predecessors regarding any one element supports and is supported by arguments for the others. And all the elements are supported by the explanatory role of the unhypothetical first principle of all. For example, it seems fairly clear that Plato's rejection of Anaxagorean explanations supports and is supported by the positing of separate Forms. But Plato insists that the hypothesized Forms are not adequate, or at least not adequate ultimately. Therefore, the cogency of antimaterialism and antimechanism requires, by Plato's own admission, explanatory and unificatory reductivism.[18] What is true in this example will be shown to be the case for every element of the foundation.

The all-or-nothing nature of the two opposing positions will be decried by some Platonizing philosophers and welcomed by Naturalists. For it is thought that at best only certain elements of the Platonic position are viable. But if they all sink or swim together and if the latter only if there is a systematic unifying principle for them all, then who can expect it to withstand the juggernaut of Naturalism? To take a different example, if

---

18. The opposition between materialism and antimaterialism or immaterialism is sometimes eschewed by contemporary philosophers in favor of a distinction between the concrete and the abstract. This is done on the grounds that there could be concrete things that are immaterial, e.g., God, and abstract things that are material, e.g., certain properties of material entities or propositions about material entities. The term "abstract" is worse than useless for characterizing the Platonic position. This is so because abstraction assumes a derivative status for the abstracted in relation to what it is abstracted from. Precisely because of the presumed derivative status, the acausality of Forms is assumed. See Hale 1987. For Plato, this is backward. Further, Platonism holds that everything in the intelligible realm is concrete if this term means extramental existence. Accordingly, I prefer to stick with the materialism/immaterialism contrast, but within the larger framework of Naturalism vs. Platonism. I take Platonism and Naturalism to be contradictory positions or at least I hypothesize that they are. See van Inwagen (2006, 75), who denies that "opposition to naturalism is the constituting factor of any possible community of intellectual interest." Van Inwagen, however, does not identify non-Naturalism with Platonism. He does, though, 82, identify one version of Naturalism with anti-Platonism, that which does not countenance abstract (Platonic) objects of any sort, including propositions, properties, numbers, functions, tensors, etc.

successfully arguing for objectivity or universality in ethics requires the positing of immaterial entities and, ultimately, a superordinate Idea of the Good, what exactly are the prospects for objectivity? Attempts to help oneself to one or another element of the foundation of Platonism while leaving the rest and ignoring the first principle of all are well documented already in the Hellenistic period. Stoicism is the stellar case, the paradigm of a philosophical position wanting to have a form of Platonism without the metaphysics. I aim to show that the consistent Stoic materialist is ipso facto denied the support of the other elements of the foundation along with the explanatory power of the first principle of all. Much of the history of philosophy since the seventeenth century has been a series of attempts to take elements of Platonism and elements of the opposing Naturalism in piecemeal fashion, seeking some sort of rapprochement among them. The birth of the new physics in the seventeenth century was taken as an invitation if not a demand to jettison as much Platonism as possible in the service of enlightenment. The insipid dialectic of the claims and counterclaims of Rationalism and Empiricism reveals much ingenuity on behalf of a deracinated and severely compromised Platonism. Only fairly recently have some Naturalists had the courage to insist that a compromised Platonism is not an acceptable substitute for the real thing. But it has been so long since Naturalists have paid attention to the real thing, that refutations or, more usually, outright summary rejections of the simulacra of Platonism ring hollow.[19]

2.2. What Is Naturalism?

"Naturalism" is obviously a term of art and so it is hardly surprising that it is used in a variety of often incompatible ways. In contemporary discussions, it refers to some sort of opposition to Platonism as described above.[20] Oddly, in my view, it is sometimes used to refer to Aristotle's philosophy, supposedly indicating his opposition to Plato's supernaturalism or transcendentalism.[21] Based on the textual evidence alone, this view is difficult to sustain. Its

---

19. It is, I think, interesting that, whereas today Platonism generally gets about as much serious attention as, say, Cartesian dualism, Platonism as a very sharply circumscribed mathematical doctrine is alive and well. But even among mathematical Platonists, full-blown Platonism seems not even to be on the horizon.

20. At *Parm.* 132D1–2, Socrates refers to Forms as "παραδείγματα ἐν τῇ φύσει (paradigms in nature)," which might lead one to claim that Platonism should be placed under the umbrella of Naturalism. But the use of "nature" here by Plato is meant in contrast to the artificial, whereas Naturalism mostly assumes the impossibility of the existence of the nonphysical or nonmaterialistic things that Plato embraces. I shall adhere to the use of "Naturalism" that sets it firmly in opposition to Platonism, even if in other contexts Plato's recognition of the reality of the natural needs to be emphasized.

21. See Irwin 2007, 4–5, on "Aristotelian naturalism" referring to Aristotle's view that human happiness is found in the fulfillment of human nature. This anodyne sense of "naturalism"

fatal flaw is in failing to distinguish debates *among* Platonists from debates *between* Platonists and their opponents. I will always use the terms "Naturalism" and "Naturalists" for the latter. As we shall see in a moment, this use corresponds pretty well to that found in many contemporary self-described Naturalists.[22]

In antiquity, the stellar example of explicit Naturalism is found among Atomists, including Epicurus and Lucretius. We do not know if Democritus was self-consciously anti-Platonic or not, though recent work on the dialogues provides a reasonable amount of evidence that the Atomism of Democritus has an implicit presence in *Timaeus*.[23] If that is the case, then he might well have seen his own philosophical position as anti-Platonic. Even if this is not so, the Atomism of Epicurus seems to be a self-conscious repudiation of Platonism in one crucial respect. The postulation of a fundamental multiplicity of atoms contradicts the necessity for positing an unhypothetical first principle of all. Atomism contradicts Plato's antimaterialism. The explanations for natural phenomena are exclusively mechanistic (including chance as an explanation). A world of atoms and void is not necessarily nominalistic since presumably one could claim that atoms may have identical shapes and sizes. Nevertheless, there is no need for the Epicurean not to embrace nominalism particularly if the only reason to reject it requires the postulation of immaterial entities to explain the phenomenon of sameness in difference. Furthermore, the hedonism of Epicurus is essentially relativistic since the arbiter of pleasure is the one experiencing it. Even if, as Epicurus says, the pursuit of some pleasures under some circumstances is unwise, this cannot be a universal truth. There are, after all, exceptions. And the individual is the final arbiter of the pluses and minuses of, say, anxiety about overindulgence vs. foregoing the pleasure itself.

---

does not clearly set Aristotle apart from Naturalism as explained here, even though I think it is obvious that Aristotle is an anti-Naturalist.

22. According to one approach to the understanding of contemporary philosophy, anti-Naturalism should not be identified with Platonism. Rather, anti-Naturalists are those philosophers, beginning with Frege, and including Russell, Wittgenstein, and Carnap, who want to carve out a subject matter for philosophy that is neither a part of the natural sciences nor Platonic, at least not Platonic in the sense in which I am using that term. This subject matter is conceptual analysis or the clarification of thought. Insofar as the target of analysis is other than the idiosyncratic thoughts or concepts of any one individual, it seems to me that either such analysis just is the analysis of the foundations of the natural sciences, in which case it does not constitute a distinct subject matter, or it is a sort of insincere Platonism, arguably attributable to Frege and Russell, which declines to make explicit its ontological commitments. See Kitcher 1992 on anti-Naturalism understood as not identical with Platonism.

23. See Hermann 2005. G. Strawson (2012, 139–140) helpfully points out that genuine Naturalism (which recognizes the reality of experience while insisting that it is wholly physical in nature) has not advanced on the philosophy of Democritus. Obviously, I find this view to be congenial in that it supports my claim that Anaxagoras and Democritus, among others, can serve as proxies for contemporary Naturalists.

In the matter of skepticism, we find the one area in which Epicurus sides with Plato. It is instructive briefly to consider why. Epicurean science is supposed to contribute to *ataraxia*, which is the way that Epicurus characterizes happiness. Understanding the causes of things is supposed to eliminate the fear of death and of divinity. Skepticism, that is, the denial of a ne plus ultra mode of cognition, undercuts the motivation for the reductivist physics.[24] Admittedly, the psychology of the true believer would seem to obviate the need that this mode of cognition be infallible.[25] Nevertheless, skepticism about sense-perception and *prolēpseis* (basic grasps) is antithetical to the so-called Cradle Argument, which seeks to show that the elementary experience of pleasure sought for by children is indicative of exactly what happiness is. If it is not necessarily true that from the evident desire for pleasure in children we can conclude to some form of hedonism, then the basis and motivation for Epicurean science is lost. For if the existence of the desire for pleasure does not entail the desirability of pleasure, then as skeptics insisted, there is no reason to take the former as evidence for the latter.[26] Epicurus insists on a form of Empiricism that can yield knowledge, not mere belief. The response to this seeming concession to Platonism is that Epicurus is not entitled to his claim to knowledge precisely because of his materialism.[27] The conclusion is that, outside a Platonic framework, antiskepticism is not sustainable.

Stoicism more closely resembles Platonism than does Epicureanism because, in addition to its embrace of antiskepticism, it also maintains a form of antirelativism and, most importantly, a postulation of a first principle of all. What is distinctive about Stoicism in antiquity is its attempt to combine this postulation with an uncompromising corporealism and mechanism. The Stoic first principle of all is active and hence radically different from any incorporeal, the principle property of which is its irrelevance to any causal explanation. For this reason it cannot be reduced to, say, a fundamental differential equation. From the Platonic perspective, the impossibility of there being a first principle of this sort resides in the fact that rationality cannot be a property of bodies. It is true that bodies can manifest or serve as a repository for the rationality of their producers, but the active principle for the Stoics has no producer; it is the ultimate source of explanation.

---

24. See Plantinga 2006, 3–32.

25. Papineau (1993, chap. 5) argues, correctly, in my view, that if there is no such thing as infallible cognition, then there is no motivation for first philosophy or, simply, philosophy as understood by Plato. But it is only the possibility of infallible cognition that is relevant, not its actuality in any particular instance.

26. Generally, a Pyrrhonian skeptic will argue against any Dogmatist that no sense-experience can provide entailing evidence for any ampliative conclusion. Although Skepticism is structured around its opposition to Stoic Empiricism, it is generally applicable to any form of Dogmatism that proposes criteria of evidence.

27. See Morel 2016, 96–112.

The commitment to the rationality of the universe on the part of the Stoics is manifested in a multitude of ways, most prominently in its teleology.[28] And with teleology comes normativity sewn into the fabric of the universe. The Stoics see the connection between antirelativism and the existence of a first principle of all. They do not see—say the Platonists—that this connection must extend to antimaterialism and so to antimechanism. They also do not see the connection between the rationality of the universe and antinominalism since rationality is found exclusively in cognition of universality, even including, say, deliberation about particulars. Cognition without universality is reserved for nonrational animals.

During the so-called period of Middle Platonism (roughly 80 BCE to 220 CE), the prominence of professional Stoicism was evidently a catalyst for a number of self-declared Platonists to try to amalgamate Stoic principles with Platonism. The mostly unimpressive results are available for inspection, even if unfortunately by means of fragmentary material. A notable exception to this—as later Platonists recognized—was in the realm of ethics and moral psychology. Platonists like Plotinus and Simplicius were, for example, full of admiration for what the Stoics had to say about rational living and even personal identity. As for Plotinus, his complaint was that Stoic materialism could not provide the principled support for these conclusions.[29]

Contemporary Naturalists are frequently conflicted, expressing doubts about whether a thoroughly consistent Naturalism can account for certain undeniable phenomena, including thinking, consciousness, intentionality, moral normativity, and subjectivity. It is helpful to have the uncompromising pronouncements of Naturalists, such as Alex Rosenberg, who strive for consistency at all costs. Here is such a statement. In "Disenchanted Naturalism" Rosenberg writes,

> Naturalism is the label for the thesis that the tools we should use in answering philosophical problems are the methods and findings of the mature sciences—from physics across to biology and increasingly neuroscience. It enables us to rule out answers to philosophical questions that are incompatible with scientific findings. It enables us to rule out epistemological pluralism—that the house of knowledge has many mansions, as well as skepticism about the reach of science. It bids us doubt that there are facts about reality that science cannot grasp. It gives us confidence to assert that by now in the development of science, absence of evidence is *prima facie* good grounds for evidence of absence: this goes for God, and a great deal else.
>
> I think naturalism is right, but I also think science forces upon us a very disillusioned "take" on reality. It forces us to say "No" in response to many

---

28. See Bobzien 1998, 44–58; and Sedley 2002, 41–81.
29. See, e.g., Simplicius's commentary on Epictetus's *Enchiridion*. Also Annas 2007, on foundations for Stoic ethics.

questions to which most everyone hopes the answers are "Yes." These are the questions about purpose in nature, the meaning of life, the grounds of morality, the significance of consciousness, the character of thought, the freedom of the will, the limits of human self-understanding, and the trajectory of human history. The negative answers to these questions that science provides are ones that most naturalists have sought to avoid, or at least qualify, reinterpret, or recast to avoid science's harsh conclusions. I dissent from the consensus of these philosophers who have sought to reconcile science with common sense or the manifest image or the wisdom of our culture. My excuse is that I stand on the shoulders of giants: the many heroic naturalists who have tried vainly, I think, to find a more upbeat version of naturalism than this one.[30]

It is not clear what Rosenberg means by philosophical problems if, as he says, the tools for answering them are those of the mature sciences. What, then, makes something a philosophical problem as opposed to a theoretical problem within one of those sciences? I take it that Rosenberg would insist that what is perhaps a mere terminological distinction between a philosophical problem and a problem within the theory of a mature science is secondary to the claim that there is no distinct content over which philosophy holds sway. I mean that, for Rosenberg, there is no objection to philosophy if, say, one is talking about a problem in the philosophy of biology, since the solution to this problem can only be successfully pursued according to the principles of that science. Naturalism maintains that there exists no realm or subject matter that is unreachable by the natural sciences, specifically the realm of the immaterial.[31]

---

30. Rosenberg 2015. Cf. Russell 1935, 243: "Whatever knowledge is attainable, must be attained by scientific methods; and what science cannot discover, mankind cannot know." Also Quine 1953, 446: "Philosophy of science is philosophy enough." Also Price 2011, 7, draft for introduction to book. Price (2008, 9–12, in typescript), in contrast to Rosenberg, thinks, like Rorty, that the "placement problems" that the Naturalist faces for explaining putatively non-Naturalistic phenomena in natural terms should be avoided by eschewing any pretense to representationalism, Naturalistic or otherwise. Thus, the question of how to explain consciousness in Naturalistic terms can be seen to be only a badly formed one. The real question is essentially the Wittgensteinian question of how discourse using language that includes the term "consciousness" functions in our human interactions. Price prefers a "subject naturalism over an object naturalism, the former of which has no representationalist aspirations." Cf. Kuhn 1970. Cf. van Inwagen (2006, 90–104), who defines Naturalism (or physicalism) as the view which holds that the world consists of those entities that possess nonteleological, nonmental, quantifiable properties, and the entities composed of these. The term "physicalism" seems to have been coined by Otto Neurath (1931, 620). He uses it in contrast to "philosophy as an independent system of definite doctrine [which is] obsolete. What can not be regarded as unified science must be accepted as poetry or fiction."

31. See Bealer 1996, 121–142, for a list of philosophical issues the addressing of which philosophers and Naturalists would certainly dispute: substance, mind, intelligence, consciousness, sensation, perception, knowledge, wisdom, truth, identity, infinity, divinity, time,

The theoretical physicist David Deutsch, like Rosenberg, argues for a type of Naturalism that is unapologetically representationalist.[32] But Deutsch is critical of Naturalists who think that Empiricism is the sole basis for arriving at scientific truth.[33] In particular, Deutsch thinks that knowledge is paradigmatically objective and universal, but that the epistemological criteria of most Naturalists do not allow them to acknowledge this. From a Platonic or anti-Naturalist perspective, the problem with Deutsch's view is that it is not possible to join universality with materialism, since a consistent materialism must be nominalistic and nominalism precludes universality as opposed to mere generality.[34] Deutsch, puzzlingly, insists on the "reality of abstractions" but refuses to identify these with nonmaterial entities.[35]

---

explanation, causation, freedom, purpose, goodness, duty, the virtues, love, life, happiness, and so forth. Sometimes, philosophers use the term "theological naturalism" for the view that they embrace a full commitment to explanatory adequacy within a Naturalistic framework at the same time as they affirm the relevance of the divine to the ontology of nature. I do not find this term perspicuous; indeed, I think it is something of an oxymoron and I shall not use it. If, however, and as I shall argue below, those who do use the term mean that Naturalism cannot in principle provide sufficient explanations for what occurs in nature, then I think that theological Naturalism is just Platonism and it is confusing and unhelpful to identify it otherwise. Another term, rather infrequently used, is "metaphysical naturalism," sometimes associated with D. C. Williams. This is an attempt to base a science of first principles on a four-dimensional Naturalistic framework. I find this term to be unhelpful also, ultimately because it rejects the idea that metaphysics has a distinct subject matter, especially if it maintains that the conclusions of metaphysical Naturalism are empirically confirmable. As such, it is insufficiently distinguished from a thoroughly Naturalistic, i.e., scientific, examination of the principles of physics. I shall discuss this more fully in the next chapter.

32. See Deutsch 2011, 39: "Scientific truth consists of . . . correspondence between theories and physical reality." See also Paul Churchland 2013, ix, for an entirely different sort of neurochemical, that is, nonlinguistic, type of representationalism: "Our knowledge is richly representational. . . . It's just that the relevant representations are not remotely propositional or linguaformal in character." See 128–138 for Churchland's reasons for resisting the antirepresentationalism of Rorty and others. Basically, he wants to defend a highly refined and up-to-date neurophysiological account of cognition as a form of scientific realism. See 215–223. On Churchland's denial that "cognition is language-like at its core," see chap. 5.

33. Deutsch 2011, 4–29, 311–312.

34. But see Armstrong (1978, 261), who says: "Naturalism, I define as the doctrine that reality consists of nothing but a single all-embracing spatiotemporal system." Yet Armstrong rejects nominalism in favor of an account of "immanent universals," an account that I find difficult to connect with Armstrong's materialism. See also Schaffer 2010a, 2010b for a rather more sophisticated version of Armstrong's position.

35. Armstrong 1978, chap. 5. The acceptance of abstract entities without a commitment to Platonic ontology is perhaps most famously articulated by Carnap (1950, 205–206). By contrast, Burgess and Rosen (2005) embrace the reality of mathematical entities, thus rejecting nominalism. They take mathematics as a legitimate science within a capacious Naturalism. So J. Brown 2012. As I shall argue, Platonism is not content with the abandonment of nominalism by Naturalism. The reason for this, briefly, is that the indispensable explanatory role of mathematics cannot be fulfilled by mathematical truths alone; they must be embedded in a richer intelligible framework.

With respect to normativity, the Naturalist Brian Leiter states that, "for naturalists, there is no real normativity, but normative judgment, and its role in the lives of creatures like us, is easy enough to explain."[36] The explanation is this: "What we call normativity is simply an artifact of the psychological properties of certain biological organisms, i.e., what they *feel* or *believe* or *desire* (or are *disposed to feel, believe* or *desire*). As long as the posited organisms are naturalistically respectable, and the mental states invoked are as well, then that is the end of the naturalist's story."[37] It seems right for Naturalism to make no pretense of giving an explanation for normativity conceived as the realm of universal moral truth. The only real alternative to denying its existence altogether is to provide some sort of genetic or evolutionary account, which cannot possibly attain to the requisite universality.

It is evident that Plato wants to anchor moral normativity in the intelligible world with the postulating of an Idea of the Good. But it is far from evident why, though he seems to retain a Form of the Good that is coordinate with other Forms, he explicitly posits a superordinate Idea of the Good, identical with the first principle of all.[38] It is Plato's view, as I shall try to show, that moral normativity is only accounted for by a unique first principle of metaphysics and that the coordinate or subordinate Form of the Good performs another task that, as Aristotle argues, cannot itself account for the universality of moral normativity. Thus, if Plato is right that normativity requires metaphysics, that is, metaphysics conceived of as a science of the intelligible world, then it would follow that without that metaphysics, there can be no such thing as moral normativity. And that is exactly the position of the consistent Naturalist.

I suppose it is reasonable for the Naturalist to claim that the Platonist has concocted an exceedingly implausible metaphysics to explain moral normativity. It is equally reasonable for the Platonist to retort that the denial of the existence of moral normativity rests entirely upon an unsupportable commitment to Naturalism. For this reason, we may suppose that we hit rock bottom when we realize the two diametrically opposed principled positions, Platonism and Naturalism.

---

36. See Leiter 2015; also, e.g., Blackburn 1984; and Papineau 1993, 98–203, on the non-doxastic expressivism of moral statements.

37. Leiter 2015, 65. Also Rosenberg 2017, 24: "Nowadays, philosophical 'naturalism' pretty much means philosophy drawn mainly by insights from Darwin." And 35: "The one thing that naturalists cannot do is seek another source of justification beyond science that could or does underwrite core morality or some component of it or a moral theory that formalizes it. To suppose otherwise is to surrender naturalism altogether." Rosenberg, 36, believes that "nihilism about moral norms" is what a consistent Naturalist must embrace. The Platonist will, of course, agree.

38. On a possible explanation for the difference between the superordinate Idea of the Good and a coordinate Form of the Good, see chap. 6, sec. 6.1.

2.3. Methodological, Philosophical Naturalism

A distinction is sometimes made between "Naturalism" as the name for the methodology of the sciences, and "Naturalism" as the name for the denial of the existence of causes or entities that are unavailable to this methodology.[39] It is perhaps unhelpful to call the latter position "philosophical" since it explicitly denies the existence of a subject matter distinct from that of the sciences, namely, the subject matter of philosophy. In any case, someone adhering to methodological Naturalism will typically appeal to this methodology as justification for the denial of a subject matter to philosophy independent of the sciences. One may be tempted to say that it is a non sequitur to hold that because a methodology rooted in the empirical can have in principle no access to the nonempirical, the nonempirical does not exist. I am not inclined to press this point, principally because I do not think that Platonists embraced a distinct methodology irreducible to the methodology of the empirical sciences. After all, logic is logic. Plato's most extensively explored account of methodology focuses on collection and division, which on any interpretation of its precise content, is concerned with the classification or taxonomical arrangement of given instances of a phenomenon. It would be odd indeed to tie the method of collection and division itself to an anti-Naturalist position.

A somewhat more serious point is made by Arthur Strahler, who claims that the methodology of the sciences which seeks out causes precludes causes that are in principle outside the ambit of the sciences. Thus,

> a specific event of history in a specific time segment must fall into either (a) divine causation or (b) natural causation. Our logic is as follows: "If *a* [divine, supernatural causation], then not *b* [natural causation]. If *b*, then not *a*." To follow with the proposal "Both *a* and *b*" is therefore not logically possible. Moreover, one cannot get out of this bind by proposing that God is the sole causative agent of all natural causes, which in turn are the causative agents of the observed event. This "First Cause/Secondary Cause" model, long a standby of the eighteenth-century school of natural theology . . . adds up to 100 percent supernatural creation.
>
> Consider the analogy of cosmic history as an unbroken chain [of causal explanations] made from all possible combinations of two kinds of links, *a* [supernatural cause, as in religion] and *b* [natural cause, as in science]. . . . When a theist declares any link in the chain to be an *a*-link (whereas all the others are *b*-links), an element of the science set has been replaced by an element of the religion set. When this substitution has been accomplished, the entire ensuing sequence is flawed by that single antecedent event of divine creation and must be viewed as false science, or pseudoscience. The

---

39. See Quine 1969 as foundational for methodological Naturalism. See also, e.g., Rea (2002, chap. 1), who takes methodological Naturalism to represent the core idea of Naturalism. Also see Kornblith 1994.

reason that replacement of a single link changed the character of all ensuing links is that each successor link is dependent upon its predecessor in a cause-effect relationship . . . that a divine act can never be detected by the scientist because, by definition, it is a supernatural act. There exists only the claim that such an act occurred, and science cannot deal in such claims. By the same token, science must reject revelation, as a means of obtaining empirical knowledge.[40]

What is especially interesting about this passage is its assumption that the natural and the supernatural are mutually exclusive putative causes. As we shall see in the next chapter, Plato has anticipated this objection, arguing that the empirical and the nonempirical are not alternative causes.[41] Rather, insofar as the latter can be shown to be necessary to explain certain phenomena, the former do not disappear. They become either necessary conditions or causes of a different sort.[42] This is the origin of the distinction between first causes and secondary causes that Strahler mentions. The justification for the distinction among causes rests upon a distinction between *per accidens* and per se causal series. A *per accidens* causal series, say, A, B, C, is one in which the fact that A causes B is ontologically distinct from the fact that B causes C. Ontological distinctness allow the possibility that A might not even exist after it causes B, such that it can have no role in the causing of C by B. By contrast, in a per se causal series, A causes C with the instrumentality of B. It could not cause C without B, but B is not the cause of C in the sense that A is. It could not be a part of the causal explanation for C if A did not exist. The causing of B by A and C by B are also per se causes but it would be misleading to call these per se causal series, unless one were to deny instrumental causality altogether. For if A is the per se cause of B, and

---

40. Strahler 1992, 345–346, quoted in Forrest 2000, 11.
41. Chalmers (2012) argues for what he calls "Fundamental Scrutability," which holds that all truths (including philosophical truths) are a priori entailed by fundamental empirical truths concerning fundamental natural properties and laws. This form of Naturalism seems implicitly to contradict Platonism, which holds that no philosophical truths are entailed by anything empirical. And yet Plato would maintain that if "S is P" is an empirical truth, where "P" stands for some natural kind, then this entails certain facts about the intelligible world. In particular, it entails that there is a Form or intelligible entity in which S participates.
42. See O'Conaill 2018 on "grounding" as the name for an attempt to show that the physical necessitates the mental, e.g., phenomenal conscious states. There are two striking features of the approach taken by O'Conaill and others. First, O'Conaill helps himself to the idea that both physical and nonphysical states can have essential properties, which is something that most Naturalists would wish to avoid. Second, he acknowledges that even if it can be shown that a given set of physical conditions or states necessitates the phenomenal, this does not in itself explain the phenomenal. That is, 726–727, there can remain an "explanatory gap" between the physical and that which supervenes upon it. As O'Conaill puts it, we might be able to say or predict *that* the physical state necessitates the phenomenal state, but not be able to say *why* it does so. As we shall see, it is such a gap that leads Plato to deny that the physical is an explanation at all, as opposed to the condition or conditions for a true explanation.

B is the per se cause of C, then if as above, B can cause C when A no longer exists, there is no instrumentality. The denial of instrumental causality can only be bought at an exceedingly high price. To deny instrumental causality is in effect to decompose such cases into *per accidens* series, the result of which is a radical inability even to describe the use of a means to an end. If I walk for the sake of health, then to decompose this event into two per se causes (me causing the walking and the walking causing the health) is to leave unexplained in principle the manifest purpose of the walking. We are thus unable to distinguish walking for health and walking for any other purpose or for no purpose at all.[43]

An obvious objection arises. If B could not cause C without A, it is no less true that A could not cause C without B. If the key could not open the door by itself, it is also true that I could not open the door without the key. Generally, when there is this sort of mutual dependence, it is because the type of causation occurring is the same kind for A and B. Thus, it is the motion or force A exerts on B that produces the motion or force that B exerts on C. But in a genuine per se causal series, A's doing something by means of B is fundamentally different from what B does. If, for example, I intend to insult you with words, my producing the intended effect is of a different order from the immediate effect of the motion of the sound waves in the air and the physiological effect they produce. It is simply false that an appeal to a per se cause nullifies the causality of the instrument. The dichotomy between the supernatural and the natural is a false one. Hence, we arrive at the failure of the argument that methodological Naturalism requires the exclusion of philosophy understood as the importation of nonnatural causes into a *per accidens* causal series. The exclusion of philosophy from where it does not belong in the first place cannot be derived from a commitment to methodological Naturalism.

Further, it would be surprising if methodological Naturalism excluded in principle the sorts of entities adduced by Platonists as per se causes. Consider the unconscious adduced as an explanation for conscious desires or actions. Whether or not this is a good explanation, it is a putative explanation in a process of abductive reasoning, that is, from effect to cause, sometimes termed inference to the best explanation. This is in principle no different from Plato's hypothesizing Forms or an unhypothetical first principle of all in his metaphysics.[44] Someone might object to the example of the unconscious on the grounds that it is an aberrant use of abduction. It is unlike neutrinos or quarks or other exotic hypothesized entities because it, unlike

---

43. It is helpful in avoiding confusion to distinguish instrumental causes from necessary conditions by limiting the use of "instrumental cause" to actions. All instrumental causes may be necessary conditions, but not all necessary conditions are instrumental causes since they are not constituents of actions.

44. Hypothesizing the unhypothetical sounds paradoxical to say the least. But the first use of the term is epistemological; the second indicates ontological ultimacy or primacy.

these, is in principle not directly observable or measurable. The exclusion of that which is in principle unobservable would have persuasive force only if a more plausible, possibly observable, cause could be found. But this is true for any putative cause.

Per se causes are introduced when the need for introducing instrumental causes arises. If per se and instrumental causes are irreducible one to the other, and if instrumental causes are one kind of condition, then at least in some circumstances, one type of cause is irreducible to a condition. But then reference to causes as necessary and sufficient conditions is problematic. For the difference between a per se cause and the condition that is the instrumental cause must be retained if per se causality is not to collapse into *per accidens* causality. Resistance to their conflation is one useful way to understand the opposition between Platonism and Naturalism.

2.4. A Rapprochement?

Many philosophers throughout the history of philosophy have found the starkness of this opposition between Platonism and Naturalism to be intolerable. I mean intolerable in the sense that it is thought that neither position taken in all its strictness gives a satisfying account of human beings and the world we live in. That is why much of the history of philosophy, beginning especially in the seventeenth century, comprises attempts by Platonists to make some strategic concessions to Naturalism. In contemporary philosophy, it is more often the case that some Naturalists have tried to make strategic but closely circumscribed concessions to Platonism.[45]

---

45. See, e.g., De Caro and Volterini (2010, 69–86), who argue that the true contradictory of Naturalism is Supernaturalism, principally the postulation of theological entities. The authors think that introducing entities such as numbers does not violate Naturalism per se because they are causally inefficacious. Thus, a sort of rapprochement may be achieved between Naturalism and Platonism so long as mechanism or causal closure is observed. As I shall argue, liberal Naturalism is unsustainable not because of its introducing the possibility of immaterial entities, but because the only reason for introducing such entities is a reason for rejecting causal closure. See also Scanlon (2010, 7–22), who argues similarly for a liberal Naturalism that allows the introduction of normativity since normative moral claims are not causally relevant. Thus, if it is a fact that murder is morally wrong, this fact does not cause anything including my acting in a certain way; it is only because I believe that murder is morally wrong that I so act. McDowell (1994, 91) calls "naturalized Platonism" the view that there are irreducible normative facts about the world. But he distinguishes this (77) from what he calls "rampant Platonism" which he identifies with "supernaturalism." If there are normative facts about a world described by Naturalism of one sort or another, it is difficult to square this with a Platonic account of normativity the ground for which is outside the sphere of Naturalism. But fitting normativity within a Naturalistic framework is problematic, to say the least. This is the point emphasized by Rosenberg and Leiter above. See also P. Strawson (1985), whose "soft naturalism" is a pioneering effort of contemporary rapprochement with the interesting feature that it is motivated by a desire to overcome skepticism, that is, the skepticism that the

The introduction of the idea of empirical knowledge, understood as the ne plus ultra of cognition, is a clear example of a strategic concession that philosophers otherwise disposed to Platonism were prepared to make. What, for Plato, is true belief as *opposed to* knowledge becomes, with suitable embellishments such as justification or evidential sufficiency, the philosophical goal. But it is not merely the case that Plato bids up cognition to include something more than empirical knowledge. He argues that the true belief supposed to be the clay out of which knowledge is to be formed is only possible if one already has nonempirical knowledge of the intelligible world.[46] Thus, the substitution of empirical knowledge for Platonic ἐπιστήμη is for Plato tantamount to the abandonment of a search for the wisdom that is thought by him to be the sole province of philosophy. With such an abandonment, the path is open for a thoroughgoing Naturalism. That is, there is no reason to think that in the search for empirical knowledge anyone, including philosophers, is better situated for success than any scientist is.

If knowledge has as its objects sensibles, it is clear that explanations of empirical phenomena cannot in principle take us outside the sensible world. For if the *explanantia* are intelligibles, that is, nonsensibles, then the knowledge of them would be constitutive of the explanations and hence not empirical. Therefore, the argument against materialism and mechanism, which is that assuming these as principles one cannot explain empirical phenomena, misfires.

Similarly, the argument against nominalism, which is that there is evidently a phenomenon of identity and difference that nominalism denies, loses its point for these identities could not be cognized according to any canon of empirical knowledge. Thus, I can see this color instance and I can see that color instance, but I cannot see that they are identical in color. The nominalist must insist that general terms are purely conceptual, serving as ways to categorize phenomena according to localized interests. These phenomena manifest no identity, but only similarity or resemblance or likeness.[47] The Platonist will reply that theories of similarity or resemblance

---

hard Naturalist has about the existence of the various phenomena to which the anti-Naturalist typically appeals.

46. Nonempirical knowledge provides the basis for the so-called Recollection Argument in *Phd.* 72A3–78B3. Cf. *Men.* 81E–86C; and *Phdr.* 246A–253C. I do not propose to take up the controversy regarding Plato's doctrine of recollection. My central point—independent of whether or not Plato means recollection literally—is that neither expressions of knowledge nor our relation to expressions of knowledge ("propositional attitudes") are knowledge; an expression of knowledge rests upon the psychical state of knowing and knowledge as a propositional attitude is not what Plato means by ἐπιστήμη. There is only ἐπιστήμη of the intelligible world which, teeming with content though it may be, has no propositions in it.

47. So Wittgenstein in *Tractatus* 5.5303: "Roughly speaking, to say of *two* things that they are identical is nonsense, and to say of *one* thing that it is identical with itself is to say nothing at all." See, e.g., Rodriguez-Pereyra 2002 for a defense of resemblance nominalism, the view

either presuppose nominalism or else they are dependent on the more basic idea of identity. That is, either we assume that the world is a four-dimensional matrix in which the inclusion of anything in it requires unqualified uniqueness and so the truth of nominalism, or else we hold that if two things are similar or resemble each other that is because they have one or more identical properties in common. If this is denied, then the opaqueness of the putative relation of similarity or resemblance leaves us wondering what makes one thing similar to or resemble another. Approximation will work no better. If the number of people in the lecture hall today is approximately the number present last week, what is the criterion of approximation? If there is none, then no definite claim is being made in asserting approximation. If there is, then this would seem to be purely subjective, and is therefore equivalent to making no definite claim about reality.[48]

Finally, the idea that knowledge of universal moral normativity could be achieved empirically seems hopeless both because there is obviously no empirical means of arriving at the conclusion of the impossibility of deviance from adherence to a universal norm. But real universality requires necessity, which is not even approached by a survey that discovers 100 percent agreement on some norm. Even if every single person in the world agrees that killing innocents is wrong, and that this fact accounts for, or, better, explains the meaning of the wrongness of murder, this does not show that it is not possible that murder is not wrong. The universality of moral normativity is not accounted for by the pseudo-universality of 100 percent agreement. If the universality is knowable, it is not knowable empirically. But if empirical knowledge is the highest type of knowledge, then either there is no such thing as moral normativity and relativism is true or else universal moral truths are inaccessible to us, which I suppose is the same thing.

Many contemporary proponents of Naturalism concede the reality or irreducibility of one or another phenomenon that the Platonist claims is only explicable by Platonism. Examples of such phenomena are well known. They include intentionality, subjectivity, consciousness, freedom,

---

that things are not called by the identical name because they share the identical property; rather, they are so called because they resemble each other, where resemblance cannot be determined objectively. If I claim that the baby resembles his father and you claim that he resembles his mother, who is right? Is there a criterion for determining who is right? And if there is not, what is the content of the claim in each case?

48. See Butchvarov (1966), who argues that there can be no such thing as a resemblance relation since all relations must have finite relata whereas if A resembles B, this is either arbitrary and subjective or else it must be expanded into: A resembles B more than C does D. But this again is either subjective or else it must be expanded into: the resemblance of A to B more than C to D is more than E to F is more than G to H, and so on.

and the truths of mathematics. This is only a partial list. There are basically three possible strategies pursued by Naturalists in the face of the recognition of such intractable phenomena. The first is to claim that the inability of Naturalism to account for such phenomena is an integral part of the advance of science where ignorance is eventually in some unspecified future replaced by knowledge. The second is to acknowledge what must be in light of the principles of Naturalism a mystery and then to argue that the mystery is unsolvable by finite minds. Third, and much more interesting, is the attempt to expand the fundamental description of Naturalism in such a way that it can account for these phenomena without recourse to anything that is even remotely Platonic. Thus, for example, the Naturalist who supports panpsychism seeks to show that consciousness is a ubiquitous natural phenomenon, present in every individual in the physical world, presumably down to the subatomic level. If this is true, then the Platonic claim that consciousness can only be explained if materialism is false is itself false.[49]

Both the first and second strategies naturally fail in light of a successful Platonic argument that accounts for these thought-provoking phenomena. The strategies cannot be maintained simply by reasserting the principles of Naturalism. We should all acknowledge the wisdom of Sherlock Holmes to the effect that when all the plausible alternatives are eliminated, the remaining one, no matter how implausible, must be true.

The third strategy opens up a new possibility, namely, that a revised Naturalism is not Naturalism after all. Thus, if molecules of water have consciousness, then either the evidence for consciousness in the first place, namely, our introspection or self-reference, is very different from the sort of evidence for the consciousness of H_2O, or else Naturalism must appeal to considerations outside those of the mature sciences for the attribution

---

49. See Skrbina 2005; G. Strawson et al., 2006. It is interesting to note that the analogous strategy of Leibniz comes from the Platonic side, so to speak. I am here more interested in the position that advertises itself as part of a rapprochement between Platonism and Naturalism than whether that position comes from the Platonist or the Naturalist. Also see Papineau (1993, chaps. 1–2), who argues for supervenience and against epiphenomenalism on the grounds that the former view acknowledges the causal efficacy of the mental, broadly speaking, on the physical, whereas the latter does not. But this causal efficacy is only acceptable if the mental is itself reducible to the physical. So, according to Papineau, Naturalism needs to be expanded beyond the strictly physical to include the mental so long as the mental is reduced to the physical. See also MacArthur (2004), who argues that the meaning of "naturalism" needs to be recognized as sufficiently expansive to include, for example, the normative or "normative fact." He calls this "liberal naturalism" and also "ontological pluralism," although the pluralism does not extend to a subject matter beyond the physical. I infer this from his claim, 45, that "where philosophy and science clash, it is philosophy that ought to give ground." Such a clash arises when, for example, Plato argues in *Phaedo* against causal closure.

of consciousness to these molecules. It is very hard to understand what evidence for consciousness other than introspection there may be, apart of course from second and third person testimonies which are themselves based on introspection. The panpsychist Naturalist seeks to undercut the anomalous nature of consciousness by gratuitously embracing an extra-Naturalistic mode of reasoning. One suspects that what is really going on here is a belief that conscious molecules of water are less absurd to contemplate than are immaterial human intellects. Intuitions will no doubt differ on this score.

It may be supposed that a rapprochement between Platonism and Naturalism should be sought in an assumption shared by both, namely, that the universe, loosely speaking, is apt for explanation. Indeed, what sets Platonism and Naturalism alongside each other is their opposition to the view that the universe is inexplicable. Everything is a mystery and nothing is perspicuous to our intellects. Viewed in this way, I suppose that Platonism and Naturalism do have a potential basis for discussion based on questions about the nature of explanation. Nevertheless, the Naturalist's commitment to causal closure and the Platonist's insistence on the principled inadequacy of causal closure to achieve real explanations seem to me to indicate a formidable impasse.

My working hypothesis is that there is no stable rapprochement between Platonism and Naturalism. I am certainly not alone in thinking that this is the case, though I suspect that I would have more support in this thought from Naturalists than from Platonists. If I am right, then the possibility of philosophy understood as a source of knowledge independent of the natural sciences depends on a defense of Platonism. I should note here that I do not take as a refutation of this position the existence of something called "philosophy of science" broadly speaking. Insofar as the traditional topics of the philosophy of science fall within the theoretical framework of the natural sciences, they are not the preserve of philosophers and they certainly do not constitute a distinct subject matter. That is, it is a mistake to conflate philosophy with theory or theoretical activity. It is not merely the case that a theoretical physicist is better placed than a philosopher to give an account of say, time or motion, but that the philosopher's theoretical efforts in this regard are entirely subservient to the evidence provided by the sciences themselves.[50] A philosopher who speculates about the theoretical foundations of physics or biology or chemistry is either an incipient natural scientist herself or else entering into the house of Platonism through a side door. Aristotle's portentous remark that the ultimate explanation for changeables qua changeable—the subject of physics or a science of nature—lies outside nature at once distinguishes philosophy

---

50. John Locke's correction of the medieval view of philosophy as "handmaid of theology" to "handmaid of the sciences" is, of course, the inspiration for Naturalists here.

from Naturalism and affirms their connection.[51] Platonism and Naturalism stand opposed, but they do so asymmetrically. That is, Platonism entails the subordination of the mature sciences, not their elimination. Naturalism, by contrast, entails the elimination of Platonism and so the elimination of philosophy, in particular philosophy understood as having a distinct subject matter.

---

51. See *Phys.* A 9, 192a30–192b1; *Meta.* Λ 7, 1072b13–15 is Aristotle's version of the identical point made by Plato in *Phaedo*: "—ἐκ τοιαύτης ἄρα ἀρχῆς ἤρτηται ὁ οὐρανὸς καὶ ἡ φύσις (Heaven and nature depends on such a principle)."

CHAPTER 3

Plato's Critique of Naturalism

3.1. Some Hermeneutical Assumptions

Like everyone else who writes on Plato and Platonism, I bring certain assumptions to my task. I shall just list them here and then go on to say a bit about each, though I shall not attempt a full-scale defense of any of them since I have attempted to do so elsewhere.

1. I reject the idea that a certain portion of the dialogues represents the philosophy of Socrates as distinct from their author's own philosophy.[1] Thus, all the dialogues represent Plato's own philosophy, generally with Socrates as spokesman, but always with the principal interlocutor the spokesman for that philosophy.
2. I reject the division of Plato's philosophy into early, transitional, middle, and late phases represented by corresponding groups of dialogues.
3. I reject the facile dilemma of unitarianism vs. developmentalism, opting instead for the position according to which there is constant or perhaps periodic development across the dialogues within a unified framework of principles.[2]

---

1. See Gerson 2014. Also Prior 1977.
2. See Gerson 2013a, 75–83. See N. Smith 2014 for a nuanced defense of developmentalism that rejects the attempt by Vlastos and others to isolate so-called Socratic ethics from the metaphysics of the so-called middle period of Plato's philosophy.

4. I reject the assumption that the manifest literary unity of each dialogue tracks a complete philosophical argument or position. The dialogues are a window on Plato's philosophy, but that philosophy is not the sum of the contents of the dialogues.[3]
5. Aristotle's testimony about Plato's philosophy (and the philosophy of the historical Socrates) is largely accurate.[4]

Here, briefly, are a few remarks expanding on these assumptions.

Ad 1. There is no evidence whatsoever that in a certain group of dialogues—called by some "Socratic" or "early"—Plato is representing the philosophical position of someone other than himself, namely, that of the historical figure Socrates.[5] On the contrary, all the evidence we have, both from Aristotle and from the indirect tradition, indicates that everything Plato wrote is an expression of his own philosophical position. This does not, of course, preclude the possibility that Plato was deeply inspired to pursue certain lines of thought both by the person of Socrates and by his teachings. Accordingly, the Plato of this book is not exactly a Plato "ohne Sokrates," as Walter Bröcker once put it. It is just that we do not know very much about the teachings of Socrates; we certainly do not know what arguments, if any, Socrates used in formulating them. According to Aristotle's testimony, Plato's most characteristic metaphysical and epistemological doctrines began to be embraced by him "starting from his youth (ἐκ νέου)," that is, probably well before Plato wrote his first dialogue.[6] If, therefore, we adhere to what the historical evidence reveals, we shall not be tempted to cleave Socratic ethics from Platonic metaphysics, thereby distorting both as these are found in the dialogues. To try to isolate ethics from

---

3. See Gerson 2013a, 83–91.
4. See Gerson 2013a, chap. 4.
5. See Benson 1992, 3–6, for a concise expression of the position according to which a certain set of dialogues called "early" represent the philosophical position of Socrates, whether "Socrates" refers to the historical figure or to a literary character. Irwin (1995, 251–254) argues that Plato rejects Socratic ethics, which Irwin takes to be found in the early dialogues. Rowe (2007, 15–20) argues, rightly in my view, that the character Socrates represents Plato's own philosophical position. I think that Rowe is mistaken, however, in identifying that philosophical position as belonging to the nonmetaphysical Socrates of the early dialogues.
6. See Aristotle, *Meta.* A 6, 987a29ff. Even those who most vociferously dispute Aristotle's exegetical remarks concerning Plato's philosophy seem disinclined to dispute the rather straightforward historical claims made in this passage. This is probably the case because what Aristotle says Plato believed "starting from his youth" is manifestly maintained in the dialogues. It is arbitrary to assign what Plato believed as a young man only to a fictitious middle period. The only reason ever given for doing so is that assigning Plato's metaphysics to the early period would contaminate the supposedly Socratic ethics of that period. For arguments against the type of developmentalism that seeks to separate Socratic ethics from metaphysics, see Prior 2004; and Fronterotta 2007.

metaphysics in Plato is one sure path to the misconception of Platonism. Or so I shall argue.[7]

Ad 2. The division of the dialogues into early, transitional, middle, and late is motivated in part by the false assumption that the "Socratic" dialogues are early and philosophically distinct from the rest. Further, attempts to confirm the doctrinal division among the dialogues have for the most part been a failure.[8] Though it is of course the case that there is a fact of the matter concerning the relative chronology of the dialogues, we do not know what that is. The spurious category of "transitional" dialogues is the fatal flaw of doctrinal developmentalism. Any attempt to link early and middle dialogues by transitional dialogues that split the difference between contrasting philosophical positions is more imaginary than it is evidence based. The above longstanding division of the dialogues has encouraged scholars to pick out the bits of Plato's philosophy they find congenial and discard the rest. Ironically, and owing to the ideological, that is, nonhistorical, presupposition of such approaches, scholars have drawn contradictory conclusions about where the real Plato is to be found. All so-called periods—early, middle, late—have had ardent proponents. The arbitrariness of all this can only be appreciated by the construction of a historically rooted account of the systematic nature of Plato's philosophy.

Ad 3. My rejection of facile developmentalism does not mean a commitment to a rigid unitarianism.[9] I am more than ready to accept that Plato's thinking evolved or developed on countless matters during the long course of discussions within the Academy. But this evolution or development pertains to the articulation of his philosophical system, to the appropriate vocabulary within which to express it, and to the consequences of embracing that system. I take the dialogues to be, as we may surmise Plato intends us to understand them to be, memoranda or dramatic records of the state-of-the-art ongoing discussions

---

7. See Brickhouse and Smith 2010, chap. 1, for a defense of the strategy of isolating Socratic philosophy—taken to be equivalent to moral psychology—from Platonism. Smith and Brickhouse do not maintain that Plato, when representing Socratic philosophy, held a view different from that of Socrates. They are, in fact, agnostic regarding Plato's view in the so-called early dialogues. I agree that Plato is not in these dialogues in disagreement with what Socrates says because I believe that what Socrates says is just what Plato believes. But he is not saying everything that Plato believes.

8. See, e.g., Ledger 1989; Nails 1995; and Kahn 2002.

9. Typically, unitarianism is selective: the middle dialogues contain the real Plato; the early dialogues contain intimations of the real doctrine; the late dialogues contain idle speculation on matters unrelated to the real doctrine or the detritus of a failing mind. See Cherniss 1936 and Allen 1970 for a taste of this way of reading Plato.

within the Academy.¹⁰ In these dialogues, we witness the invention of a technical and quasitechnical vocabulary to talk about the philosophical discoveries and arguments within a circle of thinkers at the center of which was Plato himself. It would be incredible if Plato never refined his views in any way. But all our evidence leads us to believe that he did so within a framework of principles, the articulation of which is just what Platonism is.

Ad 4. Recognizing, as everyone must, the literary integrity of each dialogue, we need not suppose that each dialogue is therefore intended by Plato to be philosophically self-contained.¹¹ That is, it is licit to appeal to one dialogue to help us understand another even under the assumption that the former was written after the latter. In that case, something like a proleptic reading of the putatively earlier claim might be hypothesized.¹² The dialogues are a window—perhaps our best window—on Plato's philosophy, but they are by no means the only one. It bears emphasizing that everyone in antiquity who wrote about Plato's philosophy assumed that the literary integrity of each dialogue did not preclude appeal to things said in different dialogues as evidence for Plato's views. It also should be noted that modern efforts to construct a literary firewall around each dialogue have generally led to results that are philosophically nugatory at best. The legend of the skeptical Plato has its roots in an arbitrary division of Plato's philosophy into literary units. There are no grounds for holding that the so-called aporetic dialogues express their author's own doubts. Further, there are no grounds for maintaining that *Parmenides* represents Plato's "honest perplexity" regarding his Forms, as Gregory Vlastos put it. Finally, there are no grounds for holding that *Sophist* reveals a Plato abandoning the Forms of the middle period in favor of something like conceptual analysis.¹³

---

10. See Gerson 2013a, 91–94, on *Phdr.* 274B6–278E3. I readily acknowledge that the dramatic situating of Plato's philosophy in the dialogues is so extraordinarily accomplished that a focus on it can seem to be irresistible. I am not, however, aware of anything in the very rich literature on this that undermines the historical evidence regarding Plato's systematic philosophy. I should add that much of this evidence comes from those who were no less impressed with Plato's literary achievement than are today's connoisseurs. It seems to me that much of Plato's literary art springs from the conclusions of his philosophical arguments about the nature of knowledge and being and the challenge of conveying these to others.

11. See Grote 1865, 1:x: "Each [dialogue] represents the intellectual scope and impulse of a peculiar moment, which may or may not be in harmony with the rest." Grote's view is taken up, in a somewhat attenuated form, by Shorey (1933), and subsequently supported by many others, both explicitly and implicitly.

12. See Kahn 1996, esp. 59–65, on the proleptic reading.

13. The so-called dialogical approach, according to which the literary integrity of each dialogue somehow guides the philosophy, is defended, e.g., in Frede 1992; and in various essays in Press 1993; Gonzalez 1995; and Griswold 1999. The hermeneutical stance according to which

Ad 5. Aristotle's testimony concerns Plato's philosophy, both as revealed in the dialogues and as communicated orally.[14] Aristotle himself distinguishes the dialogues from the oral testimony, but he does not claim to be interpreting exclusively the former. Hence, the fact that some of his testimony cannot be directly confirmed by anything in the dialogues is not sufficient reason to disparage that testimony. Nevertheless, Aristotle is certainly not a disinterested scholar dispassionately recounting the history of philosophy. The testimony of his that is not confirmed by the dialogues must be used critically and, when possible, confirmed by the indirect tradition, which can often be traced back to the Old Academy.[15] For those who find my reliance on Aristotle's testimony a bridge too far, I invite them to see my account of Platonism as only doubtfully attributable to Plato himself. In my earlier book, I tried to make the case that these scruples are not justified. In the present work, I am primarily focused on the systematic philosophical position that is Platonism and its polar opposite, Naturalism. It hardly needs arguing that this position was shared in its fundamentals by most Western philosophers until at least the seventeenth century. It seems to me than one reason for wishing to exempt Plato from the class of Platonists is not at all dissimilar to the reason for wishing to protect Socrates from Platonic metaphysical excesses. I must admit that I find this reason anything but dispositive. And in any case, it is irrelevant to the serious history of philosophy.[16] On the

---

Plato practices authorial anonymity entailing that we can attribute no doctrines to Plato based on the dialogues, has been defended by Edelstein 1962; Plass 1964; and various essays in Press 2000, including that of the editor. See next note.

14. For a brief survey of the huge literature on Aristotle's testimony and on the oral teachings of Plato, see Gerson 2013a, chap. 4. It should be emphasized that the frequent use of the term "esoteric" to refer to the oral teachings is misleading, albeit justified. I do not maintain that the oral teachings make up some secret doctrine unrelated to that which is found in the dialogues. On the contrary, the dialogues give us ample evidence for the content of the oral teachings as attested by Aristotle. The oral teaching is esoteric only in the sense that it was not written down in detail and therefore was not available generally to those outside of the Academy. Plato probably died while still working out the details of his philosophical vision. Aristotle's testimony alone is sufficient reason to reject authorial anonymity, although not without an alternative satisfactory explanation for the motive for Plato writing dialogues rather than treatises.

15. Later testimony about Speusippus and Xenocrates, Plato's successors as heads of the Academy—evidently based on written work now lost—can frequently confirm what Aristotle says about Plato. Whether or to what extent Speusippus and Xenocrates held views that differed from Plato's is, of course, another matter. But if their views were different, they were always based on the shared principles of Platonism.

16. I heartily endorse the conclusion of Richard 2005, 237: "Or eu égard aux problèmes d'authenticité posé par la transmission de l'oeuvre littéraire de Platon, nous trouvons tout à fait abusif d'*absolutisser* les *Dialogues* au point de les considérer comme l'unique voie d'accès à la pensée platonicienne et ce, d'autant plus qu'il est très difficile, voire impossible de mettre en doute l'existence et l'authenticité d'une tradition afférente à des *agrapha dogmata* de

assumption of the veracity and accuracy of Aristotle's testimony, I also reject the so-called nondoctrinal interpretation of the dialogues. According to this view, since Plato does not speak explicitly in his own voice in the dialogues, we cannot infer that he believes anything that is said therein, including or especially the conclusions reached by Socrates.[17] But once we appreciate that Aristotle's testimony includes both the dialogues and the oral teaching under the rubric "Plato's philosophy" we have no reason to follow this extreme view.

These assumptions or principles of interpretation are not new; indeed, they were the assumptions held by Platonists and interpreters of Plato up until about the beginning of the nineteenth century.[18] Still, the proof is in the pudding. I aim to show that when these assumptions are applied to the evidence of the dialogues themselves, we are plausibly led to a conception of systematic Platonism, to the conclusion that Plato was himself a Platonist in this sense, and to the reasons why it makes good sense to say that Aristotle, among many others, was a Platonist, even though he and others disagreed with Plato on a number of substantive matters. In addition, once we have Platonism clearly in view, we can see why both Plato and Richard Rorty believed that to abandon Platonism is to abandon systematic philosophy, that is, philosophy with a distinct integral subject matter. Obviously, the stark opposition between Platonism and Naturalism can only come into focus when a comprehensive, historically based account of the former is given.

3.2. The Turn from Naturalism to Metaphysics

According to the testimony of Aristotle,

> After these philosophies [the Italian schools], came Plato's system, which though it follows these philosophies in many respects, has its own peculiarities to distinguish it from the philosophy of the Italians.
> For [Plato], starting from his youth, having become acquainted first with Cratylus and with the Heraclitean doctrines that all sensibles are continuously flowing and that there is no knowledge of these, even argued this way later on. Whereas Socrates was working on ethical matters and not paying any

---

Platon: d'une part, cette tradition est bien attestée et, d'autre part, elle est issue de sources à la fois indépendentes les unes des autres et concordantes entre elles sur les éléments doctrinaux essentiels."

17. See Beversluis 2006 for a good critical discussion of those who have tried to inoculate Plato against philosophical criticism by maintaining that there is nothing to criticize in the dialogues. Also Gerson 2013a, 34–39.

18. For valuable surveys of modern Plato interpretation before and after the seminal work of Friedrich Schleiermacher, see Szlezák 1997a, 2004, 2010. See Findlay (1974, preface), who articulates a set of methodological assumptions similar to my own.

attention to the whole of nature, but seeking the universal in ethical matters and was the first to fix his thought on definitions, [Plato], while accepting Socrates's [approach], for the above sort of reason [i.e., Heraclitean doctrines], argued that this [the search for universals and definitions] is done not in regard to sensibles, but in regard to other things; for it is impossible for there to be a common definition for sensibles since they are always changing.[19]

According to Aristotle's testimony, Plato was committed to a "two-world" metaphysics "starting from his youth (ἐκ νέου)."[20] This means that, to put it minimally, Plato was oriented to the intelligible world even before writing any dialogues. But in a number of so-called early or Socratic dialogues, Plato does not explicitly introduce a realm of separate Forms or intelligibles as the objects of the knowledge sought for by Socrates.[21] One can without doing serious violence to the text suppose that the effort to define piety in *Euthyphro* or courage in *Laches* or self-control in *Charmides* may indicate something like a distinctive philosophical methodology, but they do not indicate a distinctive subject matter for philosophy. Although this view is contradicted by Aristotle's testimony, it is possible to insist on methodology rather than content if one assumes that in these dialogues Plato is representing Socrates's philosophy and not his own. There is in fact no evidence that this is the case, though I do not want to insist on the point here.[22]

In *Republic*, however, a distinct subject matter for philosophy is explicitly announced. Philosophers are distinguished from lovers of sights and sounds

---

19. *Meta.* Α 6, 987a29–b7: Μετὰ δὲ τὰς εἰρημένας φιλοσοφίας ἡ Πλάτωνος ἐπεγένετο πραγματεία, τὰ μὲν πολλὰ τούτοις ἀκολουθοῦσα, τὰ δὲ καὶ ἴδια παρὰ τὴν τῶν Ἰταλικῶν ἔχουσα φιλοσοφίαν. ἐκ νέου τε γὰρ συνήθης γενόμενος πρῶτον Κρατύλῳ καὶ ταῖς Ἡρακλειτείοις δόξαις, ὡς ἁπάντων τῶν αἰσθητῶν ἀεὶ ῥεόντων καὶ ἐπιστήμης περὶ αὐτῶν οὐκ οὔσης, ταῦτα μὲν καὶ ὕστερον οὕτως ὑπέλαβεν Σωκράτους δὲ περὶ μὲν τὰ ἠθικὰ πραγματευομένου περὶ δὲ τῆς ὅλης φύσεως οὐθέν, ἐν μέντοι τούτοις τὸ καθόλου ζητοῦντος καὶ περὶ ὁρισμῶν ἐπιστήσαντος πρώτου τὴν διάνοιαν, ἐκεῖνον ἀποδεξάμενος διὰ τὸ τοιοῦτον ὑπέλαβεν ὡς περὶ ἑτέρων τοῦτο γιγνόμενον καὶ οὐ τῶν αἰσθητῶν· ἀδύνατον γὰρ εἶναι τὸν κοινὸν ὅρον τῶν αἰσθητῶν τινός, ἀεί γε μεταβαλλόντων. See Steel 2012, 174–180, on this passage. There are many interpretative issues with these lines, but for present purposes, it is only essential to dwell on one. The words ἐκ νέου ("starting from his youth") indicate that what Plato later (ὕστερον) argued is continuous with his early view. The Greek grammar does not imply that whereas Plato became acquainted with the Heracliteans early, it was *only later* that he developed arguments for their position. This is supported by the words καὶ ὕστερον, which the Oxford Aristotle correctly renders as "even in later years." It is also supported by the fact that the main verb ὑπέλαβεν must govern the first clause as well as the second.

20. A νέος indicates a young man, most likely someone younger than thirty years old. Cf. Xenophon, *Mem.* 1.2.35.

21. See N. Smith (2018), who provides a careful analysis of Aristotle's testimony regarding the historical Socrates and his differences from the Socrates of the dialogues. On this basis, one may opt for various shades of developmentalism within the dialogues. I do not believe, however, that Aristotle gives us *arguments* for the positions of the historical Socrates. Insofar as Plato shares these positions, the only arguments we have are his.

22. See Gerson 2014. The occurrences of the word φιλοσοφία in these so-called early dialogues do indicate, broadly speaking, a methodology and a serious approach to matters.

by their love for and desire to know Forms.²³ Their desire is for knowledge (ἐπιστήμη) of the completely real or perfect being (τὸ παντελῶς ὄν).²⁴ The characterization of philosophers and philosophy is variously expressed in other dialogues, but nowhere so clearly. Yet this characterization raises a host of issues, not the least of which is the apparent surprising implication that if Forms or other intelligible entities do not exist, then neither does philosophy understood as having a distinct subject matter. Stated somewhat less drastically, if the completely real, understood to be that which is always identically what it is, does not exist, then philosophy would at least have to be conceived of in a radically different way. This apparent alternative is actually closed off by Plato given his claim that the only mode of cognition of the completely real is ἐπιστήμη along with his insistence that ἐπιστήμη is infallible (ἀναμάρτητον).²⁵ For as is shown in *Theaetetus*, there can be no infallible cognition of anything other than the completely real.²⁶ If Plato is right to identify the subject matter of philosophy with the intelligible world, then anyone who denies the existence of this subject matter would be absolutely right to reject a distinct subject matter for philosophy. And insofar as we recognize Platonism as essentially committed to the articulation of the intelligible world and to its causal role in explaining all reality, Platonism itself can hardly be expected to survive the banishment of the subject matter of philosophy as he conceives of it.

As we shall see in chapter 7, Aristotle agrees fundamentally with this claim, although he makes a terminological adjustment, calling what Plato

---

Socrates's claim that the "unexamined life is not livable for a human being (*Ap.* 38A5–6)" refers to the previous claim that φιλοσοφία is an examination of life (28E5–6). But there is no suggestion that this indicates a distinct subject matter. For example, one could engage in a serious examination of life by means of sacred texts or even historical precedents, all the while eschewing philosophy. The Atlantis story in *Timaeus* asks us to imagine an ideal political state of affairs that may serve as a template for the present. But this is not philosophy, as Plato explains. Hadot (1995) viewed Platonism (and, indeed, all ancient philosophical schools with the exception of Skepticism) as promoting a way of life, where the only distinct subject matter is wisdom about society and human beings. This view is further developed in Hadot 2002, chaps. 4–5. See also Schur 2013, chap. 3.

23. *Rep.* 476A9–D6. At 484B4–7, Socrates clearly distinguishes between philosophers and nonphilosophers by the subject matter with which they are concerned, namely, the intelligible and the sensible worlds. Cf. *Rep.* 485A10–B3; *Phd.* 79A6–7; and *Tim.* 27D6–7, where a sharp distinction between the sensible and the intelligible is made along with the mode of cognition appropriate to each. Also 51D3–E6.

24. *Rep.* 477A2–4. Later, at 479E6–7 and at 484B5, the completely real is described as things that are ἀεὶ κατὰ ταὐτὰ ὡσαύτως ὄντα (always identical). Also εἰλικρινῶς (purely), 478D6, 479D5. The implicit superlative indicates that something might have being but not completely or purely. And, indeed, it is the burden of the *Republic* argument to show that there are distinct modes of cognition for what is purely and impurely cognizable. Most important, cf. *Phd.* 79A6: δύο εἴδη τῶν ὄντων (two kinds of beings), one of which is sensible and the other is intelligible.

25. *Rep.* 477E6–7. See Krämer 2001 on the crucial role of infallibility in Plato's epistemology. Also Ferrari 2010, 605–608.

26. See chap. 4, sec. 4.4.

calls "philosophy" "first philosophy," thereby allowing for the possibility of at least "second" philosophy.[27] But second philosophy is just the theoretical foundation for the natural sciences, something hardly anathema to Naturalists. Indeed, there have been many attempts to make what Aristotle calls second philosophy the real successor to what Aristotle calls first philosophy, labeling the former "metaphysics" and thereby supposedly rescuing philosophy from extinction.[28]

A metaphysics of the natural world as conceived of by Naturalists is quite different from a metaphysics of the natural world conceived of by Platonists.[29] For Naturalists, topics like identity, existence, cause, and time, all have to be approached as principles exclusively for knowledge of entities in a three or four-dimensional framework. A concrete example of the difference is that within a Naturalistic framework, "identity" is a term that can be applied univocally to artifacts and nonartifactual entities. Indeed, artifacts are frequently adduced as paradigms for a theory of identity. By contrast, Plato assumes and Aristotle argues that identity is equivocally applied not just to artifacts and to things that exist in nature, but also to that which is immaterial. Because Aristotle thinks that "being" is an equivocal term with a focal meaning, all the per se properties of being, including identity, are analogously equivocal, always with the primary referent being in the intelligible world. One may certainly object that if this is the case, then so much the worse for Aristotelian metaphysics. My point, however, is that if this is the case, then, from the perspective of the Naturalist, so much the worse for the possibility of philosophy. For the analysis of terms in a putatively Naturalistic metaphysics does not differ from the theoretical work of scientists themselves. Quine's account of ontological commitment makes this clear: "A theory is committed to those and only those entities to which the bound variables of the theory must be capable of referring in order that the affirmations made in the theory be true."[30] Ontological commitment is the result of an account of what scientists in a particular field are prepared to count as existing. The theory relativity of the ontological commitment

---

27. Alexander of Aphrodisias, *In Meta.* 251.36–37, goes further, introducing the notion of "third" philosophy (τριτὴ φιλοσοφία). This is his interpretation of Aristotle, *Meta.* Λ 1, 1069a30–b2, where Aristotle distinguishes three kinds of οὐσία, the immovable, i.e., Forms and unmoved movers; the everlasting, i.e., the heavenly bodies; and sensible. "Third" philosophy concerns the last. The ordinality of the subject matters is clear.

28. See Kornblith 1994, 40: "For the naturalist, there simply is no extra scientific route to metaphysical understanding."

29. See, e.g., Ladyman and Ross (2007, 1), who argue for metaphysics as continuous with the natural sciences. They maintain that the aim of metaphysics is to unify the hypotheses and theories of contemporary science. So, presumably, someone who discovered the differential equation that unified gravity and electromagnetism and the weak and strong forces at the subatomic level would be doing metaphysics. This presumption would no doubt come as a surprise to working theoretical physicists and mathematicians.

30. See Quine 1948, 33.

is explicit and the theory is primarily in the hands of the scientists who formulate the theories. Of course, those trained in conceptual analysis can provide a valuable service to the primary promulgators of physical theory. But the former do not bring to the table a subject matter distinct from the subject matter of the mature sciences unless it is supposed that the conceptual foundations of a science are distinct from the science itself.[31] I do not have a clear idea of what that would mean, particularly if it is conceded, as it must be, that the actual work of scientists can impinge on discussions of the conceptual foundations of a science. If theorizing in quantum mechanics can affect putatively philosophical accounts of, say, identity, then the distinctness of the philosophical subject matter appears to evanesce. The philosophy of X, where X names a mature science does not indicate a subject matter distinct from that which is indicated by X. It refers only to the foundational issues within that science, principally, their axioms and definitions.

Plato's designation of the subject matter of philosophy as, roughly, "the intelligible world," obviously excludes an extension of the term "philosophy" to that which is nonintelligible. But the sensible world, as Plato says in *Republic*, "is and is not simultaneously, so to speak (οἷον ἅμα ὄν τε καὶ μὴ ὄν)."[32] Therefore, it participates in the intelligible world in some way. Accordingly, insofar as it does, it belongs to the subject matter of philosophy. The difference between the natural scientist and the philosopher on this account is, as Plato says, that the former "hypothesizes" its foundations, while the latter grounds these in the "unhypothetical first principle."[33] The former cut themselves off from the recovery of ἐπιστήμη. However we characterize the mode of cognition to which they aspire, it is not that which characterizes the successful philosopher. Insisting that scientists seek empirical knowledge and that this is the best that one can do is, from the Platonist's perspective, as much as to eliminate the possibility of philosophy.

In the case of *Phaedo*, however, separate Forms are explicitly introduced, along with their relevance to answering the question about the immortality of the soul. Moreover, their introduction is set within a wider framework that rejects unequivocally the sorts of explanations offered by Anaxagoras and others in favor of an entirely different explanatory path, that of philosophy. The subject matter of philosophy is thereby firmly fixed, whatever repercussions this may have for methodology.

---

31. See Papineau 1993, 3: "The task of the philosophers is to bring coherence and order to the total set of assumptions we use to explain the empirical world." Papineau then adds that *all* philosophical theorizing is of this kind. Philosophy is thus entirely in the service of the natural sciences which determine the subject matter(s) for investigation.

32. *Rep.* 478D5–9. Also *Tht.* 156A5; *Tim.* 52B3–5. Cf. Aristotle, *Meta.* Γ 5, 1010a1–4, where he rejects the view of his predecessors that "the only things that exist are sensibles (τὰ ὄντα . . . εἶναι τὰ αἰσθητὰ μόνον)."

33. *Rep.* 511A4–C2. Cf. D1–2, 533B5–C6.

3.3. Socrates's "Autobiography" in *Phaedo*

In *Phaedo* 95A4–102A9, we find the famous account by Socrates of his own intellectual history.[34] Our best evidence, including Aristotle's testimony, should lead us to suppose that this is in fact Plato's own autobiographical sketch on display.[35] It contains the most concise and complete statement of the nature of Platonism from Plato himself, both its distinction and separation from the philosophies of Plato's predecessors and the outline of its positive construct.

In this "autobiography," Socrates rejects the explanations of the natural philosophers given for problematic scientific phenomena. Instead, he posits separate Forms as the source of true explanation. The Naturalism of Plato's predecessors—explicitly here, that of Anaxagoras—presumes materialism and mechanism as the matrix for scientific explanation.[36] Thus, Anaxagoras is reported as explaining natural phenomena by, broadly speaking, the elements.[37] Socrates conjectures that Anaxagoras, if he were asked to explain why Socrates is sitting in prison, or why he is talking to his friends now, would give an explanation in terms of anatomical and physiological features of Socrates's body.[38] By contrast, Socrates had hoped for an explanation that would invoke intellect or νοῦς, for with such an explanation it would be possible to say why it was best for Socrates to remain in prison.[39]

---

34. Section 3.3 is a reworking of Gerson 2018.
35. See Sedley 1995.
36. At *Phd.* 96C4, Socrates says that Anaxagorean explanations, broadly speaking, were commonly thought to be correct, by himself and by others. I take it that Naturalism as a default position is what Plato is challenging. We may add that, at 99E1–4, Socrates rejects using his senses to arrive at explanations. So we can say that Plato is also rejecting empiricism. Cf. *Tht.* 186A6–B9 where Socrates argues that sense-perception cannot itself yield knowledge. See Furth 1991 on Anaxagoras's philosophy as an attempt to respond to the fundamental challenge of Eleaticism. Furth thinks this attempt, which he sees as an early version of logical atomism, fails. So, too, does Plato, who holds that any Naturalistic response to Parmenides must fail in principle.
37. *Phd.* 98C1–2. Aristotle, *GC* B 9, 335b9–16, assumes that Socrates is seeking explanations for sensible phenomena. Cf. *Meta.* A 9, 991b3–9, M 5, 1080a2–8. In calling Anaxagoras's explanations "mechanistic," I mean to attribute to them the assumption of so-called causal closure, meaning roughly that nature is a self-enclosed system wherein all causality originates and operates. Plato has Socrates disappointed in Anaxagoras's book precisely because his evident commitment to causal closure made νοῦς otiose in his system. See Armstrong 1978, 263–265, on causal closure as essential to Naturalism. Also Papineau 1993, chap.1, and appendix where causal closure is glossed as "the completeness of physics"; Ladyman and Ross 2007, 27–38, identify causal closure with the "principle of naturalistic closure." It should be stressed that causal closure is an assumption for which no evidence can in principle be provided.
38. *Phd.* 98C2–E1.
39. *Phd.* 98E2–99A4. Plato uses the terms αἰτία, αἴτιος, and αἴτιον seemingly indifferently through this passage. Frede (1980) argued that Plato makes a distinction that only becomes explicit in the Stoics, between a thing that is a cause (αἴτιος, αἴτιον) and the proposition that

Socrates maintains that the sort of explanation offered by Anaxagoras is not a real explanation or αἴτιον, but only "that without which the explanation would not be an explanation (ἐκεῖνο ἄνευ οὗ τὸ αἴτιον οὐκ ἄν ποτ' εἴη αἴτιον)."[40] In the case of Socrates remaining in prison, he says that his decision to do so because it is best to do so is the real explanation.[41] He thus distinguishes between an explanation and a necessary condition.[42]

---

expresses this (αἰτία). Perhaps. The main focus of the argument is, at any rate, on the entities that explain, not the expression of their explanatory role.

40. *Phd.* 99B3–4. See Meixner 2009b, 41–45, for an argument very much in the spirit of the *Phaedo* argument. Meixner argues that the Naturalist cannot coherently maintain causal closure since the sum of all physical events, taken as putative causes, can never be more than necessary conditions for the event that is supposed to be explained. To have true causal closure one must appeal to the intelligible world.

41. *Phd.* 99A8–B1.

42. At *Phd.* 99A4–5, Socrates says that it would be "exceedingly absurd (λίαν ἄτοπον)" to call the sorts of accounts given by Anaxagoras αἰτίαι. And then a few lines later, C5–6, he says that it is "the Good (τὸ ἀγαθόν)" or "that which is fitting (τὸ δέον)" that is the real αἰτία. At *Men.* 97E5–98A8, the words ἕως ἄν τις αὐτὰς δήσῃ αἰτίας λογισμῷ are specifically identified with ἀνάμνησις of Forms. That is, the Forms are here again the αἰτίαι of the truth of true beliefs. At *Tim.* 51D3–52A4, Plato says that *true* belief, as opposed to knowledge, has no account (ἄλογον). I take it that this is the identical point since an account can only be given in Formal terms. Thus, the συναίτιαι of *Timaeus*, 46C7, D1, 76D6, which are understood to be "auxiliary causes," that is, parts of the causal framework, are rather "auxiliary to the true cause or explanation." This interpretation of συναίτιαι is derived from *Phd.* 99B3, τὸ αἴτιον τῷ ὄντι (the true or real cause or explanation). At *Tim.* 46E3–6, Plato does distinguish between "two kinds of αἰτίαι," one that operates with νοῦς and one that does not. Cf. 68E4–7. The latter is identified with Necessity (ἀνάγκη). It is the "wandering cause (πλανωμένη αἰτία, 47E3–48B2)." Again, it is not a true or real cause or explanation just because it does not operate with νοῦς. Menn (1995, 38) points out that here it is assumed that soul is required for employing νοῦς and that the opponents Plato is rejecting—perhaps including Diogenes of Apollonia—are rejected because they do not recognize the need for soul in order to instantiate the workings of νοῦς. Also see *Sts.* 281E1–5, 287D3–4 with Kelsey's comments, 2004, 26–28. It is not implausible that the use of αἰτία in *Timaeus* for what are in effect instrumental causes as opposed to mere necessary conditions is the result of intra-Academic discussions reflected in Aristotle's fourfold schema of causality in *Physics*. The functional relation of material cause to formal cause in Aristotle is the explanatory successor to the functional relation of necessary condition turned instrumental cause to primary or true cause. See *Meta.* Δ 5, 1015a20–21, where συναίτιον and οὗ ἄνευ οὐκ are used synonymously. They are alternative ways of expressing that which is necessary (ἀναγκαῖον) but only derivatively explanatory. Aristotle's examples of air and food as necessary for life are nicely parallel to Socrates's examples in *Phaedo*: it would be silly to take food and air as answers to a question seeking an explanation for why something is alive. Yet, food and air can contribute to the explanation. See Johansen (2004, 103–106), who distinguishes *mere* necessary conditions (*Phaedo*) from instrumental or contributory necessary conditions (*Timaeus*). Presumably, the former would include counterfactuals. Cf. *Phd.* 95E8–96A1, 8–10; 97B3–7, C7.

It is perhaps the case that Plato mentions necessary conditions but leaves out sufficient conditions because he thinks that "sufficiency" should only be used for what is a real cause or explanation. So the putative necessary and sufficient conditions are really only a sum of necessary conditions. This sum may be said to be sufficient only in the sense that the presence of the conditions are sufficient for the true cause or explanation to operate.

Unfortunately, the full appreciation of the claim made by Socrates is impeded for modern readers by the contemporary philosophical default definition of "cause" as a product or sum of necessary and sufficient conditions and by assimilating explanation to cause.[43] By contrast, given the sort of explanation that Socrates is going to advance, conflating conditions and explanation by assimilating explanation to cause completely misses the new sense of αἰτία that is introduced here.[44] Socrates expects the true explanation to explain why it is best for something to be the way it is, including presumably why it is best that it come to be and perish when it does. This teleological dimension alone negates the possibility of assimilating αἰτία to necessary conditions. When he proceeds to sketch an approach to such an explanation, he has recourse to a method of hypothesis, hypothesizing on "each occasion" an "account (λόγον)" that seems to him to be strongest.[45] The hypothesis turns out in each case to be a Form.

The assimilation of cause to what is necessary or what is sufficient under the general rubric "condition" is to beg the question against Platonism from the start. The turn to metaphysics displayed in Socrates's autobiography should be taken to be a proclamation of the radical irreducibility of cause to condition, even the weak reducibility present in postulating their generic unity. As we shall see presently, arguing for this radical irreducibility is hampered by taking it out of its complete systematic context, in particular the ultimate causal relevance of the superordinate first principle of all. Forms may only be defended as irreducible causes if they are viewed as *instrumental* causes of the first principle of all.

Socrates's reason for rejecting Anaxagoras's account of causality is that his theory is in principle unable to eliminate the possibility that his explanation would equally serve for a property or state contrary to the property or state that he is trying to explain. The explanation is inadequate precisely

---

43. In logic or in mathematics, necessary and sufficient conditions indicate either logical connections between propositions or equivalency. According to Naturalism, causality in the world must reduce to necessary and sufficient conditions. Plato's separation of condition from cause is a hallmark of his anti-Naturalism. It leaves him immune to the criticism that the putative causality of Forms is otiose or redundant. In fact, there is no causality without Forms, though necessary conditions may be multiplied ad lib. I might add in passing that, to the extent that one conceives of causes as events, the tendency to conflate conditions and causes increases. I shall say nothing here about the dispute regarding event vs. agent causality.

44. The phrase "necessary *and* sufficient condition" is hardly perspicuous, since a sufficient condition is just a token of a necessary condition type. Henceforth, when referring to Platonic causes I shall contrast these with necessary conditions alone, stipulating that, for Plato, the necessary and sufficient conditions for the presence of a property are equivalent to a sum of necessary conditions at the type level. The main point is that no true cause is reducible to any sum of conditions. Even when what the Naturalist would call the necessary and sufficient conditions for some property are present, the cause, Platonically speaking, has not yet been ascertained.

45. *Phd.* 100A2–7. See Benson 2015, chap. 7, for some detailed analysis on how the method of hypothesis is supposed to work in *Phaedo*.

because it cannot be *causally* sufficient or adequate.[46] Much here depends on the descriptions of the terms of the Naturalist explanation. For example, one avoids Socrates's objection if one says that Helen's beauty is explained by, say, her shape arranged beautifully or that Socrates's being seated in prison is explained by the desire to stay, a desire which is itself nothing but a neurological state of the brain. Neither of these pseudo-explanations are satisfactory since it is open to Socrates to reply that at some level, Naturalistic explanations must be discontinuous with Formal explanations whether this be at the level of Anaxagorean *homoiomeres* or, in a modern version, at the level of subatomic particles. Socrates's preferred explanations must stay at the level of Form.[47] For this reason, the contending Naturalist must seek an explanation beneath the level of Form. This is where the necessary conditions for instantiation are to be found. But as soon as one tries to promote a necessary condition or sufficient condition up to the level of cause or explanation, either one reascends to Form or else one remains open to the charge that the necessary conditions for A are equally necessary conditions for non-A. If this were not the case—that is, if the necessary conditions for A were uniquely necessary conditions for A—it is difficult to see how any explanation has been provided at all. For if nature is so disposed that the putative explanation for A is uniquely an explanation for A and not any non-A, then it seems virtually impossible that there can be generalizations from any particular so-called explanation. But without generalization, there is only description and in fact no explanation at all.[48]

---

46. See Rosenberg (2018, 15, 23–24), who allows that the Naturalist must account for the possibility of "multiple mechanisms" realizing a property. He argues that this is not a problem for singular events explained by a particular mechanism. Socrates's objection to Anaxagoras cuts deeper because he maintains that no Naturalistic explanation can suffice since, expressed in purely Naturalistic terms, that explanation cannot but serve to explain the existence of a contrary property.

47. They must do so not just at the level of Forms, but hierarchically among Forms. The "cleverer hypothesis" of Socrates, 105B5–C7, states that X is f not because it participates in F-ness, but because it participates in G-ness and G-ness necessarily brings along with it F-ness. Presumably, this is a better explanation because G-ness is more comprehensive than F-ness; it explains more, that is, not only all that is implied by participating in F-ness but also all that is implied by participating in G-ness. But the exigencies of explanations mean that they all must stay within Formal confines.

48. Looking back to *Phd.* 74B7–9, sensible equals appear equal to one and unequal to another. This raises the question of whether the unreliability or diminished intelligibility of the sensible world means that no sensible ever has a definite property because it can always be said to have the opposite property. It can hardly be Plato's intention to deny the possibility that something can have a property, since Forms are adduced to explain this possibility. The question of whether that out of which an instance of a Form is constructed should be understood as a type or a token of that material is unhelpful, for the difference between type and token here presumes Forms that define types in the first place. See Irwin (1999), who thinks that they must be types.

Supposing that if the necessary conditions for some state of affairs are discovered, one has then discovered the cause naturally suggests that any appeal to a supernatural cause is superfluous.[49] The complaint has force, but only if it is assumed that a cause must simply be reducible to a conjunction of necessary conditions, with the conjunction perhaps being dubbed sufficient. I take it that Socrates's autobiography is, minimally, challenging this claim. As we shall see in the next chapter, Forms belong in the eternal world and their putative causal relevance could never be deconstructed into temporalized necessary and sufficient conditions. The Forms are, so to speak, eternally present as causes; instances of or participants in them arise in the sensible world when the relevant necessary and sufficient conditions obtain. According to this approach, it is perfectly reasonable to say that this is an owl because the necessary and sufficient conditions obtain for it participating in the Form of Owl and it is not a warthog not because the Form of Warthog is not eternally present but because the conditions for it being a warthog do not obtain. The necessary and even sufficient conditions do not preempt the causality. That is what the argument against Anaxagoras aims to show.

One might raise the objection that the supposed distinction between cause and condition depends entirely on the existence of these putative immaterial causes. But once they are eliminated, that which was held to be a mere condition can now be revealed as a cause.[50] Surely, the objector maintains, we are not constrained from talking about explanations without supposing both that there are Forms and that these Forms are the real explanations. The Platonic reply is that there would be nothing to explain without Forms, in particular, the truth-makers for predicative judgments, especially those judgments that presume that there are identities and differences in the sensible world. For this reason, necessary conditions are not, for Plato, explanations or causes waiting to do the job that Forms are shown to fail to do, but in principle things that cannot explain anything.

What is of central importance here is that Socrates's simple hypothesis seems to diverge from the sort of explanation that Socrates wanted from Anaxagoras but failed to get. For even if it is indeed the case that, say, Helen's beauty is explained by the Form of Beauty, nothing is thereby said about why it is best that the state of affairs that consists in Helen being beautiful obtains.[51] But among the examples of Forms, there is one that is

---

49. Aristotle, *Meta.* A 9, 991a8–b1, argues broadly against the causal relevance of Forms.

50. See Field (1980), who unites nominalism with materialism and mechanism, 41–46, and 68: "There are no causal connections between the entities in the platonic realm and ourselves." Thus, there would be no reason to sever cause from condition. This is essentially the Stoic complaint against immaterial entities.

51. See Lennox 1985, 203: "Socrates had much grander hopes for a theory which used Νοῦς bringing about various arrangements because they were good. In each case, goodness ought to account, not only for the *goodness* of a state of affairs, but *also* for that state of affairs itself."

mentioned, the Form of the Good, that might be thought to provide the right sort of explanation.⁵² This cannot be so, however, for several reasons. First, this Form is listed among others including Beauty and Largeness and if Good provided the requisite explanation, what about the others which are adduced as each providing the sought-for explanation on its own? More important, to say that something partakes of the Form of Good does not even begin to explain why it is good that it should do so. It is true that Socrates thinks that it is good that he remain in prison. But whether it is in fact good and why this should be so is not explained by saying that if it is good, that is because the act or decision partakes in the Form of Good. The vacuity of the proposed explanations by Socrates felt by critics from Aristotle to this day rests on the assumption that his explanations are supposed to be complete or satisfactory explanations without a teleological element.

With the hypothesizing of Forms—the simple hypothesis in each case—we are left with the problem of how this is supposed to provide the sort of explanation that Socrates failed to find in Anaxagoras and that he longed to have given to him. Gregory Vlastos and others are mistaken in supposing that when Socrates turns to his "second sailing (δεύτερον πλοῦν)," he rejects as a goal explanations that tell us why it is good that things are the way they are.⁵³ For Socrates says explicitly that his second sailing has as its destination the sought-for explanation.⁵⁴ The second sailing is not a voyage to an

---

52. See *Phd.* 100B6. I am here distinguishing a coordinate Form of the Good from the superordinate Idea of the Good. See chap. 6, sec. 1 for the basis for the distinction.

53. See Vlastos 1969, 297–298n15. Vlastos is followed by Burge 1971, 1–2n2, and Sharma 2015, 408n39, though in an earlier paper, 2009, 169, Sharma explicitly connects Socrates's rejection of materialism with teleology as necessary for adequate explanation. But this claim seems to contradict what Sharma says earlier (142), when he endorses Vlastos's interpretation. Vlastos himself followed Shorey 1933, 534, and Murphy 1951, 146. In all these works, it is assumed that if the simple explanation makes no reference to teleology, then teleology is not there. It must be insisted, however, that this self-imposed constraint on interpreting any dialogue of Plato is itself an assumption. Plato's arguments for a position seem to be like that of a Supreme Court judge who in principle seeks to settle a case on the narrowest possible grounds, always assuming that a complete down-to-principles account could be given if needed.

54. See *Phd.* 99D1. The words ἐπὶ τὴν τῆς αἰτίας ζήτησιν at D1 refer to the αἰτία that Socrates sought from Anaxagoras but did not provide at 97B8–C5, which is how νοῦς is an explanation for why things are in the best possible condition. See Vlastos 1969, 297–298n15. Cf. Aristotle (*Meta.* A 3, 984b8–22, 4, 985a18–22), who agrees with Plato that νοῦς is the appropriate αἰτία for why things are arrayed in nature as they are. See Hackforth 1955, 127n5, and Lennox 1985, 201n21, for additional supporting considerations. Crombie (1963, 161), clearly sees the reference of the sought for αἰτία. However, he ignores the full description of the hypothetical method, which ends with τι ἱκανόν and, accordingly, he is unable to give a plausible account of how Socrates's simple hypothesis has any teleological relevance. He says that the teleology comes in only by adding the Aristotelian point that in defining something, we thereby know its final cause because the formal cause and the final cause are in a way one. Cf. Kelsey, 2004, 21–43, on the "fundamentally normative dimension to how the Socrates of

alternative sort of explanation, that is, an alternative to a teleological explanation; rather, it is an alternative method of attaining the type of explanation that Anaxagoras could not give and that Socrates desired.[55] The goal is to explain the operation of intellect on the cosmos and it is this that Anaxagoras promised, but failed, to deliver. This operation is intrinsically normative since it is assumed that when intellect acts, it acts for the best. That is what "best" *means* in the context of action. It seems to me to be philosophically and dramatically maladroit to suppose that the characterization by Plato of the young Socrates as an earnest seeker of wisdom devolves into the simple hypothesis ignoring the sort of comprehensive metaphysical explanation that turned Plato away from his Naturalist predecessors in the first place.[56] So we need to keep before us the question: How are the sorts of explanations that Socrates is going to provide in his second sailing a means to the desired goal of a satisfying and true comprehensive and teleological explanatory framework?[57]

We do not have to wait long for some words that, at least, seem relevant to the answer to this question. Socrates makes two points: first, the proffered hypothesis should be examined to see if its consequences are consistent.[58] Second, the hypothesis itself should be examined, and if need be

---

Phaedo thinks about causality." Politis (2010, 100–103), agrees that teleological and formal explanations are conflated here. But he thinks that the latter are logically prior: something is F because it partakes of F-ness and it is good insofar as it partakes of the kind of goodness that F-ness has. Politis, however, thinks that the Idea of the Good in *Republic* is, too, an essence or Form.

55. Cf. *Sts.* 300C; *Phil.* 19C. At *Tim.* 46E7–47C4, the appropriate explanation for the functioning of the eye just is the explanation for its best possible functioning. The necessary conditions for this functioning are called συμμεταίτια. Aristotle makes the same point when he says that the science of X is identical to the science of good X. As we shall see, teleology is inextricably intertwined with scientific explanation in the Divided Line in *Republic*. Tempesta (2003) provides an abundance of evidence to the effect that δεύτερος πλοῦς almost certainly indicates a second-best method, not merely a method different from that of Anaxagoras. But I disagree with Tempesta who holds that the simple method of hypothesis is second best in relation to direct intuition of Forms. Rather, it is second best in relation to the attainment of τι ἱκανόν, which I argue is the unhypothetical first principle of all, the Idea of the Good.

56. See *Phd.* 97D1: "On the basis of this explanation, indeed, a man should consider nothing else but the best, the highest good." Sedley (1990, 359–384) argues that the sought-for teleological explanations are to be found in the myth at the end of the dialogue. Without denying Sedley's point that there are teleological elements in the myth, he nevertheless does not explain how the δεύτερος πλοῦς is subordinate to the sort of teleology contained in the myth. Indeed, if the afterlife has the features it has because it is better that way, this is not much of an explanation.

57. See Tait (1986), who emphasizes the mathematical nature of the scientific explanations sought by Socrates, although he does not connect these with an unhypothetical first principle of all. See also Nef 2012.

58. *Phd.* 101C2–5. See Gallop (1975, 189), who plausibly suggests that the possible contradictory consequences of the initial hypothesis of a Form are similar to those described in *Parmenides* 131A–E with respect to the Form of Largeness and Smallness. Also see Benson

another hypothesis should be offered.[59] Neither of these two methodological comments are entirely clear, though the first is clearer than the second. Presumably, the examination of consequences pertains to dilemmic reasoning about the putative properties of that which participates in the hypothesized Form. As for the second comment, there are two obvious possibilities. First, Socrates may be alluding to what he will explain later when he offers as an adumbration of his simple hypothesis a "cleverer" hypothesis, according to which it is not the original hypothesized Form that is the true explanation, but another Form which brings with it necessarily the original Form.[60] The second possibility is that the additional hypothesis could be a generic Form, for example, Virtue, offered instead of a specific Form, say, Temperance. This would be necessary, for example, if it turned out that all the Virtues were really identical. I do not see any reason to exclude either of these possibilities. My main concern, though, is to point out that in neither case would we have solved the problem about the kind of explanation that Socrates originally desired.

We do, however, get from Socrates a third point. This is that the examination of the hypothesis will proceed upward until "something adequate (τι ἱκανόν)" is reached.[61] And with this comes a warning, that once having attained something adequate, one must not confuse the beginning or starting point or principle (ἀρχή) found with the consequences of that explanation.[62] The τι ἱκανόν is the ἀρχή. Its consequences presumably include all the consequences of the hypothesizing of the Forms as well as the consequences for the Forms themselves of having attained an adequate principle.[63]

The best way to bring out the fundamental difference between the explanatory analysis offered by Anaxagoras and others that adduces necessary conditions for coming-to-be and passing away and the explanatory analysis that rejects these as truly explanatory is to begin by reflecting on the fact that no Form adduced by Socrates is the sought-for principle or ἀρχή.[64] The

---

2015, 195–204, on the relation between the hypothesizing of Forms and the explanations that Forms are said to provide.

59. *Phd.* 101D5–7.
60. *Phd.* 105B5–C7.
61. *Phd.* 101E1. It is tempting to see the adequacy here as the causal or explanatory adequacy that is in principle missing in the necessary and even sufficient conditions proposed by Anaxagoras or by any other Naturalist.
62. *Phd.* 101E1–3.
63. Cf. *Phd.* 107A8–B10 where Socrates insists on the necessity for further clarifications. Presumably, this includes a substantive discussion of the τι ἱκανόν. This suggests that τι ἱκανόν does not just indicate another Form.
64. *Phd.* 95E8–96A1, 8–10; 97B3–7, C7. See Aristotle, *Meta.* A 6, 988a14–17 with N 4, 1091b13–15, which ties Plato's rejection of Anaxagorean and Empedoclean explanations to the alternative explanation which posits the Idea of the Good identified with the One. Aristotle assumes that a full picture of Plato's account of explanatory adequacy over against the

implicit contrast is threefold: (1) the necessary conditions that are in fact "that without which the explanation would not be an explanation"; (2) the explanatory role of Forms; (3) the ἀρχή or principle that is sufficient for an explanation. It is the relation between (2) and (3) that reveals the sort of explanatory path taken here by Plato, not the relation between (1) and (2) or (1) and (3). How are the Forms supposed to be related to the ἀρχή?

At this point in our examination of the autobiography, we reach a sort of hermeneutical crossroads. On the one hand, if we resolve as a matter of principle to stay within the confines of *Phaedo*, we can insist that this ἀρχή is not necessarily, as Burnet insisted, the ἀρχή ἀνυπόθετος of *Republic*.[65] In that case, it might be *another* hypothesis although it is quite obscure what then "adequate" would mean. Presumably, it could only be adequate either for the time being or so long as investigators can find no contradictions flowing from it. But this alternative leaves us with no path to the desired conclusion of the second sailing which was, we recall, an explanation of why, broadly speaking, it is good that things are the way they are.[66]

On the other hand, if we suppose that the ἀρχή that is adequate is the "unhypothetical first principle of all" of *Republic*, every single one of the

---

deficiencies of materialists must conclude with the unhypothetical first principle of all. See Reale 1997, 143–151, on the explanatory inadequacy of Forms alone. Reale aptly calls the Socratic autobiography "the Magna Carta of Western metaphysics."

65. See *Rep.* 510B7. See Burnet 1911, 101. Bluck (1955, 199) grants that "Plato may . . . have believed that his Forms represented the best approach to a teleological explanation of causation (by comparison with which Socrates's λόγοι were only a second-best), and that these causes would be confirmed as correct and as truly teleological when the nature of the ultimate principle became clearer to him." Hackforth (1955, 141) says that "the injunction which Socrates gives in a later passage (107B), that our first hypotheses, even if we are convinced of them, ought to be further examined, does strongly suggest—inasmuch as the first hypotheses there in question are simply the existences of this or that Form—the doctrine of the unhypothetical first principle, identical with that Form of Good which is the source of all Being, and itself 'beyond Being'. Nevertheless, I do not believe that Plato is alluding to that doctrine here, in the words τι ἱκανόν: for surely the phrase could not easily be understood as carrying this vast implication; moreover Socrates is not envisioning a process of reasoning which will satisfy a philosopher's ultimate demand, but one which will serve the purpose of proving to the satisfaction of an interlocutor some particular theorem." The words "strongly suggest" and "I do not believe that Plato is alluding to that doctrine here" do not present a coherent interpretation. Further, when Hackforth says the words τι ἱκανόν "could not easily be understood as carrying this vast implication," he is assuming that the only intended readers are those ignorant of Plato's intra-Academic teachings. Why assume that? And why could it not *both* be true that some (Academics) would understand it perfectly well and some (non-Academics) would not? Further, in the passage Hackforth cites, 107B4–9, Socrates does not just say that we should examine our first hypotheses, but that if we do this, "we will follow the argument to the furthest point to which a human being can follow."

66. Horn (1995, 141) eschews any speculation about what τι ἱκανόν might signify, assuming that it is not licit to go outside of *Phaedo* for any insight into its meaning.

desiderata of the whole passage are met.⁶⁷ For, first, in the superordinate and absolutely incomposite Idea of the Good, we do have a logical stopping point for the investigation. We have the true αἰτία of all.⁶⁸ Second, as we learn from the Divided Line passage, which follows immediately after the introduction of the Idea of the Good, it is not possible to grasp the role in explanation that the Forms have without recourse to this first principle of all.⁶⁹ This means far more than: You cannot know if Justice is good without knowing that it participates in the Idea of the Good. It must mean that you cannot know what Justice is without knowing how the Idea of the Good provides "existence and essence (εἶναι τε καὶ οὐσίαν)" to all the Forms. This is so because only the Idea of the Good makes the Forms knowable. And without knowing the Forms, they obviously can provide nothing more than a nominal explanation for anything. Without knowing what F-ness is, adducing it as an explanation for why X is f would be no better than saying that X is f is explained by whatever it is that explains it. Third, with the introduction of the Idea of the Good, we not only have the principle that will serve to give Socrates the sort of explanation he desires, but we can also remove from the postulation of Forms the false assumption that they alone can provide the explanation. This does not mean that the Forms are, with the introduction of the Idea of the Good, irrelevant; rather, it means that they can only fill an instrumental role for the explanation that the Idea of the Good provides.

The instrumental causality of Forms in an adequate explanation of the "why" of coming-to-be and passing away does *not* preclude the explanatory role of Forms in a more localized or specific context. Thus, it is true that Helen is beautiful because she participates in Beauty and Simmias is tall

---

67. See *Rep.* 533C9 where the Good, the ἀρχή of all, is explicitly contrasted with "τὰς ὑποθέσεις (the hypotheses)" that dialectic "eliminates (ἀναιροῦσα)." See Stenzel 1924, 115–116; Krämer 1966; Mueller 1989, 85.

68. See *Rep.* 517B9–C1: πᾶσι πάντων αὕτη ὀρθῶν τε καὶ καλῶν αἰτία (the explanation for all that is good and beautiful in everything). Cf. 530A5–8 on a divine intellect as providing the sort of teleological explanation that Anaxagoras advertised as providing but failed to provide. C. C. W. Taylor (1969, 47) at least acknowledges that a reference to *Republic* would explain the τι ἱκανόν, though he claims that this is "speculative." Bostock (1986, 175) thinks that taking τι ἱκανόν as referring to the unhypothetical first principle of all "receives no support from the *Phaedo*." But this is so only if δεύτερος πλοῦς is, incorrectly, taken to be an *alternative* to the explicit goal of Socrates's quest for teleological explanations.

69. At *Rep.* 511B2–C2, the necessity for an ascent to the unhypothetical first principle of all is made explicit. Thus, the connection with being unhypothetical and being sufficient is clear. So perhaps one can argue that in *Phaedo* Plato held that τι ἱκανόν could be something other than that which is unhypothetical, but that in *Republic* he changed his mind and held that *only* that which is unhypothetical could be ἱκανόν, for the purposes of explanation. But in doing this, one is committed to maintaining that either Plato did not know what he meant himself by the words τι ἱκανόν or else he meant to refer to another hypothesis. Cf. the previous words: ἥτις τῶν ἄνωθεν βελτίστη. This is what Crombie (1963, 2:541–545), for example, supposes. So, too, Dancy (2004, 299). Either alternative seems quite implausible and gratuitous.

because he participates in Tallness.[70] Focusing on this sort of explanation is relevant to the answer to many questions, including the question of the immortality of the soul, the central topic of *Phaedo*. But the global account sought for by Socrates and found absent in Anaxagoras is one that adduces the Forms as instrumental to the ultimate explanatory role of the first principle of all, in *Republic* the Idea of the Good.

The attainment of the "unhypothetical first principle of all" is the *elimination* of all hypotheses. These are not, as Plato says, principles, but only stepping-stones leading to a principle.[71] Therefore, it is very difficult to envision the "something adequate" of *Phaedo* to be another hypothesis. The transcending of all hypotheses is not their elimination but their reduction to the status of instruments of the true explanation. The instrumentality of the Forms to the operation of the Good is, so to speak, the converse of the role of Forms as stepping-stones *to* the Good.

It is sometimes objected that whereas Forms might be thought to explain the being of things, they cannot explain the coming-to-be and ceasing-to-be of things—events and processes—that Socrates wanted to have explained by Anaxagoras.[72] It is true that Socrates is mainly concerned with the *why* of events and processes and not the *how*. It is generally the latter and not the former that is supposed to be the locus of causality. But Socrates's demotion of Anaxagorean causes to the level of mere conditions allows him to conclude that while the "how" is answered by Anaxagorean-type conditions, these never amount to real explanations. Socrates does not, I think, maintain that conditions are irrelevant; indeed, they are necessary for participation to occur. He insists that any true predicative judgment about nature is owing to participation in a Form, including those judgments about the results of processes or events or, in general, changes. The changes themselves, insofar as they are becoming, are not susceptible to true predicative judgment. In other words, they are not explicable. I take it that the point is that pure becoming is unintelligible and that whatever measure of

---

70. A nominalist such as Sellars will insist that (a) "x is f" and (b) "x participates or exemplifies F-ness" are synonymous. See 1963, 247–281. Plato wants to maintain that (b) explains (a). The need for an explanation depends entirely upon the claim that if "x is f" is true, then it follows that it is at least possible that "y is f" is also true, where "f" indicates that x and y are the same even though they are different. It is the sameness (or the possibility of sameness) that calls for an explanation. The nominalist assumes that there can be no such thing, in which case there is nothing to explain.

71. See *Rep.* 511B4–6. Plato is aware of the seeming paradox of hypothesizing an unhypothetical first principle. The paradox disappears when we realize that anything but the first principle (ἀρχή) cannot be a first principle. See 511B4. The unique ἀρχή of all can be hypothesized by us, but not as an instrumental cause; it is hypothesized as the logically necessary explanatory terminus. It is the impossibility of anything but the first being a true ἀρχή that explains why the hypotheses of mathematicians or, indeed, of dialecticians are merely hypothetical in the sense of provisional.

72. See, e.g., Annas 1982, 318; and Mueller 1989, 77.

intelligibility a change has, it is owing to temporary or transitory participation in Forms. Plato's reason for rejecting radical Heracliteanism is precisely that it entails the utter unintelligibility of change per se.[73] By contrast, insofar as a change *is* intelligible, participation in Form(s) is required. Forms are the only source of intelligibility.[74]

There are several additional considerations that may be mentioned here briefly in support of the claim that the autobiography of Socrates needs to be set within the wider context of Plato's overall systematic philosophy.

In *Timaeus*, the role of a divine intellect in explaining why the cosmos is as it is, and ignored by Anaxagoras, is made explicit.[75] The Demiurge wanted the world to be "as beautiful as possible (κάλλιστον)."[76] To do this is to make it as close as possible to the "Living Animal (τὸ ζῷον)" which is comprised of all intelligible, living beings.[77] That is, things are good insofar as they resemble intelligible reality, this reality including both the Forms and the Demiurge himself. Insofar as things deviate from their eternal paradigms, they are defective or evil. The Demiurge performs the task of making the cosmos like the Living Animal by imposing on it "shapes and numbers," that is, by using geometry and arithmetic.[78] The connection between the *Republic* passage and this account in *Timaeus*, that is, between the Idea of the Good and the Demiurge and Forms, is alluded to later in the dialogue where Timaeus declines to discuss "the first principle or principles" of all things owing to the difficulty of doing so within the framework of the current method of exposition.[79] This passage is especially important in indicating that not only does the explanatory role of the simple hypothesis need to be set within the hierarchical framework with the Idea of the Good at the head but also that a divine intellect is an inseparable part of that explanatory framework. How exactly the Good, the Demiurge, and the Forms are connected requires extensive investigation. Nevertheless, the fact that they are evidently connected eliminates the worry that Plato is not able or does not intend to associate teleology and the postulation of Forms.

---

73. See *Tht.* 181B–183C.

74. It might be objected that calculus shows that pure change is intelligible, at least mathematically. But the pure change postulated by radical Heracliteanism is not the ordered, e.g., constant rate of change assumed by calculus. A constant of any sort within a change negates the absoluteness of radical Heracliteanism.

75. That the works of the Demiurge are the works of νοῦς is indicated at *Tim.* 47E4: τὰ διὰ νοῦ δεδημιουργημένα.

76. *Tim.* 30A6–7.

77. *Tim.* 30C2–D1.

78. *Tim.* 53B5.

79. *Tim.* 48C2–6. Cf. 53D4–7. The reference to "principle *or* principles" perhaps suggests that the question of whether the Indefinite Dyad is a principle separate from the One or reducible to it is not yet settled in Plato's mind.

Further, in *Philebus* the Idea of the Good is said to be revealed in three perspectives, that of beauty, commensurability, and truth.⁸⁰ This is the beauty, expressed as commensurability, that is a property of the Good in *Symposium* and that the Demiurge brought to the world by the imposition of shapes and numbers.⁸¹ And it is the truth that the Idea of the Good provides to the Forms in *Republic*.⁸²

Finally, if we take Aristotle's testimony seriously, we have a clear indication of *why* the unhypothetical first principle of all, the Idea of the Good, must have the ultimate explanatory role for all Forms and, hence, for the being of all things. Plato, Aristotle tells us, identified the Idea of the Good with the One from which, along with the Indefinite Dyad or the Great and Small, it produces the Form-Numbers.⁸³ As we shall see in chapter 5, the identification of the Good with the One is not merely a gratuitous name change. Unity or oneness, specifically integrated unity, will turn out to be a substantive metaphysical and normative principle. The simple hypothesis of *Phaedo* followed by the cleverer hypothesis can thus be set within the larger framework that includes the Demiurge, all the Forms, and the Good understood as the principle of integrated unity.

Now within such a hermeneutical framework, I think it is a fair question to ask why we should favor the approach that in principle can explain nothing over the approach that can explain everything? It seems to me that the only possible reason for preferring the first approach is that one thinks that there is no evidence to support the second approach and, given this fact, it is another exegetically oriented simple hypothesis that Plato should only be approached one dialogue at a time. But to take this approach is to suppose that either Plato had no clear idea of what he meant when he wrote the words τι ἱκανόν or that he simply meant "some other hypothesis."⁸⁴ If the latter, then the mistake is corrected in *Republic*; if the former, then we shall be attributing to Plato what Vlastos called in another context his "honest perplexity" about what would count as an adequate ἀρχή. However, since we do have evidence that before Plato wrote any dialogues at all he embraced a "two-world metaphysics," and since we do have evidence, albeit far from conclusive, that in addition, probably before he wrote any dialogues, he

---

80. *Phil.* 65A1–5. See chap. 5 for further discussion of this passage.

81. See *Symp.* 204Eff. Beauty is the property of attractiveness that the Good possesses and everything insofar as it is good possesses.

82. See *Rep.* 508C10. Truth is the property of intelligibility to an intellect possessed by all Forms and provided to Forms by the Good. The principal reason why, as we shall see in the next section, the subject matter of philosophy is the intelligible world is that the intelligible world is the world of truth. See *Rep.* 475E4: τοὺς τῆς ἀληθείας φιλοθέμονας (those lovers of the sight of truth). Nagel 2012, 17, seems to endorse the Platonic position, labeling it "objective idealism."

83. See Aristotle, *Meta.* A 6, 988a8–14; cf. N 4, 1091b13–15.

84. If he meant this, one presumes he would have written the feminine τις ἱκανός instead of the neuter τι ἱκανόν. Or perhaps he would have written τις ἄλλη ὑπόθεσις instead of τι ἱκανόν.

traveled to Megara, to Cyrene, and then to Italy to study with Philolaus and Eurytus, it hardly seems defensible not to use it.[85] This evidence makes the principled position of agnosticism about what Plato thought τι ἱκανόν was when writing *Phaedo* unattractive, especially given his Pythagorean interests. Furthermore, this agnosticism is philosophically exiguous, given that the *Republic*, *Timaeus*, and *Philebus* passages along with Aristotle's testimony obviously provide the content for τι ἱκανόν whether or not it was in his mind when writing *Phaedo*.

The superordinate Idea of the Good is the obvious candidate for the referent of τι ἱκανόν. But it does not serve its purpose without the instrumentality of the Forms and without a divine intellect, the Demiurge, whose goal it is to make the cosmos as perfect as possible. But only if the Good is the One and if Forms are Numbers does the explanation role of the Good make any sense at all. This raises the following intriguing possibility. The only reason anyone has ever given for categorizing *Phaedo* as a middle dialogue and not an early dialogue is that it contains the "two-world metaphysics" that is supposedly absent in the early dialogues. But on the basis of Aristotle's testimony, Plato embraced the two-world metaphysics at a young age, almost certainly before he wrote *any* dialogues. This fact, coupled with the fact that *Phaedo* is a dramatic conclusion to the trilogy *Apology*, *Crito*, and *Phaedo* suggests that either the first two dialogues are not early or that the third one is. If the latter is the case—and I see no reason for preferring the former—then it would seem that Plato's doctrine of an unhypothetical first principle of all is not, as W. D. Ross and others have assumed, a late development in his thinking, but on the contrary, something that is rooted in his very early Pythagorean speculations.[86] The positing of the Idea of the Good seems to be of a piece with his very early rejection of natural philosophy (i.e., natural science) as the path to true wisdom.

All our evidence regarding Plato's philosophy tells us that Forms are instruments in a larger explanatory framework with the unhypothetical first principle of all at the top. The rejection of the Naturalist framework of Anaxagoras, and a fortiori that of lesser philosophers, is of a piece with the positing of the metaphysical principles of explanation.[87] It is a profoundly different approach to wisdom or comprehensive explanation. In addition, the Forms, as participatable οὐσίαι, can only fulfill their explanatory roles if nominalism is false, that is, if it is false that the only things which exist are unique individuals and their properties are uniquely possessed, for then

---

85. See Aristotle, *Meta.* A 6 and Diogenes Laertius (D.L.), 3.6.

86. See, e.g., Robin 1908; Stenzel 1924; W. D. Ross 1951, 239; and Szlezák 2011. It may be, after all, that Plato did not first postulate an Idea of the Good and then at a later date identify it with the One but rather vice versa. This is at least suggested by his Pythagorean inspiration. See Huffman 1993, 21–25, on the early influence of Philolaus on Plato.

87. No doubt, other pre-Socratics such as Diogenes of Apollonia, Archelaus, Empedocles, Heraclitus, and Alcmeon are included in the condemnation.

participation is impossible. In that case, what Plato calls the "that without which" could presumably turn into a primary cause. But this is so only at the expense of foregoing, among other things, a distinction between true and false predicative judgments. Plato announces in this passage his rejection of materialism, mechanism, and nominalism. In addition, the focus on Forms as explanatory entities is preceded by the argument that we already know these Forms prior to embodiment. So the claim of pre-Socratic skeptics that knowledge of the ultimate explanation of things is not available to us, particularly if these explanations are nonsensible, is rejected, too, albeit in a qualified way. Finally, insofar as the Forms fulfill an explanatory role, both the epistemological and ethical relativism of Sophists like Protagoras is rejected. This is owing to the universality of Forms as well as their objectivity.

But it is the Idea of the Good or the One that is needed to connect the antimaterialism, antimechanism, antinominalism, antiskepticism, and antirelativism. For without this unhypothetical first principle of all, explanatory *adequacy* is lost, adequacy in the sense of completeness without need or possibility of further steps. I take it that this is the main sense of τι ἱκανόν. Of course, a Form could well be just enough or adequate for a localized purpose, as in *Phaedo* itself, where the Forms are explicitly introduced for the purpose of proving the immortality of the soul. But even for local purposes, the Forms are explanatory only as shorthand for a more complete explanation. This fact itself speaks to the cogency of the evidence for the reduction of Forms to Numbers and their derivation from the One and the Indefinite Dyad. For both the simple and cleverer hypotheses only explain at all if the explanation can move beyond the barely nontautological claim that "X is f" because there is F-ness in it. This is possible only if F-ness is a name for an intelligible structure which is found in its instances, despite the utter diversity of, say, perceptual beauty and Beauty itself. It is Plato's intuition that intelligible structure or simply intelligibility is essentially a mathematical concept, not of course mathematical in the sense of arithmetic or geometry, but in the logically prior sense of ordering or structure.[88] This intuition is shared, for example, by Descartes in his conception of a *Mathesis universalis* and by Bertrand Russell and Alfred North Whitehead in their *Principia Mathematica*, with the crucial difference that, for Plato, logic is not independent of metaphysics but rather derived from it.[89]

We do not find anywhere in the dialogues or in the indirect tradition an actual argument for the positing of a superordinate first principle of all that is beyond existence and essence. It is, though, not difficult to discern Plato's reasons for doing so based upon four unquestionable philosophical assumptions held by him. First, he assumed that there were ultimate

---

88. See, e.g., Rodier 1902; A. E. Taylor 1926, 1927; Stenzel 1933; Findlay 1974, 54–80; Bulmer-Thomas 1983; Pritchard 1995; Blyth 2000; Vuillemin 2001; and Winzenrieth 2018.

89. See Resnik 1981, 1982.

explanations for things; the ways of the world, including their teleological aspect, were not in the laps of inscrutable gods. Second, following along the philosophical/scientific trajectory of all his predecessors—including those whose views he rejected—Plato was an explanatory reductivist. That is, he sought for explanations that were foundational and, therefore, as simple as possible. Third, and related to the second assumption, the sought-for principle must be fundamentally different from that of which it is a principle, else the putative principle is always reducible to an explanandum rather than an explanans. These three assumptions taken together led Plato inexorably to an utterly simple or incomposite first principle of all. A fourth assumption, which perhaps is not found before Plato himself, is that the first principle of all, if it is to explain the existence and essence of everything else, must also be the explanation for the end or goal of everything else. This is so because the essence of anything is to be understood as, in a way, bipolar. That is, it is both an endowment and an achievement. One attains one's own good as far as possible by fulfilling one's essence or nature. For this reason, if the Good is the source of essence, it is also the goal, that is, the fulfillment of essence. It is only the source if it provides somehow the essence and existence of all that is intelligible.[90] The Idea of the Good is the goal because it is the source. That things with different essences have different ends or goods is explained by the existence of a coordinate, generic Form of Good, which includes all possible perfections.[91] But the superordinate Idea of the Good is additionally necessary both to satisfy reductive exigency and to explain the cosmic integration of all specific goods.

These four assumptions seem to me to explain why Plato makes the first principle of all the Idea of the Good. I have already alluded to the reason for identifying this principle with the One. As the first principle of all, it must be ultimately adduced to provide explanations for cosmic phenomena alternative to the unsatisfactory explanations provided by the philosophers whom Plato repudiates. Without the Idea of the Good, the sorts of explanations that the Forms might be thought to provide—whether in the simple or cleverer hypothesis—could at best seem to be question-begging alternatives to the explanations provided by materialists and mechanists. At worst, they could only be incorporated into an explanatory framework that conflates formal cause with a set of necessary conditions for a given event or process to occur. If this is the route taken, the true place of *Phaedo* in the history of metaphysics and its elegantly concise expression of Platonism are lost.

---

90. The core idea here is in fact pre-Socratic. It follows from the bipolarity of the term φύσις (nature), indicating both what something is when it is produced and what it is meant to be in its maturity.

91. For a coordinate Form of Good, see *Phd.* 65D4–7, 75C10–D2, 76D7–9; *Tht.* 186A8; *Parm.* 130B7–9; *Rep.* 507B4–6, 608E6–609A4; *Phil.* 15A4–7. Cf. *Epin.* 978B3–4. This Good must be sharply distinguished from the Idea of the Good since the former is an οὐσία and the latter is ἐπέκεινα τῆς οὐσίας. See Gerson 2015.

There are a number of factors that together have led many contemporary scholars to the conclusion that the above interpretation—which is, in its essential components, the interpretation of the entire Platonic tradition up until the nineteenth century—is somehow outré or eccentric. The principal factor I believe is the refusal to take seriously Aristotle's testimony, and the testimony of the indirect tradition. If, to be specific, one supposes that Aristotle was, for whatever reason, mistaken in claiming that Plato reduced Forms to Numbers and that he derived these Numbers from the One and the Indefinite Dyad, the former of which is identified with the Idea of the Good, then perhaps one will, not surprisingly, also be unwilling to take seriously Plato's own words regarding the superordinate status of the Good. For to take the Good as the cause of or explanation for the existence and essence of the Forms makes little sense without the crucial Aristotelian addition. And if one takes the approach that rejects Aristotle's testimony, then it is indeed difficult to see how the τι ἱκανόν could be anything but another Form. Hence, it is also difficult to see the relevance of the procedure sketched out by Socrates beginning with the simple hypothesis to the answer to the question that he put to and failed to get a response to from Anaxagoras. As a result, Vlastos and many, many others have found in the simple and cleverer hypothesis a small bit of Platonic metaphysics completely stripped of the cosmic significance that both the philosophical and dramatic setting of Socrates's autobiography leads us to expect.

But first, it must be emphasized that writing off Aristotle's testimony rests upon the manifestly false assumption that that testimony is focused exclusively on interpreting the dialogues. It is not, not by Aristotle's own words and not by any reasonable assumption regarding Aristotle's personal contact with Plato over a period of almost twenty years. Aristotle is interpreting and arguing against philosophical claims made by Plato, not all of which are found in the dialogues nor found in the dialogues in the same form that they were transmitted orally to members of the Academy.[92]

Second, the unwillingness or even absolute refusal to use one dialogue to interpret another seems to follow from an assumption that since each dialogue is a dramatic unity, then that dialogue must be a philosophical unity which is tracked by the dramatic structure. But this is merely an unargued-for assumption, belied by the entire Platonic tradition which both recognizes the dramatic unity of each dialogue *and* maintains that there is a unified philosophical position behind all the dialogues that is variously revealed in part in each. Indeed, virtually everyone who either explicitly or implicitly assumes the self-constraint of interpreting a dialogue by the dramatic unity eventually appeals to *other* dialogues for illumination or at least for confirmation. In the very few cases where such appeals are rigorously

---

92. See W. D. Ross (1951, 143–148), who cites nine passages in Aristotle that refer to views of Plato that are not explicitly expressed in the dialogues.

excluded, the result is never anything more than paraphrase and aporia. But the licit use of one dialogue to help understand another implies that Plato's philosophy is not a collection of discrete units of philosophy, each independent of the rest. If, for example, *Philebus* can be used to help understand *Symposium*, then necessarily Plato's philosophy must be approached interdialogically. And once we overcome the groundless hermeneutic limitation to discrete units of philosophy, another reason for the exclusion of Aristotle's testimony falls. For if Plato's philosophy is, so to speak, *behind* the dialogues and not just *in* them, it seems frankly absurd to maintain that this philosophy was not transmitted orally within a community whose establishment must have been focused primarily on the discussion, that is, the oral transmission, of philosophy.

Our best, albeit inconclusive evidence, suggests that the dialogues are dramatized memoranda of discussions within the Academy recording, above all, Plato's thinking about one issue or another at the time of writing. Socrates speaks for Plato and his dramatic function is to allow Plato, through him, to confront the major philosophical views against which he is reacting. Plato's positive construct springs from his rejection of the views of his predecessors, including of course Anaxagoras. That positive construct is indeed reflected in the dialogues, although incompletely. Aristotle's testimony adds a crucial set of claims to the dialogic evidence. Plato's *Phaedo*, read in the context of all the dialogues and all the testimony about the oral teachings, provides an epitome of Platonism. If our goal is, after all, to understand critically what Platonism is, why in the world should we settle for "Plato lite"?[93]

3.4. *Republic* on the Subject Matter of Philosophy

In book 5 of *Republic*, Plato claims that philosophers are the optimal rulers of an ideal state. With a view to reaching this conclusion, he tries to show us what a philosopher is. He does this by distinguishing the objects that "lovers of wisdom (φιλόσοφοι)" pursue from those objects pursued by their counterfeits, namely, "lovers of sights and sounds (φιλοθεάμονες), lovers of crafts (φιλότεχνοι), and practical people (πράκτικοι)."[94] In the next phase

---

93. Craig (2016, introduction) distinguishes "heavyweight" Platonism from "lightweight" Platonism. I do not see a tertium quid between Platonism and anti-Platonism or Naturalism, its contradictory. Hence, there is no reason to distinguish between heavyweight and lightweight Platonism. There is just Platonism and its contradictory. This is not to say, of course, that there are not versions of Platonism whose claims may also be contradictory. But this always occurs within the framework of shared principles. The contradictions arise from the fact that these principles are underdetermining for the solutions to many specific problems.

94. *Rep.* 476A9–D6. Cf. 484B3–6. That philosophy is associated with the truth is a claim that is ubiquitous in the dialogues. See *Ap.* 29E1–2; *Cr.* 47C8–48A1; *Phd.* 65E2, 66D7, 67B1–2, 84A8–9, 99E6; *Phdr.* 249B5–C8; *Rep.* 475E2–4, 484C9, 485C3–D5, 490B5–6, 611E1–612A4; *Parm.* 135D6, 136C5, E1–3; *Tim.* 90B6–C4; and *Ep.* 7, 344A8–B2. In *Republic*, we get the crucial additional information that it is the Idea of the Good that provides truth to the Forms and

of the argument, Plato focuses on the modes of cognition appropriate to each, namely, knowledge (ἐπιστήμη) and belief (δόξα).[95] In the last phase of the argument, he focuses on a more detailed discussion of these modes of cognition.[96] Philosophers long for knowledge of the intelligible world and their counterfeits aim for belief about the sensible world. For example, a philosopher wants to know the Form of Beauty whereas all others are content to arrive at beliefs, perhaps preferably true beliefs, about beautiful things. Thus are philosophers distinguished from philodoxers.

The above distinctions seem straightforward. The subject matter for philosophy includes whatever belongs to the intelligible world, that is, "the completely real (τὸ παντελῶς ὄν)."[97] It also includes that which participates in the intelligible world insofar as it does so.[98] By contrast, the subject matter for philodoxers includes whatever belongs to the sensible world, that is, "that which is and is not real (εἶναί τε καὶ μὴ εἶναι)."[99] These two worlds cannot be identical because the modes of cognition appropriate to each are irreducible, like the irreducibility of sense modalities to each other.[100] There are many problems flowing from these distinctions, but Plato's view about the distinct subject matter of philosophy is not one of them. So if a Naturalist, like a philodoxer, wants to deal a decisive blow to Platonism, she need only deny the existence or reality of the subject matter that Plato claims is exclusively the purview of philosophy.[101]

---

that dialectic, the name for philosophical methodology, must ascend to the cause of truth to understand Forms.

95. *Rep.* 476D7–478E5.
96. *Rep.* 478E7–480A13.
97. *Rep.* 477A2–4. See Szlezák 2000 on the unambiguous meaning of the phrase οὓς μόνους ἄν τις ὀρθῶς προσείποι φιλοσόφους (those alone whom one would rightly call philosophers), 476B1–2. See Nightingale 1995, 14–20, on the use of the term φιλοσοφία before Plato and Plato's originality in this regard. Nightingale (51–52) seems to agree that Plato has introduced a distinctive subject matter for philosophy, though she stresses, rightly, its practical import. See also Dixsaut 2016, chap. 1.
98. *Rep.* 476C7–9: ὁ . . . τούτων ἡγούμενος τέ τι αὐτὸ καλὸν καὶ δυνάμενος καθορᾶν καὶ αὐτὸ καὶ τὰ ἐκείνου μετέχοντα (the one who thinks that there is a Beauty itself and is capable of seeing it and the things that participate in it). Clearly, philodoxers can also see that which participates in Forms, but they do not see these things *as* participants; they mistake them for that which is really real. Cf. 479D10–E4, 484B4–7. Because philosophers alone know the participants as participants and not as really real, they alone are fit to rule. Cf. 474C1–3, 487A7–8.
99. *Rep.* 477A9–B1; 478D5–9, which adds the word ἅμα (simultaneously), indicating that "that which is and is not real" cannot mean "was not real, is now real, and will not be real sometime later," even though it is undoubtedly true that sensibles have contingent and ephemeral being.
100. *Rep.* 478B1–2.
101. The *Republic*'s separation of the philosopher from the lover of sights and sounds is only an adumbration of the distinction found in *Phaedo*. Philosophers wish to separate from their bodies because they alone long to dwell in the intelligible world. See 61C2–9, 66A1–2, E1–2, and 67D7–8. So, too, *Symp.* 211D1–3, 212A1–2; and *Phdr.* 248D2–3, 249C4–5.

The three salient issues in the above passages for my purposes are (1) the inventory of the intelligible world; (2) the relation between the intelligible world and the sensible world; (3) and the discontinuity between the two modes of cognition appropriate to each world, namely, knowledge and belief. Under (1) are found questions about the status of soul, the Demiurge, the so-called intermediates or mathematical objects, the reduction of Forms to Numbers, and the superordinate Idea of the Good. Under (2) are all those issues pertaining to the supposed explanatory inadequacy of Naturalism as found in *Phaedo*. Under (3) are the issues pertaining to the nature of knowledge and the reasons for limiting things knowable to intelligibles. If, as many Naturalists insist, knowledge is a species of belief, then it would follow that knowledge does not have a distinct subject matter. If the Naturalist is correct, then Plato's reasons for claiming that philosophy does indeed have a distinct subject matter would be defeated. The most widely held analysis of knowledge, the so-called Standard Analysis, is that knowledge is justified true belief, where what turns belief into knowledge is not a different subject matter, but the addition of some sort of justificatory story. The origin of this story is found, ironically, among Academic skeptics, those who *rejected* the very possibility of knowledge precisely because there can in principle be no justificatory story that would turn belief into knowledge.[102] And as the Pyrrhonian Skeptic Sextus Empiricus astutely noted, to defeat the dogmatic pretensions to the possibility of knowledge is to defeat philosophy itself.[103] Accordingly, the idea that knowledge can have sensibles within its scope, even if it can also have as objects things that are only intelligible, undermines Platonism. For the reason for positing a world separate from sensibles is in the *Republic* passage derived from the fact that knowledge and belief have ontologically different objects.[104]

---

102. See Gerson 2009, 116–124.

103. See Sextus Empiricus, *M.* 9.13–14, where he identifies philosophy as the "knowledge of things divine and human." To show that such knowledge is not possible is to defeat any and all claims to wisdom. Sextus's condemnation includes Stoics and Epicureans as well as Platonists. It is, therefore, a condemnation broader than that of Platonism; it pertains to all forms of dogmatism. But the focus of Sextus's criticism is the idea held among all dogmatists that there is a ne plus ultra of cognition, an infallible grasp of the real. Plato maintains that the only infallible cognition is of purely intelligible objects and is possible only if we possess immaterial intellects.

104. See Szaif 2007. Contra: Fine 1978, 1990. Fine does not in these articles draw out the implications for her claim that, for Plato, knowledge and belief do not have ontologically distinct objects. It is not unreasonable to infer that if in fact the intelligible world does not exist, then that would not necessarily mean that philosophers would be out of work. But since Plato thinks that knowledge is infallible and there can only be infallible cognition of the intelligible world, the redescription of the knowledge that the philosopher seeks as fallible cognition of the sensible world leaves quite obscure—and I would say entirely un-Platonic—the answer to the question of how the philosopher differs from the theoretical empirical scientist. Harte (2017) defends a position similar to that of Fine, denying that *Rep.* 478A11–13 means what it says: that it is impossible that the objects of ἐπιστήμη and δόξα be identical (τὸ αὐτό). Harte

I shall have much more to say about (1)–(3) in subsequent chapters. Here, I want to dwell on Plato's account of philodoxers, surely at least first cousins of Naturalists. These are people who, for example, believe that there are many things correctly called "beautiful," but deny that there is one self-identical Form or Beauty.[105] Further, those who believe in the many beautiful things will agree that these will all appear ugly. More precisely, their accounts of what justifies us in calling something beautiful will never arrive at the true cause of the presence of Beauty, but only at conditions for its presence. So, too, for things just, double, heavy, large, and so on. It is because the many things named "f" can appear as "not-f" that such objects are not the objects of knowledge and so not the subject matter of philosophy. It seems clear that these philodoxers are akin to Naturalists like Anaxagoras in that they are unable to give the explanation for why things are as they are and why it is good that they be so. They can at best supply necessary and sufficient conditions for the true explanations to operate. The trouble with philodoxers is not that they do not know Forms, but that they do not believe that Forms exist.[106] Accordingly, they seek for the explanations for things where no explanations are to be found. They believe that some concatenation of conditions will produce a cause.

The simultaneous possession of contrary properties seems to be either inconsequential or impossible. If A is larger than B but smaller than C at the same time, no one, including Plato, I suppose, thinks that this fact can only be explained by introducing separate Forms. In addition, if A has a nonrelative property f, then so long as f is clearly delineated, it is not possible for A simultaneously to have non-f. Plato's reasons for thinking that sensibles are only objects of belief and not knowledge is rather focused on the diminished or compromised intelligibility in what is cognized when one believes that A is f. Thus, the proposition "A is f" is asserted by someone who has some measure of understanding of what "f" stands for. If this were not the case, then there would be no difference between asserting that

---

argues that knowledge and belief are "tasked" (by whom?) with working on separate, perhaps even nonoverlapping domains, but it is nevertheless possible that either one of the two modes of cognition can trespass on the domain of the other. Harte does not explain how there can be "infallible (ἀναμάρτητον)" cognition of sensibles, which is what ἐπιστήμη must be. Nor does she explain how there can be δόξα of Forms without reference to Forms, reference which would just be the infallible cognition that ἐπιστήμη is. N. Smith (2000), while distancing himself from Fine's view, argues that only the "powers (δυνάμεις)" of belief and knowledge have different objects while the states that arise from the use of these powers can have identical objects. I think that Smith is correct that if one has ἐπιστήμη of a Form, then one is cognitively better placed than anyone else in relation to the images or instances of these Forms in the sensible world. But Plato, when he is speaking precisely (see 533C8–534A1), limits ἐπιστήμη to the top section of the top half of the Divided Line. The philosopher's belief about sensibles is backed up by knowledge of Forms; she can be said to have knowledge of the former only equivocally.

105. *Rep.* 479A1–7. Cf. 480A4.
106. See *Rep.* 476C1–3.

A is f and asserting that A is non-f or g. But the understanding of what "f" stands for, in the case of the lover of sights and sounds or nonphilosopher, is necessarily constituted by what can be loosely termed the data of sense-perception, that is, spatiotemporal tokens of sensible types. In other words, the truth conditions for something being f must be understood in sensible terms. After all, the lover of sights and sounds or the Naturalist thinks that there is nothing other than sensibilia that could provide the truth conditions. But these sensibilia are in principle capable of being the truth conditions for the contrary property. Thus, whatever it is that is the truth condition for something being tall is the truth condition for it being short.[107]

This claim works just as well for nonrelative properties as for relative properties. If, to use Plato's example, the proposition is that "this is a finger," then the truth conditions for being a finger—the necessary conditions in line with the argument in Socrates's autobiography—will at some level, say, the atomic, equally be the truth conditions for being something else.[108] But if the proposal for truth conditions aspires to escape this problem by investing more and more intelligible content into them, then at some point we get the tautologous "this is a finger because it fulfills all the necessary finger conditions." To fall short of the tautologous is to introduce conditions that are not uniquely necessary and jointly sufficient for being a finger. To ascend from the tautologous to the truly explanatory is to advert to the simple hypothesis of the *Phaedo*. Alternatively, there is no truth-condition for "this is a finger"; or else, the truth-condition is, "because I say it is."

The belief that Helen is beautiful or that paying your debts is just requires that we express the truth conditions for these propositions in sensible terms. The belief is justified, to oneself or to another, on the basis of these terms.[109] It is because of her shape, or coloring say, that she is held to be beautiful and it is because he handed over a sum of money in a timely fashion that the deed was just. The reason why philosophy possesses a distinct subject matter is exactly the reason Socrates eschewed Naturalistic explanations in favor of his simple hypothesis. There is no adequate explanation for the way things are here below unless we appeal to Forms.[110]

---

107. It is worth mentioning that the argument which seeks to make causes irreducible to conditions has a contemporary analogue in arguments against type-type and token-token identity theories of mental states, especially if it is assumed that mental states are functional states.

108. See *Rep.* 523B1ff.

109. In the Pseudo-Platonic *Definitions* 414C3–4, δόξα is defined as ὑπόληψις μεταπειστὸς ὑπὸ λόγου (a defeasible cognitive state) as opposed to ἐπιστήμη, 414B10, as ὑπόληψις ψυχῆς ἀμετάπτωτος ὑπὸ λόγου (an indefeasible cognitive state of the soul). Belief is defeasible (by λόγος) because it is unavoidably inferential, and the inference can always be challenged and overturned. Typically, the inference is from a sense experience. By contrast, knowledge is direct or noninferential and so indefeasible by λόγος.

110. It is easy to construct an analogous argument against a contemporary Naturalist account for any number of contentious phenomena. For example, to account for the presence of a mental state in neurophysiological terms is to face the challenge that at some level, say,

Leaving aside for the moment the tendentious distinction between knowledge and belief, why does Plato think that the assiduous pursuit of belief relating to sensibles cannot substitute for philosophy? We have already seen the principal reason in the previous section. Insofar as one seeks explanations for things or events or processes in nature, one cannot but fail to achieve success if one does not have recourse to the intelligible world and ultimately to the Idea of the Good. But there is more.

The fundamental distinction between ἐπιστήμη and δόξα and the parallel distinction of the subject matter of philosophy and that of philodoxers does not lead Plato to maintain that the sensible world is of no use to the philosopher. On the contrary, in *Timaeus* he says that philosophy itself is derived from the study of nature.[111] But this does not in the slightest blur the distinction between the subject matters of the two. Since philosophy provides the explanatory basis for a science of nature, we might suppose that they are related analogous to the relation between a supposed scientific image and a manifest image of nature, the former providing the explanatory basis for the latter. This analogy is itself not out of line with the Divided Line in *Republic* and the analogous roles of the Idea of the Good and the Sun. For Plato, however, Anaxagoras is a representative of those seeking the scientific image of nature. The necessary conditions for the manifest image, the contents of the science of nature, are distinguished from the causal role of the intelligible world in relation to the sensible world.[112]

---

the subatomic, that account will work equally for a contrary mental state. The Platonic claim is not that if a certain brain state is really a necessary and even sufficient condition for a certain mental state, then that brain state could be present without the mental state being present. Rather, the claim is that understanding what that mental state is requires recourse to separate Forms and this recourse is not short-circuited by insisting on the conditions. This is so because, since Forms are eternal causes, the presence of the necessary and sufficient conditions does not attain to these true causes. It is only by conflating conditions and causes that one might suppose that it is possible for the necessary conditions to be present without result because *other* necessary conditions are missing. On this view, causes are the requisite sum of all necessary (and hence jointly sufficient) conditions. As we shall see in the next chapter, the failure to take into account the eternity of Forms and hence their ubiquity is fatal to an understanding of their explanatory relevance.

111. *Tim.* 47A4–B1: περὶ τε τῆς τοῦ παντὸς φύσεως ζήτησιν . . . ἐξ ὧν ἐπαρισάμεθα φιλοσοφίας γένος (regarding the investigation of all nature . . . from which we have derived philosophy). Presumably, the words "from which" indicate that the philosophically inclined investigator of nature is dissatisfied with something like causal closure and is thereby led to the subject matter of philosophy. The investigator seeks explanations *within* nature and cannot find them there, just like Socrates in *Phaedo*.

112. Fine (2016), writing about the "the two-world theory in *Phaedo*," imagines that one in possession of knowledge of Forms thereby has wisdom about the sensible world, though she concedes (562, 564) that this inference is not supported in the text. It is just that, as she maintains, the text is not incompatible with it. In fact, a successful philosopher will have well-supported beliefs about sensibles and there is nothing in principle against calling this a sort of wisdom. The crucial point, however, is that the subject matter of philosophy remains separate from the subject matter that engages the lovers of sights and sounds. And that absent this very

Philodoxers base their beliefs on their sense-experiences. But the senses as such deliver to them tainted data, the colors and sounds and shapes that are underdetermining as evidence for the presence of any formal property. More than this, they are positively misleading since they are taken to provide evidence for a property when that identical putative evidence serves as evidence for a contrary property. If one believes that there are no Forms that unambiguously explain the presence of properties, then one will naturally take the taintedness of the data to be a feature of *philodoxia*, not a bug. One can happily proceed to seek out a supposedly stable cognitive end point set forth in terms of approximations, generalizations, and so on, always with an eye to a pragmatic heuristic. Plato's criticism of the philodoxers is not simply that philosophy is more exacting or simply better at doing what it is that the philodoxers want to do. Rather, his criticism is that in the very δόξαι that constitute their achievement—even true beliefs, as Plato readily allows— there must be a recognition or presupposition of a mode of cognition radically different from δόξα and objects for that mode of cognition radically different from sensibles. As Parmenides says in his eponymous dialogue, if Forms do not exist or if they exist and are completely cut off or separate from the sensible world, then intelligible communication would be impossible.[113] For that communication depends upon our cognizing the instantiations of Forms among things and making judgments about the samenesses and differences among things owing to Forms. But the philodoxer assumes that intelligible communication is possible. It is not surprising that, ignoring the condition for this possibility, he can, like Richard Rorty, be led eventually to abandon representationalism altogether. Without the explanatory functioning of Forms, thought and language on one side and sensibles on the other are, indeed, incommensurable.

3.5. *Theaetetus* and *Sophist* on the Subject Matter of Philosophy

In the famous digression in *Theaetetus*, Socrates contrasts philosophers with orators.[114] The subject matter that concerns the former includes the nature of a human being, and the nature of justice and injustice.[115] It is from the world of the orator and to the world in which these are available for

---

specific and derivative wisdom about the sensible world, one is inevitably at sea intellectually. One can also, I suppose, call it "knowledge," as does Harte (2017, 157–159), but then this is not ἐπιστήμη; rather, it is some sort of justified true belief with all the attendant difficulties of providing a cogent account of justification.

113. See *Parm.* 135B5–C3.

114. *Tht.* 172C3–177C2. The contrast alludes to *Gorgias*, where Socrates compares orators and philosophers in his discussion with Gorgias and Polus. There, the subject matter for philosophy is primarily the nature of the soul and care for it.

115. See *Tht.* 174B4–5, and 175C2–3.

our knowledge that Socrates urges Theaetetus to flee.[116] This is just as philosophy is described in *Phaedo*.[117] The "flight (φυγή)" is described as "assimilation to god as much as is possible (ὁμοίωσις θεῷ κατὰ τὸ δυνατόν)." And this is accomplished by the practice of justice and piety along with wisdom (φρόνησις).[118] The manifest otherworldliness of the philosopher in comparison with his counterpart, the rhetorician, is another version of the contrast in *Republic* between philosophers and lovers of sights and sounds. It should be stressed that the practice of virtue with wisdom, that is, with philosophical knowledge, is an instrument of the assimilation. This assimilation, literally "making the same as," is completed when we engage in the divine activity of knowledge of the eternal world.[119]

The relevance of the digression to the main subject of the dialogue, namely, the definition of knowledge (ἐπιστήμη), is contentious and depends on whether, to use Myles Burnyeat's terminology, we opt for Reading A or for Reading B.[120] According to the former, Plato is presenting an elaborate reductio argument, showing that knowledge cannot be sense-perception (αἴσθησις) or true belief (ἀληθὴς δόξα) or true belief with an account (λόγος). On this reading, it cannot be any of these because knowledge is only of the intelligible world. On Reading B, though, like Reading A, it is admitted that none of the definitions of knowledge are successful; it is held that Plato has changed his view of knowledge in *Republic* such that he is now prepared to countenance knowledge in some sense of the sensible world. I will not here repeat arguments I have made elsewhere on behalf of Reading A.[121] Here, I shall only point out that the plausibility of Reading B depends very much on explaining why *Theaetetus* deviates from *Republic* which precedes it and from *Sophist* which succeeds it. More particularly, it needs to show that Plato is willing to allow either knowledge of contingent truths or that there is knowledge of necessary truths that is other than the knowledge of Forms. Stated thus, I can see no evidence for the former and no conceptual distance between the latter and the knowledge of Forms sought for in dialectic. The exhortation to a "flight from here" is a reaffirmation of the distinct subject matter of philosophy.

In *Sophist*, we find substantially the identical account of philosophy that we find in *Phaedo*, *Republic*, and *Theaetetus*.

---

116. See *Tht.* 176A5–9.
117. See *Phd.* 64E8–65a2, C11–D2, D11ff. The principal point is that knowledge requires separation from the body because the objects of knowledge are separate from the bodily. Insofar as we are embodied, the body is an impediment to this knowledge.
118. Cf. *Rep.* 500B8–C7, 619C8. See Lavecchia 2006, 271–272, on the connection between ἀλήθεια and φρόνησις. The latter is another name for the activity of νοῦς. See *Phd.* 65A9–C1, 66A6, D8–E4; *Sts.* 278D8–E2; and *Phil.* 58B9–D1, 59C2–D6.
119. See Lavecchia 2006, 270–273.
120. See Burnyeat 1990.
121. See Gerson 2003, 194–238; and Gerson 2009, 44–54.

And what name shall we give to this knowledge (ἐπιστήμη)? Or have we, by Zeus, unknowingly hit upon the knowledge of free persons and, in seeking the sophist, found the philosopher?

What do you mean?

Dividing according to Kinds, not taking the identical Form for a different one nor a different one for the identical one—is that not dialectical knowledge?

Yes.

And then, one who is able to see one Idea throughout many, where each one is separate, and many Ideas, different from each other, encompassed externally by one; and again, one connected into a unity through many wholes, and many separately defined. This means knowing how to distinguish the Kinds, that is, how they are associated and how they are not.

Definitely so.

And the only one to whom you would grant this dialectical ability, I think, would be none other than the one who is purely and justly said to be doing philosophy.[122]

The description here of dialectic is a slightly more detailed version of the one we find in the Divided Line in *Republic*. The ἐπιστήμη that philosophers seek is precisely of the Forms or Ideas or Kinds. Thereby, philosophers are distinguished from sophists and, by implication, statesmen.[123]

That this knowledge pertains to the identical distinct subject matter found in *Republic* is clear from the Stranger's pronouncement a few lines later, contrasting the philosopher with the sophist:

> But [contrary to the sophist] the philosopher who, by means of his reasoning, always staying near to the Idea of Being, is difficult to see because that region is so bright.[124]

The region is the intelligible world and dialectic is the methodology that the philosopher employs. It is not just the region within which the philosopher

---

122. *Soph.* 253C6–E5: {ΞΕ.} Οὐκοῦν ὅ γε τοῦτο δυνατὸς δρᾶν μίαν ἰδέαν διὰ πολλῶν, ἑνὸς ἑκάστου κειμένου χωρίς, πάντῃ διατεταμένην ἱκανῶς διαισθάνεται, καὶ πολλὰς ἑτέρας ἀλλήλων ὑπὸ μιᾶς ἔξωθεν περιεχομένας, καὶ μίαν αὖ δι' ὅλων πολλῶν ἐν ἑνὶ συνημμένην, καὶ πολλὰς χωρὶς πάντῃ διωρισμένας· τοῦτο δ' ἔστιν, ᾗ τε κοινωνεῖν ἕκαστα δύναται καὶ ὅπῃ μή, διακρίνειν κατὰ γένος ἐπίστασθαι. {ΘΕΑΙ.} Παντάπασι μὲν οὖν. {ΞΕ.} Ἀλλὰ μὴν τό γε διαλεκτικὸν οὐκ ἄλλῳ δώσεις, ὡς ἐγᾦμαι, πλὴν τῷ καθαρῶς τε καὶ δικαίως φιλοσοφοῦντι.

123. The implication rests upon the projection of the trilogy, *Sophist, Statesman, Philosopher*, each of which dialogue is supposed to discover the definition of its subject. At *Soph.* 217B1–4, the Eleatic Stranger insists that the three are distinct. And it is he who inadvertently discovers the philosopher as someone whose métier is different from that of the sophist and statesman. I have no firm opinion on why *Philosopher* was not, so far as we know, ever written.

124. *Soph.* 254A8–10: Ὁ δέ γε φιλόσοφος, τῇ τοῦ ὄντος ἀεὶ διὰ λογισμῶν προσκείμενος ἰδέᾳ, διὰ τὸ λαμπρὸν αὖ τῆς χώρας οὐδαμῶς εὐπετὴς ὀφθῆναι. The brightness of the region is a clear reference to the Good, analogous to the sun in *Republic*. The Good generates the brightness of the region.

works that is difficult to see, but the philosopher himself because he is working in that region. This is a curious claim, but presumably it means in part that what philosophers do is not, like sophists, work with words or concepts, both images of the really real. The only access that others have to this activity, however, is via the words and concepts that the philosopher uses in communication. One reason why the philosopher is difficult to distinguish from the sophist is precisely that the latter uses the same sorts of verbal and conceptual images that the philosopher uses. The direct implication of this distinction between the philosopher and sophist is that if the subject matter of philosophy did not exist, then there would in fact be no difference between philosophy and sophistry. The representations of both would be on a par, just as Rorty insisted that the representations of astronomy and astrology are on a par, according to any putative criterion of representational success.

The first of the above two passages raises problems about what it means to distinguish Forms from each other and what it means for one Form to encompass another. In an Aristotelian framework of genus, species, and differentiae, where the species is the logical composite, the genus the logical matter, and the differentia, the logical form, such an account of dialectic makes good sense. It does not obviously make sense in a Platonic framework. We shall see how Plato and Platonism deal with this problem in the next chapter. There are no grounds for supposing that Kinds are not Forms (or at least Forms in one aspect) or that dialectic is here being transformed into something like conceptual analysis. For if concepts (νοήματα) were the new subject matter for philosophy, then these would be as temporalized as anything else in the sensible world and the mode of cognition pertaining to them would be δόξα and not ἐπιστήμη.

Missing from the description of the subject matter of philosophy here is the Idea of the Good. Its absence seems to be easily accounted for by the fact that it is not directly relevant to solving the problem set by this dialogue, namely, how to define the sophist. As we shall see, however, the unifying activity of the philosopher presupposes the unificatory role of a first ontological principle of all.[125] It also presumes that the reductive analysis

---

125. This passage invites the following speculative remark. What distinguishes philosophical ability from all other abilities is being able to see unity where everyone else sees disarray and being able to see distinctions where everyone else sees indistinctness. These are what we today call imaginative and analytic skills. These do not seem to be mutually implicatory, but without both not much good philosophy gets done. What sets Platonism apart from Naturalism, wherein are found many with excellent philosophical ability, is that Platonists hold that these abilities operate on an eternal and immutable subject matter whereas Naturalists suppose that imagination and analysis operate within temporalized linguistic and conceptual realms.

leading back to a first principle of all is the mirror image of the generation of the *analysanda from* the first principle.[126]

The dialogues *Phaedo, Republic, Theaetetus,* and *Sophist,* taken together provide an unambiguous sketch of the subject matter of philosophy and of the special mode of cognition pertaining to philosophy. The problems with which these dialogues deal arise from the inadequacy of Naturalism to give adequate explanations generally. The elements of Naturalism are variously salient in these dialogues, but it is, I believe, more than just a guess that these elements are mutually implicatory. The introduction of the superordinate Idea of the Good explicitly in *Republic* and implicitly in *Phaedo* unifies the elements of Platonism and therefore those of its opposite.

---

126. Cf. Aristotle, *Meta.* H 4, 1044a23–25: διχῶς γὰρ τόδ' ἐκ τοῦδε, ἢ ὅτι πρὸ ὁδοῦ ἔσται ἢ ὅτι ἀναλυθέντοσϕ εἰς τὴν ἀρχήν (For one thing comes from another in two ways: either when one is earlier than the other in generation or when it is analyzed into its principle); *EN* Γ 3, 1112b23–24: τὸ ἔσχατον ἐν τῇ ἀναλύσει πρῶτον εἶναι ἐν τῇ γενέσει (that which is last in analysis is first in genesis).

CHAPTER 4

Plato on Being and Knowing

4.1. Forms as Explanatory Entities

The exegesis of the passage in *Phaedo* in which Plato announces a turn from Naturalism to Platonism presumes the existence of Forms as explanatory entities, albeit recognizing their instrumental role in ultimate explanation. Without a defense of the antinominalism leading to the postulation of separate Forms, the entire project encapsulated in Socrates's autobiography does not even leave the starting gate. If my hypothesis about Platonism and Naturalism is approximately correct, such a defense will have dimensions that involve all the other "antis" of Ur-Platonism. All that I can do here is offer a preface to a defense, aiming at least to focus on the elementary analytic features of Plato's antinominalism that are easy to miss.

Let us begin with a distinction between two Greek words, τὸ ἔχειν ("having") and τὸ μετέχειν ("participating"). The latter word is formed from the former, mundane Greek verb. But Plato uses the latter term to indicate the fundamental relation between sensibles and intelligibles or Forms. Helen participates in the Form of Beauty and the large table participates in the Form of Largeness and three objects participate in the Form of Threeness, and so on. The difference between "having" and "participating" may be expressed as the difference between unique and nonunique predication.[1] We define "S has f" as indicating that the predicate f is uniquely attributable to S. Within a Naturalistic framework, whether this is conceived of as

---

1. See Fujisawa (1974, 30–34), who makes the same distinction in slightly different language.

four-dimensional or three-dimensional plus time, every f may be said to have a unique identifier or ID. By definition, nothing else in the universe can have an identical ID. I leave aside for the moment the evident problem of S having f at t_1 and S having f at t_2 which would seem to require us to assign unique and nonidentical IDs to the predicate f. One kind of Naturalism will avoid the problem by confining predication within a three-dimensional matrix, leaving time aside. Another type of Naturalism will embrace the consequence of situating predication within a four-dimensional matrix, namely, that any predication is an abstract and arbitrary snapshot of a continuously flowing nature. Plato thinks that neither possibility is coherently sustainable. But Naturalism does not need to give up the constant variability of IDs so long as it is prepared to reconceptualize what cognition of the sensible world is supposed to or is able to be. In any event, by contrast, participating indicates nonunique predication or at least the possibility of f being nonuniquely predicable of another subject. It is this possibility that the nominalism of Naturalism must oppose.

The hypothesis of nonunique predication does not entail the rejection of unique predication ("having"); indeed, if S participates in a Form, then it logically follows that S uniquely has f. Stating the point this way should make obvious the question of why a Form is needed in the first place if the hypothesis of participating in Forms leaves us with unique predicates with unique IDs. The identical question may be put otherwise: If S has f, then what claim exactly is being made in saying that the name for f is identical to the name for the Form in which S participates? If, for example, Helen uniquely possesses the property which we may call "Helen's beauty," what is being claimed in saying that the explanation for this fact is the Form of Beauty in which Helen participates? Is not participation redundant to simple having?

In order to answer these questions, we need to recur to a previous distinction relied on by Plato ubiquitously and briefly mentioned earlier. This is the distinction between "sense-perceiving (τὸ αἰσθάνεσθαι)" and "thinking (τὸ νοεῖν)." The former is what we do with our five senses, whereas the latter is what we do with our intellects.[2] The point here is that in affirming "S has (is) f" we make irreducible use of our intellects. No account of the cognition of S or the cognition of f by any mechanism of sense-perception

---

2. See *Phd.* 65D9–10; *Rep.* 507B8–9, 524C13; *Tim.* 28A1–4, 51E6–52A7. All these passages stress the distinction between what is sensible and what is intelligible. One is not reducible to the other nor are they continuous as if thinking were a continuation of sense-perception, presumably only less vivid. Aristotle (*DA* Γ 3, 427a17–b6), criticizes Naturalists, here, Empedocles and others, for conflating sense-perception and thinking. Their reason for doing so is their supposition that both are corporeal (σωματικόν). They suppose this because they also believe that the cognizer must be the same in substance as that which is cognized. So cognition of a corporeal world requires corporeal cognitive equipment.

alone can yield the thought or assertion that "S has (is) f."[3] No sum of acts of sense-perception amounts to a predicative thought even when, in cases where "seeing" is cashed out as "seeing as," the sense-perception and the thinking temporally overlap or coincide. What I want to focus on is exactly how nonperceptual cognition is involved here. To cognize that S has f, even if it has f uniquely, is to transcend the unique in our cognition. The cognition of a sensible object with a unique ID is by an agent also with a unique ID. Whether this sensible is S or f, the affirmation that S is f transcends the uniqueness of S and of f, that is, the identity of each. The only way that this is possible is if f, which does not have the identical ID as does S—otherwise, there would be no difference between thinking S is S and thinking S is f—is cognizable as being other than uniquely possessed by S. But this seems to contradict the claim that f *is* unique, that it has a unique ID. How can thinking cognize that which is unique as nonunique?

The answer is found when we explore the fundamental and irreducible difference between sense-perception and thinking. The object of thinking is not a particular object of a particular sense modality, such as a smell or sound or shape, but a form or structure or arrangement or order of whatever it is that is also available to the senses.[4] The thinking of form, as opposed to the sensing of form, is always and necessarily universal, not particular. This is because form itself is *neither* universal nor particular. For example, if "f" stands for a shape, that shape in itself is neither the particular shape of that which is shaped nor is it universal. But the thinking of it is always done universally. The object of thinking is distinct from the particular or unique shape that is encountered in sense-perception. How could it not be? To grasp that the object in front of me is circular and to affirm it to be so by thinking that S is f is to cognize other than by sense-perception. We might want to maintain that any shape can be an object of sight, of course, but in claiming that S is f I am doing more than identifying S and identifying f. If I were limited to sense modalities alone I could only identify S and f; even the *reidentification* of S and f requires me to transcend my sense-perception. And here I mean to indicate more than the reidentification that, for example, a fingerprint sensor accomplishes. I mean the propositional claim that this S

---

3. This is why the δόξαι of philodoxers require a power over an above sense-perception.

4. The shapes and numbers that the Demiurge inserts into the precosmic chaos are at least paradigmatic examples of form or order. This fact becomes even clearer if we recognize that, on the *Timaeus* account, phenomenological properties or qualities as such stand outside the framework of intelligibility or thinkability. Kahn (2013, 200–206) argues that the imposition of mathematical order on the precosmic soup thereby producing a measure of intelligibility in the sensible world is Plato's final resolution to the problem of participation, that is, how one separate and self-identical Form can be present in a multitude of perishable individuals. The problem is solved by understanding intelligibility as mathematical structure so that things are given their names according to Forms because they instantiate, for example, the truths contained in Euclid's *Elements*.

in front of me now is the same as the S in front of me yesterday. Sameness here is being cognized universally. There is no sense-perception of it. The sameness is cognized universally because the identical form cognized in the two things is in each case cognized universally.

Perhaps the idea here can be expressed differently. No analysis or deconstruction of a sense-perception can yield a predicative judgment of the form "is f." This is so precisely because in sense-perception only that which possesses a unique ID is attainable. But a predicative judgment amounts to a claim that subject and predicate are, in a sense, identical, even though each has a unique ID. In thinking, what is sensed as unique is thought universally. This universality is what makes the predicative judgment other than a self-contradictory denial of a law of identity. It makes it a claim about participating and not a claim about having.

The epistemological point that thinking and sense-perception each encounter the identical form in a different way must be distinguished from the metaphysical point that a Form is a "one over many."[5] The two points are different but they entail each other. Because the Form is in itself neither universal nor particular it is able to explain how many things can be the same although they are numerically different. The universality is found in the thinking; the particularity is found in the perceiving. That the Form is "one" does not mean it is one in the identical way in which an instance of a Form or the Form particularized is one and apt for a unique ID number. That there are different ways of being one that bear on the metaphysical superstructure of Platonism and that these different ways of being one are connected with each other and with everything else is part of what the second part of *Parmenides* shows. It is not the universality of a Form that enables it to explain identity in difference or the sameness of two or more things or the possibility of predication. Rather, it is the universality of thinking that enables us to understand that unless there exists one Form in itself neither particular nor universal, no Form can explain these facts about the sensible world.[6]

---

5. See *Parm.* 132A1–4: [Parmenides is speaking to the young Socrates] Οἶμαί σε ἐκ τοῦ τοιοῦδε ἓν ἕκαστον εἶδος οἴεσθαι εἶναι· ὅταν πόλλ᾽ ἄττα μεγάλα σοι δόξῃ εἶναι, μία τις ἴσως δοκεῖ ἰδέα ἡ αὐτὴ εἶναι ἐπὶ πάντα ἰδόντι, ὅθεν ἓν τὸ μέγα ἡγῇ εἶναι (I think that you think that each Form is one for this reason: whenever there seem to you to be many large things, it probably seems to you that, looking at all of them, there is one Idea identical in all of them, for which reason you think that Largeness is one). Also *Rep.* 476A5–7.

6. Aristotle, *Meta.* M 9, 1086a32–b11, attacks Academics for a theory that supposes that universals (τὰ καθόλου) and particulars (τὰ ἕκαστα) will be "practically (σχεδόν)" the identical nature. This criticism pertains justly to a noncontextualized or truncated postulation of Forms that are both separate and are universally predicable of any "many." But there are two crucial additions to the theory that remove the sting of this criticism: (1) there is a distinction between the entity that the Form is and its nature, that which its name names; and (2) the separability of Forms is limited to separation from time and the sensible world. Forms are neither separate from each other, nor from the Idea of the Good, nor from the intellect that the Demiurge

The misconception of Forms as universals or as the subject of a realistic theory of universals has been a misguided feature of much Platonic exegesis and, indeed, a sort of enduring urban myth in the history of philosophy generally.[7] If a Form were a universal, then it could not be particularized and be the identical Form.[8] But if the particularization of the Form were not identical with Form, then the whole point of the theory of Forms, so to speak, would be lost. For the theory is supposed to explain identity in difference or, alternatively, how numerically different things can be the same. The theory explains how sameness among things not numerically identical is possible, something that nominalism finds *impossible*. If the Form were *just* a universal, it could not be particularized, in which case there could be no sameness which is explicable if and only if there is an identical Form "over and above." To say that a Form is supposed to be predicable of many things is only misleadingly elliptical for: a Form is posited to explain how it is possible to make predicative judgments in which the predicate is univocally used in multiple cases. To do this job, a separate Form does not need to be a universal, which is only a hypostatization of the activity of thinking form universally, the only way that form can be thought.

To try to maintain the claim that the Form is a universal when the Form's entire explanatory role is to show how two or more things can be the same, that is, each has the identical property, leads one to maintain that the Form

---

is. These two points only emerge clearly in dialogues that, so far as we can tell, were written when discussion of the theory of Forms was well advanced in the Academy. No doubt, Aristotle is criticizing a view held by some members of the Academy, including Plato at some time. The criticism is inoperative in light of later developments or refinements within that theory. I take the word "practically" to indicate that Aristotle is doubtful that the above two distinctions are defensible. As I shall try to show below, they are only defensible when taken together and within the larger framework of the systematic expression of Platonism. See Shields 2011, 511–523, esp. 522, for support for (1) as an appropriate response by Plato to the reading of Aristotle's criticism as foisting a contradiction on Plato's theory. For the evidence for (2), see Gerson 2005a, chap. 7.

The question of how one Form can *not* be a particular is answered briefly by insisting on grades of unity. A form is in a way more of a unity than a particular instance of it. The idea of grades of unity will be developed further in chapter 5.

7. E.g., W. D. Ross 1951, 35: "Originally the doctrine [of Forms] was simply a belief in the existence of universals as implied by the existence of individuals having qualities." Virtually every philosophy textbook that treats the so-called problem of universals asserts that Platonism is wedded to a realistic theory of universals, meaning approximately what Aristotle means in the above criticism.

8. See Allen (1965, 52–56), who rightly rejects the idea that Forms are "commutative" universals, meaning that they are univocally predicable of their instances. The straightforward reason for this rejection is that instances of Forms are deficient with respect to the Form itself whereas instances of universals cannot be so with respect to the universal which is just exactly and nothing but what all the instances have in common. Forms as universals are also rejected by Patterson (1985b, 134–135). Someone who bases his nominalism on the rejection of a realistic theory of universals misses the mark at least as far as Plato is concerned. See also Mohr 2005, chap. 12.

is both a universal and a particular. But Plato no more than Aristotle countenances this absurdity. Rather, all the universality is in the cognitive relation of thinker to Form; all the particularity is in the "having" of an instance of the Form. "Having" exclusively and "participating" nonexclusively are mutually implicating, though not identical, because the Form is in itself neither universal nor particular.[9]

It is easy to conflate the denial of the hypostatization of the objects of universal thinking with a denial of the existence of separate entities whose nature the Form's name names. It is perhaps understandable that from an argument concluding that universals should not be hypostasized, one can conclude further that Forms do not exist. From a Platonic perspective, however, this would be a non sequitur. Stated otherwise, if I encounter Forms in a cognitive modality, namely, universally, it does not follow from a denial that the intentional object of the thinking does not exist on its own that the Form does not exist on its own. Such a result would follow only if there was no real distinction between the Form and the intentional object. The closest Platonic term to indicate such an intentional object is νόημα and Plato says as clearly as possible in his *Parmenides*, that Forms are not νοήματα ἐν τῇ ψυχῇ, that is, the intentional objects that result from the activity of thinking.[10] The principal justification for the real distinction is that no intentional object can do the job that Forms are postulated to do, namely, explain identity in difference or the possibility of predication. The universality drops out of the ontological account of how two or more numerically distinct things can be the same. The temptation to think that the universality must have some relevance leads to conceptualism of some sort, according to which what makes them the same is just my classifying them under the identical concept. Plato emphatically and explicitly rejects

---

9. See *Phd.* 102D6–8: ἐμοὶ γὰρ φαίνεται οὐ μόνον αὐτὸ τὸ μέγεθος οὐδέποτ' ἐθέλειν ἅμα μέγα καὶ σμικρὸν εἶναι, ἀλλὰ καὶ τὸ ἐν ἡμῖν μέγεθος οὐδέποτε προσδέχεσθαι τὸ σμικρὸν οὐδ' ἐθέλειν ὑπερέχεσθαι (It seems to me that not only Largeness itself will never at the same time allow itself to be both large and small, but the largeness in us will never accept the small nor be willing to be exceeded). Form and form-in-us are identical in nature. That is why neither one accepts the contrary of largeness. The point is not that a universal and a particular are identical in nature; rather, there is one nature whether it be particularized in the large thing or universalized in being thought, whether by us or by an eternal Intellect. Thus, the deficiency in instances of Forms, "lacking something with respect to sameness (τι ἐλλείπει κατὰ τὴν ὁμοιότητα, 74A6; cf. 74D6, 74E4)," is not to be construed as contradicting the sameness in nature in instance and Form. The deficiency is that of sensible equality with respect to intelligible Equality where the emphasis is on the sensible not the equality. This is why we can speak of the presence (παρουσία) of the Form in the instance, that is, its presence via the nature or essence that its name names. See 100D5. Cf. *Soph.* 247A5–7. Contra: W. D. Ross 1951, 23–24; Nehemas 1975; and Kelsey 2004, 34–35. See Svavarsson (2009, 71), who identifies the deficiency in "lack [of] epistemic consistency." The idea is that sensibles will appear differently to different people, whereas Forms will not. This interpretation coheres with my own. I suggest here the reason for the lack of epistemic consistency.

10. See *Parm.* 132B3–C11. See D. O'Brien 2013 on this argument and its import.

conceptualism. Wishing to acknowledge that the phenomena that Plato wants to explain are not reasonably rejected altogether, and thinking that conceptualism is Platonism or a good substitute for Platonism produces a host of disastrous results not the least of which is to conflate universality with generalization. The main reason for resisting their conflation, a point to which I shall return, is that generalizations are always in relation to a finite data set, whereas universality transcends the finite.[11] That these are crucially different seems clear, although in mathematical induction it is easy to blur the difference.

Let us return to "having" and "participating." The idea of nonexclusive predication follows from the recognition that in predicative judgments I cognize that which is in principle not uniquely possessed or at least not necessarily uniquely possessed. This is so even though it is also necessarily true that if S is f because S participates in a Form, then S's f has a unique ID, too. If this is so, then it also seems to follow that if S is f and f has a unique ID, and we can cognize that S is f, this entails that S participates in a Form. In other words, if participation entails unique having and unique having entails participation, then these are extensionally equivalent, even though they are different in meaning. But this cannot be quite right, for a nominalist will insist on unique having without seeing a reason to admit there is participation in a Form as well. What we need to say is that the thinking that S is f entails both unique having and nonunique participating, again with these being extensionally equivalent yet distinct in our thinking. If "Helen is beautiful" is true, then it is both true that Helen's beauty uniquely belongs to her and beauty does not uniquely belong to her. That is, someone else could be beautiful. The predicative judgment that S is f either requires us to allow that S is not necessarily uniquely f, even though S's f has a unique ID or else it requires us to analyze away the relative though not formal identity implicit in a predicative judgment. If that were the case, then "S is f" would indicate a collocation of two things, not a predication. Is there any reason why such a move would be thought to be unsatisfactory?

The main argument for thinking that it is unsatisfactory is that without predication, the reidentification of S becomes impossible. This is the basis for Plato's rejection of extreme Heracliteanism.[12] If S at t_1 is to be reidentified at t_2, then this must be done by means of a predicative judgment of one sort or another. Epistemological identification and reidentification goes hand in hand with metaphysical identity. But the latter is possible only because in the former there is identity of some sort between S and f.[13]

---

11. See McEvoy (2018), who makes a similar point within the context of a defense of a priori mathematical knowledge.

12. See *Tht.* 182A4–E12.

13. Those who think that identity is just formal identity would resist the possibility that S and f should be identical. See, e.g., Rea (1998), who argues that in such cases S and f are numerically the same but not identical. Rea's scruples about identity are not necessary, certainly

The inability to provide a metaphysical foundation for predication will no doubt trouble some Naturalists who believe that there are numerous well-grounded predicative judgments in natural science. It will trouble neither those who think that natural science needs no metaphysical foundations nor those who, like Rorty, blithely accept the skeptical implications of forswearing the ability to reidentify anything.

Plato, however, does have another argument he used to try to move past this threatened stalemate. The argument is that the possibility of false predicative judgments depends on our understanding what a true predicative judgment is.[14] To understand what it is to believe falsely that Theaetetus is sitting is to presume that one understands what it means to believe truly that Theaetetus is, say, standing. Saying this does not amount to a claim that in believing that S is f one is in fact believing truly. It only amounts to the claim that false predicative judgments are only intelligible owing to the intelligibility of true predicative judgments. So the Naturalist who wants to resist this argument must say that she does not understand the difference between "S is f" is true and "S is f" is false. This is not equivalent to someone who denies that there is no evidential basis for deciding whether S is f is true or false. It is equivalent to saying that one does not even understood what it could possibly mean to say that there is a difference between S is f being true and S is f being false.

A denial of the ability to grasp this difference is curious because a manifestation of our ability to cognize difference comes to us merely with sense-perception. Without such elementary discernment (κρίσις) of differences, cognition would not be possible. Our discernment, however, goes well beyond the discernment of animals in sense-perception and certainly beyond the noncognitive discernment or discrimination in plants, enabling, for example, phototropism. Our discernment naturally results in predicative judgments of difference and of identity and so, derivatively, of sameness. For Plato, the Naturalist faces an uncomfortable trilemma: either (a) deny our cognitive ability altogether or (b) deny that it is different from that of animals or (c) admit that we can tell the difference between true and false predicative judgments. To embrace (a) is to deny what is evident, presumably on the basis of an axiom that is significantly far less evident; to embrace (b) amounts either to conflating it with (a) or to attributing to animals the ability to make predicative judgments, something for which the empirical evidence is meager at best; to embrace (c) is to admit the key premise for an argument to the effect that only with the postulation of Forms will we be able to explain how predicative judgments—judgments presupposing relative identity—are possible.

---

not for Aristotle whose position he is explicating and defending. For identity, like oneness, is a property of being, and being is *gradable*, as is identity.

14. See *Soph.* 263B6–D4.

Plato, of course, does not believe that all statements of the form S is f indicate or presuppose there is a Form in which S participates even if he does believe that our predicative judgments are a rough guide to what the population of Forms is. As Plato puts it in *Statesman*, we should not postulate a Form of Barbarian even if we claim that a certain non-Greek is a barbarian.[15] This is so because the term "barbarian" does not indicate a natural kind, used as it is by Greeks for anyone who does not understand Greek or perhaps is not conversant with Greek culture. Therefore, we should recognize once and for all that there is nothing in the so-called theory of Forms that allows us to deduce the population of the world of Forms a priori. It is not the case, however, that the discovery of the true population is entirely a posteriori as it is in the case of, say, the discovery of species in the animal kingdom. There are some Forms that can be deduced a priori, like the above Forms of Sameness or Identity or Difference. The postulation of Forms as explanatory entities is an essential part of Platonism; the discovery of the array of eternal and immutable intelligible entities is a research project within Platonism.[16]

The function of Forms is to explain the possibility of true nonexclusive predication. Plato does not doubt this possibility. He rejects out of hand the view of the so-called late learners who deny the cogency of predications other than identity statements.[17] It is not entirely clear what these late learners think, but it seems that what troubles them primarily is that any predication other than an identity statement contradicts such a statement. Thus, if S is S, then it cannot be true that S is f. If this is their complaint, then Plato's rejection of it is implicitly an endorsement of nonexclusive predication. For the nominalist generally will insist that there can be no conceptual space for nonexclusive predication. Such predication supposes a contradiction: that two things are identical. In other words, there is no room for sameness that is not identity. Conversely, when there is not identity there is not sameness. The late learner seems to long for consistency by insisting that the only thing identical with S is S. To claim that S is f, where f is not identical with S would be to countenance the impossibility that something that is S could also be somehow identified as f, since identity entails exclusivity of predication alone. Alternatively, we could allow that S is f if and only if

---

15. See *Sts.* 262D–E.
16. See Shapiro 1997, 84–106, on the Platonic "*ante rem* structures," e.g., of the natural numbers. I am using the term "array" synonymously. See Balaguer (1998, 8), who argues that "structures" must include "entities," that is, individuals. This misconstrues Forms as putative entities or particulars; rather, they are the natures of the entity that is Being. See sec. 4.2 in this chapter and chap. 5, sec. 5.3.
17. See *Soph.* 251A5–C7. See Crivelli (2012, 103–109), who interprets the passage somewhat differently. See Meixner 2009a on the view of those who hold that simple predicative judgments have no ontological import. I take it that this view is an extension of the claim of the "late learners."

there could not be something other than S that is f. In this case, S is f would only be a statement of what S is exclusively. This would be a statement of S's identity.

A nominalist who is not attracted to the extreme position of the late learners will naturally want to explain predication differently. But all nominalists, I believe, want to reject nonexclusive predication. Since Plato, as we have seen, believes that exclusive predication is a consequence of the explanation for nonexclusive predication, the real issue is the explanatory exigency supposedly met by Plato with Socrates's simple hypothesis. This is, again, an explanation for the truth of that proposition that S is f. The sort of explanation that Anaxagoras offered and with which the nominalist in principle agrees can only be an explanation if "f" stands for what is exclusively possessed by what "S" stands for. Plato's view that, minimally, it is possible that S is f indicates nonexclusive predication is as much an epistemological claim as a metaphysical one. Our belief that S is f nonexclusively rests upon the different and irreducible cognitive encounters with S and f, that is, by sense-perception and by thinking.

The way Forms explain the possibility of nonexclusive predication is by the hypothesis of an entity whose nature is such that something can have this nature nonexclusively. Without such an entity existing, the prima facie exclusive possession of f by S would be the end of the story since f has a unique ID. But because the posited entity has a nature that is in itself neither particular nor universal, there is nothing in principle to prevent the presence of this nature nonexclusively in f. Therefore, Helen is beautiful but not exclusively so, even though of course Helen's beauty is exclusively hers.

Suppose, then, that beauty is neither a universal nor a particular, but must have an ontological foundation in order to account for predication. This ontological foundation, however, does not make beauty into an eternal perfect particular. Let me here anticipate in outline a more extensive answer that I will develop later in this chapter and also in later chapters. The one ontological foundation for the array of Forms is the Form of Being. The oneness or unity of the Form of Being does not preclude absolutely its multiplicity. The unicity of the first principle of all, the Good, requires us to say that whatever is subordinate to this principle is in some way multiple.[18] The way that the specific unity-multiplicity of Being is accounted for is by recourse to an elucidation of the Parmenidean dictum "for to think and to be is the identical thing."[19] As we shall see, the Demiurge is the eternal

---

18. When Aristotle hypothesized that the first principle of all is οὐσία, he was justified in inferring that oneness is a property of οὐσία because what is first must be one and everything is one insofar as it has some share in the first. Aristotle is here evidently explicitly contradicting Plato's claim that the first is not οὐσία; on the contrary, for Plato, the first is the cause of οὐσία.

19. See Parmenides, fr. B3 DK: τὸ γὰρ αὐτὸ νοεῖν ἐστίν τε καὶ εἶναι. Cf. B 8, 34: ταὐτὸν δ' ἐστὶ νοεῖν τε καὶ οὕνεκεν ἔστιν νόημα.

intellect eternally thinking Being in its diversity or multiplicity. The Demiurge is Being viewed, so to speak, from the intellectual side as opposed to the intelligible side. It is the Demiurge that is the ontological foundation required.[20] But the Demiurge is not engaged in thinking Forms universally, for if he were, then the Forms, once again distinct from the intentional objects of the thinking, would need another ontological ground. The Demiurge just is what Beauty and Circularity are. This bald statement of the Platonic position is in serious need of exegetical and philosophical defense.

But for now, I note only in passing, again, that the theory of Forms as explanatory entities cannot without irreparable distortion be ripped out of its larger context which includes the Demiurge and, ultimately, the Idea of the Good.

The conflict between Platonism and Naturalism can be usefully viewed along the axis of explanatory adequacy. Naturalism is in principle committed to explanations within the mature sciences. These are explanations for various phenomena. Herein, explanatory adequacy indicates an explanans for which it would be a sort of category mistake to take as itself requiring another explanans of the same sort as itself. Thus, the items proposed as adequate explanations in biology may well require or admit of explanations within chemistry or physics, but their claim of adequacy means that they are foundational. In every case, the hallmark of explanatory adequacy is an entity in nature whose nature it is, roughly, to cause the sort of phenomena that are in need of explanation. A biological process like parturition is, ultimately, explained by the nature of cells whose activity it is that causes the explanandum. From this perspective, the equations that comprise mathematical laws do not themselves ever explain; rather, they describe in quantitative terms the processes themselves whose real explanation is the nature of the things causing or undergoing these processes.

It is the existence of phenomena that Naturalism seeks to explain by the things that, owing to their natures, produce the phenomena. The existence of these things themselves might be in need of explanation, but explanatory adequacy is only obtained if the new explanans is not the same sort of thing as the explanandum. Thus, if the existence of organic entities on this planet is in need of explanation, then the explanation cannot be found in other organic entities. Presumably, the inorganic or nonorganic will be needed to explain the organic by its operations. And of course if this explanation is not to be empty, then there must be something about the nature

---

20. See Perl (1999, 352), who identifies the Form with "the common nature" and infers from this that, since the common nature is the nature of many instances, the Form cannot exist without instances. But this inference is a non sequitur since (a) a Form is distinct from its "common nature" and (b) the common nature is not a generalization from instances. Plato holds that this nature is found in the eternal intellect that is the Demiurge. It is true that all Forms are instantiated owing to the goodness of the Demiurge, but this is not equivalent to saying that the common nature is just what is found in the instances.

of the inorganic that enables it to produce the organic by the manifestation of that something. In principle, then, explanatory adequacy must end up with one or more entities the existence of which cannot in principle be explained. A singularity, say, either provides an ultimate Naturalistic explanation or not. But if it does not, that cannot be because the true ultimate explanation is another singularity[1].

At this point, the proper Naturalistic position is to insist that the existence of the singularity cannot be explained because there is no possible explanation for it.[21] There is no more an explanation for that than there is for the nature of anything. Asking for an explanation for the existence of anything is illicit just in the way that asking why anything has the nature it has is illicit. But this position is vulnerable in a fairly obvious way. For explanations are habitually sought for the existence of phenomena, whereas in this case the existence of the explanans cannot be explained. But the existence of some nature is only beyond explanation if its existence belongs to its nature, that is, if it is a necessary existent. If this supposed necessity is logical necessity, then there would have to be something about the nature that made its nonexistence an impossibility. But whereas organic inorganic molecules or viviparous ovipars seem to be impossibilities, it is very difficult to see why the nonexistence of anything in nature would ever be thought to be an impossibility. If the supposed necessity is physical necessity, then this is because there is something about the nature that makes it impossible to do or to be anything other than its nature allows. But this is not at all different from implicit logical necessity.

If the existence of some nature explains the existence of a certain phenomenon, one might consider asking why the claim that the explanans does not require an explanation is not a violation of the principle that a true explanation cannot explain if it is the same sort of phenomenon as the explanandum. Perhaps the reply is that it is not the existence of the explanans that does the explaining, but the nature of it. Accordingly, it does not beg the question to hold that the existing explanans explains the existence of the explanandum. Unfortunately, however, no nature as such explains anything, since the nature is what it is whether it exists or not. It is only the existing nature that can explain. Indeed, the putative explanation may be described as the phenomenon consisting of the operation of an existing nature producing the existing phenomenon that is the explanandum. In short, explanatory adequacy within a Naturalistic framework guarantees explanatory inadequacy. Of course, one might concede that such explanatory inadequacy is irrelevant to Naturalistic purposes. It is enough to adduce such explanations as may be sought within the confines of the mature

---

21. E.g., Dennett (2006, 244) holds that the universe creates itself ex nihilo which, I take it, is equivalent to saying that it needs no explanation other than itself.

sciences and their elementary entities.[22] Is this, though, any different from saying that the realm of ultimate explanatory adequacy is in principle closed to Naturalism? If the answer is no, then the realm of ultimate explanatory adequacy is, as Plato suggests in *Phaedo*, the realm of philosophy. Regarding the existence of anything that does not exist necessarily, ultimate explanatory adequacy is in principle unavailable to the Naturalist insofar as she is wedded to methodological Naturalism, the view that all *explanantia* must be empirically available and so the sorts of things that cannot be necessarily existent themselves.

4.2. Eternity and Time

The stark opposition between Platonism and Naturalism is nowhere more evident than in the account that each gives of eternity and time. For a Naturalist, eternity is at most a purely abstract conception. Whether time is considered part of the four-dimensional complex that exhausts the world entirely or whether time is considered a dimension independent of the other three, anything considered eternal is simply a temporal or temporalized item abstracted from its temporal dimension. Thus, it might be conceded that 5+3=8 is an eternal truth, but only in the anodyne sense that it is the hypostasized, detemporalized result of a temporal act or statement or proposition.[23] It is trivially true that if all that exists is a four-dimensional matrix or a three-dimensional matrix that is "in" time, then there could be no eternal or atemporal entities that are the truth-makers for certain propositions.

By contrast, not only does Plato sharply distinguish temporal from atemporal being, but he asserts the ontological priority of the latter to the former. Indeed, it is a central tenet of Platonism that whatever is qualifiable by a temporal predicate is in some way only an image of that which is eternal. The existence of the eternal and its ontological priority is probably Plato's innovation, although it has been argued that Plato's great predecessor Parmenides had a notion of eternity.[24] The clear announcement of both the

---

22. See Ritchie 2017 on the "causal joint problem," that is, on the problem of how a supernatural principle of all could interact causally with the natural world. The Platonic position is not that the first principle explains physical regularities or natural laws generally. It is the existence of these that it is needed to explain.

23. Presumably, the concession regarding mathematical truth is owing to the supposition that such truth is acausal because the truth-makers for these truths are nonspatial and nontemporal. See, e.g., Balaguer 1998; Azzouni 2004; Leng 2010; and Colyvan 2010.

24. See Owen 1966a. The issue is whether Parmenides recognized pure atemporal being or whether he was only thinking of perpetual unchanging duration. Tarán (1979) argues forcefully against Owen that he is wrong in thinking that Parmenides conceived of the former rather than merely the latter. It does not matter for my purposes who is right here, though I suspect that Tarán is.

existence and priority of eternal being to the temporalizable comes in the famous passage in *Timaeus* on the generation of time itself.

> When the father [i.e., Demiurge] who had generated [the cosmos] saw it in motion and living, a representation of the everlasting gods, he was delighted and considered how to make it even more like its model. Since the model was itself an everlastingly Living Animal, he tried to make this universe like it as much as was possible. The nature of the Living Animal was to be eternal, but it was not possible to attach this property completely to that which was generated. Instead, he had the idea of making the cosmos a moving image of eternity, and simultaneous to his arranging the heavens, he made of the eternity that remains a unity an everlasting image proceeding according to number to which, of course, we have given the name "time."[25]

There are many things in this passage that deserve extended treatment. First, however, there is the philological point about the vocabulary of time and eternity. In this passage, Plato uses two words apparently synonymously. The words are αἰώνιος ("eternal") and ἀίδιος ("everlasting"). Neither word is used prior to Plato for that which is outside of time altogether. But here Plato wants to make a distinction between that to which no temporal predicate can literally apply and that which is everlasting, that is, without beginning and without end. Both are implicitly distinguished from that which does have a beginning and an end.[26] The word ἀεί ("always") is used by Plato in *Timaeus* and elsewhere for both that which is eternal (because it is derivatively everlasting) and that which is primarily everlasting and so temporal.[27] Nothing that has a beginning, middle, and end can be ἀεί. The

---

25. *Tim.* 37C6–D7: Ὡς δὲ κινηθὲν αὐτὸ καὶ ζῶν ἐνόησεν τῶν ἀιδίων θεῶν γεγονὸς ἄγαλμα ὁ γεννήσας πατήρ, ἠγάσθη τε καὶ εὐφρανθεὶς ἔτι δὴ μᾶλλον ὅμοιον πρὸς τὸ παράδειγμα ἐπενόησεν ἀπεργάσασθαι. καθάπερ οὖν αὐτὸ τυγχάνει ζῷον ἀίδιον ὄν, καὶ τόδε τὸ πᾶν οὕτως εἰς δύναμιν ἐπεχείρησε τοιοῦτον ἀποτελεῖν. ἡ μὲν οὖν τοῦ ζῴου φύσις ἐτύγχανεν οὖσα αἰώνιος, καὶ τοῦτο μὲν δὴ τῷ γεννητῷ παντελῶς προσάπτειν οὐκ ἦν δυνατόν· εἰκὼ δ' ἐπενόει κινητόν τινα αἰῶνος ποιῆσαι, καὶ διακοσμῶν ἅμα οὐρανὸν ποιεῖ μένοντος αἰῶνος ἐν ἑνὶ κατ' ἀριθμὸν ἰοῦσαν αἰώνιον εἰκόνα, τοῦτον ὃν δὴ χρόνον ὠνομάκαμεν. The ontological priority of the eternal to the temporal entails and is entailed by the explanatory asymmetry of the eternal and the temporal. To consider the eternal as abstracted from the temporal inverts this order. Forms can only be ultimate explanations if they are eternal. If they are in time, they are subject to change and therefore unsuitable as the sort of *explanantia* that Plato has in mind.

26. See Archer-Hind (1888, 121n6), who saw the distinction clearly. Also A. E. Taylor 1928, 186–187, who makes the important point that if something is eternal, then of course it can be said to be everlasting in the sense that at any time, it can be said to exist. But if something is everlasting, it does not follow that it is eternal; indeed, it follows that it is not outside of time. So the sense in which the eternal is everlasting is derivative; since we cannot infer from the fact that something is everlasting that it is eternal, we can infer the opposite. Also Cherniss 1962, 211–213.

27. See *Tim.* 27D6–28A4, 38A2; *Phd.* 78D5; *Rep.* 610E10–611A2, etc. Whittaker (1968, 135–138) cites a number of places in the dialogues where ἀεί, αἰώνιος, and ἀίδιος are used for that which is infinite in duration as opposed to being outside of time altogether including *Tim.*

cosmos itself, though generated, can be said to be always because there is no time at which it is not. Its generation is not "in time" since time was actually generated after it.

The philological disarray is, in my view, the result of the fact that the fundamental distinction Plato wants to make is intended to exclude what we might suppose is a real possibility, namely, that something should have infinite duration without change. It seems entirely benign to say that even if Beauty does not otherwise change, still it is temporalized in the sense that it existed yesterday and that it will exist tomorrow. In short, it perdures, perhaps without beginning and without end. What are Plato's grounds for denying this possibility?

The principal feature of intelligibles owing to which they are said to be eternal is that they are unqualifiedly unchanging, where "unchanging" follows from being exempt from "becoming" altogether.[28] The cosmic image is αἰώνιος, but not perfectly (παντελῶς) so. This use of "perfectly" puts us in mind of "perfect being (τὸ παντελῶς ὄν)" from *Republic*.[29] By contrast, the sensible is simultaneously "being and not being (εἶναί τε καὶ μὴ εἶναι)." Hence, the moving image has being in a diminished way just because it is always changing or becoming in some respect. The things in the intelligible world are typically described by Plato as ἀεὶ κατὰ ταὐτὰ ἔχειν ("always being self-identical").[30] That is, even though they can be in some sense composite, they do not have the compositeness of that which has parts outside of parts, namely, the compositeness of bodies.[31] Because sensibles are composed in this way, they have scattered being (σκεδαστὴ οὐσία) in contrast to the undivided being (ἀμέριστη οὐσία) of Forms.[32] Whatever is generated is necessarily susceptible to change because its being is scattered.[33] But why should

---

28A; *Phd.* 79A6–11; *Rep.* 611E2–3; *Symp.* 211A1, B1–2 (ἀεί); *Tim.* 37D2, 7, (αἰώνιος); and *Tim.* 37C6, 40B5 (ἀίδιος).

28. See *Tim.* 27D5–28A1: τί τὸ ὂν ἀεί, γένεσιν δὲ οὐκ ἔχον, καὶ τί τὸ γιγνόμενον μὲν ἀεί, ὂν δὲ οὐδέποτε (that which is always being, not having a generation and that which is always generated, never having being). There is a textual issue here, but little doubt I think about the sense of the passage. See Cornford (1937, 98n1, 102), Whittaker (1968, 1969), and Robinson (1979), all of whom argue that Plato does not in *Timaeus* clearly distinguish the unqualifiedly atemporal from that which has infinite, changeless duration.

29. *Rep.* 477A3.

30. See, e.g., *Phd.* 78D1–3, 80B1–2; *Rep.* 479A2–3, E7–9; *Phil.* 58A2, 59C5; and *Tim.* 38A3–4, 52A1. Luchetti (2014, 199–237) has a penetrating discussion of the derivation of eternity from unchangingness. See also Brisson 1998, 129–130. Aristotle, *DC* A 9, 279a18–22, thinks that it is changelessness that merits the use of the term αἰών, although his use of the term seems to indicate limitless duration rather than atemporality.

31. See *Tim.* 38A5–6, B6–7 on the necessary connection between being in time and being a body. On bodies as instruments of time, see 38C3–5, 42D5.

32. *Tim.* 37A5, 35A1–2.

33. The conceptual link between having scattered being and being changeable is being generated. What has scattered being is generated by being composed, parts outside of parts, that is, parts *after* parts in generation. Think of the product of a three-dimensional printer.

we suppose that something cannot just be exempt from change except in the innocent sense in which we can use a succession of temporal predicates of it? That Plato does not mean this is clear from a later passage in *Timaeus* where he distinguishes between that which is generated, that of which we can say "was," "is," and "will be," from that which is eternal of which we can only say "is," so long as we do not think this is the "is" that belongs with "was" and "will be."[34] If, indeed, Plato is in *Timaeus* using, perhaps for the first time, a sense of "is" with no implication of "was" or "will be," it is worth trying to understand why.

We have already seen why Plato situates in the intelligible world the ultimate explanatory framework for the sensible world. If the intelligible world had duration such that "was" and "will be" could be correctly said of it, then there must be some measure or reference point by which these predicates can be correctly applied. If there were no such measure, then there would be no way of telling the difference between "was" and "will be" which is as much as to say that the "is" that implies these would not be applicable. But for there to be a measure of duration for the intelligible world, this measure must be prior to that which it measures, prior in the sense in which a determinable is prior to that which is determinant. Since there can be nothing prior to the intelligible world, there can be no such measure. Of course, we can use the measure by which we measure the passage of time in the sensible world indirectly for the intelligible world.[35] Thus, we say that yesterday the Form of Beauty explained the beauty in Helen and this is exactly what it will do tomorrow. But to do this is no more than to say that we need to appeal to Being to explain becoming or the eternal to explain the temporal. The intelligible world has duration only in the sense according to which the sensible world which does have duration can be continuously related to that which explains the being of that which is essentially becoming.[36]

This is why that which is outside of time completely cannot be older or younger than itself, *Tim.* 38A2–3. Sensibles become older by leaving their past; they become younger by having parts that come to be after other parts. Thus, it is younger than what it was owing to its new parts. This is particularly evident if we include temporal predicates in the profile of any sensible.

34. *Tim.* 37E1–38B5. See A. E. Taylor 1924, 188–189; Patterson 1995a; and Patterson 1985b, 90–92. Patterson makes the important point that if the cosmos is an image of the Living Animal, that means it is not a duplicate of its model. Since the cosmos is in time, the model cannot be in time in any sense, including changeless duration.

35. The regular motion of the planets measures time. See *Tim.* 38E–39E. See Mohr 2005, 56–60, on the planets as "clocks."

36. As Plotinus will show, this fact means that while the sensible world is really related to the intelligible world, the reverse is not the case. See 6.8 [39], 17.25–27. Cf. 8.22, 11.32; 1.7 [54], 1.16–17. If the intelligible world were really related to the sensible, then participation would be characterized by simultaneity. So when Helen participates in Beauty, Beauty is simultaneously being participated in. But if this is so, then "was" and "will be" can be predicated of Beauty as indexed by the duration of Helen's beauty. This is precisely what Plato seems to want to deny.

The only modalities applicable to the intelligible world are eternity and necessity; by contrast, the sensible, changing world is temporal and contingent. Necessity follows from "always being self-identical." Contingency follows from the applicability of "was," "is," and "will be." Even if there is something such that there never was nor never will be a time when we cannot say of it that it "was," "is," and "will be," contingency alone is the modality within which we are able to refer to it. This follows from the nature of explanation laid out in *Phaedo*. For any sensible, the intelligible world will be the locus of the explanation for its nature and existence. Thus, Plato's identification of the intelligible world as providing the subject matter for philosophy, provides us with another way to demarcate Naturalism and Platonism. The former deals only with the contingent; the latter only with the necessary.[37]

Because the intelligible world is exclusively the realm of the necessary, all relations among eternal entities are internal relations.[38] That is, no one entity can exist without all the others, since all the others are constitutive of what each is.[39] This eternal complexity sheds additional light on what it means for an ultimate explanation to be τι ἱκανόν. No Form can by itself serve as an ultimate explanation since it is intrinsically complex. The interconnectedness of the elements of its complex nature are not self-explanatory. The first principle of all must transcend such complexity. That is, in part, why the Idea of the Good is the One. By contrast, all the relations in the sensible world are external. It is true, of course, that the internal relatedness of Forms is reflected in the sensible world such that, for example, anything that is five is odd or anything that is crimson is darker than anything that is

---

37. See Bealer (1987), who argues that the boundary between philosophy and empirical science is set by the distinction between the necessary and the contingent. As Bealer contends, even if it is the case that empirical science is needed for us to understand the necessity that, say, water is H_2O, if this is a necessary truth, it is because of the nature of water. And the nature of water, according to Plato, is eternally what it is. The nature of water is like the nature of triangularity, eternally unchangeable. To the extent that Plato wants to mathematize all Forms, the analogy is of course strengthened. If it is indeed possible that eternal water appears phenomenologically different from the way it appears to us, this is a function of the factor outside of the causal scope of the intelligible world, namely, the Receptacle and its contents prior to the imposition of intelligibility on it by the Demiurge. See Turnbull 1988 for some useful remarks on Forms understood as pure mathematical structures.

38. See *Men.* 81C9–D3 where the internal relatedness of all the Forms is already presupposed. See Luchetti 2014, 45–46.

39. See Shapiro 2000, 258: "The number 2 is no more and no less than the second position in the natural number structure; and 6 is the sixth position. Neither of them has any independence from the structure in which they are positions, and as positions in the structure, neither number is independent of the other." Note the implicit derivation of the cardinals from ordinals here. This is a view congenial to the Platonic metaphysical account of the being of numbers as hierarchically derivative.

pink. But the derivative nature of this internal relatedness is evident in the hypothetical nature of such claims when made about particular sensibles.[40]

If the items in the intelligible world are unchanging in their identities, how are they then supposed to enter into the explanations that Anaxagoras failed to conceive of and Socrates resolved to pursue? A seductively simple answer is provided by a straightforward reading of *Timaeus* itself. The Demiurge infuses the precosmic chaos with intelligibility by using shapes and numbers.[41] He does this because he wants the sensible world to be as good as possible, that is, to be like the Living Animal which somehow contains all that is intelligible. Either this means that the Demiurge is in time or it does not answer the question. But the Demiurge cannot be in time—except in the sense in which the eternal is in time, that is, at any time, it can be said to exist—since he is the creator of time.[42] In that case, the operation of the Demiurge is as much of a mystery as is the operation of the Forms on whose eternity Plato insists.

What is required is a distinction between change (μεταβολή) and motion (κίνησις) and an argument that the latter does not entail the former.[43] In

---

40. So *Tim.* 30D1–31A1: τῷ γὰρ τῶν νοουμένων καλλίστῳ καὶ κατὰ πάντα τελέῳ μάλιστα αὐτὸν ὁ θεὸς ὁμοιῶσαι βουληθεὶς ζῷον ἓν ὁρατόν, πάνθ᾽ ὅσα αὐτοῦ κατὰ φύσιν συγγενῆ ζῷα ἐντὸς ἔχον ἑαυτοῦ, συνέστησε (For the god, wishing to make the world most nearly like that intelligible thing which is the best and in every way complete, fashioned it as a single visible living animal, containing within itself all living beings whose nature is of the same order). Aristotle's so-called Square of Opposition clearly demonstrates the point: An A proposition entails an I proposition just as an E proposition entails an O proposition. But I and O propositions are expressed hypothetically or in terms of *de dicto* necessity, as opposed to *de re* necessity. See *Post. An.* A 24, 86a12. See Schaffer (2010b), who argues that all concrete things are internally related. What he calls "priority monism" is the sum of all the things in the universe. These are internally related because they are integral parts of the whole. Schaffer argues for the internal relatedness of all things in the sensible world, principally on the basis of their causal interconnectedness and spatiotemporal relatedness. Schaffer (2010a, 344n3) rejects Platonism and so would reject the defense of the internal relatedness of sensibles as derived from that of separate intelligibles. For Plato, however, the nonintelligible Receptacle is the irremovable impediment to the internal relatedness of the paradigms being unqualifiedly represented in their images. One way of seeing the sharp divide between these two views is that Plato allows for chance (τυχή) and Schaffer does not. Chance is a function of the nonintelligible receptacle. In Schaffer's monism, since everything is internally related, there can be no chance. The Stoics are the ancient Naturalists who come closest to this position. The permanent possibility of chance in the sensible world is derived from a property of the imagistic nature of sensibles.

41. *Tim.* 53B5. As A. E. Taylor 1928, 358, notes, numbers (ἀριθμοί) include ratios or formulas as well as integers. Geometrical shapes are determined by such numbers according to the theorems of analytic geometry.

42. The disorderly motion in the Receptacle clearly exists independently of the Demiurge. If that motion is taken to be in time or measurable by time, then in some sense the Demiurge must also be in time. But since Plato wants to defend the existence of a sort of motion that is apart from change and therefore not in time, it seems that the disorderly motion is another sort of motion that is not in time, even though it is ceaselessly changing.

43. At *Parm.* 162C2, μεταβολή is taken to be a species of κίνησις, leaving open the possibility that there should be another species of motion that does not involve change. *Tim.* 38A3

addition, if only that which changed is temporalized, then the possibility emerges that the atemporal and unchanging motion of the intelligible can somehow be adduced to explain the presence in the sensible world of such intelligibility that it has.[44] It might be thought that to infer the existence of motion in the intelligible world on the basis of the thinking activity of the Demiurge is a mistake since it is at least possible to interpret all these references as mythological. But it is also possible to interpret these references as mythological only in the sense that they represent atemporal activity as temporalized, for example, when the text says that the Demiurge "having calculated, he discovered (λογισάμενος οὖν ηὕρισκεν)."[45] The Demiurge acts on the cosmos because of his goodness and his knowledge of the Living Animal. These acts occur without the motion that is measured by time. But to exclude these from motion altogether, that is, atemporal motion, is to be committed to the view that the entirety of the description of the Demiurge is mythological. This possibility, frequently embraced by scholars, dwindles in plausibility in light of the famous passage in *Sophist* in which motion is specifically attributed to the intelligible world. "Are we really going to be so easily persuaded that motion, life, soul, and thought have no place in that which is completely real; that it has neither life nor thinking, but stands immovable, holy and solemn, devoid of intellect?"[46] Here, I do not want to dwell on the interpretative issue of whether "the completely real" refers to the intelligible world—as it does in *Republic*—or whether Plato is now extending its use to the sensible world such that the attribution to it of the life, and so on, that it indubitably already has would seem to be entirely pointless. Rather, I want to focus on the question of why Plato would want to insist—if indeed that is what he is doing—on the cognitional life of the intelligible world.

Briefly, the explanations provided by Forms in *Phaedo* are first, the simple hypothesis that something is f because it participates in F-ness and second, more elaborately, that something is f because it participates in G-ness and G-ness always brings with it F-ness. Therefore, we can say that something is hot because it participates in Hotness or, better, that it is hot because it participates in Fire and Fire always brings with it hotness. The extremely important point of these homey examples is that somehow or other the Form of Fire and the Form of Hotness must be necessarily connected or internally

---

describes intelligibles with the adverb ἀκινήτως. This does not contradict the claim that there is κίνησις in the intelligible world, for what is here being denied of intelligibles is that it has the type of motion such that "was" and "is" and "will be" can be said of it.

44. As Scolnicov 2017 shows, Plato's atemporal teleology is essentially hierarchically ordered and it is reflected in the sensible world insofar as that is possible.

45. *Tim.* 30B1, 4–5.

46. *Soph.* 248E6–249A2: Τί δὲ πρὸς Διός; ὡς ἀληθῶς κίνησιν καὶ ζωὴν καὶ ψυχὴν καὶ φρόνησιν ἦ ῥᾳδίως πεισθησόμεθα τῷ παντελῶς ὄντι μὴ παρεῖναι, μηδὲ ζῆν αὐτὸ μηδὲ φρονεῖν, ἀλλὰ σεμνὸν καὶ ἅγιον, νοῦν οὐκ ἔχον, ἀκίνητον ἑστὸς εἶναι. See Perl 1998; and Gerson 2006.

related such that whatever participates in the one necessarily participates in the other. But the Forms are supposed to be "monads (μονάδες)" and "in-composites (ἀσύνθετα)." How, then, is it possible for them to be eternally necessarily connected? Plato returns to this puzzling fact again in *Sophist* where he speaks about the "association of Forms (κοινωνία τῶν εἰδῶν)," their "plaiting (συπλοκή)," and "their being mixed with each other necessarily forever (συμμειγνυμένω μὴν ἐκείνοις ἐξ ἀνάγκης ἀεί)."[47]

It is not too difficult to see how cognitive motion has a role to play in solving this puzzle. Indeed, it is very likely that in *Sophist* the introduction of cognitive motion a few pages prior to the various descriptions of the Forms' interconnectedness is intended at least to indicate this. The general point is made by Aristotle. A and B can be one in being (εἶναι) but two in essence or account (λόγος).[48] For example, teaching and learning. The relevant point here is that accounts are cognitional activities. The important lesson is that what is one in reality is multiple in the intellect.[49] This is also true for knowledge (ἐπιστήμη) in which one intellectually sees that the subject of a proposition and its commensurately universal properties are one in reality but multiple in their account.[50] Along the same lines, the very idea of a λόγος of a Form implies complexity, though not in the Form in itself, but in the one providing or grasping the λόγος.[51]

It seems clear that Plato needs an intellect to think that what is one in reality is yet multiple. Therefore, Hotness and Fire are hypothesized as one in reality but multiple in their intellection. Since Forms are unchangeable in their identity and atemporal and so necessarily interconnected if they are interconnected at all, the guarantor of their eternal interconnectedness must be an intellect that is equally unchangeable and atemporal. For if it were possible that the intellect were temporal and so changeable, it would be possible that it should not think the necessary interconnectedness of the Forms, in which case that interconnectedness would not be necessary.[52] On this interpretation, what is "one in being" is intelligible Being itself. But it

---

47. See *Soph.* 254Dff. Also 245B7–C3 for Being as ἓν-ὅλον (one-whole), meaning a whole of parts.

48. See, e.g., Aristotle, *Phys.* Γ 3, 202b16–22. Plato makes the identical point at *Lg.* 895E5–8, where the name of something and its definition have the identical referent.

49. It is important for Aristotle and Plato and for many other issues treated in this book that the locus of "manyness" be an intellect, which is uniquely possessed by rational beings and not in the senses, possessed by animals as well. For both Plato and Aristotle, a nonhuman animal is incapable of thinking that teaching and learning are one in reality though two in their account precisely because no animal is rational or has λόγος. Without λόγος, it cannot "externalize" its putative rationality in a λόγος.

50. On knowing as seeing, see Beierwaltes 1957, 65–66.

51. See *Phd.* 78D1: αὐτὴ ἡ οὐσία ἧς λόγον δίδομεν τοῦ εἶναι (the essence itself of whose being we give an account). Cf. *Tim.* 35B2; and *Rep.* 531C9–D4, 532A1–D4.

52. See *Crat.* 440B4–C1 which seems to be making this point or at least assuming it. Cf. *Phd.* 76E5–7; and *Phdr.* 247E1–2.

is also multiple in the eternal intellection of it. Here, we have yet another reason why only that which is absolutely simple and "sufficient" for explanation must be "above" οὐσία or Being, that is, the Being with οὐσία.[53] Being is a "one-whole" or a "one-many."[54] It has the unity of a whole or many. But that wholeness or manyness is identical with the thinking or cognition of it.

In Aristotle's example of two things being one in reality but two in λόγος, there is a clear distinction between reality and thinking. But applying this distinction to the Demiurge and his eternal cognitive identity with Forms is more complicated.[55] For the thinking is, so to speak, both on the metaphysics side and on the epistemological side. The reality, analogous to the real identity of teaching and learning, is at the least a complex identity such that we can say that the Demiurge is cognitively identical with the entire array of Forms.[56] And these Forms must be many, but not just *quoad nos*. I shall return to what sense can be made out of a reality that is eternally one-many. For now, I shall only point out that the cognitive identity of Demiurge and Forms is not the same thing as our embodied thinking of intelligible reality. This is something we do with λόγοι. The "manyness" of the elements of a proposition representing eternal reality is not the manyness of the Forms eternally cognized by the Demiurge. Therefore, my account of a mathematical theorem represents as conceptually complex what is in reality unified, although the unity is not and could not be unqualified unity. Eternal Being has a unity, a minimally complex unity perhaps, that is distinct from the absolute unity of the first principle of all.[57]

On this interpretation, intellect and Forms are cognitively identical in reality but distinguishable *quoad nos*. To be aware of our own intellect, as when we are self-reflexively aware of a unity amid some diversity, is implicitly to be aware of the Forms that are in fact cognitively identical with that intellect of which we are images. I would suggest that recollection may be understood as our making actual this implicit awareness. But there is an insuperable bar to our thereby having embodied knowledge. It is that we

---

53. See Halfwassen 2004.
54. Cf. *Phil.* 16C9–D7 where each single Form is shown in dialectic to be a many (πολλά). Its oneness does not contradict its manyness for it is not many in the sense in which it is one. What is true for each Form is true for the generic Form Being. See Cornford (1934, 263–273), who makes some useful albeit misleading remarks on this, especially on the containment of all Forms by the Kind Being.
55. The term "cognitive identity," as distinct from "formal identity" indicates extensional equivalence plus a real distinction between the thinking and the object thought.
56. See Halfwassen 2000, 50–62; Karfik 2004, 127–138; and Ferrari 2008, 98–102.
57. See *Tim.* 37D6 in reference to the Living Animal: μένοντος αἰώνιος ἐν ἑνί (remaining always in unity). This is so despite its manifest complexity, including Forms of all living things. Again, the different sorts of unity are explored in the second part of *Parmenides*. In the second hypothesis (142B5–143A1), the properties of a minimally complex unity are deduced. Here, we get the a priori deduction of the most general or categorical Forms, such as Identity, Difference, Sameness, Number, and so on.

can only think the identities-in-diversity representationally, in words, even "mentalese" or in images. And to do this requires a temporalized existence. To see that 5+3=8 is not to do what an eternal intellect does eternally. But doing this in a temporalized manner does give us an intimation of eternity. And the difference between, on the one hand, seeing 5+3=8 as an eternal truth eternally cognized as a unity-in-diversity in an eternal intellect and, on the other, seeing it as an abstraction from the temporal is that in the former case we see that it is an eternal truth, whereas in the latter case its truth is purely stipulative or tautologous. Therefore, it is only in the former case that 5+3=8 could be an explanans since no tautology explains anything.[58]

Thus, the atemporal motion of an eternal intellect, what Plato calls κίνησις νοῦ ("motion of intellect"), is not the motion of any temporalized being; it is, therefore, not subject to change.[59] It is exactly what Aristotle describes by introducing the new term ἐνέργεια ("activity") to indicate what the Unmoved Mover does, even though it is not so clear that the Unmoved Mover is an eternal intellect.[60] But even granting that the Demiurge must be eternally active, we still have no explanation for his incursion into the temporal, that is, for an activity that is not wholly removed from the temporal. In order to answer this question fully, we shall need to bring in the Good, which I do in chapter 5. But here I briefly note the following. The Demiurge's creation of time is posterior to the disorderly motion in the Receptacle prior to the Demiurge's intervention.[61] For this reason, the Demiurge's creative activity is circumscribed. In order to fully appreciate the causal role of the Demiurge it will be necessary to see it as an instrument of the Good, exactly in the way we saw earlier in this chapter how the Forms are instrumental to the ultimate explanatory role of the Good. The intellect of the Demiurge is cognitively identical with the Forms, although what it is to be an intellect is distinct from what it is to be a Form.

Naturalism cannot countenance eternity, especially the thought that that which is eternal can have an explanatory role for the temporal. It is for this reason, I suggest, that Naturalists are at best diffident about the patent success of mathematics in explaining countless features of the sensible world.[62] The diffidence is all the more egregious once we distinguish cause from necessary condition and separate the latter from the causal explanation.

---

58. Those who hold that the truths of mathematics are analytic generally avoid the obvious question of why mathematics works in the world, not just in the sense that we use it to make predictions, but in the sense that we use it to explain. Analyticity is an antimetaphysical substitute for necessity, indeed, for *de re* necessity.

59. See *Lg.* 897D3.

60. See Aristotle, *Meta.* Λ 7, 1072b26–27: ἡ γὰρ νοῦ ἐνέργεια ζωή, ἐκεῖνος δὲ ἡ ἐνέργεια· (For the activity of intellect is life, and [the Unmoved Mover] is that activity).

61. See *Tim.* 52D–53C on this disorderly motion which is a fact about the material on which the Demiurge is constrained to operate.

62. See, e.g., Kitcher 1988.

It is owing to eternal truths about mathematics, given physical conditions, that things happen in nature in the only way they could happen as opposed to the infinite number of ways they cannot. This is vividly evident in biology and botany.[63] The eternal array of Forms expressed in the variety of nature are not *possibilia*, but the eternal natures that explain possibilities, possibilities actualized with the appropriate physical conditions. Since the Form of Mouse is eternal, it is eternally present to the temporalized cosmos. When the physical conditions for the evolution of a mouse allow, then a mouse comes into existence. And it is no more plausible to deny that participation in the Form of Mouse explains why this is a mouse than it is to deny that mathematical laws explain aspects of organic morphology.

In this example, the Form of Mouse must be understood as a stand-in for the paradigms of whatever real organic identities and differences there are. If it turns out that, as many modern biologists hold, the notion of species or biological essentialism is outmoded, then the Platonic paradigm is the eternal explanation for the real irreducible possibilities in nature, whatever these may be. That is, if it turns out that species are actually adventitious collocations of simpler biological entities, say, protein molecules or amino acids, then the Platonist will adduce Forms for these, the real explanations for one protein molecule or one amino acid being irreducibly distinct from another.

The causality of the eternal in relation to the temporal is best appreciated when we dwell on the omnipresence of the intelligible. Wherever there is identity, sameness, and difference there is intelligibility. Thus, Being is present everywhere and always. The immateriality and eternity of Being means that it is not present at one time but not another nor present in one place but not another. It is present and available to our cognitive powers whenever and wherever there are the necessary conditions for its presence. And the specificity of its presence—a mouse and not a rat—is determined precisely by the presence of the necessary conditions for the one and not the other. Assuming that the intelligibility in the sensible world is not an arbitrary construct, it can only be explained by invoking eternal Being. The omnipresence of eternal Being is as evident as is the omnipresence of mathematical truth. It is obviously question-begging to assert that the eternal has no explanatory relevance to the temporal because causality is a temporal phenomenon. The Platonic position is that, once that relevance is granted, the intelligible must then inevitably become the focus in an explanatory framework, reducing what was hitherto thought to be the sole locus of causality to the status of necessary condition.

Once the ubiquity of eternal complex Being is grasped, it is easy to understand why mathematics works, that is, why eternal mathematical truths

---

63. See Thompson 1945, 1094–1095, and the following epilogue; Denton 2016; and Wagner 2017.

explain why the sensible world is the way it is and not another way. These mathematical truths are expressions or λόγοι by embodied intellects of what eternal Being is. Since, as Plato says, the eternal Being that is the array of Forms owes its existence and variegated essence to the Good, understanding eternal Being as derived from the Good is exactly what Socrates in his autobiography longs to be able to do. With that understanding, it is possible to have adequate explanations for the way the sensible world is. This is how a mathematical explanation can be teleological.

4.3. Nominalism and Its Connection to Relativism

When Timaeus describes the composition of souls, including both the soul of the universe and individual souls, he specifies their composition thus:

> Between eternal being that is always in the identical condition and divisible being found in bodies, he compounded a third form of being from both. Again, in the case of the nature of identity and difference, he followed the identical procedure and made a compound midway between indivisible identity and difference and divisible identity and difference found in bodies. Then, taking the three, he compounded them into one form, forcefully mixing the nature of difference with identity, hard as it was to make it be harmonious it, mixing them with being and from the three making one.[64]

Setting aside for the moment the cosmological and even ethical significance of this passage, I want to focus on the epistemological point that is being made. As Timaeus goes on to explain, the soul's composition enables it to make judgments about being, identity, and difference among intelligibles and among sensibles.[65] Thus, the theory about the soul's composition is offered to explain how it is that we are able to do what we manifestly are able to do, namely, cognize identity, difference, and being. On the basis of this cognition, we make further judgments about sameness and are thereby led

---

64. *Tim.* 35A1–8: ἀμερίστου καὶ ἀεὶ κατὰ ταὐτὰ ἐχούσης οὐσίας καὶ τῆς αὖ περὶ τὰ σώματα γιγνομένης μεριστῆς τρίτον ἐξ ἀμφοῖν ἐν μέσῳ συνεκεράσατο οὐσίας εἶδος, τῆς τε ταὐτοῦ φύσεως [αὖ πέρι] καὶ τῆς τοῦ ἑτέρου, καὶ κατὰ ταὐτὰ συνέστησεν ἐν μέσῳ τοῦ τε ἀμεροῦς αὐτῶν καὶ τοῦ κατὰ τὰ σώματα μεριστοῦ· καὶ τρία λαβὼν αὐτὰ ὄντα συνεκεράσατο εἰς μίαν πάντα ἰδέαν, τὴν θατέρου φύσιν δύσμεικτον οὖσαν εἰς ταὐτὸν συναρμόττων βίᾳ.

65. See *Tim.* 37A2–B3. See Cornford 1937, 64–65n3, on the principle "like knows like." In *Phd.* 78B4–84B4, in the so-called affinity argument, Socrates argues that the soul is more akin to immaterial Forms than it is to sensibles. I take "invisible (ἀιδές)" as equivalent to "immaterial." The argument, following the recollection argument, takes as proven that we have knowledge, but that we could not have it unless our souls had a composition more akin to Forms than to sensibles. And yet it is implicitly assumed that we can also have cognition of the intelligible aspects of sensibles. The *Timaeus* description of the composition of the soul seems to provide an explanation for the dual capacity of what is essentially immaterial.

to posit separate Forms to account for the puzzling phenomenon of two or more things being the same even though they are numerically different.[66]

The identity, difference, and being of the intelligible world are eternal and they are a function of Being as necessarily a one (whole)-many. The identity, difference, and being of the sensible world are temporalized and are what we first encounter with our five senses and regarding which we make predicative judgments. Because of the soul's bipolar ability, it can judge temporalized identity, difference, and being as deficient in relation to intelligible paradigms.[67] This deficiency, as we have seen, pertains to the forms particularized in sensibles. The conditions for the manifestation of Forms compromise the intelligibility of forms since these conditions suffice for the manifestation of contrary forms. No combination of conditions will amount to a cause or explanation for the truth of true predicative judgments.

Plato makes substantial use of the ability we have to cognize identity, difference, and being in the argument against Protagorean relativism in his *Theaetetus*. He does this in the course of the larger examination of the claim that knowledge (ἐπιστήμη) is to be identified with sense-perception (αἴσθησις). The claim that knowledge is sense-perception has already been shown to be in need of Protagorean relativism and Heraclitean flux theory in order to meet the criteria laid down for knowledge at the beginning of the argument: knowledge must (a) always be of what is and (b) it must be inerrant (ἀψευδές).[68] In order for sense-perception to have a chance at meeting these criteria, Plato adduces Protagoras and Heraclitus. Thus, only if in sense-perception we attain what is and only if what is is what is always becoming (for us), will sense-perception be knowledge.

Protagoras is represented as arguing that "human beings are the measure of all things, of what is that it is and of what is not that it is not." But this is only plausible if "what is and what is not" exist privately or subjectively (τὰ ἴδια).[69] That is, this is only plausible if "what is" and "what is for me" are identical. And this in turn is only plausible if "what is" is identical with the result or product of an act of sense-perception (αἴσθησις). Someone who maintained that in sense-perception we attain to what is will no doubt agree

---

66. I take it that our ability to make predicative judgments is a variant on the judgments of sameness among things that are different. If I judge that S is f, I am able to do this because I can distinguish S from f, even though f is an aspect of the identity of S. From this, I can infer that S that is f at t_1 is the same as S that is f at t_2. Judgments of sameness are always derived from judgments of identity and difference.

67. This is the conclusion of the so-called recollection argument at *Phd.* 72E3–78B3.

68. *Tht.* 152C5–6. I translate ἀψευδές thus in order to be neutral between "true," "incorrigible," and "infallible." In fact, in the course of the argument, all three senses will be deployed. It will, however, turn out that only in the last sense can both criteria be met.

69. *Tht.* 166C4.

that the objects of different sense modalities are different.[70] But then, no sense modality is capable of making the judgment that both exist or have being and that each is self-identical and different from the other.[71] The strategy for the defeat of Protagoras is based on showing that we do make judgments about the existence or being of the things we perceive and that these things are self-identical and different from each other.[72] But these judgments are not acts of sense-perception. And the objects of these judgments are not, therefore, reducible to τὰ ἴδια; rather, they are "common" or "objective (τὰ κοινά)."[73] For this reason, their being is not exhausted by the result of any one act of sense-perception. That is the antirelativistic point.

Our ability to judge identity and difference is also the ability to judge that two or more things are the same (ὅμοιον).[74] But identity is not sameness. Thus, for example, the judgment of identity regarding a color or a sound sensed is a judgment that the color or sound has an identity different from any other but that on a different occasion, that identical color could be found in another sense-experience which would be the same as the first owing to the identical nature being encountered. Similarly, the judgment of identity of any composite, say, something having a number of properties, entails that we can make a judgment to the effect that those properties are the same owing to the fact that they belong to the identical thing. To judge that S at t_1 is identical to S at t_2 entails that S-at-t_1 is the same as S-at-t_2 even

---

70. *Tht.* 184E8–185A2.

71. Contra: Aristotle, *DA* Γ 2, 426b14–15, says that we sense the difference (ὅτι διαφέρει) between two sensibles of different sense modalities.

72. *Tht.* 185A4–12.

73. *Tht.* 185E1. For reasons given above, I do not think that τὰ κοινά should be understood to be universals. Universality occurs only in thinking. Universals are only a conceptual and linguistic hypostatization of this activity. To understand τὰ κοινά as universals is particularly maladroit in the context of the argument, since the argument will conclude that any mode of cognition, if it is going to be knowledge, must attain to extramental reality.

74. It is important that we do not understand ὅμοιον ("same") as "like" or "similar" or "resembling" for these three terms do not and could not entail that there is some identical nature or essence "over and above" them. If two things are merely like, nothing follows from this; if they are like in a certain respect, then either they are merely like in that respect, in which case still nothing follows since we do not know if they are more or less like two other things that are like in the same respect or else their being like in some respect means that they are the same in that respect, that is, the identical nature is present in them. Only in this case, does the theory of Forms come in. So there are no grounds for understanding ὅμοιον as "like" in the first place. See Quine (1969, 69–90), who tries to explain sameness in terms of similarity. The obvious problem with this is that similarity admits of degrees and since *exact* similarity, i.e., sameness, is treated as a form of similarity not entailing identity, there is no criterion for a degree of similarity. If, for example, we maintain that x is more similar to y than it is to z, this must mean that it is more similar to y than is some w to y. But there can be no criterion for determining whether or not this is so. Only if there is exact similarity that is equivalent to sameness can degrees of similarity be scaled. And it is only exact similarity, synonymous with sameness, that generates Forms. So we should understand Plato's one-over-many argument to start with the datum of sameness.

though they cannot be identical since they have at least different temporal properties. And their sameness entails that there be something identical in virtue of which the claim to sameness can be made.

The main thrust of the argument is to the effect that thinking (διάνοια) is different from sense-perception. If the proponent of the view that knowledge is sense-perception must admit this, then it will turn out that relative to sense-perception, only thinking attains to existence or being.[75] But it was agreed that being must be attained if a candidate for knowledge is to be successful for knowledge is of what has being. Note that even one who supports the definition of knowledge as sense-perception must agree that knowledge must attain being; but he is forced to equate being with becoming in sense-perception in order to be able to claim that sense-perception is knowledge.

This simultaneous attack on nominalism and on relativism can be met either by insisting that thinking is not different from sense-perception or by insisting that it is not necessary or even possible to attain to being in order to have knowledge where being is understood to be something κοινός and not something ἴδιος. The first alternative was, according to Aristotle, maintained by Empedocles, Parmenides, and Democritus.[76] Plato's reason for rejecting this view is, however, slightly different from Aristotle's. Whereas Aristotle argued that sense-perception is always true (ἀεὶ ἀληθής), while thinking sometimes errs, Plato argued that judgments of identity and difference are implicit in claims to perceive anything and therefore the thinking involved in judging cannot itself be sense-perception. For example, if one judges that one is perceiving a sound and a color, it is not any sense that makes this judgment. And surely it is possible to make such a judgment. And the judgment assumes that the color and sound are different and that each is self-identical.

What would it be like to deny that such judgments are even possible? Presumably, the denial would amount to the claim that someone who says he is making such a judgment is mistaken. But that would mean that the two sensibles are not identical and not different and that they do not exist or have being. But the intelligibility of such a denial presumes the possibility that the claim is not or could not be mistaken. Therefore, if it is possible that someone is either mistaken or not mistaken in making a judgment about sensibles, then thinking is not sense-perception.

This conclusion illuminates the response to the second objection. If one does not need to attain being in order to have knowledge, then how are we to assess the judgments of being, identity, and difference? Again, if it is

---

75. *Tht.* 186B11–C10.
76. See Aristotle, *Meta.* Γ 5, 1009b12–28. Anaxagoras is in the same passage mentioned as holding that things are as they are believed to be (ὑπολάβωσιν), which Aristotle perhaps thinks is tantamount to the identification of sense-perception and thinking. Cf. *DA* Γ 3, 427a18–428a14, where Parmenides and Democritus are not mentioned.

insisted that these judgments can be mistaken, then it is possible that they are not, too. In either case, the judgment is true or false. And if this is so, then it is difficult to see why a correct judgment is not to count as knowledge. If it is admitted that true judgments do count as knowledge, then it is also difficult to see how the word "knowledge" is being used when applied both to sense-perception and to the true judgment. We have already seen that the judgment is not an instance of sense-perception. Then, since sense-perception is not a judgment, either sense-perception is knowledge for a reason other than that it is a judgment or else it is not knowledge. The first alternative would require that, although sense-perception does not attain being, it is knowledge because it attains to something else, presumably becoming or nonbeing. It will be recalled that the original reason for proposing that knowledge is sense-perception was that sense-perception attains to becoming and being is just becoming. Therefore, if it is agreed that being is not becoming, then sense-perception's claim to be knowledge is completely undermined. But it is obscure, to say the least, what it would mean to agree that becoming is not being but that attaining to becoming is knowledge.

The triad identity-difference-being contains the primary constituents of thinking. This includes thinking about intelligibles as well as about sensibles. The nominalist refuses to acknowledge the possibility that two or more things can be the same, thereby entailing both that they are different (at least numerically) and that there must be a self-identical nature of some sort distinct from them to account for this.[77] Plato's response to this refusal in the *Theaetetus* passage is to dwell on our capacity to think with these primary constituents. To claim that it is impossible for two or more things to be the same because they would then be different and so not the same, rests upon an error analogous to the error of equating sense-perception with thinking. For the reason for insisting that if two or more things are the same, they then cannot be different is that if they are the same, they are identical and therefore *not* different. Thus, sameness and identity are conflated. But then the above example of diachronic judgments regarding S at t_1 and S at t_2 would not even be intelligible much less true.[78] Once identity is distinguished from sameness, the possibility of making true or false judgments about sameness in difference

---

77. See *Parm.* 132A1–4.

78. It seems that the real problem is in supposing that identity is always strict or formal identity, whereas Platonists will want to argue that identity is gradable. Gradable identity removes the force of the claim that there is no conceptual space for sameness that is not identity. Identity other than formal identity *entails* difference. Short of embracing radical or extreme Heracliteanism, we can hardly deny our ability to cognize identity and difference and *therefore* sameness. But an embrace of radical Heracliteanism certainly does not appear to be a promising principle for Naturalism, whose very idea of nature or physical reality requires identities and differences. For the Platonist, the acknowledgment of even a single case of sameness opens a door to the eternal intelligible world.

reemerges. And with that possibility the argument for the impossibility of there being such judgments disappears.

Plato construes the relativism of Protagoras in such a way that the relativist is forced to concede that thinking is irreducible to sense-perception. The reason for this is that sense-perception by definition only attains to what is ἴδιος whereas thinking attains to what is κοινός. I have interpreted this distinction as between that which is private or personal or subjective and that which is public or interpersonal or objective. But it might well be maintained that the distinction between sense-perception and thinking can be retained without granting that the latter has that which is public, and the like, as its objects. For example, one might say the following. Thinking is an activity the currency of which is concepts. And concepts are not public. In fact, they are anything but that. The relativist need not insist that sense-perception and thinking are identical in order to be able to maintain that thinking is as nonpublic as are the concepts with which thinking is done. Therefore, when Protagoras or any other Naturalist who embraces relativism says, "Man is the measure of all things, of what it is that it is and of what is not that it is not," he need not be committed to the apparently self-contradictory position that man is the measure of that of which he cannot be the measure, namely, that which is public, and so on.

The relativity of concepts (νοήματα), held to be irreducible to percepts, which are themselves also relative, does not take into account Plato's implicit distinction in the *Theaetetus* argument between concepts and the objects of thinking. This is the distinction made above between form and universal. The concept, or better, conceptualizing of form must be kept distinct from form itself. Thus, to use Plato's own example, hardness and softness are cognized by the soul by touching something hard or soft.[79] When someone then says, "this is hard" and "this is soft," she no doubt conceptualizes or expresses with a concept the experience or the act of sense-perception. It is possible to maintain that the expressions "this is hard" and "this is soft" are as relativizable as are the experiences themselves. But in thinking or believing the proposition "this is hard" or "this is soft" one cognizes hardness or softness. That is, one thinks the forms of hardness and softness universally. This must be the case since "this is hard" goes beyond the sense-perception of the hard thing; it goes beyond the mere report, "I am experiencing what I am experiencing right now regardless of how I wish to characterize it." This is evident in my thinking that "this is hard" and "that is soft." But these expressions certainly involve universality or at least generality as distinct from particularity. If, however, form is neither universal nor particular, the form that is perceived by touch is identical to the form that is being thought universally. The universality is expressed in a concept. But it is a mistake to conflate the expression of the form universally with the form itself. The

---

79. *Tht.* 186B2–4.

relativizing of concepts amounts to nothing more than the relativizing of the expression of thinking. It is trivially true that concepts are relative because all thinking is by particular subjects and all thoughts or concepts are properties of thinkers. But this does not entail that form is relative. And that is what thinking is of, albeit always in a universal manner, a manner whose expression can be legitimately held to be both distinct from sense-perception and also private.[80]

Plato's claim is in effect that whereas one's concept or conceptual act can be relative, the content of the concept is public. The reason why this claim is rejected out of hand is that if concepts are relative, then conceptual content seems to be relative, too. This is because one assumes that the concept occupies its own realm, namely, the realm of the personal or private. But Plato maintains that conceptual content is just form cognized universally and then hypostasized as if the mode of cognition had its own content because it is an independent or distinct entity. But that claim belies our contact with the objects of sense-perception. For we do not just perceive them but we think them as well. That is because in perceiving them, we perceive form—particularized—and at the same time think form—universally. Even if we insist that in saying "this is hard" and "this is soft" we are applying antecedently acquired concepts, concepts that are private, to judge that "this is hard" and "this is soft" is to think that the form we are experiencing falls under those concepts or that these concepts apply to them. Only if we conflated thinking with perceiving could we maintain that thinking is relativized in its content. But maintaining that thinking is relativized in its content is to confuse the expression of thinking with thinking itself, the content of which is not the expression of the experience of that content.[81] One is only tempted to do that if one thinks that content is particularized, as surely the expression of the experience of content is. But if content is form, form is neither particularized nor universal in itself. The content, therefore, could not itself be particular.

Here is an experiment. Try to relativize the content of your concept of circularity. Let us say that you do so by "personalizing" it, for example, by endowing it with a unique location in your conceptual space via an ancient

---

80. The concept is a variation of the universal, the hypostasized act of thinking, which is always cognition of form universally. Since this hypostatization is always expressed in language, which is public, there is an almost irresistible tendency for us to move from "my concept of P" to "*the* concept of P" where the latter is supposed thereby to attain some measure of objectivity. Unfortunately, the passage from cognition of form universally to the objectivity of concepts via language is fraught with difficulties, as Sellars, Davidson, and Quine, and many others have noted. I am arguing that these difficulties are not Plato's difficulties.

81. Plato says that thinking is internal speech or discourse. By "expression of thinking" I mean an assertion or a doxastic state resulting from thinking. Whether one talks to oneself silently or out loud, the expression is different from the thinking. See Duncombe 2016; and Corcilius 2018.

mnemonic technique. Say this is the particular printer on your desk. But in doing this, all you succeed in doing is qualifying the universality of the concept. You qualify the adverb "universally" so to speak. Thus, your concept of circularity is stipulated to have its unique location in conceptual space. But you have not succeeded in relativizing the form circularity, only the manner in which you cognize it. What circularity is is independent of how we cognize circularity even if it is necessarily true that we can never encounter circularity except by cognizing it, universally in thinking and particularly in sense-perception.

That form is neither particular nor universal in itself and that it is form that we encounter in sense-perception is driven home in the continuation of the argument. "But their being [hardness and softness] and the fact that they exist and their contrariety and the being of their contrariety are what the soul reveals itself as trying to judge altogether with respect to each other."[82] Plato is referring to judgments regarding the content of sense-experience. Our ability to experience something as hard as opposed to soft depends on our ability to think the forms of hardness and softness. And it is only because these are forms that we can perceive them as particularized *and* think them universally. Our ability to make judgments of their being, whether they exist as properties, and of what their contrariety consists in depends on content belonging to form, not to concepts of form. One might wish to conflate thinking with sense-perception, but that would be at the cost of forgoing any sort of intersubjective communication, that is, any dialogue. But insofar as thinking is, as Plato says, dialoguing with oneself, the conflation of thinking with sense-perception is to forgo thinking, too. Plato seems to assume that the only reason why one might even be remotely tempted to take on this self-destructive position is that one is unable to see that the particularization of form does not mean that form is particular. This inability to recognize the difference between form and form-as-particularized is just what nominalism is. And nominalism's twin is relativism.

Plato's argument against relativism concludes with this line of reasoning: we cannot attain the truth without attaining being; we cannot attain (τυχεῖν) being by sense-perception; therefore, we cannot attain truth by sense-perception. But if we cannot attain truth, we do not have knowledge.[83] I take it

---

82. *Tht.* 186B6–9: Τὴν δέ γε οὐσίαν καὶ ὅτι ἐστὸν καὶ τὴν ἐναντιότητα πρὸς ἀλλήλω καὶ τὴν οὐσίαν αὖ τῆς ἐναντιότητος αὐτὴ ἡ ψυχὴ ἐπανιοῦσα καὶ συμβάλλουσα πρὸς ἄλληλα κρίνειν πειρᾶται ἡμῖν.

83. *Tht.* 186C7–D5. This interpretation is along the lines of Cooper 1970, though I do not share Cooper's conclusion that Plato in this argument intends to affirm the possibility of knowledge of the sensible world. I assume that the referent of "being" in "attaining" being is dialectical, meaning that can refer either to the intelligible world or to the sensible world so long as cognition of being in the sensible world is infallible (cf. 152C5–6). But it turns out that it cannot be so; attaining being means attaining to the intelligible world. See Gerson 2009, 44–55.

that by this point in the argument, Plato already believes that he has shown that sense-perception attains only to becoming, not being. But it is still open to the relativist to insist that the connection between being and truth is not unique. That is, there can be truth in sense-perception just insofar as the perceiver reports her own sense-experience, or, what becomes for her. Is not someone who says "this feels hard to me" saying something true? I think Plato would reply that it is true as a report of how something appears to me. But unless reality is reduced to appearance, the report does not attain to the truth. The sense-perception itself is literally unintelligible.[84] It is, by definition, only of the particularized form with no separation from the particularization. That is, the experience as such is nonrepeatable. Even to consider its repetition is to bring in thought and to separate the form from its particularization. I suspect that Plato's connecting οὐσία and ἀλήθεια is because he is using the latter term in the sense of "ontological" truth. This is what the Idea of the Good is said to provide to οὐσίαι in *Republic*.[85] Truth here is a relational property of intelligibles. It is that which makes them perspicuous or transparent to an intellect. It is what makes intelligibles "attainable." By comparison, that which is unintelligible is that which is opaque to an intellect. That is why, in *Timaeus*, the "Receptacle" is only graspable by a sort of "bastard reasoning."[86] Therefore, without attaining to οὐσία, there is no cognition of anything intelligible. Without intelligibility, there can be no thought. "Semantic" truth as a property of propositions is just the expression of the ontological truth that is attained when being is attained. Thought is the only way to attain being as opposed to becoming and so the only way to attain truth.

The close connection between relativism and nominalism in *Theaetetus* is made evident in the argument against the claim that knowledge is sense-perception.[87] That is, if relativism is true, then knowledge could not be possible since relativism only attains to what is ἴδιος whereas knowledge attains to what is κοινός. If nominalism is true, then the judgments that have been shown to be possible and to disqualify sense-perception from being

---

84. The term αἴσθησις which like most -σις words in ancient Greek indicates a process of some sort, can be used for what we would call the "raw sensation," that is, the beginning of the process or the result of the process where perceiving is usually conflated with "perceiving-as." I take it that Plato believes that only if Protagoras understands αἴσθησις in the former sense, can his theory that knowledge is sense-perception have a chance of being defensible. So the more the perceiver eschews contact with form that is κοινός, the more unintelligible the act of sense-perception becomes.
85. See *Rep.* 508D10–E2.
86. See *Tim.* 52B2. The Receptacle is cognized even without sense-perception. This is because in sense-perception, there is a measure of intelligibility insofar as sensibles partake of Forms.
87. Goodman (1978, 2–19) spells out the connection between his nominalism and "radical relativism." His idea of truth as relative to "world" and "world" as equivalent to "frame of reference" or "alternative descriptions" seems to be a close analogue to the position of Protagoras.

knowledge would not be possible. Relativism, nominalism, and skepticism understood as the denial of the possibility of knowledge are in this dialogue mutually implicating. I take it that efforts to deny the mutual implication, for example, by supporting nominalism and the possibility of knowledge but denying relativism belong to the class of theories aiming at some sort of rapprochement with Naturalism. It seems inevitable, however, that a stable position can only be reached by discounting knowledge, that is, by denying both that it is what Plato says it is and that it is possible for us to attain. In the next section, I want to consider Plato's arguments for holding that knowledge is exactly what he says it is and that it is possible to attain.

4.4. The Nature and the Possibility of Knowledge

As we saw in the previous section, Plato gave us the criteria for knowledge: knowledge must (a) always be of what is and (b) it must be inerrant (ἀψευδές). It might occur to one that it is somewhat suspicious that these criteria are found in a dialogue that raises the question "What is knowledge?" and ends by failing to find an answer to that question. The identical criteria are, however, found in *Republic*.[88] It will perhaps lessen the suspicion to point out that these criteria may without distortion be taken hypothetically so that the three claimants to knowledge in the dialogue—sense-perception, true belief, and true belief with an account (λόγος)—can be examined and found wanting according to them. This would, of course, still leave the criteria as hypothetical at the end of the dialogue, although since the most obvious claimants to knowledge cannot meet them, the option of finding knowledge elsewhere as opposed to amending the criteria seems most promising. But the criteria are not adventitiously adduced, since they are manifestly defining criteria, as are all the λόγοι in the dialogues offered by Socrates and his interlocutors.[89] If this were not so, then there would be no basis for their being criticized. It is very difficult to see how, if (a) and (b) above are defining criteria, they could be independently satisfied since the unity of each object of definition precludes any "overlap." And so if it can be shown that either of the two criteria cannot be met without meeting the other, then the possibility of amending the criteria seems even more

---

88. See *Rep.* 477B9–10 (knowledge is of what completely is, τὸ παντελῶς ὄν); and 477E6–7 (knowledge is infallible, ἀναμάρτητον).

89. That is, defining criteria for a real, as opposed to a stipulative, definition. Within the context of "Socratic" definitions, the real criteria may be taken as a map for locating instances of a Form. So if we had defining criteria for the Form of Piety, we could use this as a guide for deciding whether or not a putative instance of Piety really was so. If multiple criteria were not defining, then one could not tell from the presence of one criterion alone whether the Form was present. It is surely not the case that with respect to eternal and immutable Forms that are internally related, multiple defining criteria could be independently satisfied. What would make such putative criteria defining rather than derived from the defining criteria?

unattractive. For amending them would mean jettisoning both, with the result that knowledge is of something other than what is and fallible or capable of being errant.⁹⁰ But what fallible cognition of what is other than what is would amount to, for Plato, fallible cognition of what is and what is not simultaneously or becoming, in which case we return to supposing that knowledge is true belief. But in that case we have to face Plato's objection that if knowledge just is true belief, then there is no difference between the true belief adventitiously arrived at and the true belief with some sort of justificatory basis.

Apart from the dialectical argument that the most plausible claimants to knowledge cannot actually be knowledge according to the hypothesized criteria, Plato does in fact offer a transcendental argument for the definition of knowledge as the inerrant cognition of what is which is at the same time an argument that we do in fact possess exactly this. This is the argument from recollection, set forth most explicitly in *Phaedo* but also referenced in *Meno* and *Phaedrus*.⁹¹ The argument is elegant and its basic structure is simple. There is a certain cognitive activity that we could not perform unless we had knowledge (ἐπιστήμη); we can perform this activity; therefore, we must possess knowledge. The cognitive activity Plato is referring to is the identification of a group of items that (a) are correctly said to have a certain predicate predicated of them and (b) are nevertheless deficient with regard to the nature indicated by the predicate.⁹² Therefore, equal sticks or stones may be said to be equal at the same time that it is recognized that their equality is deficient equality. The deficiency resides in the fact that any account (λόγος) of the attribute in them in virtue of which the predication is made will be compromised because it must include information that would necessarily be in the account of a contrary predicate. For example, in giving an account of the equality of two or more equal things, I must necessarily

---

90. This is the position that Philo of Larissa (158–84 BCE) took, a position that became easy prey for skeptics. See Brittain 2001. Philo apparently wanted to argue that there could be fallible ἐπιστήμη, something that is precluded by the argument against the identification of true belief with knowledge in *Theaetetus*. That is, the failure of true belief to be ἐπιστήμη turns upon the fact that false belief is possible. But if there is no false ἐπιστήμη, then true belief cannot be identical to ἐπιστήμη. In other words, for it to be possible to say "I know, but I might have been mistaken" is to identify knowledge with true belief. But we have seen that this is not possible. For if one knows, one cannot possibly have been mistaken. Modern versions of the position that Philo takes vary, but they are all essentially reliabilist. That is, they take knowledge to be a natural or physical state arising from a process of discovery that normally reliably achieves a certain given practical result. This is also the default Naturalist position. See, e.g., Papineau 1993, 142–152.

91. See *Phd.* 72E3–78B3; *Phdr.* 249C; and *Men.* 82B.

92. As discussed in sec. 4.1, the predication is also indicated by the term μετέχειν which may be glossed as "nonexclusive having" as opposed to ἔχειν, which is "exclusive having." Every subject has exclusively the numerically distinct attribute it has; it has nonexclusively the nature or essence that is manifested in the numerically distinct attribute.

include the quantity or magnitude of each sufficient to make it equal to the other(s). But this quantity or magnitude would necessarily be included in an account of why one or the other thing was unequal to any other.

The activity of judging something to be equal although deficiently so is distinct from the activity of merely making the predicative judgment of equality when that judgment implies no awareness of deficiency. If one learns to apply the word "equal" to things as a result of having acquired the concept of equality, there is in principle no conceptual space for deficiency. This is so because the application of the concept requires the conceptual exclusion of anything not relevant to the objects falling under this concept. Thus, it is irrelevant to the conceptualization of a group of objects as equal that they may be composed of material that would also be a part of the account of their inequality. That is, concepts are primarily univocally predicable of objects and whatever falls outside the univocal predication is logically unrelated to it.

Because all thinking is of form universally, conceptual thinking is like this, too. But the universality in conceptualizing does not, unfortunately, guarantee the authenticity of the formal content, so to speak. To take a simple and obvious example, one's concept of a fish indicates a rule for using the word "fish." But that rule may be defective because one's concept is defective, for example, if it entails the use of the word "fish" for a whale. Therefore, to have a concept of a fish is not automatically to cognize the Form of Fish. Indeed, insofar as our concepts are generally formed from our sense-perceptions, it is not just that our concepts do not guarantee authentic formal content, but it seems actually impossible that our concepts should attain to formal content. It is, though, possible to criticize or refine our own concepts by means of the Forms which are deficiently instantiated.

There would seem to be a fine line between thinking that some objects are equal and thinking that they are equal despite the fact that they are deficient with respect to that which the Form of Equality's name names. Indeed, one might suppose that the latter thought is inconsistent or self-contradictory since the claim of equality precludes the claim of deficiency. But this is only the case if one confuses the concept of equality with Equality. It is the latter, not the former, that accounts for the equality in equal things.[93] The concept of equality only describes our thinking and in fact entails nothing about the objects. As the argument shows, the judgment of deficient equality is a very particular sort of judgment, one which could not be made unless one already knew that in relation to which the deficient equals fall short. They are not equal and then, independently, deficient. They are deficiently equal. Thus, if a property is deficiently f and therefore F-ness cannot be identified with any f, we have a premise in an antimaterialist argument.

---

93. See *Parm.* 132B2–C11.

The knowledge that one must possess in order to make this judgment is the knowledge of Equality. It is not the putative knowledge of a λόγος of Equality. This is because such knowledge would not only be the knowledge of the Form of Equality; it would also be the knowledge of the equality in the equal objects insofar as they are equal. But our cognition of their equality would require an additional feature in our account, namely, that which necessitates their being deficiently so. This point will be easier to see with a brief thought-experiment. Suppose that I declare that there is an array of things in my office labeled A, B, C, and D, two of which are equal in number, while two of which are equal in magnitude. If you had a true account of equality, you could know independently of each pair of equals that that account would apply to them. But if I asked you what makes A equal to that to which it is equal and what makes C equal to that to which it is equal, you could not say since you do not know if the equality is in number or magnitude. Just so in the present case; even if you know that A is equal to B in number and C is equal to D in magnitude, just by knowing that B is equal to A, you could not know what it took to make B equal to A, and D equal to C.

In the argument discussed in the previous chapter, an argument that occurs later in the dialogue, we saw that Socrates insisted that even that without which something could not have the properties it has—a necessary condition—could not serve as the explanation for the possession of the property. Similarly, in the recollection argument, a stick would have to be one meter long to be equal in magnitude to another stick one meter long. That without which the one stick could not possess equality in relation to the other is also not the explanation for the equality. The explanation for the equality will be the Form of Equality and a λόγος of it could not include any mention of number or magnitude much less of a specific number or magnitude. But the way to make one object equal to another thing—the way to import that without which equality is not present—is to make the object into a specific magnitude or number.

The knowledge of the Form of Equality that enables us to judge equals to be deficient is, according to Plato, analogous to cases where sense-perception (αἴσθησις) of one object causes us to "think (ἐννοήσῃ)" of another.[94] What he thinks of is that of which he has "another knowledge (ἄλλη ἐπιστήμη)." The knowledge he has is thus not equivalent to the thinking of that which he knows. Insofar as the thinking is equivalent to having recollected, this is still not the original knowledge. The point is of some significance in leaving open the possibility that no embodied thinking could be equivalent to the knowledge of the Forms, a possibility that reinforces and is reinforced by the distinction between the knowledge and the ability to

---

94. *Phd.* 73C4–D1.

give a λόγος.⁹⁵ One may well surmise that the searching for and the giving and receiving of a λόγος belongs to the thinking that is recollecting but is only asymptotically related to the knowing, as it were.

The knowledge of the Form, if it is to be had in a preembodied state, cannot be propositional, at least if propositions are λόγοι and so expressed in language.⁹⁶ It is best described as mental seeing, analogous to the mental seeing achieved when one, for example, sees some pattern and so is able to continue it.⁹⁷ And even in such cases, the seeing of the pattern is distinct from the ability to express that pattern in a formula or, generally, in a λόγος. The representation of knowledge is not the knowledge. Far from thinking that all knowledge is representational, when Plato considers ἐπιστήμη, he denies that it is representational altogether. This is at least part of the reason why, in the so-called affinity argument, Socrates argues that in order for us to have knowledge of Forms, our souls must be more like the immaterial objects of knowledge than any body.⁹⁸ If knowledge of Forms were representational, there would be no such inference available since any representation would seem to be in need of a material medium.

We recall that the antirepresentationalism of Rorty or Price claims that all representations whether linguistic or conceptual are, so to speak, incommensurable with what they purportedly represent. The antirepresentationalists are right that the token "cat" doesn't represent a cat. It only does so indirectly when it is used to represent a cat by someone otherwise cognizing that object. When representation occurs, this requires a three-term relation, including (a) the one who represents, (b) the representation, and (c) that which is represented. In the recollection argument, Plato maintains that the ability to cognize two or more things as equal albeit deficiently so requires a *nonrepresentational* cognition of that in relation to which they are deficient. The reason for this is quite simple. An account or representation

---

95. From *Phd.* 74B2–3 and 76B8–12 we can infer that everyone knows the Form but not everyone can give an account of it. Knowing the Form is, then, necessary for being able to give an account, but not sufficient. So the knowing cannot just be the account or the ability to give it; otherwise, the one who received the account, even from the one who knows, would then know it.

96. Sorabji (1982) strenuously objects to the possibility of nonpropositional thinking generally, a position which in my view does not take into account the claim for the infallibility of ἐπιστήμη. But see Sorabji 2000, 298, where he retracts this view, agreeing that "there are no propositions in the intelligible world." Hence knowledge of the contents of the intelligible world is not knowledge of propositions.

97. See, e.g., *Rep.* 524C6–8, 525A2, 527D8–E3 for such mental "seeing." Mohr (2005, 248–250), lists some fifty passages over more than a dozen dialogues in which knowing is described in terms of seeing. See Crombie 1963, 2:450–451, on cognition as a unificatory process, particularly his remarks on degrees of unification correlated with degrees of cognition and being. "Seeing" is essentially how cognitional unification works. We see the unity in an apparently random data array. Also Nagel 2012, 82–83; and Braine 1993, 435–445. We can express what we see propositionally, but the seeing is not of a proposition.

98. *Phd.* 79B16–17.

of equality itself is logically and epistemologically posterior to the cognition of equality.[99] These are accounts or representations of direct or unmediated cognition. Hence, the infallibility. Without this unmediated cognition, we could not recognize the deficient equals. That we could ever recover that unmediated cognition while embodied and constrained to represent whatever we experience is doubtful. Or so Plato seems to think, perhaps anticipating Aristotle's insistence that imagination (φαντασία), that is, imaginative representation of some sort, must accompany all thinking.

Plato's doctrine of knowledge tends not to be taken seriously because it is couched within an argument that the soul preexists embodiment. So, it is supposed, if this is highly implausible, then the doctrine of knowledge that underlies the argument must be suspect. More than that. If all cognition, even the highest form, is embodied, then the distinctions made above, between knowledge and the ability to give a λόγος, between knowledge and conceptualization, and between knowledge and representation, seem to be unnecessary. But it is salutary to reflect on the fact that Aristotle, despite denying the immortality of the soul, endorses the force of the above transcendental argument.[100]

If our embodied cognition of form is always qualified with the adverb "universally," and if the medium of this cognition is an image of some sort—linguistic or otherwise—a problem remains regarding disembodied cognition, presumably the cognition of the Demiurge and the cognition to which we appeal in ourselves when we make judgments of deficient sameness in instances of Forms. Leaving aside the Demiurge for now, I want to focus on how Plato can respond to the antirepresentationalist who seizes upon the admitted presence of images as proof that nonrepresentational thinking is impossible for us. The criticism is not deflected by insisting on the distinction between thinking and the representation of thinking in, say, a proposition. Rather, the criticism pertains to the thinking itself, apart from its propositional representation, and the fact that representations of some sort are intrinsic to it.

Plato's response is that the reason why thinking must be distinguished from the propositional representation of thinking is the identical reason why thinking must be distinguished from the representational images intrinsic to it. Thinking is the presence of form in the intellect universally. But every representational image is a particular, however one supposes that particularity is to be analyzed. For this reason, if for no other, thinking is not "having" a representational image, just as it is not the expression of the

---

99. Suppose that disembodied cognition of Forms is representational. How is the representation of F supposed to differ from the representation of G? Presumably, the disembodied person says, "My representation is of *this* not *that*." The reference is a sort of acquaintance, that is, it is nonpropositional. The expression or representation of the acquaintance in a proposition is a function of the acquaintance or the "seeing."

100. See chap. 8, sec. 8.2.

completion of a thought in the affirmation of a proposition. The principal ground for denying this is, I believe, the Naturalist assumption that thinking must be identical with a brain state, that is, a particular brain state, a token-token relation. This is what someone committed to materialism must say. But if it is claimed that thinking is of form universally, and that this is not possible unless the thinker is an immaterial intellect, it is question-begging to dismiss the argument out of hand just because it turns on the denial of materialism. And that is what the antirepresentationalism of Rorty and Price does.

Why, then, should we accept that thinking universally would not be possible if the intellect were not an immaterial entity? Aristotle and Plotinus and, in fact, the entire Platonic tradition thematize this subject to a far greater extent than does Plato. And I shall return to it in chapters 7 and 8. Here, I briefly discuss Plato's intimation of the argument underlying the immateriality of the subject of universal thinking.

Once again in *Theaetetus*, part of the argument that true belief is not knowledge turns upon showing that if it were, then false belief would not be possible. But false belief is possible, for which reason true belief is not knowledge. The reason for the first premise is that knowledge is a direct seeing of something knowable, analogous to the actual seeing or sensing of something sensible. This direct cognition is at least incorrigible, even if it is not infallible. By way of defending the second premise, Socrates introduces the metaphor of an aviary in which we possess, like birds, many pieces of knowledge.[101] Suppose that one bit of knowledge is that 7+5=12. But knowing this, we sometimes think mistakenly that 7+5=11. There may be many mundane and exotic explanations of *how* this is possible, but it is surely beyond doubt that it *is* possible to make such a mistake. This is not the mistake of someone who is learning math for the first time and does not antecedently know that 7+5=12; it is the mistake of someone who in one sense knows this, but in another sense fails to make occurrent the knowledge at the moment when the question of the sum of 7+5 arises. If true belief were knowledge, then the problem would not be with the possibility of making the calculation error. Rather, the problem would be with occurrently knowing, that is, seeing that 7+5=12 and at the same time thinking that 7+5=11. But this is impossible. The relevant point here is that the error is possible despite our knowing, but not in the sense of occurrently knowing. This error, therefore, requires us to distinguish the dispositional knowing and the occurrent knowing.[102] This is a distinction that cannot, in principle, be

---

101. See *Tht.* 196D–199C.
102. See *Tht.* 197B–D. The distinction in Greek is between κεκτῆσθαι (possessing) knowledge and ἔχειν (having) knowledge, where the former is what we have when we learn something and the latter is what we have when what we have learned becomes occurrent. The distinction is expressed by Aristotle as between first and second actuality (ἐντελέχεια).

made within a material entity. The reason for this is that the disposition to give the right answer in the material entity can only be defined in terms of the necessary conditions required for that disposition to be realized. When those conditions are met, the right answer must be given; if it is not, either the conditions were not met or else there was no such disposition. By contrast, it seems extremely difficult to give the necessary conditions for realizing the disposition in a human being. To try to realize the disposition is to try to add correctly. But adding is not a brain state, for adding requires the cognition of form universally whereas all brain states are particular.[103]

It will be replied that there is nothing easier than making a distinction between the dispositional and the occurrent for a material entity. The calculator has, dispositionally, the knowledge that 7+5=12, and occurrently the knowledge that 7+5=12 when I ask it for the sum of the two numbers and it gives the correct reply. But this is not exactly the distinction that Plato is making. Plato is not distinguishing between a disposition and the use of that disposition, where the latter can be defined operationally or behaviorally. The "having" as opposed to "possessing" is a state, not an action or operation. It is a state ("having") in which one is aware of the state ("possessing") that one is already in. Without this self-reflexive awareness, there is no difference between the having and the regurgitation of information. When the calculator gives the right answer, it is more than implausible to suppose that it is aware that that is the right answer. If one wants to simulate awareness, then one installs a self-checking mechanism that applies an algorithm to the occurrent state. But then the self-checking mechanism must, for a material entity, be really different from the mechanism that is checked. In that case, there is no self-awareness, which requires that the subject that possesses the knowledge be identical to the subject that is aware that one has the knowledge.

The initial dispositional knowledge is the possession of a form, that is, the form that is the sum of 7+5 in the intellect.[104] The occurrent knowledge is the awareness of the presence of that form in the intellect by the intellect universally. The thrust of this line of thought is that only an immaterial intellect can be the place of forms, as Aristotle puts it, and be self-aware that it is the place of the form that is the subject of recall.

One not unreasonably supposes that there is a necessary connection between the immateriality of thinking and its universality. One reason for this is that if the intellect is immaterial, then all the particularity of the form in its material instantiation is eliminated. Instead, there is the particularity or perhaps, less confusingly, the specificity of the form itself (not its instantiation), cognized universally. To cognize the shape that is the sum of 7+5 is

---

103. See Ross 1992b.
104. All functions, e.g., x+y=z, are forms, particularized when values are inserted for the variables, and universalized in an intellect.

to cognize a form different from that which is the shape of 7+6. But in both cases, the particularity of the material is irrelevant. Thinking is paradigmatically self-reflexive and universalizing.

The above argument must be understood in its dialectical context. Plato is not here claiming that the cognition that 7+5=12 is knowledge in the sense of ἐπιστήμη. He is denying that true belief can be knowledge because if it were, then false belief would not be possible. This is so because knowledge is a mental seeing of form and one either sees or fails to see, whereas false belief is a complex cognitive state in which one cognizes a subject and then fails to attribute the correct predicate to that subject. There is no false knowledge precisely because this would require a similar complexity wherein one cognized the subject and failed to attribute to it the correct predicate. But to cognize the object of knowledge is to see it, where the question of what exactly the "it" must be is left open here. But if what is known is a Form and a Form is internally related to all the other Forms and these are only knowable in light of the Idea of the Good, then the knowledge must be comprehensive, either as comprehensive as the entire array of intelligible Forms or as comprehensive as a reductive heuristic would demand. In other words, Plato's rather elusive remarks about the immateriality of thinking should not be taken as evidence for anything like a commitment to propositional knowledge.[105] The difference between the dispositional and the occurrent is strictly an embodied phenomenon where we should not expect to find knowledge paradigmatically. If, however, we do have paradigmatic knowledge dispositionally, then however we may describe the occurrent state, that state, although not knowledge, is better than a wild guess. And if all embodied cognition requires images, then the ne plus ultra of embodied cognition, though short of knowledge, is better than what any material entity could do.

4.5. Some Exigencies of Knowledge and Belief

Our ability to make predicative judgments or to have propositional beliefs depends upon our ability to cognize Form universally. When we do this, we are able to see that two things—subject and predicate—are one, though not unqualifiedly so. It is, of course, possible to represent the grasp of the one-many in a sentence or other set of symbols. But it is in principle not possible for the grasp to be reducible to the representation in the technical sense of "reducible" according to which A is reducible to B if, given B, there is nothing left over to which A refers. I take the reductivism of, say,

---

105. Corcilius (2018) emphasizes the comprehensive or systematic nature of the cognition of the world soul, which he takes to be propositional. Whether or not the world soul may be said to have propositional knowledge, the relevant point for my purposes is that there is a system to be cognized, both in the intelligible world and in its sensible image.

eliminative materialism, to be of this sort. Good examples of such reductivism would be the replacement of phlogiston with oxygen as the source of combustion or the replacement of the retrograde motion of the planets with the correct astronomical planetary motion. A more liberal sort of reductivism according to which all intelligible content of A is in B, but the term "A" still has a legitimate reference seems to me to be incoherent, but nothing turns on this distinction here since Platonists want to argue that if we were nothing but extended bodies, it would not be possible for us to have beliefs, in which case no sort of reduction would be possible.

The cognition of the relative identity of that to which a subject term in a sentence refers and the nonexclusively possessed property represented by the predicate could not in principle be reduced to a state (say, a brain state) of an entity describable exclusively in physicalistic terms. This is so because no finite state could be the thinking of relative identity. It could, of course, be a representation of that. But the brain state must have, expressed in physicalistic terms, an unequivocal identity, not a relative identity. Call the putative brain state B, and give it the appropriate electrochemical description. That description identifies the state. There is no room, as it were, for relative identity. No particular brain state could be the thought that the Morning Star is identical with the Evening Star. The cognition of nonformal identity, which entails difference, could not be one brain state because if A is A, and B is B, then A is not B. It would seem that the only way to configure a state in which A is B, would entail the denial that A is A and B is B. The identity conditions for A have to be different from those for B, in which case A could not be B. If the identity conditions were not different, then it would not be the case that A is B. The universality in the thought that A is B is found in the concept of relative identity, instantiated by A and B.

If we are persuaded that a material entity cannot have beliefs, we may suppose that we have proven too much. Why should we think that an immaterial entity is any better at doing what we are supposed to be doing when we make a predicative judgment? Recall that, in *Republic*, in the detailed characterization of the philosopher and his counterfeit, the lover of sights and sounds, Plato describes the objects of belief (δόξα) as "in a way being and not being simultaneously (οἷον ἅμα ὄν τε καὶ μὴ ὄν)."[106] The word οἷον ("in a way") tells us two things. First, Plato is not here denying the law of noncontradiction which he elsewhere in the same book strongly affirms.[107] Second, he is pointing to the relative identity of S-under-one description and S-under-its contrary, say, Helen who is beautiful in relation to Xanthippe and ugly in relation to Aphrodite. The lovers of sights and sounds are fixated on δόξα and ignore ἐπιστήμη. But even philosophers, who are lovers

---

106. *Rep.* 478D5–6.
107. See *Rep.* 439B–C.

of ἐπιστήμη, have beliefs and aspire to have only true beliefs. The ability to have beliefs is part of our human endowment.

Only an immaterial entity can have beliefs about the sensible world, namely, that which is in a way simultaneously being and not being because of the cognition of a one-many requires self-reflexivity and, by definition, only an immaterial entity can have that. Self-reflexivity occurs when a person is in a cognitive state and is aware of being in that state. This is only possible for an immaterial entity because the subject of the cognitive state must be identical with the subject that is aware of the subject being in that state. For example, I believe that Theaetetus is sitting or, what amounts to the same thing, I believe that "Theaetetus is sitting" is true. To put the core analysis of this crudely, I believe that Theaetetus is and is not identical with what the word "sitting" is taken by me to refer to. I have to be able to decompose this belief into what I perceive and what I judge to be the case regarding what I perceive. I perceive one thing and I judge that it is relatively identical with another. But the judgment regards the perceptual state I am in. It is not a judgment that Theaetetus is more than one thing. It is a judgment that the intentional object of my perception is a one-many. This sort of judgment could not be made by a material entity because the part of that entity consisting of the putative perceptual state would have to be physically distinct from the part consisting of the judgment that what is perceived is relatively identical with its property. No representation of the belief, whether behavioral or symbolic, could be the reductive base for the belief.

As Plato puts it in *Phaedo*, the theory of Forms and the immortality of the soul stand or fall together. But the soul can only be immortal if it is immaterial as are the Forms. The need for an unhypothetical first principle of all that provides the unity that is expressed in all beliefs thus provides the doctrine justifying Plato's antinominalism and antimaterialism. Not only could we not have beliefs if we were not immaterial entities, but there would be nothing to believe if the unifying first principle of all did not exist. Thus, the positive doctrine of a first principle of all lends support to the account of what, according to Plato, is not possible if Naturalism is true. Beliefs are not possible if knowledge is not possible and knowledge is not possible if the immaterial world does not exist. But this world is necessarily a unified world in which all the parts are internally related in relation to the Good or One.

In this chapter, I have tried to sketch some of the arguments underlying Plato's anti-Naturalism. The rejection of skepticism, nominalism, and relativism are interwoven with the rejection of the materialism and mechanism of Anaxagoras. Plato's antiskepticism is most vulnerable considering his argument that in order to show that we can have knowledge, we must show that we do have knowledge, but that this knowledge must have been acquired in a preembodied state. Aristotle, despite his rejection of the immortality of the soul, appeals to a strikingly similar argument to show that without an immortal and eternal agent intellect we could not think. Without the possibility of thought, understood as universalizing cognition of form, Naturalism could no more be defended than anti-Naturalism could be. With the possibility of thinking established, Aristotle is as firmly set against Naturalism as is Plato. For this possibility depends on a rejection of materialism, mechanism, nominalism, skepticism, and relativism.

The positive construct that is Platonism rests upon the need to postulate a first principle of all without which there would be no such thing as explanatory adequacy. Illusions of explanatory adequacy attainable without such a first principle arise generally from a confusion of empirical or predictive adequacy and explanatory adequacy. The former is always situational; the latter is unqualified. The exceedingly heavy demands made upon the latter do not justify a kind of arbitrary or stipulative exclusion of the existence of any given explanans from the ambit of explananda. If we start with the existence of natural things (as Aristotle does in his *Physics*), surely we do not thereby exclude the possibility of the explanation for the existence of such things. This would only occur within a Naturalistic framework according to which philosophy, as Plato understands it, would not be possible.

CHAPTER 5

The Centrality of the Idea of the Good in the Platonic System (1)

5.1. The Idea of the Good, Unhypothetical First Principle of All

All Platonists have acknowledged the need for a first unifying metaphysical principle of all. That the need for such a principle is recognized in Plato's dialogues, in Aristotle's testimony, and in the indirect tradition was never doubted. All this despite the fact that disputes regarding its nature and its relation to everything else evidently existed even in the Old Academy itself.[1] As we saw in chapter 2, Plato does not provide arguments for the existence of such a principle, although it is not difficult to construct one on the basis of the assumptions with which he was most likely working. In fact, Aristotle and Plotinus focus on such arguments, arriving at decidedly different conclusions about the nature of this principle. I shall consider these later. In this chapter, I want to set out first the evidence from the dialogues concerning a first principle of all. Then, I shall briefly consider Aristotle's account of the nature of this principle and the evidence of the indirect tradition.

We begin with those passages in *Republic* referring unequivocally to a superordinate first principle of all, the Idea of the Good (ἡ ἰδέα τοῦ ἀγαθοῦ).[2]

---

1. See, e.g., Krämer (1964) 1967; and Dillon 2003. See Fronterotta 2001, 137n38, for a useful categorization of the major lines of interpretation of the Good in the twentieth century along with their principal supporters. Fronterotta divides these into four: (1) the Good is the Demiurge of *Timaeus*; (2) the Good is the ontological foundation of Forms; (3) the Good is the source of axiology or teleology in the universe; (4) the Good must be understood historically as identical with the One, as per Aristotle's testimony.

2. The list is based in part on that of Szlezák 2003, 111–112.

1. There is a "greatest study (μέγιστον μάθημα)" for humankind. This study is of something more important (τι μεῖζον) than the study of the Forms (504D2–E5).[3]
2. This study is of the Idea of the Good (505A6–7).[4]
3. The sun in its active causal role is analogous to the Idea of the Good. Each is "overflowing (ἐπίρυττον)" (508B6–7).[5]
4. The analogy between the sun and the Idea of the Good is convoluted so that the sun itself can be seen as the offspring of the Good (506E3, 508B13, 517C3).
5. The Idea of the Good is the end point of all striving (505D11–E1).
6. The Idea of the Good is the principle of knowledge (ἐπιστήμη) and intellection (νοῦς) and truth (ἀλήθεια) of things, especially Forms (508E1–4 with 508A9–B7, 509B6, and 517C2–3).[6]
7. The Idea of the Good is the principle of the existence and essence (εἶναι τε καὶ τὴν οὐσίαν) of Forms (509B9–10).
8. The Idea of the Good itself is "beyond essence in rank and power (ἐπέκεινα τῆς οὐσίας πρεσβείᾳ καὶ δυνάμει ὑπερέχοντος)" (509B9–10).[7]
9. The causal reach of the Idea of the Good extends beyond (or below) the Forms (516B10, 517C1–2).

---

3. Cf. Plato, *Ep.* 7, 341C5–6: ῥητὸν γὰρ οὐδαμῶς ἐστιν ὡς ἄλλα μαθήματα in reference to the study of first principles. The sentence means minimally that the μάθημα of the Good is not like others. That is, it is not expressible or capable of being practiced like others, which would follow from the fact that its subject is beyond essence. As we shall see in the next section on *Parmenides*, part of the μάθημα of the Good, which must be absolutely simple since it transcends οὐσία, will consist in a logical or conceptual investigation of the senses of "one." It is noteworthy that the μέγιστον μάθημα is introduced (*Rep.* 504E8, 505A3) as something Socrates has spoken about many times (οὐκ ὀλιγάκις, πολλάκις) before. Yet there is no previous discussion in the dialogues. The remarks end, 509A7, with Socrates saying συχνά γε ἀπολείπω (I am really leaving out a lot). Cf. 506D8–E3, expressing the same reticence. Those who regard *Republic* as a middle dialogue in which Socrates is representing Plato's own views, cannot I think give a plausible account of these words that does not indicate that it is Plato who spoke frequently about this first principle of all. It is difficult to reconcile all these remarks with the unargued-for claim that the Idea of the Good is not the subject of the unwritten or oral teachings of Plato. On the unwritten teachings generally, there is a huge literature continuing to grow from the seminal writings of Krämer (1959) and Gaiser (1963). Much of their further work on this topic and their responses to criticism are collected in Krämer 2014 and Gaiser 2004. See also Wippern 1972; Szlezák 1985; Krämer 1990; Halfwassen 1992a; Reale 1997; Richard 2005; and Nikulin 2012.

4. Independently of the fact that the Good is beyond οὐσία, because the study of the Good is more important than the study of the virtues, we should resist any attempt to make the Good coordinate with Forms, that is, with a genus of the Forms of the Virtues.

5. This text suffices to refute the claim that the Idea of the Good can only be a final cause. See Teloh 1981, 136–137, for the view that the Good is only a final cause, despite his recognition that "the Good creates Being."

6. The Good makes Forms intelligible just as the sun makes objects visible. Truth is the property of being in relation to an intellect.

7. That the Good is beyond essence in rank and power does not mean that the Good is an essence of the greatest rank and power as, for example, Brisson (2002, 89–90) would have it.

10. The Idea of the Good is "in a certain sense the cause of all things (ἐκείνων ὧν σφεῖς ἑώρων τρόπον τινὰ πάντων αἴτιος)" (516C1–2).[8]
11. Attaining to or grasping the Idea of the Good is necessary for knowing Forms (511B5–C2).[9]
12. The Idea of the Good is apprehensible (γιγνωσκομένην)[10] itself and an account (λόγος) of it can be given (508E4, 517B8–C1, 532B1, 534B3–D1).
13. Dialectic is the sole means of attaining knowledge of the Idea of the Good, the unhypothetical (ἀνυπόθετον) first principle of all (510B6–7; 511B5–6; 533A8–9, C7–D4).[11]

---

8. This is inferred from the analogy of the sun which is the cause of all things in nature. See *Rep.* 509B1–3. See Johansen 2013, 98. As Johansen points out, if the Good is the cause of the sun and the sun is the cause of becoming in the sensible world, then in some sense the Good is the cause of the latter. Santas (1980, 379n9) denies that the Good is a cause of the being of things. But this seems to go against the text, including the words τὸ εἶναί τε καὶ τὴν οὐσίαν ὑπ᾽ ἐκείνου αὐτοῖς προσεῖναι (the existence and essence are present to them [the Forms] by that [the Good]) which are one ordinary way of indicating causality as in the preceding line τὸ γιγνώσκεσθαι . . . ὑπὸ τοῦ ἀγαθοῦ παρεῖναι (knowability is present [to the Forms] by the Good).

9. At *Rep.* 511B6–7, it is quite explicit that the Forms are deduced from the first principle (τῶν ἐκείνης ἐχομένων). I take this to imply that there is no ἐπιστήμη of Forms without ascending to the Good and then descending to the Forms themselves. This requirement itself follows from sec. 5.1, 7. Deductions within the intelligible world depend on internal relatedness and, ultimately, on the integrative unity of the parts of being proceeding from the Good.

10. Reading γιγνωσκομένην with the manuscripts against S. R. Slings's emendation to γιγνωσκομένης. The reason for the emendation is so that the word should be taken with ἀληθείας and not with αἰτίαν. But taking the words ὡς γιγνωσκομένης to mean something like "insofar as truth is apprehensible" is grammatically and philosophically unpersuasive. See Adam 1921, appendix to bk. 6, 2:83–84.

11. See Sayre (1995, chap. 6), who argues against the identity of the Idea of the Good and the unhypothetical first principle of all. Sayre (174) is puzzled by how the Idea of the Good could be the source of the existence and essence of Forms or the source of their knowability. But he takes no account of the evidence for the identity of the Good with the One. At *Rep.* 509D2, the Good is said to rule (βασιλεύειν) over the intelligible world. If it is not the unhypothetical first principle of all, then the primacy that ruling implies is inexplicable. Sayre argues (177–181), that the unhypothetical first principle of all is the "interconnected field of eternal Forms." It is true that the Forms are eternally interconnected, but as we shall see, that is owing to the first principle of all which causes this interconnectedness. Vegetti (1992, 282–283) thinks that the Good (different from the One), makes the Forms knowable by making their cognitive attainment good for humans. But if this were true, then the Good would just be the cause of the fact that the Forms are good to know, not their being knowable at all. Vegetti's position conflates "desirable" and "knowable." Baltzly (1996) seeks to identify the unhypothetical first principle of all with a proposition, particularly, "a proposition is unhypothetical if its contradictory could not even be formulated if its truth-conditions actually obtained." It seems to me implausible in the extreme that that which is the cause of existence and essence to the Forms could be a proposition, including a proposition something like the principle of noncontradiction. Furthermore, one might well ask why we need to ascend to the first principle of all, thus understood, to know the Forms and what "descent" from this principle is supposed to mean. Sillitti (2005, 95) seems to hold the same position. Nails (2013) guesses that the unhypothetical first principle of all is the principle of sufficient reason and/or the

14. This dialectical knowledge of the Idea of the Good is the means to the highest human happiness (498C3, 532E2–3, 540B6–C2).

The following are not separately listed by Thomas Szlezák:

15. The Idea of the Good is the "happiest of that which is (εὐδαιμονέστατον τοῦ ὄντος)" (526E4–5, referring to E2), the "brightest of that which is (τοῦ ὄντος τὸ φανότατον) (518C9)," and the "best among things that are (τὴν τοῦ ἀρίστου ἐν τοῖς οὖσι)" (532C6–7).[12]
16. The Idea of the Good is "more beautiful (κάλλιον)" than knowledge and truth (509A6).
17. The Idea of the Good is a source of exact measure (μέτρον) (504C1–4, E2–3).
18. The Idea of the Good is the explanation (αἰτία) for everything right and beautiful (517C1).
19. Forms are "Good-like (ἀγαθοειδῆ)," but not the Good itself (509A3–5).
20. No one can act wisely, either in private or in public, without seeing the Good (517C3–4).
21. The Idea of the Good is a model (παράδειγμα) to be used by philosopher-rulers for ordering states and individuals (540A7–B1).

We should add, though the passages are found in *Phaedo* and *Philebus* and not *Republic*, and do not obviously refer to the *Idea* of the Good,

22. That which is good (τὸ ἀγαθόν) or binding (δέον) truly binds things or holds them together (*Phd.* 99C5–6).
23. The Good cannot be captured in one idea (ἰδέα) but rather in three ideas united. These are beauty, commensurability, and truth (*Phil.* 65A1–5).

These passages raise profoundly difficult problems, but they leave no doubt whatsoever that the Idea of the Good, in *Republic*, is held by Plato to be the focus of his philosophy. And because of its unique, superordinate, and comprehensive causal scope, it is the focus of his *systematic* philosophy.

---

law of noncontradiction. She argues this because she thinks that the first principle of all must have a wider scope than the Good which is "anthropocentric." I believe her worries are addressed by the identification of the Good with the One as per the testimony of Aristotle and the indirect tradition. See Krämer (1966) 2014, 36n10, on the abundance of evidence and the overwhelming scholarly consensus on the identity of the Good with the unhypothetical first principle of all.

12. Note that all these passages imply that the transcendence of the Good in relation to οὐσία does not mean its transcendence of existence or being altogether. See de Vogel (1986, 45), who notes that the superlatives in these passages (εὐδαιμονέστατον, φανότατον, ἄριστον) can be taken in a comparative sense, therefore not implying that the Good is on a par with οὐσίαι.

Here are just some of the obvious problems raised by these passages. How, for example, can the Good exist or be in any way if it is beyond being or essence? How, so conceived, can it be the cause of anything? What does it mean for the Good to provide the knowability of Forms?[13] Why cannot Forms be known unless the Good is known? And, perhaps most puzzling, why is the first principle of all identified as the Idea of the Good? These are by no means the only problems or even the only serious ones, but they can hardly be avoided if the dialogues are held to be primary data for the systematic construction of Platonism.

It is no exaggeration to say that this evidence for the postulation of an unhypothetical first principle of all has been increasingly dismissed or even ignored in the last two generations or so in the English-speaking world of Platonic scholarship. I shall not attempt here to provide a list of what I take to be obviously false interpretations of the Idea of the Good or of those scholars who profess Plato's metaphysics and epistemology without any mention of this principle. Suffice to say that if the Good is beyond essence, it cannot have an essence, as it must if being an essence is a property of Forms or if it is the sum of the essences that are Forms or if it a *summum genus* of the Forms, the Form of Forms, so to speak. Nor can its being the cause of the existence and essence of Forms amount only to its being the explanation for why it is good that such entities exist, even though this is true. Nor can it just be the Demiurge, who, among other things, has the property of being good and who is, minimally, qualified by the essences he cognizes.[14] In light of such interpretations, one can perhaps understand the inclination to ignore the matter of the Idea of the Good altogether. I believe, however, that the correct lesson to learn from such efforts is the one that undeniably meets anyone who examines the writings of Platonists and Platonic scholarship prior to Friedrich Schleiermacher. The lesson is that interpreting Plato and Platonism correctly requires that we do not confine ourselves to the dialogues, much less to a disjointed set of dialogues each one hermeneutically sealed off from all the rest.

In the remainder of this section, I want to address several technical issues first on behalf of answering the above questions. These are issues the clarification of which will be of assistance in arriving at a clearer picture of the role of the Idea of the Good in Plato's system.

First, the words τὸ εἶναι τε καὶ τὴν οὐσίαν (sec. 5.1, 7). There are two related points here. First is whether Plato is using the words τε καὶ to indicate redundancy so that εἶναι and οὐσία may be supposed to refer to the same

---

13. Less colloquially, the Good gives the power (δύναμις) of knowing to knowers. It makes the Forms knowable.

14. See Krämer (1997) 2014, 194–200, for a brief survey of some relatively recent, though unpersuasive, interpretations of the superordinate Idea of the Good.

thing.[15] This seems highly unlikely in this case because while the Good is said to be "beyond" οὐσία, it is not beyond having a form of the verb εἶναι said of it (sec. 5.1, 15). Thus, we should suppose that the Good is beyond εἶναι only in the sense in which this is attributable to something with οὐσία; it is not beyond being or existing altogether. It is beyond the existence of anything composed of existence and essence. Since the primary connotation of οὐσία is that of limitedness or circumscription or "whatness," I translated the word in this context as "essence." Thus, the Good is beyond essence, but not beyond being or existence.[16] The implication is that insofar as the Good can be said to have an essence at all, its essence is infinite or unlimited. This point will be clarified in the second part of *Parmenides* wherein we find a logical analysis of what follows for that which is without essence or οὐσία.

The second point is that the Good is itself said to be "apprehensible" (sec. 5.1, 12) which might be thought to be problematic if what we apprehend generally is an οὐσία.[17] But there is also a study (μάθησις) of

---

15. For examples of this, see *Euthyd.* 303C3: ἐπὶ τὸ ἐπαινεῖν τε καὶ ἐγκωμιάζειν; *Phd.* 81C5: ἡ ὁμιλία τε καὶ συνουσία; and *Soph.* 249D4: τὸ ὄν τε καὶ τὸ πᾶν. At *Rep.* 508D4, 5, 6, 7, we have repeated rhetorical uses of τε καί which may well be taken as cases of hendiadys, although τὸ γιγνόμενόν τε καὶ ἀπολλύμενον (D6) surely indicates some distinction. Hitchcock (1982, 69 with n. 28), citing *Rep.* 479C7 (μεταξὺ οὐσίας τε καὶ τοῦ μὴ εἶναι), takes the phrase as a hendiadys. Krämer ([1997] 2014, 195n9), followed by Ferrari (2003, 309), seems to take the καί as epexegetical, so that the phrase means something like "being in the sense of essentiality." But I can find no case in which τε καί can clearly be so understood.

16. See Baltes (1997), who shows with an abundance of evidence that the transcendence of the Good does not mean that the Good does not exist or is beyond being altogether. Baltes's positive interpretation, however, according to which the Good is being itself or the sum of all beings is based on no evidence. Aristotle, *Meta.* N 5, 1092A14, says that the One (= the Good) is μὴ ὄν, meaning, I take it, that the One does not have the being that anything with οὐσία has. See Irwin (1995, 272), who takes the words "beyond οὐσία" to indicate that the Good "is not independent of the totality of Forms whose goodness it explains." This appears to be the view of Gosling (1973, 67–68), too. See Ferber (2003), who argues against Baltes that the being or existence of the Good does not negate its transcendence. As I shall try to show later on (chap. 6, sec. 6.1), the supposed tension between a Good that is beyond being but nevertheless has being is owing to a confusion between the superordinate Idea of the Good and a coordinate Form of the Good. Kahn ([1976] 2009) argues that existence does not emerge as a distinct concept in Greek philosophy; rather, the primary use of εἶναι is "veridical," that is, the verb indicates what is true or what is the case. If Kahn is correct, it would be wrong to understand εἶναι as existence in sec. 5.1, 7. But it seems to me that Kahn's blanket denial of the existential use of εἶναι is actually contradicted by this passage as well as by *Phil.* 14B1–2 where the existence of "monads" (read: "Forms") is the direct question. Kahn (72) mistakenly believes that, for Plato, "to be" always means "to be something." This is not so for the Good which is not something, though the Good exists. In addition, even for things whose existence entails that they exist as something, we can distinguish their existence from the nature they must have if they are to exist. See Halfwassen 1992a, 259–261, for an argument for why εἶναι and οὐσία must be distinct.

17. See *Rep.* 534A3: νόησιν δὲ περὶ οὐσίαν (thinking is related to essence). See Dixsaut 1991 on οὐσία as the mode of being of Forms. Form is what is intelligible or νοητόν.

the Good and that word does not necessarily indicate that only an essence can be studied. The Good is apprehensible but only by inference as the necessary unhypothetical first cause. "Apprehensible" should thus be taken to have a wider scope than ἐπιστήμη which can *only* have essence as its object. The Good can be known, but as a power, it can only be known by its effects or what it does.[18] Because the Good is unlimited in its nature, it is unlimited in its power and therefore, unlimited in its effects. In other words, anything that has limited being (which is to say everything that is other than the Good) is directly or indirectly an effect of the Good. Thus, the Good is necessarily implicated in the explanation of the being of everything or, stated otherwise, in the being of everything for which there is an explanation.[19] If this were not the case, this would indicate a limitation in the Good, a case where an ultimate explanation is available but for one reason or another the Good is limited in being unable or unwilling to contribute. If this is impossible, we have before us the foundation stone for the systematic nature of Platonism, namely, explanatory unity. All philosophical explanation converges on the Good. The contributions of Forms, therefore, must be as instrumental causes, not as ultimate causes or explanations.

The third point is that the Forms are "Good-like (ἀγαθοειδῆ)" but not the Good itself (sec. 5.1, 19). How can an οὐσία or that with an οὐσία be like that which is beyond οὐσία? To say, as is certainly the case for Plato, that an effect must be like its cause, just pushes the problem into a different arena. Here is a striking example of a claim made within *Republic* for which there is no clarification elsewhere in the dialogue, whereas when we appeal to Aristotle's testimony matters become substantially clearer. But an answer to this question should be framed by the following consideration. Everything comes from the Good (sec. 5.1, 10), directly or indirectly, and everything desires the Good (sec. 5.1, 5). The answer to the question of how Forms can be Good-like will be found in what the Forms do generally.[20] Each is a principle of integrative unity, making all their participants one this or that.

---

18. See *Rep.* 477D1–3 on the principle that a δύναμις is known by its effects. The passage also says that a power is known by "what it is set over (ἐφ' ᾧ)." What is the supremely powerful Good "set over"? The being of everything with an essence.

19. There is, of course, the problem of whether or how the supremely powerful Idea of the Good is the explanation for the existence of evil. Plotinus and Proclus provide two slightly different answers to this question well within the systematic framework erected by Plato. An example of that for which there is no explanation (at least of the sort here envisioned by Plato) is chance or luck.

20. At *Rep.* 534B8–D1, the examination of the Good is supposed to take place not κατὰ δόξαν, but κατ' οὐσίαν. This seems to mean that, as per sec. 5.1, 18, together with 505D5–9, the Good can be examined via the Forms that participate in it as opposed to the apparent goods that most people pursue. So, for example, showing that justice is good would amount to showing how justice is an integrative unity, whereas showing why some pleasure is not good would amount to showing why it is not such a unity. The unlimitedness of pleasure is the point here.

Therefore, what makes a heap of flesh and bones a human being is what makes it one human being, namely, participation in the Form of Humanity. As we shall see below, Plato identified the Good with the One. The Forms will be like the Good insofar as each is a principle of integrative unity. But none of these principles of unity are themselves unqualifiedly one; each is internally complex. A Form is Good-like by being a principle of unity. Yet, since each is an οὐσία, it is like the first principle of all in a diminished or inferior way. The Good is the One *because* it must be beyond οὐσία or principles of limit and therefore unqualifiedly simple.[21]

I will be returning to the above texts in this and in subsequent chapters, especially the next. In the following four sections, however, I want to show that the references to the Good in *Republic* are certainly not obiter dicta; rather, the Good is in fact ubiquitous.[22]

5.2. First Principles in *Parmenides*

For many modern scholars, a constructive metaphysical interpretation of *Parmenides*—particularly its second part—is the outstanding distinguishing mark of later Platonism, or as most prefer to call it, Neoplatonism. I wish to emphasize two points here at the outset, though I shall have much more to say later on. First, as Proclus amply shows, Platonists offered widely different interpretations of this dialogue.[23] There is no one "Neoplatonic" interpretation of it. Second, as I am trying to show in this chapter, for the majority of the Platonists that dialogue is not so much the central focus of their metaphysics as it is a systematic expression of principles drawn from other dialogues, from Aristotle's testimony, and from the indirect tradition. I think it is most accurate to say that, generally, they took *Parmenides* as providing confirming rather than decisive evidence.[24]

---

21. See Proclus, *ET* Prop. 13; *PT* 2, 7, 49.14: ἁπλότητος ὑπερβολή (superabundance of simplicity).

22. The following four sections are, I hope, not intolerably brief. I am aware that in each one many problems remain unaddressed and many interpretations remain unexplored.

23. See Proclus, *In Parm.* 6.1051, 34–1064, 12, and the very useful analysis of Saffrey in Saffrey and Westerink 1968, lxxix–lxxxix. More recently, see Migliori 1990, 56–68; Halfwassen 1992a, 265–307; Brisson 1999, 285–291; Westerink and Combès 2002a, 1:ix–xx, on Platonists before Damascius, and xx–xxxvii, on Damascius.

24. As we shall see, this claim requires some qualification. Probably from Syrianus onward, and owing to his idiosyncratic interpretation, *Parmenides* does loom very large indeed in the line of sight of Platonists. This does not, however, negate the point that were *Parmenides* to have been lost early on, there would still remain ample and relatively unambiguous evidence on the basis of which late Platonic metaphysics would have been reconstructed pretty much as it is now. See Miller (1995), whose important paper shows in great detail how Aristotle's testimony about the identification by Plato of the Good and the One is supported by *Parmenides*. Also see Desjardins (2004), who connects Aristotle's testimony with *Republic* and *Philebus*. Hitchcock (1982, 73ff.) derives the identification of the Good with the One, while eschewing any appeal to Aristotle's testimony or to the testimony of the indirect tradition.

In *Parmenides*, Plato has the great man himself pose a number of problems for Socrates's so-called theory of Forms. Actually, these problems amount to a sort of superdilemma: either Forms are unqualifiedly separate from the sensible world, in which case they have no explanatory role to play therein, or else they are somehow implicated in the sensible world owing to sensibles participating in them, in which case the status or integrity of every Form as a "one over many" is threatened. Parmenides himself says that if these problems are not solved, then all discourse will be destroyed, for it is the Forms that explain the grounds of intelligible discourse by accounting for the samenesses and differences among things, that which makes language possible.[25] He suggests an exercise in order to train one to solve the problems.[26] The exercise is to consider the logical consequences of hypothesizing the existence of something both for itself and for everything else; in addition, it must consider the consequences of denying that subject's existence, both for itself and for everything else.[27] At the urging of his interlocutors, Parmenides agrees to offer as an example of his proposal his own hypothesis regarding that which is one, considering the consequences of its existence and nonexistence both for itself and for everything else.[28] That is, for any "one," the consequences of its posit are to be examined along with the consequences for anything related to that "one" insofar as it is one in the posited sense.

---

25. Plato, *Parm.* 135B5–C3. The words ἡ δύναμις τοῦ διαλέγεσθαι (the power of discourse) might be taken to be a reference to the technical methodology of the philosopher in *Republic*, namely, διαλεκτικὴ μέθοδος (the dialectical method). See, e.g., 533C7; and *Phil.* 17E6–7. If, however, Forms do not exist, that is, if the theory is reduced to absurdity, then *of course* there can be no science of Forms. It is more likely that Parmenides is making the powerful point here that if Forms do not exist, then it will not be possible to grasp the samenesses and differences among things that are communicated in discourse. With the possible exception of proper names and demonstrative pronouns, all language presumes the existence of sameness and difference among things in this cosmos. Without Forms, language would be purely constructivist, something upon which the Naturalist will be inclined to agree.

26. Plato, *Parm.* 135C8ff. This dialogue, along with *Sophist*, is classified by D.L. 3.58 as λογικός. See Aristotle, *Meta.* Λ 1, 1069a27–28. Cf. Z 4, 1029b13; and N 1, 1087b21. It may well be that Aristotle has *Parmenides* in mind in all these passages. Cf. *Phys.* Γ 5, 204a34ff. On the present interpretation, Plato is making logical, that is, nonsubstantive, remarks about the nature of oneness or unity and being. These remarks certainly apply to the solution to the problems raised by Parmenides in the first part of the dialogue. But they do not do only that. They also apply to that which is the unhypothetical first principle of all. W. D. Ross (1951, 99–101) argues that the second part of *Parmenides* is strictly a logical exercise with no direct substantive application. One of his main reasons for maintaining this position is that he does not think that Aristotle ever refers to *Parmenides*, which he would have presumably done if there was substantial doctrine there. But see contra Ross, Allen 1983, 269–273, who shows clearly that Aristotle was immersed in the arguments of *Parmenides*.

27. *Parm.* 135D7ff.

28. *Parm.* 136E5ff. See O'Brien 2005, 2006 on the meaning of the hypothesis. It will turn out that that which is one in H1 is the One that Aristotle identifies with the Idea of the Good.

Parmenides's own hypothesis is summarized by Socrates earlier in the dialogue as "the all is one (ἕν ... τὸ πᾶν)."[29] The claim is obviously both obscure and ambiguous and efforts to eliminate at least the ambiguity seem to me to miss the point. If there is an "all," then how can it be one? Stated differently, if the all is one, then it seems equally worth insisting that in whatever sense the all is one, we still have to assert that it is all or many or not-one.[30] In addition, if the all is one, then the oneness that the all shares cannot be oneness in the sense in which each member or part of the all is one. This point has particular relevance for the Forms. Parmenides has cautioned Socrates that he needs a preliminary training before he seeks to define (ὁρίζεσθαι) each one of the Forms (ἓν ἕκαστον τῶν εἰδῶν).[31] Therefore, if indeed the all is one, it cannot be one in the sense in which each Form is one. For the identical reason, insofar as that which is one has the status of a paradigm for any of its participants, we cannot suppose that the oneness of each one of these will be exactly that of the paradigm. That is, the oneness in which all the participants share, is not the oneness of each participant. And this goes both for the oneness of the all and for the oneness of the Forms. For this reason, it is a mistake to think the ensuing exercise has as its subject only Forms or even a Form of Unity. Only when the various senses of "one" are sorted out will we be in a position to see how exactly a Form is one and how this determination affects the responses to Parmenides's objections. As we shall see, the *derivative* oneness of a Form implies the *underivative* oneness of a first principle of all. Forms cannot be unqualifiedly first because of their structural complexity.

Our concern for now is primarily with the first and second hypotheses (H1 and H2) of the second part of that dialogue. In H1, Parmenides works out the consequences for the hypothesis that "if there is a one, of course the one will not be many."[32] On this hypothesis, it follows that the One cannot be a whole or have any parts (137D1–2); it can have no limits or boundaries (137D7–8); it can have no shape (137D8); it can be nowhere nor in anything that is anywhere (138B5–6); it cannot be in motion or at rest (139B2–3); it cannot be identical (ταὐτόν) with or different from itself or from anything else (139E4–5); it cannot be the same (ὅμοιον) or not the same (ἀνόμοιον) as itself or anything else (140B4–5); it cannot be equal to or unequal to itself or anything else or greater than or lesser than itself or anything else (140D6–7); it cannot be older or younger or the

---

29. *Parm.* 128A8–B1. Cf. D1. Cf. *Soph.* 242D6, 244B6.
30. See Palmer 1999, 92–108, on the complexities of the thesis that all is one.
31. *Parm.* 135C9–D1.
32. *Parm.* 137C4–5: εἰ ἕν ἐστιν, ἄλλο τι οὐκ ἂν εἴη πολλὰ τὸ ἕν. As Cornford (1939, 116n2) notes, the sentence is most naturally understood as saying that "if there is a one, of course the One (τὸ ἕν, *either* "the One in question" *or* "that which is one") will not be many." Thus, the consequences drawn will apply to any "one." But as we shall presently see, the first two hypotheses define their subjects differently, meaning that different "ones" are in view.

same age as itself or anything else, in which case it cannot be in time at all (141D4–5); since the One is not, was not, and will not be, it cannot partake of being (οὐσία) (141D9); it cannot even be to the extent of being one (141D10–11); there can be no name (ὄνομα) for it, no account (λόγος), no knowledge (ἐπιστήμη), no sense-perception (αἴσθησις), nor belief (δόξα) of it (142A3–4).

H2 ostensibly returns to the original hypothesis, or more accurately to the original first clause of the hypothesis, "if there is a one."[33] This time, however, Parmenides argues that if there is a one, it must partake of essence (οὐσία).[34] This explicitly contradicts the above consequence at 141E9 that if it is one, the one cannot partake of essence. Here, it seems we have conclusive evidence that the subjects of H1 and H2 are not identical, that is, they are defined differently.[35] The immediate consequence that *we* should draw in relation to the problems set forth in the first part of the dialogue is that the senses in which each of the elements of Plato's metaphysics are "one" are likely to be different or distinct. Thus, if a Form is a "one over many," the sense in which it is one needs to be made precise. And, if the first principle of all, the Idea of the Good is, as Aristotle says, and as *Philebus* seems to confirm, the One, the sense in which it is one needs, too, to be made precise.

H2 will reverse the string of consequences drawn in the first. Thus, all the properties denied of that one will be attributed to the one that partakes of essence. It is hardly surprising that Platonists should identify the subject of the first hypothesis with the first principle of all.[36] But far from clarifying matters, this identification is the starting point for an array of deep problems, not the least of which is how that which is in no way can have any causal functioning or, generally, any relevance to anything in Plato's philosophy. The identification of the subject of H2 is, among Platonists, more controversial and more complicated. Minimally, what H2 tells us is that anything that has any essence whatsoever is really distinct from the

---

33. *Parm.* 142B3. In H2 there are three additional attributes said of the one (and therefore implicitly denied of the one in H1): "being many," which is distinct from multiplicity (143A4–144E7); "being a whole," which is distinct from wholeness (142E8–145A4); and "touching" and "being touched," which are altogether absent from the first hypothesis (148D5–149D7).

34. *Parm.* 142B5–6.

35. Proclus, *In Parm.* 6.1041, 1–20, refers to some unnamed person or persons who want to take "one" univocally throughout the hypotheses. Dillon (1987, 386) suggests that the reference may be to Plotinus's contemporary, the Platonist Origen, who did in fact maintain the univocity of "one" in the hypotheses. Proclus rejects this not just because the subjects of H1 and H2 are defined differently but for the more profound reason that, given the uniqueness and nature of the first principle of all, "one" is in principle radically equivocal. Nothing can be one in the way that the One is one. And everything else, according as it is composed, will be one in its own way, meaning that it will also be many.

36. See Gerson 2016.

essence in which it partakes.[37] In addition, it is really distinct from its oneness. This is so because if something is really distinct from its essence, then there is a unified being consisting of that which partakes of the essence and the essence itself. But that means that there is a real distinction between that which is one and the oneness it has.[38]

The general point is that wherever something with an essence is found, we must distinguish within it the essence, the thing that has the essence, and the unity of the two. As we learn from *Timaeus*, *Philebus*, and *Statesman*, Plato recognizes that οὐσία is found in the sensible world, albeit in a diminished manner.[39] So, for example, whereas there is no cognition of the one of H1, there can be sense-perception, belief, and knowledge of the one of H2.[40] This claim, therefore, covers the oneness of purely intelligible objects as well as the oneness of anything that partakes of an intelligible object. In H2, then, we have a critical distinction between, on the one hand, the array of intelligible objects and their participants, and on the other, the one which completely transcends intelligibility.

Complexity is not necessarily divisibility whether discretely or continuously. But the one of H2 is divisible in both ways. As acknowledged in the Old Academy by Plato's successor Speusippus, this is owing to the presence

---

37. *Parm.* 142B5–8: ἓν εἰ ἔστιν, ἆρα οἷόν τε αὐτὸ εἶναι μέν, οὐσίας δὲ μὴ μετέχειν; {—} Οὐχ οἷόν τε. {—} Οὐκοῦν καὶ ἡ οὐσία τοῦ ἑνὸς εἴη ἂν οὐ ταὐτὸν οὖσα τῷ ἑνί· (If it is one, then is it possible for it to exist and not to partake of essence? No it is not possible. Then the essence of that which is one would not be identical with that which is one).

38. A small point: The oneness of the nature of which something nonexclusively partakes must be different from the oneness of the instance of the property. Beauty is one and Helen's beauty is one, but here "one" is being used equivocally. Thus, Helen's beauty is one owing to her participating in the one Form of Beauty but that beauty is not one in the way that Beauty is one. This is so because Beauty is a "part" of Being; its oneness is internally related to all the other parts. Also see *Phil.* 15B1–8, a passage with a notorious ambiguity in the number of questions being put there. Nevertheless, it is clear that one of the questions is: How can a monad, i.e., a single Form, be one and also be many? The question is supposedly puzzling because one and many are contraries. The answer is, broadly speaking, that the Form is not many in the sense that it is one. This answer will require a distinction within the Form between that in virtue of which it is one and that in virtue of which it is many. In other words, the nature of the Form present multiply is to be distinguished from that which remains one.

39. See *Tim.* 37A5 on the "scattered essence (οὐσίαν σκεδαστὴν)" belonging to the sensible world. Nevertheless, at 27D5–28A4, Plato maintains the sharp distinction between the realm of becoming (τὸ γιγνόμενον) and that which is really real and eternal. At *Phil.* 26D8, we find γένεσις εἰς οὐσίαν and at *Sts.* 283D8–9, there is measurement concerned with τῆς γενέσεως ἀναγκαία οὐσίαν. See Owen 1953 and Cherniss 1957 for a seminal debate on whether or not Plato changed his view on the presence of οὐσία in the sensible world. Rather than a change in doctrine, it appears more likely that there is a change of vocabulary such that οὐσία can be attributed to things in the sensible world because there is there a measure of intelligibility or essence. Every "unit" of intelligibility in the sensible world bears the mark of the more perfect unity of nonsensible intelligibility.

40. *Parm.* 155D5–6.

of the principle of the Indefinite Dyad.[41] Anything that is complex in being is composite and so divisible discretely or continuously.[42] Therefore, the being of everything other than the one of H1, the Idea of the Good, has within it a principle of indefiniteness or limitlessness. The principle of limit, therefore, is the one of H2. The Indefinite Dyad is the principle of unlimitedness. Much of the confusion in relation to this dialogue can be traced to the fact that it is easy to conflate the one of H1, which is transcendent, with the one of H2 which is coordinate with the Indefinite Dyad, and which together comprise or represent logically the One-Being. The confusion is compounded by misreading the one of H1 as irrelevant to what follows and therefore not possibly identical with the Idea of the Good. When the latter confusion is internalized, so to speak, it then seems impossible to identify the Good with the one that is coordinate with the Indefinite Dyad. Not the least reason for this is that it participates in essence.

It is hardly the travesty of Platonic exegesis that some make it out to be to infer that the one of H1 is extensionally equivalent to the Good of *Republic* which is "beyond essence (ἐπέκεινα οὐσίας)" and beyond the existence of that which has essence.[43] Nevertheless, we are still left with the problem of how the one is supposed to have not just *a* causal role, but the ultimate causal role in Plato's system. In addition, if the one of H1 is the Idea of the Good, how do the multiple effects of the Good as set forth in *Republic* belong to the one? We must recall that if the one of H1 is the Good and therefore is beyond essence, then if it does possess causal efficacy, it is unlimited in doing so. Its "overflowing" does not cease at some point short of what is logically possible. By contrast, the one of H2 is, as that hypothesis assumes throughout, limited by its essence. But it is only limited in this way. That one is present wherever its essence is present.[44] Suppose, for example, that the one of H2 were a Form F. Then F is present wherever and whenever anything can be said to be nonexclusively f. According to the negation of the list of properties which the one of H1 cannot possess, anything that is f nonexclusively can possess these properties, including being extended, in time, and being the object of sense-perception and belief. It is also divisible insofar as it is extended. In short, the intelligible

---

41. See Halfwassen 1992a, 1993. See below in this chapter, sec. 5.4 on *Philebus*.

42. See Horn (1995), who takes the one of H2 to be the Indefinite Dyad. Also Hösle 1984, 473–490. But on this view, the οὐσία in which the one participates is left unexplained. I take it rather that because the one in H2 participates in οὐσία and so is composite, we must assume that the principle of the Indefinite Dyad is in it. This principle is treated directly in H7 (164E–165E). Plotinus is the only Platonist to offer an account of how this is to be explained. See below, chap. 9.

43. In H1 at 141E12, the conclusion that the one does not exist is derived from our inability to say "was," "is," or "will be" of it. At *Tim.* 37E5–38A2, we learn that what is eternal cannot have "is" said of it if this implies "was" and "will be." So the denial of the existence of the one in H1 should be taken as a denial of its existence in time only.

44. See sec. 5.5, on "scattered essence" in *Tim.* 37A5.

world goes right up to or down to the limit of intelligibility, which is the unintelligible or formless. With the logical tools to be able to distinguish the oneness of a Form and the oneness of an instance, we are then supposed to be able to march between the horns of the dilemma posed by Parmenides. We do not have to accept either that Forms are irrevocably separate from the sensible world, in which case they are irrelevant to the explanation of anything here below, or else that they are impossibly implicated in the sensible world such that the regress arguments destroy the claim that these Forms are "ones."

The putative causal scope of the one or Good of H1 in relation to the causal scope of the one of H2 gives us a hint as to what this causality is.[45] It is not the paradigmatic causality possessed by a Form or by Being in general. It is not the efficient cause of any complex being in the precise sense of complexity according to which the cause is one existent with an essence.[46] The efficient causality operates eternally. It is eternally present such that when the necessary conditions for the existence of anything are present, then that thing exists. This is analogous to the way that the eternal truths of mathematics are eternally present and applicable to anything when the necessary conditions for their operation are present.

As we have seen, and as I shall discuss further below in *Sophist*, the claim that the Good or One is beyond Being means that Being is multiple or complex. It is complex in the sense that all the natures of the Forms are internally related. Each is one in one sense of "one" and all together are "one" in another sense of "one," that sense which is salient in H2. H2 gives us a logical map according to which we can at least begin to understand intelligibility in the sensible world. This is significant because the intelligibility found in the sensible world is diminished and the reason for rejecting nominalism, materialism, mechanism, skepticism, and relativism is only as strong as the reason for maintaining that the intelligibility of the image can

---

45. Cornford (1939, 131–134) execrates the so-called Neoplatonic interpretation of *Parmenides* on the grounds that the one of H1 cannot be the Idea of the Good of *Republic*. Cornford, like many others, thinks that the one of H1 is utterly beyond being of any sort and so cannot do what the Good does or be what the Good is. He argues that the one of H1 is "bare unity." This, though, cannot be right if this one is unique; it is not the unity that is unequivocally present in anything else. In order for Cornford's criticism to stick, he needs to show how the Good which is beyond essence and absolutely simple or incomposite causes anything as supposedly the one of H1 does not. My point here is that if the causality of the Idea of the Good in *Republic* can be explained, then the causality of the one in H1 of *Parmenides* can be explained. Their identity means that the negative deductions of H1 do not indicate that the one is nothing; rather, they indicate that only a so-called negative theology pertains to it, for to say anything "positive" about it, is to incorrectly imply its lack of absolute simplicity.

46. See *Parm.* 142C4–5: Οὐκοῦν ὡς ἄλλο τι σημαῖνον τὸ ἔστι τοῦ ἕν (Then the "is" signifies something other than the "one"). The "oneness" here is not that which, say, is abstracted from an array of Forms; for example, if there are five Virtues, each is one. It is the oneness that belongs uniquely to any essence.

never be adequately explained in Naturalistic terms. Plato does not think he has a better explanation than Anaxagoras in Anaxagorean terms or in terms congenial to any of his materialist predecessors. He thinks that the correct terms of the explanation are entirely of a different sort. What is available to our thought via sense-perception is explicable ultimately only in terms of that which is available to thought alone.

Let us savor for one moment the paradox underlying the claim that Plato's unhypothetical first principle of all, the lynchpin of his system, has not even sufficient being to be said to be one. But then let us go on to acknowledge that Plato has evidently embraced the Parmenidean point that the first principle of all must be absolutely and unequivocally simple such that, among other things, no legitimate predicative judgments can be made in relation to it. And further, as absolutely simple, its causality must be unique as well as indispensable for the being of everything else. It is eternally producing its effects (sec. 5.1, 3). Pace F. M. Cornford, and a slew of other scholars, if the Idea of the Good is *not* the one or One of H1, it is very difficult to discern its position as the unhypothetical first principle of all.[47]

One obvious criticism of the view that the one of H1 is the Good which is identical with the One is that there is a study (μάθησις) of the Good (sec. 5.1, 10) and it is apprehensible with an account (sec. 5.1, 11), whereas as we have just seen, there is no λόγος of the one of H1 nor any other cognitional relation to it. The answer to this objection is that the subject of H1 is unavailable to cognition precisely because of its absolute simplicity. There is nothing that can be said about it because that would involve a predicative statement and that would in turn imply complexity in it of some sort. The cognitive unavailability of the subject of H1 is exactly like that of the Idea of the Good insofar as we agree that its being beyond οὐσία indicates its lack of complexity of any sort. This would seem to be inevitable if having any sort of complexity means that there is *something* that it is, which in turn means that it has οὐσία in some sense. So, what is the study of the Good supposed to be and what sort of account of it can be given? The core of that answer is that we are able to study and cognize it only via abductive inferences, that is, as the necessary cause of given effects. Apart from everything else, this is a daunting task since everything that is is an effect of the causal activity of the Good. This broad abductive approach may be narrowed insofar as we can isolate a specific effect or a property of a specific effect and therefore name the Good as the cause of that. For example, if self-sufficiency is a property of good insofar as something is good, then we can name the

---

47. Here is a small selection of those whose rejection of the Neoplatonic interpretation of *Parmenides* ranges from the mildly disdainful to the contemptuous. See Allen 1983; Miller 1986; Meinwald 1991; Gill 1996; Sayre 1996; Brisson 1999; Silverman 2002; and Scolnicov 2003.

Good unqualifiedly self-sufficient. I take it that the "happiness" of the Good (sec. 5.1, 15) follows from its self-sufficiency which follows from the fact that it is the cause of the existence of all cases of goodness, and goodness has the property of self-sufficiency.

The analysis of the meaning of "one" in H1 gives us a picture of what an absolutely simple one must be. The denial of this one's identity with the unhypothetical first principle of all, that is, the Idea of the Good, seems arbitrary and unjustified, particularly when we realize that the explicit logical exercise that is the entirety of the second part of *Parmenides* must not identify that of which absolute simplicity or oneness applies.[48] As Parmenides says, one has to go through the exercise in order to see how to solve the problems in the first part of the dialogue. It is true that nowhere in the first part is there said to be a problem the solution to which is going to require the positing of an absolutely simple first principle of all. On the other hand, *Republic* tells us that without "ascending" to this first principle, Forms are unknowable.[49] And if Forms are unknowable or uncognizable in any way, then as Parmenides says, the "power of discourse" is destroyed.[50]

5.3. First Principles in *Sophist*

The nominal subject of *Sophist* is the discovery of the métier of the sophist.[51] It turns out that he is a purveyor of falsehoods or counterfeits

---

48. See Lavecchia 2012, 363–382, for an argument to the effect that the Good is prior to the One. Lavecchia rejects their identity because while the Good is unequivocally simple and unique, the One is, according to all reports, always paired with the Indefinite Dyad. But if the Indefinite Dyad is itself dependent on the One, then this objection is diffused. This is the case if the Indefinite Dyad is found in H2 and not H1. Lavecchia (370–372) objects further that if the Good is the One as examined in *Parmenides* H1, then nothing can be derived from it, which is manifestly not the case with the Good. A similar argument is found in Vegetti 2003, 5:273–280. But as I have already argued, the examination of the One in *Parmenides* is an examination of the various senses of "one" and does not concern itself with derivation among the hypotheses. To give an account of that derivation would be to go beyond the confines of the logical exercise that is the second part of *Parmenides*.

49. Hitchcock (1982, 70) says that it is "absurd" that one has to ascend to the unhypothetical first principle of all, the Good, in order to understand Tallness or Shortness.

50. In H4 (159B–160B) and H8 (165E–166C), we find deductions for "others" on the assumption that the one of H1 is separated (χωρίς) from the others (H4) and on the assumption that the one of H1 does not exist (H8). We learn that the others cannot be ones if the one of H1 is separated from them and that they cannot even exist if the one of H1 does not exist. At this point, I shall not pursue the question of what hints are to be found here regarding the causality of the One or Good. I offer only the suggestion that the One is the cause of the being of everything else. This being decomposes into existence and essence and the oneness of the existent. If, as in H4, the One is separated, the others would exist but they could not be ones, that is, one this or one that. If, as in H8, the One did not exist, the others could not exist as well.

51. See *Soph.* 216C2–D2. Socrates avers that the philosopher is sometimes mistaken for a statesman or a sophist. The Eleatic Stranger, when asked about the three names "sophist," "statesman," and "philosopher," unambiguously replies that these names indicate three "kinds

of that which is real. But this identification raises the problem of how that which is not real can somehow still be. The problem of the reality or existence of nonbeing in turn is unsolvable unless the nature of being itself is revealed. The central part of this dialogue (242B–251A) is focused on various accounts of being or existence or realness (τὸ ὄν), in particular those offered by Pluralists and Monists, Materialists and Idealists. Not surprisingly, Platonists were seriously engaged with this discussion.[52]

The above problem introduces the central metaphysical discussion of the dialogue. The Stranger attempts to provide a survey of those who have spoken about being. He adduces first various Pluralists who tell us what things they think have being (εἶναι).[53] They do not, however, explain what they mean by the word "being." If, for example, the Hot and the Cold make up reality, then being is not real or part of reality. If, though, saying that the Hot and the Cold are the only things that exist implies that "being" means something different from either "Hot" or "Cold," then an accurate account of reality must not only include the Hot and the Cold, but also their being. If, for example, "Hot exists" gives us one piece of information and "Cold exists" gives another single piece of information, then "exists" conveys no distinct information. It would be as if we said "Cold is different from Hot." But if they are different, then each must exist and "exist" seems to convey something different from "Cold" or "Hot."

The argument seems hopelessly inadequate since the claim that, say, only the Hot and the Cold exist or have being does not commit one to including being among existents even granting that "being" means something different from either "Hot" or "Cold." But consider again. If "being" means something different from either "Hot" or "Cold," then even if the latter two terms exhaust the kinds of things that have being, the fact that they have being is different from the fact that they are the only beings. This is so because, failing to provide an argument that Hot and Cold are the

---

(γένη)." That the philosopher is a different kind from the statesman at least raises the question of whether their identity in *Republic* is now being questioned. Whether a philosopher is or is not the best statesman or a statesman at all, does not affect the nature of the subject matter of philosophy.

52. It was one of the ten dialogues in the Platonic curriculum probably set up by Iamblichus. See *Anonymous Prolegomena to Plato's Philosophy* 26 Westerink-Trouillard on the curriculum. D.L. 3.58 says that the title of the dialogue is Σοφιστὴς ἢ περὶ τοῦ ὄντος, λογικός. It is thus held to be parallel to *Parmenides* which is also a "logical" dialogue. Revealingly, Iamblichus, fr. 1 Dillon, says that the subject of the dialogue is the "sublunary demiurge," distinct from the heavenly Demiurge. The underlying point of Iamblichus's identification of the subject of the dialogue is that the study of being is not the study of the first principle of all, which is the One. The semantic range of the nominalized participle τὸ ὄν of the verb "to be (εἶναι)" is not covered by one English word. This is also true for οὐσία, an abstract noun formed from the same participle. "Exist," "being," and "real" are all needed to express the distinctions that Plato is developing here.

53. *Soph.* 243D8–E2.

only two things that are real or have being, the possible being of something else entails that "being" means something different from Hot and Cold. If "being" does mean something different, then the default Platonic position, which is a referential theory of meaning, is that there is something that is real or has being that enters into the explanation for the being of Hot or Cold (and, implicitly, the nonbeing of everything else), something which neither the nature of Hot nor the nature of Cold could do. We recall that the hypothesizing of the absolutely simple first principle of all, the Idea of the Good, leads Plato to distinguish the existence and the essence of the Forms, the reason being that if the first principle is unique, everything else that exists must be a composite of existence and essence. The failure of Pluralists is not a failure to get right the number or kinds of things that have being, but to suppose that in making a claim about the number or kinds, they are thereby giving an account of being or existence. Lurking in the background, however, is the problem that if an account of being requires that a Form of Being exist, then we shall face the difficulty of whether that account pertains to the nature of Being or to the fact that the Form itself exists or has being.

The problem underlying Pluralism is the mirror image of the problem faced by the Eleatic Parmenides who, the Stranger says, maintain that "the all is one (ἓν τὸ πᾶν)."[54] That is, if Eleatics claim that the One has being, to what does "being" refer? Either it refers to the identical thing that "One" refers to, in which case there is no claim that the One exists or has being, or else it refers to something different, in which case it is not true that the One alone has being, that is, it is not true that "being" and "One" refer to the identical thing.[55] In addition, if either "one" refers or "being" refers, then each of them must exist sufficiently to be able to refer.[56]

The Stranger argues that the question "What is being (τὸ ὄν)?" cannot be coherently answered by the Parmenidean claim "the all (τὸ πᾶν) is one" or, alternatively, "the One alone is."[57] The principal reason for this is that

---

54. *Soph.* 244B6–7.

55. *Soph.* 244B6–245E5. The phrase "to what does 'being' refer" is my expression of 244C1–2 where the question is: Are "one" and "being" two "names (ὀνόματα)" "attributable (προσχρώμενοι)" to one thing or not. For Plato, a name is only a name if it refers. So if "being" and "one" are two names, then they must refer to different things. I am of course using "things" in the widest possible sense, further specification of which is provided a few pages later by Plato. If something is composite in any way, then there can be two or more names that refer to the distinct elements of the composite, even if this composite is also one. See *Parm.* 137C4–D3 to which *Soph.* 245A8–9 is probably referring. The Parmenidean One cannot be absolutely one or simple as the first principle of all must be. The words ὄν καλεῖτέ τι (Do you call being something?) are in line with a common pattern in the dialogues. If x is τι, then x has being. The general point is taken to apply to being itself.

56. *Soph.* 244C8–E13.

57. *Soph.* 244B6–10. The alternatives ἓν τὸ πᾶν and ἓν μόνον εἶναι seem to be intended as synonymous.

to say that "the One alone is" is in effect to claim two things: (a) the only thing that has being is the One and (b) it has being.[58] That is, what has being (only the One) and the fact that it has being are distinct. This distinction cannot be merely conceptual, like the distinction between "brother of John" and "brother of Mary" when applied to the identical individual. For if "one" and "being" indicated merely a conceptual distinction, there would in fact be from Parmenides no answer forthcoming to the question "What is real?" For when he replies, "the One," this must be taken as equivalent to replying "the real is real" or "being is." Since Parmenides (at least according to Plato) does actually want to make a substantive claim about the nature of reality, namely, "all is one," it cannot be the case that "one" and "is" or "being" refer to the identical thing. Similarly, if Parmenideans now say that the all is one, meaning that the all is a whole consisting of all its parts, then the sense in which the all is one requires that there be a real distinction between "one" and "being." For what is unequivocally one is without parts.[59] Therefore, if being or reality is a whole, we can say that it has a sort of oneness, but that it is not unqualifiedly one; rather, it has oneness as a property (πάθος).[60]

It may be supposed that the conclusion reached about the distinction between that which is truly one and the oneness of that which is real or a whole is unproblematic. For a similar conclusion can be reached as to the distinction between being and the being of whatever is real. But the insight that the Platonic tradition will eventually seize on with full force is that the cases are not parallel. Plato himself will later in the dialogue argue that the being of real things is distinct from those things.[61] But that which provides being to Forms is "beyond" the real things (τὰ ὄντα). At least, it is beyond the things that are real owing to their partaking in οὐσία. Putting this together with Aristotle's claim that for Plato the first principle of all is the One invites the conclusion that the way a real thing's being is distinct from that real thing is different from the way its oneness is distinct from it. This in turn suggests that the oneness of that which partakes of oneness, either the whole that it is or as a part of the whole, is different from that which

---

58. *Soph.* 245B12–C2. This line of reasoning obviously matches that of *Parm.* 137Cff. The difference is that Parmenides is represented here as not acknowledging the ambiguity in the words "the one is" meaning either "the One is one" (H1) or "the One has being" (H2).

59. *Soph.* 245A8–9: Ἀμερὲς δήπου δεῖ παντελῶς τό γε ἀληθῶς ἓν κατὰ τὸν ὀρθὸν λόγον εἰρῆσθαι (Surely, that which is truly one must be said to be without parts according to the correct account). This is probably a reference to the one of *Parm.* H1.

60. *Soph.* 245A1–3.

61. *Soph.* 254B–255E. Indeed, if that which makes real things real is their participation in a Form of Being, τὸ ὄν, then that Form, too, is real, and it is real owing to *its* participation in Being. At 255E2–6, this argument is applied to all the Greatest Kinds and their difference from one another: each (including implicitly Difference) is different from the rest by partaking of Difference. So, too, it would seem to follow that each Kind is real owing to its partaking of Being, including the Form of Being. On the identification of "Kind" and "Form," see below.

the first principle is for the first principle is not really one, where "one" indicates a predicate.

The second part of the examination of theories of being is the confrontation with the Materialists and Idealists or "Friends of the Forms," the former identifying realness with that which is sensible and the latter with that which is intelligible.[62] The response to the first group is a definition (ὅρος) of the being of real things: "I say that all that which really has being is whatever by nature possesses some power either to affect or to be affected by anything else whatsoever in the smallest way by the smallest amount even if for only an instant. I propose that we should say that the definition for the being of real things is nothing but power."[63] The definition is meant to include what moderate Materialists will not want to exclude from the real, that is, properties of bodies which themselves cannot be three-dimensional solids.[64] They agree that in bodies and their properties alone realness or essence (οὐσία) is found.[65] But the definition of being as power does not, of course, tell us what is real or even what realness is. It only gives us a property (πάθος) of the real. If we compare this definition with the passage in *Republic* above (sec. 5.1, 8), we would naturally draw the conclusion that the Idea of the Good is most real, not only because it is said to exceed all else in δύναμις but also because it unqualifiedly affects everything that has being in the most profound way, by causing everything to exist. Therefore, the defining property of the real is possessed in the highest degree by that which transcends essence, though it does not, apparently, transcend existence or being. But the fact that this does not undercut the absolute simplicity or incompositeness of the Good directs us to see, at least in the case of the Good, power not such that it *has* it, but as what it *is*.[66]

The response to the second group, the so-called Friends of the Forms, who want to insist that only the unchanging intelligible realm is real, the Eleatic Stranger asks the rhetorical question: "For heaven's sake, are we really going to be so easily persuaded that motion, life, soul, and wisdom are not present in that which is perfectly real or that it has neither life nor thinks,

---

62. *Soph.* 246A7–B8. Here, "realness" is synonymous with "exist." See 246A11. It is difficult to say whether these Materialists are supposed to include one or more historical figures. Probably, Plato would have used the label "Materialist" for a number of his predecessors, including Democritus and Antisthenes.

63. *Soph.* 247D8–E4: Λέγω δὴ τὸ καὶ ὁποιανοῦν τινα κεκτημένον δύναμιν εἴτ' εἰς τὸ ποιεῖν ἕτερον ὁτιοῦν πεφυκὸς εἴτ' εἰς τὸ παθεῖν καὶ σμικρότατον ὑπὸ τοῦ φαυλοτάτου, κἂν εἰ μόνον εἰς ἅπαξ, πᾶν τοῦτο ὄντως εἶναι· τίθεμαι γὰρ ὅρον ὁρίζειν <δεῖν> τὰ ὄντα ὡς ἔστιν οὐκ ἄλλο τι πλὴν δύναμις. Cf. *Phdr.* 270D2–7.

64. *Soph.* 247A9–10.

65. *Soph.* 246B1.

66. A δύναμις is functionally related to the being of that which has the δύναμις, that is, it is functionally related to its οὐσία. Since the Good's being is beyond οὐσία, it is unlimited in its δύναμις. There is no οὐσία to determine its δύναμις in one way rather than another.

but that it stands unchanging in holy solemnity, having no intellect?"[67] This passage has been widely misinterpreted to indicate that Plato is here, so to speak, announcing the rehabilitation of the sensible world as now being on a par with the intelligible world. But taking the passage in this way would require us to assume that the Friends of the Forms had hitherto denied not the relative unintelligibility of the sensible world but that it has being at all. Although there is nothing anywhere in the dialogues to point to as evidence that Plato ever held this view, one could suppose that the Friends do not represent Plato himself at an earlier stage of his development, but rather, for example, other members of the Academy. This is possible. But if the sensible world does not have being at all, what is the point of positing Forms in the first place? As we learn from *Parmenides*, Forms are posited to explain the possibility that things can be the same even though they are not identical.[68] More broadly, they are adduced to explain the possibility of predication. But if the sensible world does not have being, then there is nothing to explain. It seems much more reasonable to suppose that the correction to the theory of the Friends is in fact a correction to their view that the intelligible world is bereft of life, especially intelligent life and the sort of motion that this entails.[69]

---

67. *Soph.* 248E7–249A2: Τί δὲ πρὸς Διός; ὡς ἀληθῶς κίνησιν καὶ ζωὴν καὶ ψυχὴν καὶ φρόνησιν ἦ ῥαδίως πεισθησόμεθα τῷ παντελῶς ὄντι μὴ παρεῖναι, μηδὲ ζῆν αὐτὸ μηδὲ φρονεῖν, ἀλλὰ σεμνὸν καὶ ἅγιον, νοῦν οὐκ ἔχον, ἀκίνητον ἑστὸς εἶναι; Cf. *Phd.* 79D1–7; 80B1, 7; and 81A5. See Gerson 2006; Abbate 2010, 129–136; and Perl 2014.

68. See *Parm.* 132A1–4.

69. The concluding words of the refutation of the Friends, *Soph.* 249C10–D4, namely, that τὸ ὄν τε καὶ τὸ πᾶν must be understood to include ὅσα ἀκίνητα καὶ κεκινημένα, should be translated as: "such things as are both unchangeable and changing," *not* "such things as are unchangeable and such [other] things that are changing." If we understood it in the latter way, the claim would not have been one with which the Friends would have ever disagreed. The second way of reading these words assumes that τὸ ὄν τε καὶ τὸ πᾶν refers to the entire world (not to the intelligible world alone). But that would mean that the Stranger is no longer talking about τὸ παντελῶς ὄν (248E8); he would have shifted the subject of discussion from the intelligible world to the intelligible world plus the sensible world. See Perl 2014, 152–153. It should be noted that this passage is proposed as a reconciliation between Idealists and proponents of constant change, e.g., Heracliteans, not as a reconciliation between Idealists and Materialists. So the tendency among scholars to take the proposed reconciliation to be between Idealists and Materialists should be resisted. Menn (1995, 1–24 with notes) argues that τὸ παντελῶς ὄν must refer to the entire universe, not just the intelligible world because the "agreement achieved between the gods and giants" demands a concession to each. But the concession to the giants is that if something does not have a δύναμις to make any difference in the world, then its claim to exist should be rejected. The giants no doubt think this criterion will exclude all the inhabitants of the intelligible world. Menn is also mistaken in supposing that what he calls "the neo-Platonist" interpretation, which restricts τὸ παντελῶς ὄν to the intelligible world, maintains that the intelligible world is just the world of Forms. L. Brown (1998, 201) rejects what she calls the "mystical view" according to which perfect Being contains motion, life, etc., "all these attributes." Here, "mystical" is evidently being used as a rhetorical term of abuse, not a legitimate conceptual category.

The principal import of this text is that intelligible reality is alive and possessed of intellect, something that, as we shall presently see, is confirmed by *Timaeus*. The dilemma posed by this claim for the Platonist is patent: either the first principle of all is beyond life and cognition altogether, in which case its causal role, to say nothing of its happiness, is utterly opaque or else it does have life and cognition, in which case it is equally opaque how it can be "beyond οὐσία."

We recall that the words τὸ παντελῶς ὄν are used by Plato in *Republic* to describe the subject matter of philosophy.[70] What we have here is an explicit expansion or at least substantive clarification of the contents of the really real. As a result of this expansion, we may infer that change, life, soul, and wisdom insofar as these are found in the sensible world, have their paradigms in the intelligible world. Accordingly, any fruitful study of the former must grasp these as images of the latter. Insofar as Platonism and Naturalism engage on psychological and cognitive issues pertaining to human beings, the Platonic position will be an extension of the argument in *Phaedo* according to which Naturalists can in principle only provide necessary conditions for the true causes of embodied phenomena. Thus, say, embodied thinking can only be understood as a diminished version of the thinking that occurs in the intelligible world. A Naturalist will, of course, agree that an image can only be understood if one understands what it is an image of. They will disagree that psychological and cognitive phenomena in the sensible realm are images of anything. Therefore, their denial of the subject matter of philosophy as identified by Platonism leaves them, according to the Platonist, with only a Naturalist account of these phenomena. If such accounts are adequate, then the motive for seeing the phenomena as images evanesces; if they are held to be inadequate, the way is open for Platonic accounts.

The recognition of the presence of life in the intelligible world is related to the analysis that yields a first principle of all that is uniquely incomposite. That is, if there is an intelligible world at all, something that even the reformed Materialists are poised to accept, it is intrinsically complex. Hence, relations are possible among intelligibles. But as we have seen, in the intelligible world all relations must be internal relations. For example, if Justice and Virtue are Forms and Justice is a species of Virtue, then the relation between these is intrinsic and eternal. It belongs to what Virtue is that a part of it is Justice and it belongs to Justice to be a part of Virtue. Thus, the complexity among Forms is more than the minimal complexity that follows from a real minor distinction within each Form between its existence and its essence. The essence of each Form is itself complex and this complexity

---

70. *Rep.* 477A3. Cf. 477A7, 478D6–7, 479D5: τὸ εἰλικρινῶς ὄν; and 597D2: ὄντως ὄν.

cannot exclude the existence of each of its complex essential parts really distinct from the essence of each part.[71] But what of its life?

There are many things that Platonists will say about this, as we shall see. Here, it will perhaps suffice to point out that the internal relations among eternal entities must still leave each intelligible to be what it is. Virtue remains uniquely Virtue even though it is, say, composed of Forms of individual Virtues. And Justice remains Justice even though what it is is a part of Virtue. Obviously, it will not do to represent such relations as ontological correlates of class inclusions and exclusions. Nevertheless, it is possible for intellects to think the samenesses, identities, and differences among Forms, that is, to represent these in λόγοι or necessarily true propositions. Thus, if Justice is a part of Virtue, the proposition that justice is a virtue both represents the difference between Justice and Virtue and their relative identity. What is needed for an intelligible world that is constructed to provide explanations for predication here below is an intellect eternally thinking all that which is represented by us in necessarily true propositions.

What need is there, though, for the middleman, the eternal intellect? The reason is that the requisite simultaneous identity, difference, and sameness is purely a property of cognitional activity. It is only in thinking that two different things can be one. Consider the following analogy. To maintain that the Morning Star is the Evening Star is, roughly, to maintain that two things are really one. But they are only two in the intellectual act of their identification either by referring to one or the other or by affirming the identity of each with the other. There must be eternal intellection because the eternal identity of each Form is inseparable from its internal relatedness to all the other Forms.[72]

Sophist provides further confirmation that Plato is working along this line of thought. It will be recalled that the exploration of Being (τὸ ὄν) was undertaken to understand how nonbeing (τὸ μὴ ὄν) is real. It turns out that Being, though somehow present in things that are in motion and

---

71. Owing to this compositeness, we should reject the claim made by a number of scholars (e.g., Lavecchia 2010, 44–45 and n. 6; and Halfwassen 2000, 46n16) that, for Plato, ὄν, οὐσία, and εἶναι are equivalent as are the phrases οὐσίας μετέχειν (μεταλαμβάνειν) and μετέχειν (μεταλαμβάνειν) τοῦ εἶναι. See *Parm.* 141E7–8, 11; 142B8–C2, C5–6; 143A6–7, B3; 152A2–3; 156A1–2, 4–5; and 162A6–B2. The mistake made by these scholars in my opinion is that they assume that if A and B are mutually implicatory, then this entails their identity. Not only is this not true for any A and any B that are internally related, but from the unique superordinate status of the Good, it follows that in everything else there must be a real distinction between A and B within the (relatively) self-identical thing.

72. Gill (2012, 150–155) thinks that because each Kind is "outside" the others, it can have accidental properties. On the contrary, among eternal and immutable entities, all its properties must be essential or internal to it. The array of intelligible entities necessitates the complexity of Being, not a realm in which accidental properties may be found. Accidental properties, along with chance and becoming are not features of the eternal.

things that are at rest or are stable, is distinct from both.[73] Nevertheless, the association (κοινωνία) of the Kinds Motion and Stability with Being is necessary for each to exist.[74] That Motion or Stability exists cannot, however, mean that "Motion" and "exist" are two names that apply equally to Motion, that is, that there is a mere conceptual distinction within Motion between its essence and its existence.[75] Motion and Stability and Being are three entities.[76] Therefore, their association is of a different order from the association that is made in a predicative statement such as "Motion exists." Because Motion and Being associate in some way, we can give Motion two names, "Motion" and "exist," without thereby falling prey to a sophism. Or can we?

The association of eternal entities each one and immutable is not obviously defended by saying that unless Motion exists, then (on the postulation of Forms) things will not be able to participate in Motion, that is, they cannot be said to move or be movable. For one good reason for adhering to the nominalism of an Antisthenes is precisely that allowing predication means either saying that one thing is many or saying that there is nothing wrong with one thing being many so long as we postulate an intelligible world in which one thing can be said to be many. Conceptual distinctions can be maintained so long as the problem they are supposed to resolve is displaced into the eternal realm. This does not seem satisfactory.[77]

An association among Forms (or a disassociation) is *expressible* in thoughts and statements the ontological foundations for which are difficult to see. But since the eternal is ontologically prior to the temporal, the association of individual Forms cannot be reduced to their expression. Motion and Being must be eternally associated.

It is at least possible that the introduction of thinking into the really real is intended to provide the solution to this problem. Here is a way of considering this solution. Suppose an array of Forms that provides the ontological foundation for (1) every necessary truth simpliciter and (2) every

---

73. *Soph.* 250B8–C4.

74. *Soph.* 251D5–252A4. Their association will, therefore, also be necessary for anything to participate in Motion or Stability.

75. See *Soph.* 251A8–C6, evidently directed against Antisthenes. If this is so, the position he is supposed to have held is that all conceptual distinctions are real distinctions and all real distinctions are real major distinctions such that no one thing can have many names, for if it did, it would not be one thing. But the Eleatic Stranger says that this is nonsense. The unity of something is not compromised by many names being said of it. If Socrates is tall, using the words "Socrates" and "tall" of him does not compromise his unity. This is because the predicates or names are not themselves entities. The sophism here dismissed is of a different order from the kinds of distinctions that will follow. Cf. *Tht.* 201D–E.

76. *Soph.* 254D12.

77. I think it is licit to take participation in Forms as implicit in the argument against Antisthenes given Parmenides's challenge in *Parmenides*, namely, that discourse would not be possible if Forms were unqualifiedly separate from the sensible realm.

contingent truth that depends on a necessary truth. Examples of (1) are naturally found within mathematics, though there is in principle no limitation on what the necessary truths are truths about, for example, moral properties. Examples of (2), at the most simple, are predicative judgments of the sort "S is f" where "f" stands for a property instantiating a Form. So, S could not be f unless the Form of F exists or unless "F exists" is a necessary truth. What is still wanting is an explanation of how the postulated array of Forms is an association. That is, the association must somehow represent a unity so we can say that what one Form is is to be relatively identical with another Form such that there is a necessary truth that, for example, Motion exists. Relative identity ensures that participation in one Form entails participation in another.

The problem with this as it stands is that relative identity seems to be a reciprocal relation, but although it may be the case that Motion exists, it is not the case that Being is in motion or, less contentiously, that Oddness is three. What is needed is a generic Form that unites all the Forms in their articulated differentiations. This seems to be the Form of Being itself. But this virtual identity is not sufficient, since the necessary truths in (1) and (2) above depend on the nonidentity of the Forms that are associated. This is why an intellect eternally thinking all these necessary truths in their relative identities and differences is required. The ontological foundation for the necessary truth "three is odd" is in eternal thinking. The relevant intellect is eternally cognitively identical with what it is thinking which is, generically, Being itself. The array of Forms is one because the thinker is one and the thinker is cognitively identical with the Forms. The Forms appear as an articulated many to anyone expressing in a λόγος or in a thought a necessary truth.

In the *Sophist* passage in which the properties of the "Greatest Kinds (τὰ μέγιστα γένη)" are deduced, there is additional information relevant to the above interpretation. The five Greatest Kinds are Motion (κίνησις), Stability (στάσις), Identity (ταὐτόν), Difference (ἕτερον), and Being (τὸ ὄν).[78] We have already seen that Motion exists because it partakes of Being, which must be distinct from it. But Being is different from Identity.[79] It is

---

78. *Soph.* 254B8–255E6. "Stability" is a better translation for στάσις than "Rest" since rest implies an absence of motion, whereas, as the text makes clear, the στάσις of the intelligible world does not preclude its motion. Further, "Identity" is the appropriate translation for (τὸ) ταὐτόν rather than "Sameness (ὁμοιότης)" because the latter term implies multiplicity and is logically posterior to Identity, which does not. Sameness is not a Greatest Kind. It is not clear that we can infer from the fact that two of the Greatest Kinds, say Motion and Identity, partake of Being, then Motion and Identity are therefore the same. This is so because from sameness we can infer *numerical* difference, not merely otherness or distinctness. But I think that Plato is reluctant to say that Forms are numerically different from each other if they are internally related. It is true that there are *five* Greatest Kinds, but Form-Numbers at any rate are not countable.

79. *Soph.* 255B11–C4.

also different from Difference.[80] Being is different from Difference and different from Identity not owing to its own nature, but owing to its partaking of Difference.[81]

The designation of Being as a Kind, even one of the Greatest Kinds is, to say the least, odd. The apparent oddness should be mitigated by the fact that this Kind is not equivalent to the subject of first philosophy for Aristotle, namely, being *qua* being. The equivalent functional role of being qua being for Plato is that of the Idea of the Good which is beyond Being. More important for present purposes is that Being is both "in itself (καθ' αὐτό)" and "in relation to something else (πρὸς ἄλλο)," meaning that *within* Being there is a real distinction between what Being is in itself and the difference it has in relation to the other Kinds (and the other Kinds in relation to it).[82] We have already been prepared for this startling conclusion by Plato's previous rejection in the dialogue of Parmenides's claim that Being is one. But now we have a better sense of why this is so. The "in itself" refers to each essence and all together; the "in relation to something else" indicates their internal relatedness.

Being must be complex or a "one-many" if there is to be an intelligible world. This complexity requires that the first principle of all be beyond Being in the sense of being other than that which exists by having a finite nature or οὐσία. The Idea of the Good or the One or, if one insists, the nameless first principle of all, is a postulate inseparable from the postulate of an eternal intelligible world. And as we have seen, an eternal intellect eternally cognitively identical with the array of intelligibles is an additional postulate without which the first two would be insufficient.[83] Neither the Good nor Forms alone, nor the Good and the Forms together achieve explanatory adequacy, the τι ἱκανόν of *Phaedo*. The Kind Being seems most perspicuously represented as a summum genus of all intelligibles analogous to the *Form* of the Good (not the Idea of the Good),

---

80. *Soph.* 255D3–E1.
81. *Soph.* 255E3–6.
82. The distinction between two kinds of Being, τὰ αὐτὰ καθ'αὑτά and τὰ πρὸς ἄλλα, 255C13–14, has been taken to be alluding to the One and Indefinite Dyad. See Dancy 1999. This perhaps makes sense if the One and the Indefinite Dyad are what is found in H2 and not in H1. Silverman (2002, 162–181) offers an ontological interpretation of the two kinds of Being, different from my own, but close enough to set him squarely against the linguistic interpretation of Frede (1967, 12–29) and others. Plato is not in this passage focused on types of predication, but rather on the ontological foundation for predicative judgments, including the false judgments of sophists. As Silverman (176) argues, τὰ αὐτὰ καθ'αὑτά indicates participation in Being; τὰ πρὸς ἄλλα indicates "to be in any other way." This does not I think bring out the (internal) relational aspect among the Forms.
83. The Good, being absolutely simple, must be beyond thinking, whereas the reductive unity of a predicative assertion is inseparable from thinking. Apart from thinking, what are many are really only one.

the genus of perfection, according to the interpretation of Proclus.[84] Both are distinct from and subordinate to the Idea of the Good or the One. In addition to containing all the Forms, Being is essentially connected to an eternal intellect. Being, though one, is intrinsically complex or many as it comprises all intelligible reality. If an eternal intellect is cognitively identical with Being, we can speak both of the intellectual side of the intelligible world and of the intelligible side, recognizing that these are ontologically inseparable.

The inseparability of intellectuality and intelligibility and the consequent fact that whatever partakes of the one partakes of the other apparently yields a surprising result congenial to the panpsychist Naturalist. If an electron partakes of the Form of Electron, it thereby partakes of the intellect that is cognitively identical with all intelligible reality. But apart from the fact that embracing this conclusion means detaching panpsychism from Naturalism, there is a further consideration. There are necessary conditions for an electron's participation in the Form, just as there are necessary conditions for something having a life, that is, a particular kind of life. In addition, Platonists insist that there are necessary conditions for the presence of an immaterial intellect in human beings. The necessary conditions for being an electron are, so far as we can tell, other than and probably incompatible with the necessary conditions either for life or for intellect. If this is so, then electrons could not partake of life or intellect after all. They are limited in this way by having only the necessary conditions for partaking of the Form of Electron. As Platonists will later express the point, things partake in as much of Being as they are able to, according to the essence of each. It is not the case that Being is itself variously dispersed; it is altogether one and entirely present wherever it is present. But the necessary conditions for participating in Being *are* variously dispersed such that, for example, when the necessary conditions for being a worm are present, the necessary conditions for being a flea are not and the worm is thereby deprived of what is completely available to it in principle.

Our embodied intellects represent Being in λόγοι and in thought. Presumably, what allows us or compels us to represent Being in all its variegations is our experience in the sensible world of the instances of Forms, the products of the creative activity of the Demiurge. The ability that rational animals have to engage in such representations and to express, affirm, and deny them is owing to the knowledge that we have had prior to incarnation. On the hypothesis that Being and intellection are two sides of the same coin, our immortal souls or intellects are, too, identical with Being. According to the story of the soul's creation in *Timaeus*, however, our souls are made of a mixture of the type of οὐσία that is found in the intelligible world and the

---

84. Cf. *Soph.* 254A8–10 for the connection between philosophy and Being as a summum genus. See chap. 6, and Gerson 2015. Also Beierwaltes 2004, 103–108.

type of οὐσία that is found in the sensible world.[85] On the basis of this mixture, it is not clear whether the soul, when separated from the body, sheds the sensible type of οὐσία or whether it retains this, making its reconnection with the intelligible world more problematic. Speaking for the first alternative is that the composition of the human soul precedes its "seeding" among stars prior to the incarnation of individuals.[86] In the preincarnate state, the Demiurge addresses human souls regarding the nature of the cosmos and the laws of destiny. Therefore, we may infer that the postincarnate soul or its immortal part is capable of reconnecting with the knowledge it was given prior to incarnation. It is, therefore, owing to being a soul in a body that we are unable to cognize Forms directly without representation.

Prima facie, it is a major concession to Naturalism to admit that incarnated souls—human beings—have access to the intelligible world only via representations. For as Rorty insisted, representation is not mirroring. Caught within the web of conceptual thinking and language, we do not seem to have direct access to an intelligible world as Plato conceived of it since we do not even have direct access to the sensible world. The relation between Being and cognitional representations remains a crucial stress point in the debate between Platonism and Naturalism. It must be added, however, that the fact that there is no access to intelligibles without representation certainly does not entail that thinking is just representation.

The internal complexity of the Kind Being is, I claim, strong evidence in support of the role of the Good or One in the Platonic system. If there is a first principle of all, it must be beyond Being because a first principle of all must be absolutely simple whereas Being is intrinsically complex. Stated otherwise, since the first principle of all must be absolutely simple, it must be beyond Being, since the being of anything is intrinsically complex. That is, minimally, its being is comprised of existence and essence. In the *Sophist*, Plato explicitly limits his discussion of Being and Not-Being or Difference only to that which is necessary for identifying the sophist.[87] For this reason, we do not get a full-scale discussion of this complex topic. It is clear, however, that the complexity of Being does not just allow for the possibility of an absolutely simple first principle of all. It demands such a principle.

5.4. First Principles in *Philebus*

Philebus is a dialogue in search of the human good, that is, the best sort of life for a human being. The central problem for the dialogue is the relative

---

85. See *Tim.* 35A–B, 41D–E.
86. *Tim.* 41D4–42A3.
87. See *Soph.* 254B8–D2; and Krämer (1990, 108–109), who suggests that if *Philosopher* had been written, that would have been the natural place to find a discussion of the principle beyond Being and Nonbeing.

weight that should be given to intellect (νοῦς) and pleasure (ἡδονή) in that life. In search of the correct answer, general ontological principles are adduced in a number of passages. The central principle is that of νοῦς. "Should we say, Protarchus, that everything, I mean that which is called the universe, is governed by irrationality and by chance or, on the contrary, as those who have gone before us have said, that it is governed by some wonderful organizing intellect and wisdom?"[88] The introduction of νοῦς as a supreme organizing principle immediately complicates the picture. For even though in *Republic* the Idea of the Good is said to be "the happiest of that which is"—a claim that is hardly perspicuous—there is no indication that the Good is intellect; indeed, the Good would seem to be beyond intellect insofar as it is beyond οὐσία. How, then, are the two supposed to be related?

The role of the intellect itself is not entirely clear, for it is implicitly introduced within a tetrad of principles underlying the composition of everything in the universe.

> Let us divide into two—or rather, three, if you don't mind—all the things said now to be in the universe. . . .
> We said, if you recall, that god has shown us that among things there is the unlimited and there is the limit.[89]
> Let us posit these two forms, with the third being the mixture of the two. . . .
> Look for the cause of the mixture of these two with each other and add it to the other three as a fourth.[90]

The cause of the mixture is νοῦς which operates by imposing a limit on an unlimited principle in order to produce the mixture. The specific mixture in the good life that the dialogue is meant to ascertain is that of intellect and pleasure, a kind of unlimitedness, admitting of more and less indefinitely. Even if there be some doubt as to the status of the unlimited as a principle, there can be no doubt that intellect and limitedness have

---

88. *Phil.* 28D5–9: Πότερον, ὦ Πρώταρχε, τὰ σύμπαντα καὶ τόδε τὸ καλούμενον ὅλον ἐπιτροπεύειν φῶμεν τὴν τοῦ ἀλόγου καὶ εἰκῇ δύναμιν καὶ τὸ ὅπῃ ἔτυχεν, ἢ τἀναντία, καθάπερ οἱ πρόσθεν ἡμῶν ἔλεγον, νοῦν καὶ φρόνησίν τινα θαυμαστὴν συντάττουσαν διακυβερνᾶν;

89. A reference to *Phil.* 16C–17A.

90. *Phil.* 23C4–D8: Πάντα τὰ νῦν ὄντα ἐν τῷ παντὶ διχῇ διαλάβωμεν, μᾶλλον δ', εἰ βούλει, τριχῇ. . . . Τὸν θεὸν ἐλέγομέν που τὸ μὲν ἄπειρον δεῖξαι τῶν ὄντων, τὸ δὲ πέρας; Τούτω δὴ τῶν εἰδῶν τὰ δύο τιθώμεθα, τὸ δὲ τρίτον ἐξ ἀμφοῖν τούτοιν ἕν τι συμμισγόμενον. . . . Τῆς συμμείξεως τούτων πρὸς ἄλληλα τὴν αἰτίαν ὅρα, καὶ τίθει μοι πρὸς τρισὶν ἐκείνοις τέταρτον τοῦτο. Cf. 16C7–10. Cherniss (1945, 28) takes the above two passages to be limited in their application to the sensible world (πάντα τὰ νῦν ὄντα). See Richard 2005, 143–144, for a refutation. If, like Cherniss, one rejects those texts which state that the Good is the first principle of all, along with those texts in which Plato is said to have identified the Good with the One, it would not be unreasonable to infer that the *Philebus* passages are not to be understood as manifestations of this principle. The unreasonableness in Cherniss's position is in his rejection of the evidence for the supremacy of the Good and for the identification of the Good with the One.

a fundamental role that transcends the sensible world. This is evident is the identification of νοῦς as a divine nature only two pages later.[91] We do not have, though, any clear evidence of how these principles relate to the Idea of the Good.

On the other hand, the primary aim of this dialogue is to discover the human good. Socrates lays down three criteria for this good: that it be perfect (τέλεον), sufficient (ἱκανόν), and that it be the object of choice.[92] The human good will be found in a characteristically human life. But this good can only be one finite expression of the Idea of the Good. If, after all, it is true that we all desire the Good for ourselves, this is only obtainable by a choice of a specific good or set of goods perfecting human activities and desires. The human good will be so because it is a specific instance of the Good itself. Something possesses the predicate "good" because it participates in the Good which, judging from *Republic*, is the superordinate Idea.[93] In the concluding passage of *Philebus* we read: "So if we are not able to capture the Good in one idea, let us get at it with three, with beauty and commensurability and truth, and say that we would be most correct to treat these as in a way one and responsible for what is in the mixture [of the elements of the good life], and that it is owing to this [the three taken as one] being good that it becomes so."[94]

Note that the first sentence does not deny the existence of the Idea of the Good, only that we cannot capture it in one idea, something that would follow immediately from the Idea being "beyond οὐσία."[95] The three available ways of capture are via beauty, commensurability, and truth. We have already seen above (sec. 5.1, 6) that the Idea of the Good provides truth to Forms.[96] And truth, that is ontological truth, is transparency or availability to an intellect. As for commensurability, we learned earlier in the dialogue that it is a proportion or ratio of measures, which themselves are

---

91. *Phil.* 30D1–4. Cf. 28C6–8.

92. *Phil.* 20D1–10; cf. 67A1–8, which makes clear that whatever the mixture of reason and pleasure that constitutes the good life for a human being, this good cannot be the Good itself. Reason is, indeed, closer to the Good but that is because reason has no unlimitedness in it. See *Ep.* 7, 342D1–2.

93. See Van Riel 1999, 253–267; Ferber 2002, 187–196; and Desjardins 2004, 55–90, on the implicit referencing of *Republic* in discussions of the Good in *Philebus*.

94. *Phil.* 65A1–5: Οὐκοῦν εἰ μὴ μιᾷ δυνάμεθα ἰδέᾳ τὸ ἀγαθὸν θηρεῦσαι, σὺν τρισὶ λαβόντες, κάλλει καὶ συμμετρίᾳ καὶ ἀληθείᾳ, λέγωμεν ὡς τοῦτο οἷον ἓν ὀρθότατ᾽ ἂν αἰτιασαίμεθ᾽ ἂν τῶν ἐν τῇ συμμείξει, καὶ διὰ τοῦτο ὡς ἀγαθὸν ὂν τοιαύτην αὐτὴν γεγονέναι.

95. See esp. Krämer (1969) 2014, 1–30. See also Delcomminette 2006, 505, 563, 577, 619, on the identity of the Good here and the Idea of the Good in *Republic*. The Good is not captured by identifying it with the One presumably because absolute oneness is no more transparent than is absolute goodness. By contrast, beauty, commensurability, and truth are cognitively available to us.

96. On ontological truth, see Szaif (1996) 1998, 132–152; and Ferrari 2003, 304.

combinations of limit and unlimited elements.[97] That is, commensurability results when various limits are applied to various unlimited bases and then combined according to an appropriate or ideal proportion. As for beauty, we have also seen above (sec. 5.1, 16) that the Idea of the Good is more beautiful than knowledge and truth.[98] Thus, even if the Idea of the Good is not directly in view in *Philebus*, the attentive reader can hardly avoid the conclusion that this dialogue enriches our understanding of the first principle of all.

If commensurability, truth, and beauty are "in a way one," and they are various expressions or aspects of the Good, which is itself "beyond οὐσία," it seems to follow that the Idea of the Good is itself in a way a principle of unity or oneness in the sense of incompositeness.[99] It should also be noted that the three aspects are referred to in the singular (τοῦτο) when the cause of goodness in a mixture is cited. That is, commensurability, beauty, and truth are ultimately unified in some way. Admittedly, the connection between the Idea of the Good and unity or oneness is, on the basis of this passage alone, tenuous. Given this passage, though, it is difficult to see why Aristotle's testimony, which explicitly identifies the Good with the One, should be discounted.

As Platonists understood it, the One and the Indefinite Dyad are the principle of limitedness and unlimitedness in all composites, which is to say, everything other than the One itself.[100] The One is itself not the limit in each thing nor is the Indefinite Dyad the unlimited; limit and unlimitedness are manifestations of the principles. As the above passage makes clear, the unity that something has is the result of the imposition of limit on unlimitedness and it is this unity that defines the goodness of the thing, that unity and goodness being indexed to the kind of thing it is. This is integrative unity, which implies that the One, being incomposite, is not that, but rather its principle.[101] The assimilation of the Idea of the Good to the One is, accordingly, the metaphysical foundation for Plato's antirelativism.

---

97. See *Phil.* 25A6–B3. Συμμετρία is a combination of μετρία or measures. Also *Sts.* 265E7–266B7, 283C3–285C2.

98. Cf. *Tim.* 87C4–6: πᾶν δὴ τὸ ἀγαθὸν καλόν, τὸ δὲ καλὸν οὐκ ἄμετρον· καὶ ζῷον οὖν τὸ τοιοῦτον ἐσόμενον σύμμετρον θετέον (Now that which is good is always beautiful, and that which is beautiful is never without measure; a living creature, then, who is going to be [good and beautiful] will possess commensurability).

99. See Sayre 1983, 168–174; and Desjardins 2004, 105–112.

100. See Van Riel 1997, 39–43, on Iamblichus in particular and his account of how the first principles are expressed as limit and unlimited.

101. Sayre 1983, 173, says, "Limit and Unity are ontologically equivalent." Sayre does not say that by "unity" he means "integrative unity." But I take it that this is what he means. For an attempt to base an account of the nonrelativity of the good in *Philebus* without reference to the Good or to its identity with the One or without explicitly identifying goodness with integrative unity, see Cooper 1977a (1999). Cooper's otherwise exemplary analysis is missing only a connection between the passage at 65A1–5 with the passage at 23C4–D8. On integrative

The puzzle about how the Good provides truth to the Forms is solved by looking at the Good from the aspect of integrative unity. Ontological truth is a relative property of intelligibles, the property of being transparent to an intellect. This means seeing the unity of the parts of an intelligible complex or whole; for example, seeing a pattern in an array of numbers or seeing the unified functionality across the organs among biological homologues or seeing a unifying cause behind various medical symptoms or, to take an unquestionably Platonic example, seeing that physical and psychical beauty are really one thing. In all these cases, the Good provides truth to the intelligibles manifested in these examples because the Good is the One. Owing to the uniqueness of the Good or One, all unity other than its own is complex. The unity as opposed to the disarray of the complex is integrative unity and without it there would be no intelligibility. That is, to be able to understand anything at all, it is necessary to see the unity of its parts, where unity is indexed to kinds or essences and parts can be either static or dynamic or both. The unified paradigms are, as instruments of the Good or One, relative principles of unity and hence of intelligibility.

Returning to νοῦς as the cause of any good mixture, this seems to be the Demiurge. Because the Demiurge is Good-like, he manifests proportion, beauty, and truth and this is what he communicates to the cosmos.[102] What he produces for each natural kind is an integrative unity. Deviations from this unity, for whatever reason, may be judged over against the Form he instantiates in each case. Hence, for human beings, our ideal achievement is determined by our endowment and this is expressible in terms of an integrative unity of the parts of the soul and of the soul/body complex. The best life for a soul/body complex is a particular sort of integrative unity. But this is not the best life for a soul capable of living separate from the body. The ideal integrative unity of the soul consists in cognitive identity with all that is intelligible. Beauty, commensurability, and truth are ways of attaining the Good. The combination of the three criteria forms an integrative unity, that is, the unity of a complex. One of the things it means to say that the Good is the One is that the Good is achievable only via an integrative unity of the criteria, the sort of unity appropriate for a human being. Any such unity obviously approaches the Good or One itself asymptotically, as it were. There is no integration into or with the absolutely simple first principle of all.[103]

---

unity as goodness see Miller 1995, 630–633. He uses the term "complete and well-apportioned whole." Recall that at *Phd.* 99C5–6, the Good is that which "binds (συνδεῖν)" and "holds things together (συνέχειν)."

102. Cf. *Sts.* 269D, 270A, 273B–C.

103. See Desjardins (2004, 12–51), who presents a persuasive analysis of the overall structure of the dialogue that shows the central theme of the dialogue to be integrative unity (of knowledge and pleasure in a good human life) under the governance of the first principle of all.

5.5. First Principles in *Timaeus*

The principal texts in the dialogues in which Plato indicates the mathematical tendency in his thought are in *Timaeus*. The Demiurge, says Timaeus, "wanted to make the cosmos as near as possible to being like himself."[104] Just one page later, he says, that the Demiurge wanted to assimilate (ὁμοιῶσαι) the cosmos to the most beautiful of intelligibles, that is, to the Living Animal that contains all intelligible living kinds within it.[105] It is possible, of course, to take these wishes on the part of the Demiurge as two and not one. If this is true, then being like the Demiurge is not identical to being like the Living Animal. One desideratum could possibly be achieved without the other. But on that interpretation, it is a mystery how both desiderata are to be independently achieved. For when the Demiurge acts, he does one thing and one thing only, namely, imposes mathematical order on the precosmic "soup" using "shapes and numbers (εἴδεσί τε καὶ ἀριθμοῖς)."[106] This presumably achieves both desiderata. The shaped and numbered elements are themselves composed into living beings here below according to the mathematical formulae that guarantee assimilation to the Living Animal.

Both desiderata are simultaneously achieved if the eternal intellection of the Demiurge is cognitive identification with all that is intelligible. There are within the entire Platonic tradition three ways to understand such intellection. According to the first, what the Demiurge has in his intellect are concepts (νοήματα) or thoughts of intelligibles, which are separate from these concepts. According to the second, intelligibles just are such concepts. According to the third, the Demiurge is cognitively identical with the intelligibles themselves.

On the first view, it is difficult to see how a concept of an intelligible, not derived from sense-perception, differs from the intelligible itself. More important, this view requires the separation of the desiderata, in which case it is not clear how the cosmos is made to be like the Demiurge in addition to being made to be like the Living Animal. That is, how is the element of fire made to be like the Demiurge where this likeness is other than its likeness to Fire in the Living Animal? On the second view, Plato would be held

---

104. *Tim.* 29E1–3.
105. *Tim.* 30C2–31A1. There is an ambiguity here as to whether this claim suggests that there are intelligibles outside the Living Animal or not. I return to this question later. See Ferrari 2008, 83–94, esp. 88–91, on the identity of Demiurge and Living Animal. Also Perl 1998; Halfwassen 2000; and Abbate 2016. The cognitive identity of Demiurge and Living Animal is the primary inference made from the passage at *Soph.* 248E6–249A5 wherein life and soul cannot be excluded from τὸ παντελῶς ὄν. This cognitive identity is essentially dynamic. Cf. Plotinus, 6, 2 [43], 7.3–15.
106. See *Tim.* 53B4–5. See A. E. Taylor 1928, 358, on the meaning of εἶδος as "geometrical shape." These are the shapes of the particles that will enter into the composition of the elements and then of the things composed of the elements. Cf. *Rep.* 529D8–E3.

to be contradicting his claim in *Parmenides* that Forms are not concepts, but rather that which concepts are of.[107] This leaves the third view, according to which the Demiurge is eternally cognitively identical with all that is intelligible. Thus, real or true Being and paradigmatic intellection are extensionally equivalent.[108] Therefore, we can say that the association of Forms is the thinking by the Demiurge of all necessary truths including those that make contingent truths intelligible. The unity of Being is the unity that Intellect has by being cognitively identical with Being. This is an integrative unity that is of an irreducible many.

If the Demiurge is an intellect cognitively identical with Being but distinct from it, the unity that Intellect has with Being is extrinsic to Intellect, and extrinsic to Being since Being is an array of intelligibles. The unity is evidently supposed to be provided by the Good which provides both existence and essence to intellect-intelligibles. Presumably, owing to the fact that the Good is the source of this unity, its alternative name is, not inappropriately, "the One," just as Aristotle tells us.

In *Timaeus*, the principle that is νοῦς is identified as the cause of the transformation of the precosmic chaos into the orderly universe we presently inhabit. The Demiurge is not explicitly said to be νοῦς, but the imposition by the Demiurge of "shapes and numbers" on the receptacle are said to be "the things crafted owing to intellect (τὰ διὰ νοῦ δεδημιουργημένα)."[109] The Demiurge does this by using as his paradigm "the Living Animal (ὁ ζῷον)" which somehow contains within it all the "intelligible Living Animals" as parts.[110] He "looked (ἔβλεπεν)" to the eternal (τὸ ἀίδιον) in order to have the paradigms for use.[111] The looking is, presumably, an intellectual awareness which, since it occurs before the generation of time, is an eternal intellectual relation between νοῦς and intelligibles (τὰ νοητά). Given this, we can hardly suppose that the Demiurge is identical with the Good which is "beyond οὐσία." For first, the Demiurge has an οὐσία because it has a distinct activity, that of thinking. We may add in this regard that the Demiurge is also himself good, a property he has, presumably, by participating in the Idea of the Good. Second, if the Demiurge is eternally in cognitive relation to Forms, these Forms, or if one insists their simulacra, must inform his οὐσία. Finally, there are two passages later in the dialogue in which Timaeus states that this dialogue will not consider

---

107. See *Parm.* 132B3–C11.
108. The root idea here is no doubt an interpretation by Plato of the claim of Parmenides that τὸ γὰρ αὐτὸ νοεῖν τε καὶ εἶναι (for the identical thing is thinking and being) B3 DK.
109. *Tim.* 53B5, 47E3. See Xenocrates fr. 15 Heinze (= fr. 213 Isnardi Parente).
110. *Tim.* 30C2–D1. That these Living Animals are Forms is clear from 51E6–52A4.
111. *Tim.* 29A3. That "the eternal" is a description of the Living Animal is clear from 37D1: ζῷον ἀίδιον ὄν.

the "principle or principles of all things."[112] This alone should be taken as conclusive proof that the Demiurge (or Demiurge and Forms) is not those principles.[113]

The function of the Demiurge serves to reply to the criticism that Forms are "metaphysically idle."[114] As we have already seen, Forms taken alone—separate from intellect, the Good, and from each other—could justly be said to be metaphysically idle. That is, they are not able to account for their instantiation. But this is not Plato's position. Nor is it his position that an eternal intellect eternally contemplating itself, including all that is intelligible, supplies the remedy to idleness. Rather, the Demiurge, cognitively identical with Forms, is an instrument of the inexhaustible causal power of the Good. Forms are not metaphysically idle because Forms were never intended by Plato to be independently causally efficacious.

The introduction of the Demiurge seems prepared for by the passage in *Sophist* above which insists on the inclusion of life, intellect, and so on, in the intelligible world and in *Philebus* in which a divine intellect governs the cosmos. The nonsensible world, then—the subject matter of philosophy—includes the Good or One, Forms, the Demiurge or divine intellect, and souls insofar as they are composed of eternal nonsensible essence.[115]

The integration of these elements of intelligible reality in a systematic manner was the central task of Platonism. There are here so many moving parts—literally, one is inclined to say—that it is not surprising that disagreement was endemic. On one side, the systematic construction proceeded apace within the framework provided by the canonical texts. On the other, engagements with Naturalists required appeal to whatever happened at the time to be the favored version of a systematic construct. It is probably the case that no Platonists of antiquity considered the possibility

---

112. *Tim.* 48C2–6 and 53D4–7. The last passage should be connected with 53B4–5 where it is said that the Demiurge brings intelligibility into the precosmic chaos by imposing shapes and numbers on it. The "first principles of all" are the principles of these shapes and numbers. Plato at 48B8 also calls these principles "elements (στοιχεῖα)" which is how Aristotle characterizes the One and the Indefinite Dyad. See *Meta.* A 6, 987b19–20.

113. Despite the intense scrutiny of *Timaeus* among Middle Platonists, the tendency to conflate the Demiurge and the Good or the One seemed to them to be irresistible. This is the case, too, in contemporary scholarship. See, e.g., Benitez 1995, 128: "It is clear that the Demiurge occupies the place held by the Good of the *Republic*." See Ferrari (2018), who takes a somewhat more nuanced view, although he is still attracted to the conflation.

114. See, e.g., van Inwagen 2014, chap. 10. See d'Hoine 2008 on Proclus's analysis of Plato's argument for design in his *In Parm.* 3.790.5–791.20, according to which the causal role of Demiurge and Forms in producing the order in nature are mutually implicatory. Mohr (2005, 77–80) sees a paradox in the claims that the Forms are causally inefficacious and also that they are the causes of being known. On the present interpretation, Forms alone were never intended by Plato to be the cause of their being known. The Idea of the Good is the cause of the knowledge and knowability of Forms (sec. 5.1, 6).

115. The status of gods, apart from the Demiurge, is interestingly ambiguous as a potential philosophical topic. See *Tim.* 40D–41D.

that there was in fact no coherent account of first principles to be had from Plato. This is particularly so in light of the fact that Aristotle seems to assume that there is a genuine account of this sort even though it does not ultimately stand up to criticism.

In the second part of this book, I shall turn to some of the outstanding figures in the Platonic tradition with an eye to their unique contributions to the system exposed in the first part. These contributions include both exegesis and the replies to arguments arising from anti-Platonists or Naturalists. Occasionally, we shall see the system applied to the solution of hitherto unremarked philosophical problems. Amid the manifest disagreements among Platonists regarding how to understand what Plato says and what is implied by the truth of what he says, there is, with some notable exceptions, an impressive agreement about principles and what the denial of these principles amounts to.

5.6. Aristotle's Account of First Principles in Plato

I have left to the end of this chapter Aristotle's testimony regarding the Good and the One. I do this because I have tried to show that from the dialogues alone we can derive considerable information on two central points: (1) Plato posits an unhypothetical explanatory first principle of all that is absolutely simple or incomposite. It does not even have the minimal compositeness required for an entity to be something or other, that is, to have any true predicative judgments made of it. (2) One suitable name for this principle is the Idea of the Good. It is so called because entities, including the Demiurge, are good owing to their participation in it. But the explanatory role of this principle remains mostly obscure if we insist that it is only a principle of goodness. Much of what the first principle of all is said to do is owing to its being a principle of unity or oneness, though we need to keep constantly in mind that the first principle is neither good nor one predicatively. With these points in view, Aristotle's testimony to the effect that Plato identified the Good with the One is more confirmatory than a bolt from the blue. It is certainly not the outrageous misinterpretation that many make it out to be.

In chapter 6 of book A of *Metaphysics*, Aristotle moves from a survey of pre-Socratic philosophers to Plato, whose "treatment (πραγματεία)" of ultimate causes is a centerpiece of Aristotle's dialectical history.[116] Aristotle begins by distinguishing the ethical philosophy of the historical Socrates from the metaphysics of Plato, which begins with the positing of separate Forms as the objects of knowledge. He adds that, in addition to Forms and

---

116. See esp. Miller 1995 for *Parmenides* as a major source of this testimony.

sensibles, Plato posited Mathematical Objects which are "intermediary" between the two.[117] He then reports:

> Since the Forms are the causes of all other things, he thought that the elements of Forms are the elements of all things. As matter, the Great and the Small are the principles; as essence, it is the One. For from the Great and the Small and by participation in the One come the Forms and these are Numbers. In saying that the One is essence and not another thing that is said to be one, he spoke like the Pythagoreans, and also like them in saying that Numbers are causes of the essence of other things.[118]

The evidence that Plato did indeed identify Forms with Numbers in some sense is extensive.[119] Aristotle does not introduce this identification as a late development in Plato's thinking; indeed, Aristotle throughout the corpus and the scores of references to Plato's philosophy never even suggests that that philosophy is not a unified system.[120] The reduction of Forms to

---

117. Aristotle, *Meta.* A 6, 987a14–18. See also B 1, 995b15ff.; Z 2, 1028b19–21; K 1, 1059b2; Λ 1, 1069a33ff.; M 1, 1076a19ff.; M 9, 1086a11–13; and N 3, 1090b35–36.

118. *Meta.* A 6, 987b18–25: ἐπεὶ δ' αἴτια τὰ εἴδη τοῖς ἄλλοις, τἀκείνων στοιχεῖα πάντων ᾠήθη τῶν ὄντων εἶναι στοιχεῖα. ὡς μὲν οὖν ὕλην τὸ μέγα καὶ τὸ μικρὸν εἶναι ἀρχάς, ὡς δ' οὐσίαν τὸ ἕν· ἐξ ἐκείνων γὰρ κατὰ μέθεξιν τοῦ ἑνὸς τὰ εἴδη εἶναι τοὺς ἀριθμούς. τὸ μέντοι γε ἓν οὐσίαν εἶναι, καὶ μὴ ἕτερόν γέ τι ὂν λέγεσθαι ἕν, παραπλησίως τοῖς Πυθαγορείοις ἔλεγε, καὶ τὸ τοὺς ἀριθμοὺς αἰτίους εἶναι τοῖς ἄλλοις τῆς οὐσίας ὡσαύτως ἐκείνοις. W. D. Ross (1924 ad loc.) argues for omitting τὰ εἴδη. Jaeger (1957) and others, including Primavesi (2019), omit τοὺς ἀριθμούς. Berti (2017) retains both. Neither omission is found in the manuscript. Steel (2012, 186–188) argues that neither omission is desirable or necessary. An important additional piece of information is found in *Phys.* A 9, 192a3–12, where Aristotle contrasts his own principles of change—underlying subject, form, and privation—with those who posit a "triad" of Great and Small and One as principles. This leads them to conflate matter and privation. That Plato is being referred to here is confirmed by the previous explicit reference at A 4, 187a16–20. Cf. Alexander of Aphrodisias, *In Meta.* 55, 20–35; Simplicius, *In Phys.* 454, 28–455, 3; and Sextus Empiricus, *M.* 10.276–277. See W. D. Ross (1951, 216–220) and Reale (2008, 209–212), who argue that the Forms are not literally reduced to Numbers but rather that what Aristotle means is that the Forms are *derived* from Numbers. I do not propose to adjudicate this issue here principally because I think the evidence for adjudication is lacking. There are numerous details in Plato's doctrine of principles that may well have remained unsettled in his mind at the time of his death.

119. Cf. *Meta.* A 8, 990a29–32; Z 11, 1036b13–25; Λ 8, 1073a18–19; M 6, 1080b11–14; M 7, 1081a5–7; M 8, 1083a18; M 8, 1084a7–8; M 9, 1086a11–13; N 2, 1090a4–6; and N 3, 1090a16. M 4, 1078b9–12 is especially important because it makes a clear distinction between an early (ἐξ ἀρχῆς) phase of the theory of Forms and then a subsequent reduction of Forms to Numbers. There is, however, no indication by Aristotle of when in Plato's career this reduction occurred. For this reason, it is left to students of Plato to discover indications of the reduction in the dialogues. See Gerson 2013a, chap. 4, where this evidence is discussed at greater length. Also see Richard 2005, 211–218; and Krämer (1969) 2014, 206–207.

120. As Burnet (1914, 313) pointed out more than a century ago, "One thing, at any rate, seems clear. Aristotle knows of but one Platonic Philosophy, that which identified Forms with numbers. He never indicates that this system has taken the place of an earlier Platonism in which the Forms were not identified with numbers, or that he knew of any change or

Numbers is not presented as a development but rather as an integral part of Plato's causal analysis.

The testimony continues:

> It is evident from what has been said that he [Plato] uses only two causes, the cause of the whatness and the cause according to matter (for the Forms are the cause of the whatness of the other things, and the cause of the whatness of the Forms is the One). It is also evident what the underlying matter is, in virtue of which the Forms are predicated of the sensible things, and the One is predicated of the Forms; this is the Dyad, or the Great and the Small.[121]

Aristotle's testimony is that the ultimate principles of Plato's philosophy are the One and the Indefinite Dyad. It is not unreasonable to infer from this that this One must be another name for the first principle of all, the Idea of the Good. This inference is supported by the following passage: "Among those who posit immovable substances, some say that the One itself is the Good itself; at least they thought the essence of the Good to be, most of all, the One."[122]

A number of features in the above report deserve attention. The first is the claim that Plato viewed Forms as having elements.[123] The second is that these elements are the One and the Great and Small, also called "the Indefinite Dyad (ἀόριστος δυάς)" as the next passage indicates.[124] The third

---

modification introduced by Plato into his philosophy in his old age. That is only a modern speculation." Cf. Steinthal 1998, 67; and Szlezák 1998.

121. *Meta.* A 6, 988a8–14: φανερὸν δ᾽ ἐκ τῶν εἰρημένων ὅτι δυοῖν αἰτίαιν μόνον κέχρηται, τῇ τε τοῦ τί ἐστι καὶ τῇ κατὰ τὴν ὕλην (τὰ γὰρ εἴδη τοῦ τί ἐστιν αἴτια τοῖς ἄλλοις, τοῖς δ᾽ εἴδεσι τὸ ἕν), καὶ τίς ἡ ὕλη ἡ ὑποκειμένη καθ᾽ ἧς τὰ εἴδη μὲν ἐπὶ τῶν αἰσθητῶν τὸ δ᾽ ἕν ἐν τοῖς εἴδεσι λέγεται, ὅτι αὕτη δυάς ἐστι, τὸ μέγα καὶ τὸ μικρόν.

122. *Meta.* N 4, 1091b13–15: τῶν δὲ τὰς ἀκινήτους οὐσίας εἶναι λεγόντων οἱ μέν φασιν αὐτὸ τὸ ἓν τὸ ἀγαθὸν αὐτὸ εἶναι· οὐσίαν μέντοι τὸ ἓν αὐτοῦ ᾤοντο εἶναι μάλιστα. A bit further on, 22–25, Aristotle contrasts this position with that of Plato's successor as head of the Academy, Speusippus, who, owing to problems with the identification of Good and One, abandoned this, claiming that good arises from the One; it is not identical with it. The contrast seems to support the surmise that Plato (among others) is the one who is referred to in this passage as holding the identity of Good and One. Cf. also *EE* A 8, 1218a15–32, which refers to those who hold that τὸ ἕν is αὐτὸ τἀγαθόν. See Brunschwig 1971 for a comprehensive argument that the crucial *EE* passage is focused on the metaphysics of Plato, not that of Pythagoras or Xenocrates.

123. The "elements" of Forms cannot be the superordinate One and the Indefinite Dyad, but must be the One of *Parmenides* H2 and the Indefinite Dyad. The superordinate One is above elemental status. Aristotle, *Meta.* Δ 3, 1014a26–27, says an element is that out of which a thing is composed. But this is distinct from an ἀρχή or principle. See 1, 1013a7–8. An element is an internal constituent; a principle is not that.

124. See *Meta.* N 7, 1081a22, etc. where whoever is the subject of Aristotle's criticism, it is clear that "Dyad" is a shortened form of "Indefinite Dyad." At A 6, 987b25–26, Aristotle says that Plato differed from the Pythagoreans in making the Indefinite a duality. See *Phil.* 16C1–17A5, and 23C–27C on the Unlimited and the Limit. I take it that even if we suppose

feature of the above account is Aristotle's expression of the two principles as matter and essence or form. We must assume that Aristotle knew that the Idea of the Good is specifically said by Plato to be beyond essence. If the Good is the One, in what sense is it the essence in relation to matter? We may recall that the One-Being of H2 of *Parmenides* partakes of essence.[125] We are left with no indication by Plato of how One-Being can partake of essence if that in which it partakes has no essence. Alternatively, if it does not partake of the essence of the One, then in what sense is the One or Good the first principle of all? And, again, if One-Being does partake of the One and thereby shows that it has an essence, how can the One be absolutely simple?[126]

In addition, note Aristotle's careful distinction between outright identification of Good and One and a more nuanced possibility that, though the two may be identical in reality, they may yet be somehow distinct in λόγος. One suggestion that I shall explore in the next chapter is that the first principle of all is the Good insofar as it is an end or goal and the One insofar as it is the metaphysical cause of all things. The idea is that in reality the first principle of all must be identical with the goal of all things. As we shall see, this is the axiom which leads Platonism to claim that ethics is inseparable from metaphysics. The axiom is open to the obvious challenge that there simply is no one good that all things seek, but rather that good is equivocal. This is Aristotle's objection to a coordinate Form of the Good, a genus of all types of goods.[127] But the Idea of the Good cannot be a summum genus since it is above essence. Still, radical equivocity in the meaning of "good" is a bedrock of any type of Naturalism. With the rejection of metaphysics, it goes without saying that a Naturalist account of ethics cannot appeal to any metaphysical foundation.[128]

---

that in *Philebus* the Unlimited refers to a principle of sensibles, we may suppose that it is an instantiation of the first principle of the Indefinite Dyad. See Sayre (2006, 139–170), who provides what I take to be conclusive evidence in favor of regarding as equivalent the various expressions for the Indefinite Dyad in antiquity.

125. Plato, *Parm.* 142B5–6.
126. See chap. 9 for Plotinus's solution to this problem.
127. See *EN* A 6. At 1096b5–7, where Aristotle contrasts the Good he is criticizing with the Pythagorean claim that the One is in the column of goods. Aristotle says that this way to think about the good is more promising, suggesting that what he is criticizing here is the coordinate Form of the Good not the superordinate Idea of the Good which is identified with the One. At *EE* A 8, 1217b1–1218b27, however, Aristotle seems to be aware of Plato's positing a superordinate Good that is identical with the One, and to deny that this means that it enables Plato to avoid the problems with a coordinate Form of the Good.
128. At *Meta.* Δ 6, 1016b20–21, Aristotle says: ἀρχὴ οὖν τοῦ γνωστοῦ περὶ ἕκαστον τὸ ἕν (so, the principle of knowability regarding each thing is that which is one). Cf. I 1, 1052b31–35, and 1053a31–33. For example, we know a quantity by applying a unit of measure to it. But knowability surely extends beyond the quantitative. In scientific knowledge or ἐπιστήμη, we know when we are able to see that a subject (the species or genus of an individual subject) and a predicate (the species or genus of a commensurable property) are in reality one. That which

The identification of the Good with the One is also supported by a fragment from a student of Aristotle, Aristoxenus, in his *Elementa Harmonica* in which he reports that Aristotle said that in a public lecture *On the Good*, Plato defied the expectations of his audience and instead of talking about traditional human goods such as wealth, health, and strength, he discoursed on mathematics, culminating in the claim that the Good is One.[129]

The glaring problem in understanding this testimony is not the identification of the Good with the One, but with the postulation of the Indefinite Dyad as a supposedly coordinate principle.[130] If the Good/One and the Indefinite Dyad are distinct principles on the identical ontological level, then each must possess sufficient complexity in order to be distinct from the other. But then the absolute simplicity of the first principle of all is

---

is the principle of their unity is the definition or essence. Cognition is, generally, a unificatory process. We recall that at sec. 5.1, 6 the Good is the principle of knowability for the Forms. Aristotle must have recognized the appropriateness of the identification of the Good with the One if the Good is such a principle. Cf. *Rep.* 537C7, ὁ συνοπτικὸς διαλεκικός (the one capable of attaining a unified vision is the dialectician). This person alone can attain the highest degree of truth. See *Phil.* 58C3. The Good as One does what the essence does in scientific knowledge according to Aristotle. So Aristotle presumably infers that the One is supposed to be the essence of all things, that which unifies ontologically and so cognitively. Also see *Tht.* 186D3; *Gorg.* 479C5–6, 498E10; and *Phil.* 41C9. In all these passages, we find cognition as a unificatory process, particularly with regard to belief formed from acts of sense-perception.

129. Aristoxenus, *Harm. Elem.* 2.30–31 (= *De bono*, p. 111 Ross). Brisson (2018) tries to deflate the value of this testimony. The words ὅτι ἀγαθόν ἐστιν ἕν (that good is one) (without the definite articles) can certainly be understood in the anodyne sense according to which Plato is reported to have said that good is one as opposed to being many or diverse, as most people think. Plato does, of course, believe that. But these words conclude the account of what Plato talked about, namely, mathematics and astronomy, with the conclusion that "good is one." This brings to mind the education curriculum of Plato's rulers culminating in their vision of the Good. But "good is one" would be a rather odd way to describe this conclusion. After all, many opponents of Plato—for example, hedonists and certain other Socratics who held that virtue is alone sufficient for happiness—would agree that the good is one. Given Aristoxenus's own testimony, it seems more reasonable that Aristoxenus is reporting that the Good is to be identified with the metaphysical first principle of all. It should be noted that Aristoxenus says specifically that he got his information from Aristotle. A passage in *Magna Moralia* should also be considered here, even if this work is not genuine. See A 1, 1182a27–30: τὴν γὰρ ἀρετὴν κατέμιξεν εἰς τὴν πραγματείαν τὴν ὑπὲρ τἀγαθοῦ, οὐ δὴ ὀρθῶς· οὐ γὰρ οἴκειον (For he incorrectly mixed in virtue with the treatment of the Good, for that is inappropriate). This πραγματεία would seem to be a reference to a technical lecture on the Good such as the one Aristoxenus mentions; otherwise, it would be bizarre for Aristotle—or the author of this work, if a student of Aristotle—to criticize Plato for connecting the study of good with virtue. This is confirmed by the next line: ὑπὲρ γὰρ τῶν ὄντων καὶ ἀληθείας λέγοντα οὐκ ἔδει ὑπὲρ ἀρετῆς φράζειν· οὐδὲν γὰρ τούτῳ κἀκείνῳ κοινόν (for when speaking about being and truth, he should not have spoken about virtue, for the two have nothing in common). It should be added that Simplicius, *In Phys.* 151, 6–19, 453, 22–30, and 545, 23–25, who endorses the identification of Good and One, cites three distinct accounts of Plato's lecture or lectures by Aristotle, Speusippus, and Xenocrates.

130. See Gaiser 1963, 12–13, on the centrality of this problem for understanding Plato's doctrine of principles.

destroyed along with the rationale for positing such a principle in the first place.[131] The interpretive and philosophical choices seem to be either to somehow subordinate the Indefinite Dyad to the Good/One or else to subordinate both the Indefinite Dyad and the Good/One as coordinate principles of the Form Numbers to another superordinate Good/One. In the latter case, we can maintain the interpretation of the first hypothesis of the second part of *Parmenides* as referring to a remote, uncognizable first principle and the second hypothesis as referring to the One and its coordinate Indefinite Dyad.

The path to a solution to this problem should begin by recognizing that the Indefinite Dyad has its own sort of unity. It has a unity which nevertheless entails complexity since the One is uniquely simple. And it is the One's simplicity that entails its absolute priority. Accordingly, the Indefinite Dyad cannot be really coordinate with the primary One.[132] The Indefinite Dyad *is* a coordinate principle of Being, but the first principle of all is beyond Being. Undoubtedly, this alternative involves its own severe problems.[133]

Why, though, is the Indefinite Dyad a principle at all? The simple answer is that the Indefinite Dyad is the principle of πλῆθος or magnitude or size, which includes both continuous and discrete quantities.[134] With the principle of number alone, there could be no lines or planes or solid figures.[135]

---

131. See Plato, *Parm.* 140A1–3: ἀλλὰ μὴν εἴ τι πέπονθε χωρὶς τοῦ ἓν εἶναι τὸ ἕν, πλείω ἂν εἴναι πεπόνθοι ἢ ἕν, τοῦτο δὲ ἀδύνατον (if, however, the one has any property apart from being one, it would have the property of being more than one, but this is impossible). This consequence also follows if the one is one.

132. See Aristotle (*Meta.* N 1, 1087b9–12), who says that the Great and Small is one, although the proponents of the principle do not say if it is one in number or in λόγος, too. Cf. Sextus Empiricus, *M.* 10, 261; and Simplicius, *In Phys.* 454, 8–9. See Halfwassen 1997 on the combined monism and dualism of principles in *Parmenides*. This is (16) "a monism in the reduction to an absolute with a dualism in the deduction of being." That is, a dualism subordinate to the primary monism. There is dualism *within* being and monism in the explanation for the generation of being.

133. Already Aristotle, *Meta.* Λ 10, 1075b18–20, notes that those who posit Forms need a superordinate principle as cause of participation by sensibles in Forms. This causal role, however, does not seem to be easily assumed by an absolutely simple first principle.

134. Thus, πλῆθος can refer to a plurality of units or "ones." See *Parm.* 132B2, 144A6, 151D3; and *Phil.* 16D7. But it can also refer to a continuous quantity. See *Parm.* 158C4; and *Phil.* 29C2. In the latter sense, πλῆθος is used synonymously with τὸ ἄπειρον. See *Phil.* 26C6. Also μέγεθος. See *Parm.* 149C5 and 150B8. This is quantity or extension apart from number.

135. Sextus Empiricus, *M.* 10.281–283, describes two ways in which the generation of bodies from numbers was thought to occur by different Pythagoreans (including Plato). The first mentioned describes the generation of bodies from numbers via the usual dimensional levels using the verb ῥυεῖν which, it will be recalled, is the root verb used for the Good (§1, 3). It is hardly surprising that if like produces like, the mode of production will be like in all cases. How, say, a line "flows" from a point (or an indivisible line, as Aristotle explains, *Meta.* A 9, 992a20–22, M 8, 1084a37–b2) is a special case of how a many is derived from a one. That is, the reduction of bodies to numbers is the epistemological analogue of the generation of bodies

The apparent paradox facing Plato is this: if everything is generated from the One, then so is the Indefinite Dyad. But magnitude cannot be generated from the One. For example, a line is not generated from a point or an aggregation of points. The paradox is mitigated to a certain extent by the fact that One-Being is not number, but the principle of number, in which case number is generated from One-Being as much as is magnitude. This is why number and magnitude are both generated in H2 of *Parmenides*. They are coordinate principles of One-Being. It is simply not the case that the Indefinite Dyad is coordinate with the One, first principle of all. The general idea, I think, is that generation of Numbers up to the generation of three-dimensional volumes may be conceived of as a geometrical construction eternally carried out and eternally completed by a divine intellect, that is, the Demiurge. Plato does not have to worry about how lines are composed out of points; rather, lines are constructed from a starting point in thought and planes from a given line, and so forth. The ontological hierarchy is manifested by constructive mathematical analysis. The generation of bodies in time is that of an image of this mathematical order. Without the Indefinite Dyad, not only could bodies not exist, but even their paradigmatic geometrical volumes could not exist.[136] Neither could the Mathematical Objects. In fact, without the Indefinite Dyad, there could not even exist that which is minimally complex, that in which existence and essence are distinct. But complexity is, apparently, maximally instantiated. In that case, the One (from H1) and One-Being (from H2), which comprises the Indefinite Dyad and the array of essences and with which an eternal intellect is cognitively identical, must exist.

Aristotle's testimony regarding the reduction of Forms to the principles of the One and the Indefinite Dyad is, along with the texts in *Republic* on the Good as unhypothetical first principle of all, the most important piece of evidence for the claim that Plato's philosophy is systematic. This evidence also informs us that the system is a *Derivationsystem*, hierarchical in terms of logical or substantial proximity to the first principle.[137] Simply stated, the greater unity there is, the closer something is to the first principle. And the

---

from numbers. Everything that exists along this line of reduction/generation is ultimately accounted for by the unlimited fecundity of the first principle of all. The proof of the unlimited fecundity is just the existence of bodies. See Richard 2005, 190–205, for some helpful remarks about the complexities of the various accounts of generation from the first principle.

136. See Dumoncel 1992.

137. See *Rep.* 511B8 on "the things that depend (τὰ ἐχόμενα)" on the first principle; and Aristotle, *Meta.* M 8, 1084a32–34, on the "things that follow (τὰ ἐπόμενα) the first principle." Here together are dependence and hierarchy. If the Forms depend on the Good for their being and knowability, the Good cannot represent a property of these Forms, e.g., their goodness. Theophrastus (*Meta.* 6b11–15) speaks of a γένεσις of Forms and Numbers from the principles, but no further information is supplied. See Krämer 2014. Merlan (1953, 166–177) concisely examines the considerable evidence for the claim that Plato was committed to a system of the derivation of all things from a first principle.

identification of Good and One means that unity is also an index of goodness or at least of proximity to the achievement of goodness. I am happy to allow that absent this evidence, there is little reason to insist that Plato is a systematic philosopher. Nevertheless, I see no reason whatsoever for rejecting the evidence, either of *Republic* itself and elsewhere or that of Aristotle's testimony or that of the indirect tradition, much of which certainly does not rest upon Aristotle's testimony but on that of other Academics. For the sake of historical accuracy, it is essential that the engagement of Platonism with Naturalism follow upon a systematic exposition of the former. Indeed, many of the forms of Naturalism in antiquity—most notably Stoicism—were systematic as well. The fundamental grounds of their opposition will be most perspicuously available to us if we see the engagement at a systematic level. But apart from the history, any philosophical illumination resulting from the consideration of the opposition of Platonism to Naturalism needs the *Derivationsystem* as the grounds for its antinominalism, antimaterialism, antimechanism, antirelativism, and antiskepticism.[138]

---

138. See Erler 2007, 406–429, for a valuable and concise account of the evidence for Plato's doctrine of first principles and of its most prominent interpretations. Guthrie 1978, chap. 8, is still well worth consulting.

CHAPTER 6

The Centrality of the Idea of the Good in the Platonic System (2)

In this chapter, I turn to the centrality of the Idea of the Good for Plato's ethics. It is certainly a remarkable fact that just as the Idea of the Good has little presence in the bulk of Anglo-American scholarship on Plato's metaphysics, so it has little presence in accounts of Plato's ethics. I aim to show that any account of Plato's ethics is seriously deficient if the superordinate Idea of the Good is not the main focus and if the Good is not identified as the absolutely simple first principle of all, the One.[1]

6.1. The Form of the Good and the Idea of the Good

There may be a number of reasons for the lack of interest in the Idea of the Good among students of Plato. At least one of these is that it is supposed that Aristotle's critique of the Form of the Good in his *Nicomachean Ethics* is decisive.[2] In that case, any hope for the preservation of the value of Plato's ethics should not depend on the Good. The underlying point of the barrage of arguments Aristotle marshals against the Form of the Good is that "good" is equivocally predicable of things that are said to be good whereas a Form should, on Plato's terms, be univocally predicable of all that partake of it. For example, "good" in the category of "when" means one thing, say,

---

1. See Fronterotta 2001, 137–144, especially on the interdependence of ethics and metaphysics in Platonism.
2. See Aristotle, *EN* A 6. See Baker (2017, 1849–50 with n. 23), who argues, rightly, in my view, that Aristotle's rejection of a Form of the Good does not apply to "the Good itself" which I take to be equivalent to the Idea of the Good.

the right time to plant crops, and another thing in the category of "how it is" or state, say, the health of an animal. The word "good" is not univocally predicable of these, in which case we should stop supposing that there is such a Form. And if we do stop, we will have no reason to appeal to the Form of the Good in any argument for any Platonic position in ethics.

There are a number of places in the dialogues in which Plato seems to group indifferently a Form of the Good along with other Forms.[3] And as Plato frequently maintains, a Form is an οὐσία or essence.[4] Yet, in *Republic*, the Idea of the Good is said to be "beyond essence (ἐπέκεινα τῆς οὐσίας)."[5] Hence, a seemingly simple and obvious question is this: "Is the Good an essence or beyond essence?" Indeed, the force of the question seems to increase when we discover that in *Republic* itself, barely three Stephanus pages prior to the superordination of the Good, the Form of the Good is, once again, apparently classed along with other Forms, each of which would presumably be an οὐσία.[6] Therefore, it would seem that Aristotle's objections to the putative univocity of a Form of the Good could not apply to the Idea of the Good since the latter is not an οὐσία and so could not be univocally predicable of anything. If it should turn out that *some* immaterial Good is a central part of Plato's ethics, there is then at least some reason to believe that this will be the superordinate Idea of the Good and not the coordinate Form of the Good. That does, of course, leave us with the problem of what the latter's role is in Platonism.

Briefly, Proclus has the most plausible explanation for what the Form of the Good is supposed to do. This explanation is found in his remarkable but sadly underutilized *Commentary on Plato's Republic*.[7] Essay 11 is devoted to the question "What is the Good in *Republic*?" Proclus faces squarely the exegetical and philosophical problem of how there can be two Ideas of the Good, one that is coordinate with other Forms or οὐσίαι and one that is ἐπέκεινα τῆς οὐσίας. One gratifying feature of all of Proclus's writings on

---

3. See *Phd.* 65D4–7, 75C10–D2, 76D7–9; *Tht.* 186A8; *Parm.* 130B7–9; *Rep.* 507B4–6, 608E6–609A4; and *Phil.* 15A4–7. Cf. *Epin.* 978B3–4.

4. See, e.g., *Eu.* 11A7; *Phd.* 65D13, 77A2, 78D1; *Crat.* 386E1; *Sts.* 283E8; *Parm.* 133C4, etc.

5. *Rep.* 509B8. It is true that these words are qualified, for the Good is ἐπέκεινα τῆς οὐσίας πρεσβείᾳ καὶ δυνάμει ὑπερέχοντος. However, the previous words are unqualified: οὐκ οὐσίας ὄντος τοῦ ἀγαθοῦ. Cherniss (1932, 237), followed by Brisson (2002), argues that the qualification requires us to reject the superordinate status of the Idea of the Good. Among other things, this interpretation effaces the distinction between the superordinate Idea and the coordinate Form. So if on other grounds we decide that Plato wants to posit a Form of the Good and the Idea of the Good, that would be another reason for insisting on the latter's unqualified superordination.

6. *Rep.* 507B4. Each of the Forms here is said to bear the mark ὅ ἐστιν, indicating a certain specific nature. This would seems to preclude the Form of the Good from being beyond οὐσία.

7. See Kroll 1899, 1901. An English translation of this work is being prepared under the direction of Dirk Baltzly. An Italian translation with commentary by M. Abbate (2014) is available. See Gerson 2015.

Plato's dialogues is that he takes seriously everything Plato says, which is not to say that he takes everything literally. As a result, he is in no doubt that Plato intends to posit a Form of the Good among other Forms and also a superordinate Idea of the Good.[8] The way he explains the difference is, first, to distinguish among coordinate Forms those that name kinds of things or substances (οὐσίαι) or properties of things and those that name certain perfections (τελειώσεις) of these. Among the former are Forms of substantives like man or horse, but also Forms of kinds of being, in particular the μέγιστα γένη of *Sophist*, namely, Being, Self-Identity, Difference, Motion, and Stability, and presumably, the types or species of these. Among the latter are good, beautiful, just, health, strength, and so on.[9] Among the former, the Form of or Kind of Being is the γένος of the rest; among the latter, the Form of Good is the γένος.[10] Any substance or individual exists or has being because it partakes in a particular type of Form which is a (Platonic) species of the γένος that is Being or One-Being. Analogously, anything has the perfection of a property owing to its partaking of a specific type of perfection, the γένος of which is the Form of the Good.[11] As a result of this way of ordering the Forms, we can say that something exists because it partakes of a Form that necessarily brings existence or being with it. Analogously, something is good because it partakes of, say, the Form of Justice and Justice necessarily brings goodness with it because Justice is a species of perfection, that is, a species of the coordinate Form of the Good.[12]

The reason Plato apparently does not jettison the coordinate Form of the Good at the moment he introduces the superordinate Idea of the Good takes us to the heart of Plato's ethics. Let us assume for the moment that a coordinate Form of the Good is the genus of all specific "perfections." The standard term for human perfection is "virtue (ἀρετή)." Throughout the dialogues and the treatises of Aristotle, virtue is the human good, that is, it is the perfection of human kind. It seems entirely possible, however,

---

8. Proclus, *In Remp.* 1.278.22–279.2. Cf. his *Platonic Theology* (*PT*) 2.7, 46.13–20 Saffrey-Westerink. Cf. Plotinus, 6.7 [38], 25.1–16, on the two Goods. Also Halfwassen 1992a, 245n73; and Beierwaltes 2004, 103–108.

9. *In Remp.* 1.269.19–270. 20. Cf. *In Parm.* 3.810.2–3. Note that Proclus is not troubled by the problem of how there can be a genus of Forms that apparently cannot have a genus univocally predicated of them.

10. *In Remp.* 1.270.20–24.

11. Cf. *Rep.* 357C6, where εἶδος ἀγαθοῦ clearly refers to a species of the Form of Good. It is that which is painful in the application, like medicine, but beneficial in its consequences. This is in contrast to another species of Good (357B5) including those things that we desire for themselves and not for their consequences, like pleasures.

12. At *In Remp.* 1.271.20–26 (cf. 273.11), Proclus, in addition to the superordinate Idea of the Good (ὑπερούσιος) and the coordinate Form of the Good (οὐσιῶδες), distinguishes a third use of "good," referring to the kind of perfection itself which can be in us, for example, pleasure or wisdom. These are the specific "goods" people seek. See also *Rep.* 367C–D where seeing, hearing, knowing, and being healthy are all goods.

for someone to agree that virtue is the human good and at the same time question whether virtue ought to be pursued. For though everyone wants what is good for themselves, one might suppose that virtue, though it is a perfection, is not one's own good. This is, I take it, the central conundrum that motivates the discussion of *Republic*. If one asks, "Why should I strive to be a virtuous human being?," this question does not even suggest a rejection of the claim that virtue is human perfection. Nor does it even suggest a rejection of the claim that one wants only the real good for oneself. It is just that one may doubt whether achieving virtue is necessarily in one's own interest, that is, whether it is in fact good for oneself even granting that it is a perfection. The cogency of the questioning of the value of virtue to oneself is what makes intelligible the question put by Glaucon and Adeimantus regarding the benefit of being just.[13] No facile appeal to the fact that virtue is human excellence or human good can make the challenging response, "I accept that, but still, why should I be good?," into a solecism or open one to the accusation of having committed a logical fallacy.

There are all sorts of prudential arguments that can be deployed to show that pursuing virtue is, on balance, in one's interest. Epicurus provides a stellar example of why being virtuous is in fact beneficial to us.[14] But the prudential case for virtue cannot, in principle, rise to the level of an absolutist argument to the effect that it cannot possibly be in one's interest to be anything other than virtuous.[15] The reason for this is quite simple. An

---

13. See Dasgupta (2017), who clearly describes the problem of the normative authority of nonnatural properties. Dasgupta cites Nowell-Smith, Korsgaard, and Nagel among others as posing the same problem. He goes on to argue that in fact there can be no normative nonnatural property, good, such that to recognize something as good is ipso facto to desire to do it or to have it done. Plato's position, as we shall see, is that the only way to meet this argument is if there is a superordinate Good (in the technical sense of "superordinate" described above), identical with the One. Dasgupta's paper presents a nice Naturalist counterpoint to the Platonic doctrine.

14. See Epicurus, *Ep. Men.* (= D.L.10.132). Note that here Epicurus contrasts his prudential advice with the deliverances of philosophy, perhaps expressing the Naturalist response to Platonism.

15. See *Ap.* 28B5–9, D6–9; and *Cr.* 48C7–D6 for expressions of the absolutist prohibition of behavior that is nonvirtuous. I find the modality ("cannot possibly be in one's interest") clearly implicit in the repeated claim that it is better to die than to do an injustice. See Penner (2003, 2007a, and 2007b), who makes a heroic effort to support prudentialism—what he also calls "pure prudentialism"—by offering an interpretation of the Idea of the Good that makes it a universal of sorts, equivocally instantiated by the particular good of each individual. I find his account of the Good's transcendent status deficient on many counts, but most of all because if the Good is beyond οὐσία, it cannot be a universal which is in any case univocally predicable of whatever shares in it. But apart from this, Penner seems to me to assume, wrongly, that a transcendent Good must be quite separate from the good of each individual and also that pursuit of it must be in conflict with pursuit of one's own good. As I have tried to show, however, Plato does not think that it is possible to separate pursuit of one's own good from pursuit of the Good any more than it is possible for one to have "one's own" correct answer to a mathematical question different from *the* right answer. It is precisely because the Good is beyond οὐσία

exhortation to virtuous living—the sort of thing that Socrates habitually expresses—can only propose or sketch out alternate scenarios for virtuous and nonvirtuous behavior and then present the consequences of the former as preferable to those of the latter. But what if someone actually prefers these consequences, all things considered? In the case of Epicurus, and his exhortation to virtuous behavior to his acolytes, someone might prefer the rewards of licentious behavior with all its attendant risks to the rewards of virtuous behavior accompanied by the certain loss of the benefits of licentiousness. It is, for example, easy enough to imagine a Thrasymachus or a Callicles being unimpressed with an exhortation to self-restraint even granting its benefits. Indeed, they might well acknowledge the superiority of virtue to vice for those who are too feeble to overcome or avoid the consequences of bad behavior. But as for themselves, things are different. Prudentialism is the respectable face of the real view that the only relevant question is "What's in it for me?" It is irrelevant to Plato's ethics that for many or even most a recital of the beneficial consequences of virtuous behavior will be an adequate answer to the question.[16]

There is within the realm of practical reasoning no way in principle to achieve the universality in ethics that Plato evidently thinks he is aiming for in *Republic* and elsewhere. For both means to ends and the constituents of ends are always ordinally ranked by the human agent. There is no way to guarantee that the ranking of one of Socrates's interlocutors will correspond to the ranking that Socrates himself would make. If, for example, Socrates exhorts Callicles to prefer ἰσονομία (equality) to πλεονεξία (greed), he has no hesitation in replying that this is suitable for the weak

---

that it can be equivocally instantiated as an end of the full array of natures that pursue it. Penner rightly rejects attempts by Cooper (1977b), White (1979), Annas (1981), and Irwin (1995) to separate the Good in such a way that pursuit of it means abandoning one's own interests. Penner's crucial mistake, in my view, is a mirror image of the one he rightly rejects. He thinks that one's own interest must be separated from an absolute impersonal Good. In order to make the case for the former as opposed to the latter, in contrast to his opponents who make the case for the latter as opposed to the former, he must offer an implausible interpretation of the metaphysics of the Idea of the Good. Penner also seems to me to conflate the coordinate Form of the Good with the superordinate Idea of the Good. Another major effort at defending prudentialism by isolating "Socratic moral psychology" from metaphysical Platonism is Brickhouse and Smith 2010, esp. chap. 3. Prudentialism, of course, follows from absolutism if the latter is true. What appear to be prudentialist lines of argument in *Republic* and elsewhere in the dialogues are correct, but only if we assume absolutism. Thus, it is prudent to be virtuous if one wants one's own good. But this prudence is only indefeasible if one's own good is inseparable from the Good.

16. Vasiliou (2015, 61) recognizes that knowledge of virtue is not alone motivating. He thinks (62) that it is "upbringing" or habituation that supplies the motivation. It is not clear, however, how, if this is the case, the desire for the real Good, for the Idea of the Good, does not drop out as relevant to fixing motivation. He seems to admit as much when he assimilates Plato's view to the view of Aristotle.

but unsuitable for the truly superior.[17] But it must always be this way. Naturally, one could pitch one's exhortation to the preferential calculus of the interlocutor, arguing that on his own terms one course of action, the virtuous course, would have superior consequences to the nonvirtuous course. Thus, it would be possible to achieve a sort of objectivity since the analysis of an expressed preferential ranking can take it out of the subjective. This is presumably what psychological therapy aims to do. But objectivity cannot rise to the level of universality since this objectivity is functionally relative. It is, after all, possible to revise one's ranking and the acceptance of one course of action based on the fact that the ranking does not have any implications for the rankings of someone else.[18] Indeed, the ranking does not even have any implications for one's own ranking at another time, say, tomorrow. Nor does the ranking necessarily remain stable when one has it made explicit to oneself.

The problem with prudentialism, in my view, is twofold. First, it confuses subjective value with objective truths. Second, it fails to see that objectivity is not, at least not for Plato, enough for moral absolutism. For that, the superordinate Idea of the Good is necessary. The prudentialist thinks that it is sufficient to criticize one's subjective ordinal valuations according to the supposedly agreed-upon principle that everyone desires their own good. But "one's own good" is a perfectly legitimate way of expressing the goal of the subjective ordinal valuations. In reply, the critic will want to distinguish the apparent good from the real good. And rightly so. But this distinction in order to work in the way that the prudentialist wants has to be severed from the subjective ordinal valuations. And this is not possible unless one transcends objectivity and attains to universality. For at the level of objectivity, it is an open question whether one's valuations do or do not achieve one's own good.

A coordinate generic Form of the Good will do for providing the objective basis for perfection of a kind, but no universality can result from this. I would like to forestall an obvious objection which seeks to identify Forms with universals or at least claims that the objectivity of a Form renders it

---

17. See *Gorg.* 483B4–C6.

18. See Wreen 2018, 338–341, on the distinction between objectivity and universality. Something like objectivity without universality is found in various neo-Aristotelian ethical theories. See, e.g., Hurstouse 1999; and Foot 2001. All these philosophers seek to ground normativity in human nature or in nature generally. A good human being is one who fulfills her nature; so, too, a good animal or a good plant. But this view conflates nonnormative and normative rationality, assuming that these are identical. Thus, a good person is supposedly one who is rational. If, though, we have a rational nature, it is not possible not to be rational even when we are violating some putative universal standard of goodness. It makes no sense to exhort someone to be other than what he is necessarily. According to Plato, there must be such a universal normative standard in order to avoid begging the question of why a Thrasymachus or a Callicles is not good just because he is rational. See Lott 2014, 761–777, for the identical criticism of this view.

universally predicable. According to this objection, if there is a coordinate Form of the Good, that is sufficient for universality. If virtuous behavior is good, then it is universally good, meaning always and everywhere. I believe this objection rests upon a confusion. First, the universal is a hypostatization of an act of thinking of any intelligible. It is, as we have seen, the way one cognizes a Form, enabling one to make predicative judgments. The Form as such is not a universal and so it cannot be that within the Form there is universality independent of cognition. The universality of the Good or of any impersonal or nonsubjective entity (as opposed to the so-called universal) is a property of being and the principle of being roughly equivalent to ontological truth, indicating its ubiquitous availability. Second, and more crucially, a Form is an οὐσία, a limited or circumscribed nature. It is always possible to ask whether participating in that nature is good not in the sense that a virtue is good because it is one type of perfection, but whether it is unqualifiedly and ultimately good for the individual regardless of his preferential rankings.[19]

Plato in *Republic* has Socrates say, "Is it not also clear that many people would choose to do or acquire or think things that seemed to them to be just or beautiful, even if they are not so, whereas the acquisition of things that seemed to be good would be acceptable to no one; rather, they seek things that are really good. In this case, at least, everyone disdains the mere seeming."[20] This passage, preceding by only a page the introduction of the Idea of the Good, would seem to suggest that Plato thinks he can show that only the Idea of the Good is that which everyone seeks. No one finds acceptable something that merely seems to be good as opposed to being really good for oneself. The challenge is not to establish a distinction between what seems to be good and what is really good for me since this is something that no one can seriously deny. The challenge is to show that what is really good for me is in fact good period. That is, the challenge is to move from objectivity to universality. If this can be done, then the problem of nonnatural normativity is solved. My motive for doing what is good simpliciter is exactly the same as my motive for doing what is really good for myself, something that I cannot but want.

The reason why a generic Form of perfection cannot deliver universality is that the perfection has to be somehow presented to a person as his good.

---

19. Cf. G. E. Moore 1903 for the argument that it is a fallacy of Naturalism to identify "good" with any natural property, e.g., pleasure. Various Naturalist responses have held that "good" is indeed not identical in meaning with any natural property, but that to which "good" refers and some natural property or other are extensionally equivalent. See Lott 2014 on the "normal-normative gap" meaning the failure of entailment from virtue in a human being to moral goodness.

20. *Rep.* 505D5–9: τόδε οὐ φανερόν, ὡς δίκαια μὲν καὶ καλὰ πολλοὶ ἂν ἕλοιντο τὰ δοκοῦντα, κἂν <εἰ> μὴ εἴη, ὅμως ταῦτα πράττειν καὶ κεκτῆσθαι καὶ δοκεῖν, ἀγαθὰ δὲ οὐδενὶ ἔτι ἀρκεῖ τὰ δοκοῦντα κτᾶσθαι, ἀλλὰ τὰ ὄντα ζητοῦσιν, τὴν δὲ δόξαν ἐνταῦθα ἤδη πᾶς ἀτιμάζει; Cf. *Phil.* 20D7–10.

It can only be received either as what seems to be good or not. And the latter is always an option. The criterion that any person applies in making a choice is whether the proffered perfection, that is, the virtue, is one's real good as opposed to seeming good. Everyone wants only the real good. The problem with this, of course, is that no one can pursue anything without a definite nature. One cannot simply act to achieve the Good; rather, one has to act to achieve something that he thinks is really good, that is, an instance of the Good. This instance has to be understood as being really good, not merely seeming good. And yet any good appears *only* as what seems to be good, even if it does so appear because it really is good.

Of any perfection, especially virtue, it can be asked if that perfection is really good or only seems good. What Plato needs to show is the unity of good such that its universality is evident. That is, he needs to show that the question, "Is virtue, which is a good, good for me?," is no more coherent than the question, "Is the Pythagorean theorem which is true, true for me?" In other words, the perfective good just is an instance of the real good that everyone wants.[21]

What needs to be shown is that the Idea of the Good is the source or cause of the goodness of every perfective good.[22] This is what is claimed when it is said that Forms are "Good-like (ἀγαθοειδῆ)" (chap. 5, sec. 5.1, 19) because they are produced by the Good. They are "Good-like" because they manifest the Good itself. Their cause is virtually all that they are. Since every good is an end, it is not possible to achieve a real good without achieving a manifestation of the Good. There is no scenario under which "good for me" is not identical with "good."[23] If, say, Justice is Good-like, meaning

---

21. See *Phil.* 64A1-3: ἐν ταύτῃ μαθεῖν πειρᾶσθαι τί ποτε ἔν τ' ἀνθρώπῳ καὶ τῷ παντὶ πέφυκεν ἀγαθὸν καὶ τίνα ἰδέαν αὐτὴν εἶναί ποτε μαντευτέον (in this [approach to discovering the role of pleasure in the good life] trying to learn what is the nature of the good for human beings and in the universe and to intuit what form it has). Note the singular ἰδέαν. As the passage goes on to emphasize, the Good is one thing, though variously conceptualizable, that is, conceptualizable as this or that οὐσία. As we have seen in the previous chapter, the Idea of the Good is virtually all of these οὐσίαι.

22. See Oderberg 2014, 353–354, on the logical priority of "good" to "good for x." Precisely because of this logical priority, nothing can be good for x that is not good for y even though it is the case that the λόγος of "good" is distinct from the λόγος of "good for x" or "good for y." More precisely, we should say that it cannot, logically speaking, be possible that if something is good for x, then it is not good for y that that something is good for x. This analysis ignores for the sake of simplicity the possibility that if something is good for x, then it is possible that it is neither good nor not good for y that that something is good for x. So-called indifferents may be set aside for present purposes.

23. In the continuation of the above passage (505E1–506A2), Socrates says that people have an "inkling (ἀπομαντευομένη)" that there is a real good, but they do not know what it is. I suggest that this "inkling" accompanies a vague awareness that one cannot attain the real good at the expense of anyone else. It is perhaps what gets to be represented as "conscience." "Conscience" is a systematic concept derivable from Socrates's daimon which always restrains him when he is about to pursue some apparently exclusionary good. See *Ap.* 31D–32A, 40A–C;

that it is a real good and therefore that it is incoherent to claim that if A is just that might involve injustice for B, then that is because the Idea of the Good is the cause of the essence and existence of Justice (chap. 5, sec. 5.1, 7). Being Good-like is a part of the essence of Justice. That is what it means to say that being just is good for "its own sake," a deeply obscure claim outside of the present metaphysical context.[24]

The Naturalist critique of normative universality in Platonism draws strength from the fact that the desire of everyone for their own real as opposed to apparent good can only be satisfied by achieving some specific goal. And it is very difficult from a Naturalist's perspective to imagine universalizing from that agent-specific goal. Plato's position, however, neatly circumvents this objection. For a desire for one's true good means that if it turned out that what one thought was one's real good was in fact not so, then one would immediately disavow a desire for it.[25] Therefore, I could not coherently claim that x was my real good but that I do not want it. The Naturalist then strategically retreats to the position that my wanting x does not entail that anyone else wants x, too. And that is where Plato means to insert a superordinate Idea of the Good or One. The requisite universality comes from specific Forms and their instances manifesting the Good. The requisite particularity of the agent's desire for his own real good is linked to the Good by these specific Forms. If achieving an instance of Justice is really good for me, that entails that it cannot be other than good for anyone else. Someone might suppose that recognizing that a deed is just does not entail that one must desire to do it. And one can even suppose that recognizing that a deed is really good for me does not guarantee that it is good period. For Plato, it is left to the philosopher to show that in fact there is such a guarantee.

---

and *Phdr.* 248B–C. In *Tim.* 90A–D, Plato identifies the daimon with reason, the "most authoritative" part of the soul. It is the impartiality of reason that makes it a guide to the Good. Reason, when it is authoritative in action, does not seek what is good for oneself independently of what is good simpliciter. To suppose otherwise is to employ reason in the service of desire which could only attain an apparent good. The question of whether this apparent good is really good cannot be answered by speculation about how things might appear to one on one's deathbed. It can only be answered in light of the discovery of the superordinate Good and its identification with the One.

24. B. Williams (2008) thinks that the Idea of the Good is supposed by Plato to be that which alone is intrinsically good but that in fact when in *Republic* Socrates answers the question "Is justice intrinsically good?," he does so without regard to the Good, holding that being a just person is an end in itself or valuable for its own sake. He does this without regard to the Idea of the Good which is virtually contentless and incapable of providing a foundation, metaphysical or otherwise, for Plato's primary ethical concerns. Williams pays no attention to the content provided for the Good by its identification with the One and the consequent "content" of integrative unity.

25. See Penner 1971, 1973, 1991.

The Good is both the source of Being (chap. 5, sec. 5.1, 7, 9) and the end of all striving (5). This is not coincidental.[26] Part of our understanding of the Good is inferred from its products; another part is inferred from how we strive to possess it. What this means is that the Good is (1) virtually all that is intelligible and (2) that which is virtually attained by knowing all that is intelligible. Stated thus, there could not be other than an identity between the Good as source and the Good as goal.[27] By contrast, the disruption of the two aspects of the Good renders each unintelligible. To argue that there is no universal Good is to argue that there is no unique, universal source of Being, and vice versa. Intimations of the Good are found in beauty, proportion, and truth, all expressible in terms of integrative unity.[28] In principle, then, a proof of the existence of a first principle of all that is, as we have seen, essentially self-diffusive, is a proof of the universality of Good, and vice versa. Thus, Plato's antirelativism supports and is supported by his first principle of all. Since the universal Good is transcendent, relativism entails and is entailed by materialism.

In *Gorgias*, there is a good example of the connection between τέχνη and the ability to impose an integrated unity. "If you like, look at painters, or house builders or ship builders or any other craftsmen you like, how each one puts whatever he does into a certain order and forces one thing to be suitable for another and to be fitted to it until the entire object is constructed in an ordered and arranged manner."[29] This is achieved by the imposition of a form (εἶδος) of some sort. It is the unity of the form that provides the integrative property. The divine craftsman that is the

---

26. Cf. Plotinus, 6.8 [39] 15, 1–2: Καὶ ἐράσμιον καὶ ἔρως ὁ αὐτὸς καὶ αὐτοῦ ἔρως, ἅτε οὐκ ἄλλως καλὸς ἢ παρ' αὑτοῦ καὶ ἐν αὑτῷ (And it [the Good] is itself an object of love and love, that is, love of itself, inasmuch as it is only beautiful by reason of itself and in itself). Plotinus perhaps has in mind *Symp.* 192C–D on love as an achievement of integrative unity (ποιῆσαι ἓν ἐκ δυοῖν).

27. The fact that the Good is a goal is manifested by instantiations of Forms being said to desire (ὀρέγνυμι) their Forms. See *Phd.* 74E9–75B2. See Papineau (1993, 44–48), who argues that sciences that have a teleological dimension, such as psychology, are not reducible to physics. Papineau thinks that psychology is an exception in this regard. The teleological dimension, however, does not suggest the universality of goodness. From Plato's claim that all sciences study that which has a teleological dimension, none of these are reducible to physics done in the "Anaxagorean mode."

28. Beauty is the integrative unity provided by form to whatever is informed. For this reason, Plato can have recourse to an ambiguity according to which we can speak either of a separate Form of Beauty or of all the Forms together, having the unity of Being, as what Beauty is. And, in addition, the Good, the source of the being of all the Forms, can also be said to be beautiful.

29. *Gorg.* 503E–504A2: οἷον εἰ βούλει ἰδεῖν τοὺς ζωγράφους, τοὺς οἰκοδόμους, τοὺς ναυπηγούς, τοὺς ἄλλους πάντας δημιουργούς, ὅντινα βούλει αὐτῶν, ὡς εἰς τάξιν τινὰ ἕκαστος ἕκαστον τίθησιν ὃ ἂν τιθῇ, καὶ προσαναγκάζει τὸ ἕτερον τῷ ἑτέρῳ πρέπον τε εἶναι καὶ ἁρμόττειν, ἕως ἂν τὸ ἅπαν συστήσηται τεταγμένον τε καὶ κεκοσμημένον πρᾶγμα. Cf. *Phdr.* 264C, 268D on the integrative unity of a speech and a tragedy.

Demiurge is the paradigm of this orderly imposition. The reception of integrative unity(-ies) is how the cosmos receives the Good.

As we saw in chapter 3, the τι ἱκανόν of explanation in *Phaedo* is most plausibly taken to be the Idea of the Good. With the identity of the Good as source and as goal, we can add that its explanatory role also pertains to action. The Good produces, indirectly, through the array of Forms, the beings that act to fulfill their natures. As Socrates says, the explanation for his action which consists in his refusing to run away from prison, is that it is good for him to do so. It is good, an instantiation ultimately of the Good because, broadly speaking, it is an act contributing to the fulfillment of his nature. But his nature is that of a human being, and the Good is virtually the Form of Human Being. Nothing else can explain his staying in prison, especially not the relaxation of his body on his cot in a sitting position. The question "Is it good *for* Socrates to stay in prison?" and the question "Is the universal Good manifested in the act of Socrates staying in prison?" are identical questions with identical answers.

The universality guaranteed by the Idea of the Good is derived to forms in the sensible world via the intelligible Forms. But as we have just seen, this does not make the Idea of the Good otiose in the sense that a generic Form of the Good would suffice to guarantee universality. The Idea of the Good is not, therefore, a property of a specific Form. This would follow straightforwardly from the fact that it is beyond οὐσία.[30] But it is not thereby emptied of content. On the contrary, it has an exact content expressible in a λόγος. The pseudo-name "One" indicates that content. The content is absolute incompositeness. But more substantively, that content is expressed in every integrative unity. If the One is the cause of the being of the integrative unity of everything, then the desire for the really good for ourselves is the desire for that which we do not possess but would satisfy the desire of beings such as ourselves. The One accounts for the essence and existence of everything with any measure of intelligibility. The Good is just the One as desired. The Good provides the ultimate explanation for everything because, as the One, it is the source of the structured desire of everything.

6.2. Virtue, Knowledge, and the Good

Throughout the dialogues, Plato consistently maintains that no one errs willingly.[31] The words οὐδεὶς ἑκὼν ἁμαρτάνει may be understood in a way

---

30. Thomas Aquinas, while recognizing that Aristotle's criticism of the Form of the Good does not preclude Aristotle himself from positing a separate universal good, thinks that Plato's error was in positing a determinate Idea (*quamdam ideam*) whose nature it was to be the goodness common to all goods (*communem omnium bonorum*). See *In EN* 1.6. Aquinas's exegetical error is in failing to distinguish the Form of the Good from the Idea of the Good.

31. See *Men.* 77C1–2; *Ap.* 37A5; *Gorg.* 488A3; *Protag.* 345D8, 358C7; *Rep.* 589C6; *Tim.* 86C7–D1; and *Lg.* 731C–D.

that makes the claim an analytic truth. For the word ἁμαρτάνει indicates that one tried and failed to hit a target. Presumably, no one *tries* to hit a target and willingly fails. Plato, however, certainly means more than this. He means at least that no one fails to achieve the real good they seek willingly, since no one would ever be satisfied with anything other than the real good. If they fail, it is because they have wrongly identified a seeming good as the real good. They do this because of some cognitive failure. They simply do not know that what they take to be the real good is not so. If, though, we understand the real good which people only fail to achieve because of ignorance as conceivably detachable from the Idea of the Good itself, we shall be back to the prudential conception of good and the prudential interpretation of Plato's claim.[32] It might well be the case, as Socrates insists against Polus in *Gorgias*, that tyrants do what seems best to them but not what they want since what they want is what is really good, not just apparently good.[33] Still, there is a gap between the true claim that tyrants want what is good for themselves and the contentious claim that what they want is what is universally good because this is nothing other than what is good for themselves. It is certainly contentious because if it is true, then the tyrant would have to agree that he does not want to be a tyrant after all, assuming, of course, that tyranny is unqualifiedly not good.

If this is so, then it casts a new light on the sort of knowledge that is supposed to be missing from someone who goes wrong in moral matters.[34] The most common understanding of this knowledge is that it is a knowledge of the Forms, at least the Forms of the Virtues.[35] If one knows what Justice is, then one will be able to identify just acts. But unless we add that by knowing Justice one knows that Justice is Good-like, then it seems perfectly possible that one should know what Justice is and be unimpressed with its instrumental value. As we have already seen, one must ascend to the Good not in order to know that Justice is good, presumably meaning that Justice is one subspecies of the species Virtue which is one species of the genus of perfection, the Form of the Good. One must ascend to the Idea of the Good in order to know Justice. Whatever else this means, it must mean that since Justice is Good-like, knowing Justice means mentally seeing it as

---

32. So Penner 2003.

33. *Gorg.* 466A4–467C4. Of course, what is in fact the apparent good here must be taken by the agent as the real good.

34. On the connection between knowledge and virtue see, e.g., *Protag.* 313B; *Tht.* 153B; *Alc* 1 133B.

35. Many scholars who hold this view either identify it as the view of Socrates as distinct from the view of Plato or as the view of Plato in the "Socratic" dialogues. See, e.g., Santas 1979, chap. 6; Brickhouse and Smith 1994, chaps. 2–4; Irwin 1995, chaps. 3–4; and Vasiliou 2008, chaps. 1–4. The extensive works of Penner and Vlastos are essential in guiding much of the scholarship along this line. Even if one nuances the claim about knowledge of the Virtues to have it include the "craft (τέχνη)" of virtue, this craft is, for Plato, presumably, grounded in the knowledge of the Forms, which is only available in relation to the Idea of the Good.

the product of the first principle. That is, its nature is determined by the first principle. If it is not possible that it is good for me to be unjust, this is because of the universality of Good. Therefore, it would make no sense for someone to aver that, while Justice is a perfection, it is not good for me. Perfection according to kind is a manifestation of the Good. To move intellectually from objectivity to universality requires the positing of a first principle of all which is the cause of the existence and essence of those Forms that are the determinants for specific actions and soul-states that are unqualifiedly good. If the Idea of the Good is not an integral part of the ethics, then the establishment of the nature of a perfection such as justice could only produce a prudential motivation. But these are, as we have seen, eminently negotiable.

It would seem that the knowledge that guarantees virtue or, stated otherwise, that guarantees that one does not go morally wrong is the knowledge obtained in dialectic as sketched in the Divided Line. No one without this knowledge would be able to understand why it is necessarily not the case that attaining a good life is a zero-sum game. The point is vividly made at the very end of *Republic* where Plato considers the man who practices virtue by habit without philosophy.[36] Such a man, given the opportunity to choose another life, opts for the life of a tyrant, surely Plato's paradigm of someone who thinks that life is a zero-sum game. It is important to see that the philosophy he is missing is quite far removed from philosophy understood in the Socratic sense of "a critical examination of life." What the hapless unnamed character is missing could not be supplied by refuting the unsupported and unreflective views of Socrates's interlocutors on how to live. For as Socrates is represented as understanding his divinely inspired mission, he is continually exhorting others to care for their souls.[37] Apart from the deliverances of dialectic, however, soul-care can certainly be practiced, along with body-care, as essential for a good life, but this could well be a life following prudential lines, just like the life of the decent man who chooses the life of a tyrant.[38] And it matters not at all that he immediately regrets his choice, for he only does so for prudential reasons. Even if one insists that soul-care has to be understood as care for the most important thing, it is a crude informal fallacy to suppose that this means not caring for things, like the body, that are of secondary importance. And this means that, on occasion, it is certainly possible that this or that action on behalf of body-care would preclude a focus on soul-care. A good example of this would be

---

36. *Rep.* 619B7–D1: ἔθει ἄνευ φιλοσοφίας ἀρετῆς μετειληφότα. This man is presumably much like the "decent people (τοὺς ἐπιεικεῖς)" at 606A7–8 who are capable of being corrupted by imitative poetry. Cf. 518D11. Also *Phd.* 82D2–3, and 87A11–B3.

37. See esp. *Ap.* 29B–30D. Cf. *La.* 187D–188C; *Gorg.* 457B–C, etc.

38. Note that "body care" includes care for the subject of bodily states. If the true self is the soul, this does not include such states. The true or ideal self is an immaterial entity, capable of existing separately from the body. Obviously, no Naturalist will want to go there.

someone who held that Socrates should escape from prison if *he* thinks that he is innocent of the charge upon which he was convicted. Such a person could reasonably argue that the harm done to others by escaping does not equal the benefit to Socrates (and to others) by escaping. The mere fact that an injustice would be done would not be dispositive. What would settle the matter would be a proof that if an injustice is done by escaping, then it is not possible for Socrates or for anyone else to benefit from this. Indeed, that is what Socrates's absolutist prohibition on wrongdoing would seem logically to imply even if that is not explicit in the dialogues promoting soul-care as philosophy.

The difficulty of appreciating the reductive identity of "good for me" and "good" is evident in the account of Plato's infamous lecture (ἀκρόασις) on the Good.[39] The disappointed listeners expected to hear some bit of wisdom about a recognized human good, some species or subspecies of the genus of the Form of the Good. Instead, what they got was a mathematical lecture leading up to the claim that "good is one (ἀγαθόν ἐστιν ἕν)." I will focus on the mathematical denouement in a moment. I want to point out first that anything Plato might have said on behalf of recognizable human goods and their contribution to happiness would have, in principle, been open to the possibility of rejection on prudential grounds. To argue, as no doubt Plato would wish to do, that overzealousness in the pursuit of wealth is not conducive to happiness, is to leave one open to the obvious objection that what counts as overzealousness is highly circumstantial or situational. It is, of course, possible to suppose that, apart from the evidence, Plato's position might have been more or less a version of prudentialism. But then there is the evidence, all of which converges on the interpretation according to which prudentialism is exactly what Plato opposed, probably from a time even before he decided to put his thoughts down in writing.

The way that the Form of the Good is connected to the universal Idea of the Good is via the integrative unity that is expressible according to the parameters of beauty, truth, and commensurability as found in *Philebus*. What this means is that one is precluded from thinking that it is possible that if A is good for x at a certain time, then it could be the case that it is bad for y that A is good for x at that time. Accordingly, one could not suppose that it is possible to achieve one's own good as a zero-sum game, a game in which one's own benefit automatically results in something that is the opposite of beneficial for someone else. This is the case because if anything is really good for oneself—and we recall that this is all that *anyone* ever wants—then that is because this good has an integrative unity assessable according to truth, beauty, and commensurability. If that which appears to be good for oneself is really good it is because it indirectly

---

39. See Chap. 5, n. 129.

manifests or instantiates the Idea of the Good, the principle of measure and the source of truth and beauty.[40]

The threefold parameter, then, provides criteria for assessing ethical claims according to Plato. The Idea of the Good is the source of truth, measure or commensurability, and beauty. In order to see how these three are one, it is best to recur to Aristotle's testimony. We recall that Aristotle says that Plato reduced the Forms to the first principles, with the Great and Small as matter and the One as essence.[41] Thus, the One is, in Aristotelian language, the essence of that which has essence, but everything that has essence is complex because its existence is distinct from that essence. Every Form is one distinct way of manifesting that which the One is virtually.[42] In addition, each Form is, in a specific sense, one way that Being is. Insofar as something partakes of a Form, it partakes of its unity, although in a diminished manner owing to materiality or physicality.[43] Normativity enters the picture when we are in a position to judge any gap between the endowment and the achievement of the thing with the nature it has. For present purposes, the most critical gap is between the endowment that is human embodiment and the potential achievement of an ideal personal integrative unity.

I understand the criteriological function of truth as indicating the natural kind under investigation. That is, its role is to tell us what Form is partaken of. The determination of the natural kind is the result of a successful

---

40. One might object that if the Idea of the Good is beyond οὐσία, then nothing can really instantiate it for any instantiation will be of an οὐσία. But this objection fails to take account of the fact that οὐσίαι are instrumental causes. That is, something or someone instantiates the Idea of the Good by instantiating one or another Form. The instantiation is of a certain kind of integrative unity that each Form is.

41. Aristotle, *Meta.* A 6, 987b20–21; N 4, 1091b13–15: τῶν δὲ τὰς ἀκινήτους οὐσίας εἶναι λεγόντων οἱ μέν φασιν αὐτὸ τὸ ἓν τὸ ἀγαθὸν αὐτὸ εἶναι·οὐσίαν μέντοι τὸ ἓν αὐτοῦ [τὸ ἀγαθόν] ᾤοντο εἶναι μάλιστα (Among those who say that there are immovable substances, some say that the One itself is the Good itself; but they thought that the essence of the Good is, most of all, the One). Plato is very likely to include among those who think (ᾤοντο) that the One is the essence of the Good. Also *EE* A 8, 121825–30.

42. Cf. *Phil.* 15B1–2 which asks the question of whether or not one should believe that Forms exist. These Forms are called "monads" or "ones (μονάδες)." The puzzle set forth for Protarchus is how these ones, while retaining their identity, can each be directly present in a multitude of things, or mediately present via subordinate ones. The connection between the One, the oneness of a Form, and the normative role of a Form in providing measure to the unmeasured or unlimited is straightforward. See Adam (1920, 2:62), who believes that all οὐσίαι are "specific determinations of the [Idea of the] Good." Also appendix 3, *Rep.* bk. 7, 176: "expression[s] or embodiment[s] of the Good." I think he is basically right, but Adam does not consider the causal role of the Good. Nor does he consider the identification of the Good with the One without which it is, to say the least, puzzling how, say, the Form of Circularity is a specific determination of the Good. Further, the expressions of the Good are so by being expressions of Being.

43. See esp. *Rep.* 476A5–8, where the one Form appears (φαίνεσθαι) to be many owing to its association (κοινωνία) with actions and bodies.

collection and division. Thus, to identify a Form in its integrative unity is one way of cognizing the Good. The criteriological function of measure or commensurability indicates the integrative unity that consists in a balance of elements in the constitution of the thing. The criteriological function of beauty is as an indicator of the attraction that any integrative unity has for anyone capable of perceiving it. Thus, apparent beauty, as we have seen, will be attractive for some, while only real beauty will attract the philosopher. This is so because only real beauty is really good, that is, a manifestation of the Good.

The most vivid illustration of the principle of integrative unity is in *Republic* where the virtuous person is said "to have become altogether one out of many (παντάπασιν ἕνα γενόμενον ἐκ πολλῶν)."[44] In this case, the integrative unification is the result of separation from the body or, more accurately, separation from the transitory subjects of bodily states and concentration of the self into the intellect. The normativity resides in the fact that this concentration or integration is the fulfillment of one's true nature. It is unification of one's endowed or empirical self with the "human being within the human being (τοῦ ἀνθρώπου ὁ ἐντὸς ἄνθρωπος)."[45]

The argument for the identification of "good" and "good for me" is a move from mere objectivity to universality. To admit that what is good for me can differ from what appears to be good for me now is to admit an objective criterion for one's own good.[46] Once objectivity is admitted, then the passage from objectivity to universality is provided by the Forms that are Good-like. To limit Good to a genus of perfection would still leave us short of the requisite universality. For there is no *necessity* that achieving that perfection is good for oneself. Only if what is good for oneself is

---

44. *Rep.* 443E1–2. See Korsgaard 2008, 100–109. Cf. *Rep.* 554E4–6 and *Phd.* 83A7–B2 on the role of philosophy persuading the soul "to gather oneself into oneself." Gathering into oneself is an act of integrative unity. See also *Tim.* 31B4–8 and 32A7–B2 on the Demiurge as imparting integrative unity to the cosmos. On the Allegory of the Cave as showing the starting point of self-transformation and the achievement of true identity, see Lavecchia 2006, 236–249; and Gutiérrez 2012. The end point of the ascent from the cave is, of course, the vision of the Idea of the Good. Without self-knowledge, one cannot know what is really good for oneself. And what is really good for oneself is identical with that which is the Good. This conclusion only appears empty if the Good is not identified with the One and one's real good is "becoming one out of many" in accord with one's nature. Also see Lavecchia 2006, 179–183; and Luchetti 2014, 460–461. We have already seen that integrative unity is provided by the Good at *Phd.* 99C5–6. Also see *Rep.* 422E–423B on the geographical requirements for the unity of the ideal city and *Lg.* 739D on the unity of the state as a desideratum.

45. *Rep.* 589A7–B1. Hitchcock (1982, 76) finds the integrative unity in the "consistency in thought and desire."

46. See the argument with Thrasymachus in *Republic* and Callicles in *Gorgias* both of whom are forced to admit that it is possible that what is good for someone can be other than what that person thinks is good for him at any moment. The path from subjectivity to objectivity is much more easily trodden that the path from objectivity to universality. This is evident in the decades-long education of the philosopher-rulers.

extensionally equivalent to what is good simpliciter is the universality of goodness established. This is found only in the superordinate Idea of the Good which is revealed to us according to the threefold criterion of beauty, truth, and commensurability. These are aspects of integrative unity. For all we know, prudentialism was the view of the historical Socrates. There is no evidence, however, that it was ever Plato's view or the view of his literary character Socrates. In all likelihood, Plato opposed prudentialism beginning early on in his philosophical career.

The argument for the universality of goodness whose content is integrative unity seems to be easily countered by one who insists that the recognition of objectivity does not conduce to universality because what is objectively good for oneself is uniquely so. That is, there is no intelligible object available in the search for the objective referent. One cannot look to the Form of Human Being (which is Good-like because it partakes of the Idea of the Good) in order to determine what is objectively good for oneself. Hence, universality is blocked. The appearance-reality distinction is reflected in and only in the subjective-objective distinction.

This is an entirely different sort of objection, one that is in line with the tenets of Naturalism. Even if one were to concede that it is possible to arrive at correct conclusions about what is good for oneself from empirical generalizations about what works for others, one would still face the problem of the scope of the term "others." It cannot be the natural kind, since there are no such things. Objectivity joins with nominalism to atomize the normative. Moral prescriptions would be as individualized as genetic-based medicine. Does Plato have any systematic resources to meet this sort of objection? Many scholars have thought that Plato has such resources, whether his own or in the guise of Socratic ethics and moral psychology.[47] But in no sense do these require any appeal to a superordinate Idea of the Good.

6.3. Platonic Ethics without the Idea of the Good

Since almost all discussions of Platonic ethics in the contemporary scholarship ignore the Idea of the Good as irrelevant, it will be helpful to see why this is a mistake or, more precisely, why to exclude the Idea of the Good is to make a nonnaturalistic ethics impossible.[48] Recall, first, that Plato has said that the subject matter of philosophy is the intelligible world broadly

---

47. A good example of this way of approaching Platonic ethics is Kamtekar 2017.
48. Cf. Annas (1999, 102), who says that "it is unpromising to look in the *Republic* for a direct way in which [the theory of Forms] has impact on the content of the dialogue's moral theory." Annas (108), following Irwin, thinks that the Idea of the Good is just the "ordered structure of the realm of Forms." She goes on to argue (115) that Plato is confused if he thinks that "ethical conclusions can be obtained from metaphysical premises." This is indeed what Plato thinks, but it is not a confusion, for it is the only way that universal ethical conclusions can be derived. The normativity is found in the interstice between endowment and achievement

speaking. He has also maintained that the determination of what is good and bad, right and wrong is a philosophical matter. Plato thinks that the Naturalist, whether as relativist or hedonist, does not have the resources to defend a coherent position about these. For on Naturalistic terms, they have the resources only to express what is ἴδιος, not what is κοινός, whereas what is really good belongs to the latter not the former.

Discussions of Plato's ethics typically either invoke the coordinate Form of the Good as the basis for a claim that virtues are good or else they eschew any appeal to metaphysics altogether. The latter alternative has its roots in a strategy first to set apart a Socratic nonmetaphysical ethical doctrine.[49] Then, with this in place, the manifestly metaphysical framework for ethics in the so-called Platonic (as opposed to Socratic) dialogues can be ignored as irrelevant or unnecessary for the ethical doctrine. On the former alternative, a coordinate Form of the Good serves as the anchor for the general argument: everyone desires the real good; the virtues are the real good; therefore, everyone desires the virtues. Since it is obviously the case that many people do not desire to be virtuous, it is concluded that this must be a failure of knowledge. If one knew that the virtues were the real good, then one would desire them. It is not clear, though, whether, say, the knowledge of Justice or the ability to give a λόγος of Justice is supposed to suffice for knowing that Justice is good or that knowing that Justice is good is supposed to be an additional piece of knowledge.[50] For someone who wants to be just, knowing what Justice is would seem to suffice; however, for someone who has no particular inclination to being just, knowing what Justice is in itself could not motivate just behavior, even granting that one desires the real good for oneself.

The nexus virtue-knowledge-happiness or the human good is the focus of most studies of Plato's ethics. The relation between virtue and knowledge and the relation between virtue and happiness are central. It is within this nexus that the so-called Socratic paradoxes are critically examined.[51] Thus, the claims that it is better to suffer than to do evil, that a bad person is worse off if he is not punished than if he is, that no one does wrong willingly, that tyrants do what seems best to them but not what they want, and that a worse person cannot harm a better person are analyzed in order to

---

where achievement is articulatable as integrative unity expressed in terms of beauty, truth, and commensurability all of which are determinable by unencumbered reason.

49. See, e.g., Santas 1979; Vlastos 1991; Penner 2003; Penner and Rowe 2005; and Rowe 2007.

50. See *Rep.* 505A1–4 where Socrates says that it is the Idea of the Good that makes just things useful and beneficial. Usefulness and benefit are among the things assumed to be unqualifiedly good. Cf. 367C6–D3. As Socrates will go on to explain, however, we cannot know what Justice is unless and until we connect it with the superordinate Idea of the Good.

51. See O'Brien 2005, chap. 1, and Santas 1979, chap. 6, for helpful introductions to the paradoxes.

reveal the assumptions according to which these claims would be true, even if paradoxical. Thus, a typical analysis of the paradoxes would aim to show that virtue is necessary and sufficient for happiness and accordingly that vicious behavior cannot make one happy.[52] The evildoer cannot be better off than the one who suffers evil; a bad person unpunished is deprived of the possibility of rehabilitation in virtue; wrongdoing is exclusively the result of lack of knowledge of virtue; a tyrant is ignorant that wrongdoing is conducive to happiness; and a virtuous person is somehow impervious to the intended harm inflicted upon him by a vicious person.

Such an analysis depends on a certain understanding of virtue. As we saw above, Plato thought that there is a considerable difference between virtue with and without philosophy. The difference is evident in the fact that someone who is virtuous without philosophy is not completely happy. And insofar as he is not happy, then it is not clear why such a person would be better off suffering rather than doing evil or why he would not be better off going unpunished for an occasional bad deed or why the knowledge that he must have if he is virtuous is not sufficient to prevent him from wrongdoing.

Those who are committed to staying within the ambit of the paradoxes and who simultaneously eschew any recourse to the superordinate Idea of the Good should be troubled. For though they can agree that philosophy does transform ordinary virtue into something else and that it is only this something else that is the foundation for the truth of the paradoxes, this conception of philosophy must necessarily exclude what Plato says philosophy is in *Republic*, the desire for knowledge of perfect Being, knowledge which, as he then tells us, is only possible in light of the superordinate Idea of the Good.

There are perhaps two possible paths that one can take in order to integrate philosophy into the account of virtue such that virtue remains necessary and sufficient for happiness and the paradoxes can be defended on that basis. One path takes philosophy as refutation in the manner of Socratic elenchus. According to this, one embraces one's own ignorance or at least is continuously open to refutation of any claim. But this stance cannot be what turns mere popular virtue into true virtue.[53] The unnamed virtuous individual in *Republic* 10 discussed above chooses the life of a tyrant

---

52. Whether or not virtue is in fact held by Plato to be sufficient for happiness has been doubted since virtue alone does not preclude bad luck and bad luck may inhibit the attainment of happiness. See *Ap.* 30C6–D5, 41C8–D2; *Cr.* 48B8–9; and *Charm.* 173D3–5, 174B11–C3 for evidence of the sufficiency thesis. See Irwin 1995, 58–60, 236–237, for the suggestion that even if virtue is not sufficient for happiness, it contributes to happiness more than anything else. This issue does not affect the present discussion.

53. See Sedley (2013, 82–84), who argues that it is the purificatory virtues of *Phaedo* not the popular and political virtues that are within the purview of philosophy. The popular and political virtues are those defined at the end of book 4 of *Republic*; the purificatory virtues are

because there is something he is ignorant of not because there is something he believes he knows that in fact he does not. There is no indication that he embraces the wicked life for any reason other than his ignorance of the ineluctably bad consequences of such a life. But that ignorance is not the so-called Socratic ignorance.

Second, there is the rather weak recourse to philosophy as an examination of life, the soul-care Socrates pronounces himself devoted to in *Apology*.[54] But soul-care in itself is highly problematic as a basis for defending the paradoxes and the absolutism of Platonic ethics. For someone might well acknowledge the desirability of soul-care at the same time as they are insisting on the necessity of body-care. Given a devotion to both, circumstances could well indicate attention to one rather than the other. For example, Socrates might be well advised to flee from prison on behalf of body-care, even if he thereby neglects soul-care temporarily.

In order to make soul-care robust enough to be the substance of the philosophy that turns ordinary virtue into the virtue that is sufficient and necessary for happiness, one would need to argue that soul-care alone is self-care, that is, that the soul is the self.[55] On this basis, one could argue that body-care is only care for one's possession and care for one's possession over care for oneself is never a rational strategy. This may well be the case, but it is disingenuous to claim that body-care is care for a possession like the "externals" that one may possess. For though it may be that caring for one's fingernails as opposed to one's soul is indefensible, the situations in which body-care and soul-care are in tension are those in which the subject of bodily states and the subject of nonbodily states conflict. The most obvious examples in the dialogues are those in which one is faced with a choice between pursuing appetites and refraining from their pursuit because one believes their pursuit would be harmful. Since the subject of the appetites is, according to Plato, a psychical subject, the conflict is not between soul-care and body-care, but between care for one part of the soul as opposed to another. It is mere rhetoric to suppose that this is a choice which is always obvious.[56] One can easily imagine a Callicles endorsing the

---

those belonging to the philosopher who has seen the Idea of the Good and how the Forms are derived from this.

54. See, e.g., Penner 1992, 134–137; Brickhouse and Smith 1994, chap. 4; and Brickhouse and Smith 2010, 44–49.

55. See Gerson 2003, chap. 1. A calculation of the relative value to oneself of soul-care vs. body-care is occluded or even made impossible by the division of the subjects of each. Who decides between the subject of the bodily states and the subject of the psychic states? Only if the subject of the latter is the true self does measurement of comparative value become perspicuous.

56. See Vlastos (1971, 5–6), who proclaims, "If you have just one day to live, and can expect nothing but a blank after that, Socrates feels that you would still have all the reason you need for improving your soul; you would have yourself to live with that one day, so why live with a worse self, if you could live with a better one instead?" The texts Vlastos cites on behalf of this

desirability of soul-care so long as it does not conflict with the duties of a grown-up Athenian citizen.⁵⁷

The implausibility of both of these interpretations of the philosophy required for happiness diminishes even further in light of Plato's unambiguous description of the nature of philosophy in *Republic*. Someone devoted to philosophy seeks knowledge of τὸ παντελῶς ὄν. But Plato also tells us that this knowledge depends upon a cognitive assent to the Idea of the Good. Therefore, it is puzzling to say the least how we are to arrive at a non-question-begging, nonprudential defense of the Socratic paradoxes without recourse to metaphysics, specifically to the first principle of all. In other words, the alternatives are a question-begging response to Naturalism or Plato's systematic metaphysics.

6.4. The Good, Ethical Prescriptions, and Integrative Unity

From the above, it would be easy to conclude that if Plato's ethics does indeed rest on the metaphysical first principle of all, it either proves too much or, what amounts to the same thing, it proves nothing at all. Let there be a superordinate Idea of the Good such that everything that can be said to have "good" predicated of it does so because it partakes indirectly or directly of the Good. If just acts are good because just acts instantiate Justice and Justice partakes of the Good or is Good-like, this does not even begin to tell us whether a contentious ethical or political or social act is just or not. If, to take another example, Euthyphro agrees that piety is good ultimately because of the Idea of the Good and the Form of Piety, how does that concession help us to know whether prosecuting his father for the homicide of a slave is pious or not? This problem remains, of course, even when we have agreed that "good" and "good for me" are identical or at least extensionally equivalent. The problem also remains even if we imagine Socrates to have at his disposal a λόγος of Piety and a willingness to share this with Euthyphro, and even if we imagine that Euthyphro is disposed to take this λόγος as more than empty words.

I believe that the answer to this question rests entirely on understanding goodness as integrative unity. That is, something is good insofar as or

---

view (*Ap.* 28B5–6, 28D6–10; and *Cr.* 48C6–D5) do support the thesis of what Vlastos calls "the sovereignty of virtue," but they do not reveal, nor does Vlastos try to explain, why one should be absolutely devoted to the sovereignty of virtue as opposed to maintaining that on occasion this sovereignty is defeasible.

57. See *Gorg.* 484C4–E3. At *Tim.* 88A9–B2, Plato has Timaeus say that human beings have two sorts of desire, one owing to embodiment and one of the divine or immortal part of the soul. Thus, the human being is a bifurcated subject. Psychical conflict pertains to these two subjects, both of which are rational subjects, though the rationality of the former is occluded by embodiment.

to the extent that it is an integrative unity.[58] Every Form is an integrative unity by definition because it is an eternal and unchangeable one apt for integrating its sensible instances, that is, making each one instance of the Form. But the integrated unities of these instances are necessarily more complicated because Forms are manifested in things that "are and are not simultaneously." In addition, since Forms can be variously manifested, the integrated unity of a just act, a just person, a just city, and a just law may all be manifested differently. To say this is only to elucidate the obvious point in *Symposium* that a beautiful body and a beautiful institution both manifest Beauty but they do not do so in the same way. As a first attempt at understanding how integrated unity provides a criterion for ethical prescriptions, the proper question would be: Does this action or policy arise from or contribute to the integrative unity of the natural kind to which it is attached? For example, the polis is, according to Plato, an integrated unity when all the essential parts are doing their job.[59] So social or political policies can be judged if they arise from the actions of the legislators, doing their job of conserving the unity of the polis, or if they arise as attempts by the legislators to repair or preserve that unity. A similar account would apply to the actions of the virtuous individual. In the case of both, the integrative unity entails the rule of reason for the benefit of the whole polis or the whole individual human being. It is reason in the soul or reason in the person of the rulers that unifies or integrates all the parts optimally. As we have seen, cognition is, generally, a unifying activity.[60] The possibility of suboptimal unification having as its terminus disintegration provides us with a hierarchical axis on the basis of which we can make moral and political judgments.[61] The more unity according to kind the better; the less unity the worse. Further, an integrative unity

---

58. See *Rep.* 422E–423B, 462A–B, where it is clear that the difference between a successful or good state and a bad one is the presence or absence of integrative unity. Also cf. *Symp.* 192C–D on love as integrative unity. See Aristotle, *EE* A 8, 1218a19, discussing the Good, on justice and health as τάξεις. See C. Moore (2015, 193–196), who understands integrative unity as "self-constitution." This, roughly, is the way that Plotinus understands it. See *Enn.* 5.8 [31], 13.20; 6.6 [34], 1.10–14; 6.9 [9], 9.11–13.

59. See *Rep.* 423B9–10, D4–6; 551D5–7. See Pradeau 1997, chap. 2.

60. See Chap. 4, secs. 4 and 5. At *Phil.* 16Cff., in the example of literacy, it is especially clear that the ability to read is a unificatory skill, a skill in which all the letters of the alphabet are unified cognitively into various λόγοι.

61. The taxonomy of decay both in individuals and in states in books 8 and 9 of *Republic* makes it evident that integrative unity is gradable with the absolutely unified at one end and the absolutely disunified at the other. This is intraspecific unity, so to speak, a scale of better or worse people or states. But Plato also sets forth the metaphysical foundation for interspecific unity such that we can say that the optimal integrative unity of a human being is better (that is, closer to the One) than the integrative unity of another animal and worse than the integrative unity of a god and also that the integrative unity of the immortal soul that each person is is better than the integrative unity of a human being.

with fewer parts to integrate is closer to the paradigm than one with more parts to integrate.[62]

Rationality has a unifying effect on the nonrational and the soul has a unifying effect on the body. In general, form unifies the formless; limit unifies the unlimited. What drives the idea of *integrative* unity is the imposition of unity by a higher function on a lower without the elimination of the latter. Thus, for example, rationality normally orders the appetites without extirpating them. But when appetites begin to be extirpated, one approaches disintegration of the composite that generates appetites. Philosophy is "practice for dying and for being dead" precisely because the identification of the self with one's intellect has as a necessary consequence alienation from the appetites. It is not just that philosophy has a proprietary subject matter but that acquiring knowledge of this subject matter, that is, achieving cognitive identity with it, is "assimilation to the divine" by advancing to a higher integrative unity.

The rule of reason in the virtuous individual is established in book 4 of *Republic* with the definition of the virtues. But the rule of reason there described, although it produces virtue does not produce virtue with philosophy, which is not even thematized until book 5. Book 4 establishes the integrative unity of the human being; not until book 9 do we arrive at the integrated unity of the philosopher. This is a higher unity since it achieves separation from the body, separation in the sense of psychological distancing or alienation. Living thus according to the rule of reason is to become detached—or as much as is physically possible to be detached—from the idiosyncratic, that which is ἴδιος. Adhering to the deliverances of universal reasoning, the identity of "good" and "good for me" becomes as obvious as the identity of "true" and "true for me."

It is not, I think, a serious criticism of this interpretation to say that it leaves many or perhaps even most actions and states below the threshold of relevance to integrative unity. There will be many actions that, as the Stoics insisted, will be indifferent. But the absolutism that Socrates insisted on in *Crito*, namely, that one must never under any circumstances commit an unjust deed, thinking that it is unjust, remains and is clarified. For to do that, is to be oriented to self-disintegration. And there can be no scenario under which one could benefit from this. We can, though, readily concede that this claim would make no sense unless the soul were the self and the soul were immortal. An integrative unity unlocatable within Plato's metaphysical hierarchy cannot be claimed to be universally desirable. Everyone has his or her own way of unifying their lives or of constructing an integrative self-narrative. The privileging of one of these over another depends entirely on a hierarchy with the superordinate Idea of the Good at the top. One life

---

62. "Parts" here being understood as extended parts. An organic individual may have more parts than an inorganic individual, but his psychical integration involves no extended parts at all.

is better than another life only because it is closer to the Good itself, the absolutely simple first principle of all. "Closer" here, of course, means more of an integrative unity.[63]

An integrative unity is just the product of the imposition of limit on the unlimited as explained in *Philebus*.[64] Normativity enters the picture with the idea of "measure (τὸ μέτρον)" which indicates the correct or exact imposition of mathematical order as opposed to a deviation from this.[65] An optimal integrative unity possesses the correct or exact ordering of the instantiations of the principle of unlimitedness by the instantiations of the principle of limit. The integrative unity of the parts is the best possible instantiation of the paradigm. In *Republic*, we saw that integrative unity of the soul is that of the parts of the soul ordered according to the rule of reason. In *Philebus*, a different question is raised, namely, that of the optimal integrative unity of a human being which, being a complex of soul and body is different from the soul and, ideally, is the subject of the immortal part of the soul. The embodied soul is the subject of both psychical states and acts and the subject of bodily states, including pleasure and pain. And this dialogue raises the very specific question of what constitutes optimal integrative unity for the human being, the locus of multiple states or acts of subjectivity whether these be synchronic or, more typically, diachronic.

The Good is manifested in integrative unity.[66] To put it in Aristotelian terms, integrative unity is the essence of the manifestation of goodness. That is why the principle of limit—not limit itself—is the One and also why it is repeatedly emphasized that the manifestation of the Good for a human being will be in integrative unity. The problem with which *Philebus* wrestles is that, though we are really intellects for whom bodily pleasure is nothing, we are in fact now embodied and embodied souls do desire pleasure. But the strictures that the dialogues discover for pleasure, the distinction between true and false pleasure, is intended to minimize the self-disintegration of the intellect while embodied, thereby impeding its destiny. This desideratum is the basis for the distinction between true and false pleasures.

Built upon this metaphysical foundation, ethical prescriptions can be judged according to whether or not they inhibit or promote integrative

---

63. See *Rep.* 540A9 where the Idea of the Good is appealed to as a "paradigm (παράδειγμα)" for instantiating goodness in actions and in souls. My claim is that the superordinate Good as such cannot be a paradigm; only considered as the principle of integrative unity can it serve this function.

64. *Phil.* 16C9–10, 23C9–10. Hackforth (1945, 41) rightly rejects the identification of limit with the Forms, but he is then thrown into confusion about what the limit is.

65. See *Phil.* 26B10: νόμος καὶ τάξις; 28E3: "διακοσμεῖν; 30C5: κοσμοῦσα τε καὶ συντραττοῦσα; 64B7: κόσμος.

66. It seems obvious that the description of Forms as "units (μονάδες)" at *Phil.* 15B1–2 within the context of the broader metaphysical doctrine of that dialogue is meant to indicate integrative unity. But we recall from *Parmenides* that no Form can be unqualifiedly one; its oneness is derived.

unity. The quantitative nature of the optimal integrative unity renders futile the claim that unlike "true" and "true for me" which are identical, still "good" and "good for me" can diverge. It is, for Plato, a mathematical impossibility that my good can be achieved at your expense even if you or I or anyone else may take it to be so.[67]

It would take us too far afield to explore all the ways that Plato's educational vision depends on the inculcation of integrative unity according to the aspects of beauty, truth, and commensurability. These are all evident in *Republic, Statesman, Timaeus,* and *Laws*.[68] Music, physical training, mathematics, astronomy, and dialectic are concrete ways of achieving the Good, that is, producing an ever greater integrative unity in the human being and, more importantly, in the soul which is identical with the person.

6.5. Eros and the Good

The connection between the Good as principle and the Good as end is made explicitly by Plotinus in one of the most remarkable passages in his *Enneads*: "And it [the Good] is itself an object of love and love, that is, love of itself, inasmuch as it is only beautiful by reason of itself and in itself. And indeed whatever is present to itself would not be so if that which is present and that to which it is present were not one or identical."[69] The three most remarkable features of this passage are (1) that the Good is identified with eros; (2) that unlike other predicates or "names" that are denied of the Good or said to belong to it only "in a way (οἷον)," the Good is unqualified eros; and (3) that the Good is beautiful because it is eros. There is no suggestion here that the identification of the Good with eros insinuates complexity or multiplicity into the Good in any way. It is eros that is supposed to explain how the goal of all striving is identical with the source of all being.

Is this claim a fair inference from what Plato says in the dialogues? There is certainly solid ground for saying that Plato held that (1) all things desire or strive for the Good; (2) eros for possession of the beautiful is identified with the desire for the Good; and (3) the Good is the principle

---

67. See Rist 2002, chap. 2, for an argument that a transcendent metaphysical foundation is necessary for an objective morality both for Plato and in fact.

68. See Miller (1980) 2004, especially the supplementary essay "Dialectical Education and Unwritten Teachings in Plato's *Statesman*" to see integrative unity front and center in its three aspects. Also see Burnyeat 2000.

69. Plotinus, *Enn.* 6.8 [39], 15.1–4: Καὶ ἐράσμιον καὶ ἔρως ὁ αὐτὸς καὶ αὑτοῦ ἔρως, ἅτε οὐκ ἄλλως καλὸς ἢ παρ' αὑτοῦ καὶ ἐν αὑτῷ. Καὶ γὰρ καὶ τὸ συνεῖναι ἑαυτῷ οὐκ ἂν ἄλλως ἔχοι, εἰ μὴ τὸ συνὸν καὶ τὸ ᾧ σύνεστιν ἓν καὶ ταὐτὸν εἴη. Cf. 16.13; 6.7 [37], 22.8–9. See Pigler 2002 for a monograph-length study of 6.8 [39], 15.1–4. Proclus, *In Alc.* 30.16–17, says οὕτω δὴ καὶ ἡ ἐρωτικὴ πᾶσα τάξις ἐπιστροφῆς ἐστὶν αἰτία τοῖς οὖσιν ἅπασι πρὸς τὸ θεῖον κάλλος (in this way, the entire class of erotic desires is the explanation for reversion in all beings toward the divine beauty).

of all things.⁷⁰ Therefore, everything desires that from which it comes in some sense. The problem with Plotinus's expression of this doctrine resides in the identification of the Good with eros. But the account of eros in *Symposium* and Plotinus's commentary on that dialogue acknowledge and expatiate upon the relative defectiveness of eros, its lacking that which it aims to possess.⁷¹ How can it serve to characterize the unqualifiedly nondefective first principle?

A facile first step in the direction of an answer is that since the Good is virtually all that it produces, it must be virtually eros.⁷² This point does not, however, speak to the centrality of eros in the overall metaphysical construct that is Platonism. The Good, as Plotinus says, is also eros of itself. That is, the Good is essentially an activity of self-loving. But the Good, as Plato says, is overflowing.⁷³ Therefore, this self-loving is essentially productive. That is why, at the apex of the ascent of the philosopher in the higher mysteries in *Symposium*, the achievement of the Good necessarily and spontaneously produces true virtue in the aspirant.⁷⁴ True virtue, that is, not popular or political virtue. This is because the achievement of the Good, in the only way that achievement is possible for us, by cognition of all that is intelligible, produces just what the Good itself produces. This is what happens when philosophy is added to mere popular virtue. It is also why Socrates's maieutic activity can be said to be self-motivated.

And it is why Vlastos was so far wrong in maintaining that Plato's theory of the erotic was a failure because it cannot endorse the love of whole persons over the love of Ideas.⁷⁵ The individual as initial love-object is indeed seen only as an image of the really real. For Plato, to say anything else would simply be untrue. But love for persons in the sense in which Vlastos, I think, meant it, is the result of attaining the Good. This does not mean, of course, that only the successful philosopher can love persons. It does mean, though, that love for persons is gradable according to the extent that Goodness is instantiated in the life of the lover. If the Good is essentially overflowing, wherever and however the Good is present, there is overflowing, too.⁷⁶ If the Good were not eros itself, the presence of eros in everything else would not be a desire for the Good but for something else. And in that case,

---

70. For (1) see *Rep.* 505D5–506A2 (chap. 5, sec. 5.1, 5); for (2) see *Symp.* 204D–206B, esp. 204E1; for (3) see *Rep.* 516C1–2 (chap. 5, sec. 5.1, 10).

71. At *Symp.* 202D13, we learn that Eros is a daimon, whose status as *intermediary* is certain, regardless of how exactly that is so. A first principle of all cannot conceivably be an intermediary.

72. See *Rep.* 509B9–10 (chap. 5, sec. 5.1, 8).

73. See *Rep.* 506E3, 508B6–7 (chap. 5, sec. 5.1, 3).

74. See *Symp.* 212A.

75. See Vlastos 1973, 30–31.

76. So the Demiurge creates because he is good. See *Tim.* 29E1–2, 42E5–6. Plotinus, *Enn.* 4.8 [6] 6, 6–16; 5.4 [7] 1, 34–36.

it would be false to maintain that what everyone wants without exception is the Good. It is not, for Plato, paradoxical to say: eros for the beautiful is eros for the Good which we do not possess; but in possessing the Good, or to the extent that we possess it, we possess eros itself.[77]

I take it as a strength of the above interpretation that the integrative unificatory process of cognition, whether of contingent or necessary truths, mirrors the dynamic integrative unificatory process that is the desire for the Good.[78] Aristotle's statement that the ultimate object of desire (ὀρεκτόν) and the ultimate object of thinking (νοητόν) are identical is precisely the Platonic point.[79] That is why the Good is the One. All beings desire the Good and so strive for integrated unity. For human beings, this is generally true, too. But as subjects uniquely capable of higher cognition, there is a twofold striving for integrated unity. The first is to identify with our intellects and the second is to strive for knowledge, cognitive identity with all that is intelligible. That is how an intellect achieves the Good.

The above may provide a suitable background to appreciate why later Platonists, intensely conscious of the connection between the Good as principle and the Good as goal, took as emblematic of Platonism the famous exhortation in the "digression" in Plato's *Theaetetus*. Socrates's counsel to "assimilate to the divine as much as possible (ὁμοίωσις θεῷ κατὰ τὸ δυνατόν)" has disconcerted Plato scholars for a variety of reasons.[80] Not the least of these is that it does not seem possible for a mortal to assimilate himself to that which is immortal.[81] This is particularly the case because the method of assimilation is said to be virtue, whereas the divine is in no need of virtue. Even the addition of wisdom does not turn human wisdom into divine wisdom.

Given the above, the ascent to the Good should be understood as the reversion of the effect to its cause. Expressed systematically, the fundamental dynamic structure of the universe is "remaining (μονή)," "procession (πρόοδος)," and "reversion (ἐπιστροφή)." The most extensive treatment of

---

77. As Proclus remarks in his *In Alc.* 30, 16–17, the fact that everything is charged with eroticism is the explanation for the reversion of all things to the divine. Cf. 52, 10–12; and 141, 1–5. See Vasilakis 2017 for further apt remarks on the identification of the Good with eros.

78. See Halfwassen 1992a, 226–236, esp. 229, and Desjardins 2004, 64, on cognition as a unificatory process as reflected in the stages of the Divided Line. The μέγιστον μάθημα of the Good (as One) is both the presupposition and the culmination of this process.

79. Aristotle, *Meta.* Λ 7, 1072a25–26.

80. See *Tht.* 176B1. Cf. *Rep.* 613B1; and *Tim.* 90D. See Lavecchia 2006 for a comprehensive survey of the Platonic treatment of this exhortation. It has exceedingly disconcerted Peterson (2011, 59–89), who finds the exhortation to assimilation to the divine so absurd that she refuses to believe that this was Plato's view.

81. Given what is said at *Phdr.* 245C5–246A2, the soul is immortal because it is a self-mover. And that which is immortal is divine. So the task of assimilation is to *recognize* one's own immortality, hence one's own divinity.

this structure is found in Proclus's *Elements of Theology*.⁸² As we have seen, procession and reversion are grounded in the overflowing of the Good and the desire of all things for the Good, that from which they originate. Remaining is based on the text in *Timaeus* in which it is said that the Demiurge "remained in himself in his accustomed manner (ἔμενεν ἐν τῷ ἑαυτοῦ κατὰ τρόπον ἤθει)" while ordering the cosmos.⁸³ The structure is dynamic owing to the essential activity of the first principle of all. The dynamism does not result ultimately in dissolution because reversion is guaranteed by the remaining and the procession. It is so guaranteed because the procession is from the self-loving first principle. If its self-loving were a property of it, that is, if it were distinct from its self-loving, then procession from it would not produce eros in everything else. Procession, if it is to be part of a system, must be from the essence of that which proceeds.

This dynamic structure, it will be recalled, is primarily eternal. In the eternal realm, procession and reversion are no less eternal than the remaining of the Good. Because the temporalized cosmos is an image of this eternal dynamic structure, it represents it imperfectly. Thus, in all erotic activity the relation between eternal intellect and the Good is recapitulated in a diminished way. That is, the lover satisfies his desire for the Good by achieving the fulfillment of his own nature as intellect. Beauty is the Good as attractive. But the intellects of embodied human beings are the intellects of temporalized souls. The desires of embodied souls are themselves images of intellectual desire. The reversion of all embodied souls to the Good is, in one sense, a quest for the unknown. But no one seeks for that which is completely unknown, a point made in a limited and focused manner in Meno's paradox. The quest for the unknown is a reversion because it is a quest to return to the source of one's own being. The soul that reverts is engaged in an attempt to recover itself as it is found in its cause.

The reversion to the Good is the metaphysical foundation of the passage in the *Republic* previously quoted, where Socrates asserts that, though people are content with the seeming just or beautiful, no one is content with the seeming good.⁸⁴ Platonists connect this passage with the numerous passages, also mentioned above, in which Plato says that no one willingly does

---

82. See Proclus, *ET* Props. 25–39. There is a good concise exposition in Chlup 2012, 64–69. Also see Gersh 1973, 49–53. I discuss this further in chap. 9.

83. See *Tim.* 42E5–6. The point of the imperfect, as Archer-Hind (1888, 147) and A. E. Taylor (1928, 266) note, is that both before and after ordering the cosmos, the Demiurge abided in his eternal customary state. Presumably, this is the state of contemplation of the Living Animal with which the Demiurge is cognitively identical. Broadie (2012, 23) seems to concur. Cf. Plotinus, *Enn.* 3.8 [30], 10.5–10, where remaining is paradigmatically in the One or Good. Cf. 4.8 [6], 6.1–18; 5.1 [10], 3.11–15, 6.27–30; 5.2 [11], 1.7–21; 5.5 [32], 12.40–49. Also see Proclus, *In Tim.* 1.282, 26–31.

84. *Rep.* 505D5–9.

wrong.⁸⁵ Plato does not ever say, however, and he certainly does not mean to imply by this, that no one willingly does right either. On the contrary, our freedom is found entirely and exclusively in our pursuing the Good. The asymmetry underlying this theory of action is anathema to any Naturalist since the Naturalistic explanations for action cannot discriminate between those that are oriented to the good—whatever that means—and those that are oriented to the bad. Indeed, a Peripatetic such as Alexander of Aphrodisias, counters the Stoic compatibilist position by insisting that only if we are free to choose contraries ("to do otherwise") are we free at all.⁸⁶ There are few things that more vividly express the systematic nature of Platonism than the asymmetry of human action which is only explicable if there is a distinction between the real good and the apparent good and if the real good is universal. For if the real good is only objective for each individual and not universal, there is no way to maintain asymmetry. For in that case, every action will have as its goal the apparent (objective) good. It cannot be the case that we are free when we do what we think is good for ourselves and not free when we do what we think is good for ourselves even though objectively it is not. This is so because the difference between the two cases is something that is external to the psychology of the agent.⁸⁷ Without the universal Good, we have no grounds to resist symmetry, whether it be that of the Naturalist or that of the Peripatetic.

If "what is up to us" is limited to the pursuit of what we are hardwired to pursue, the real Good, how does this differ from determinism? After all, the metaphor of being hardwired, representing genetic evolution instead of ontological necessity, is music to the Naturalist's ears. But whereas the Naturalist claims that we are hardwired to do what we do even when what we do is bad, Plato claims that being hardwired to pursue the Good does not eliminate our moral responsibility when we do bad.⁸⁸ The answer to this question is not thematized by Plato, though both Plotinus and Proclus take it up. It is possible, however, to get a glimpse of how Plato's solution would go. First, begin with the fact that, though we all desire the real Good, we can only pursue what appears to us to be the Good, whether it is in fact so or not. But whether or not things appear to us to be good is as much a function of our desires as it is of our intellects. The differences among the virtuous, the encratic, the akratic, and the vicious, are precisely gradable according to desire: the virtuous does not have the desire for what is bad,

---

85. See, e.g., Plotinus, 3.1 [3], 9.4–16.
86. See Alexander of Aphrodisias, *De fato* 169, 13–15; 181, 12–14; 196, 24–25; 199, 8–9; 211, 21–23.
87. See Aristotle, who assumes that the distinction between the apparent and real good is external to the account of the action, which is always for the apparent good. *Top.* Z 8, 146b36–147a11; *Phys.* B 3, 195a23–36; *DA* Γ 10, 433a27; *Rhet.* A 10, 1369a2–4.
88. See *Rep.* 617E5: θεὸς ἀναίτιος (god is not responsible). That is, god is not responsible for our wrongdoing.

the encratic has it but does not act on it, the akratic has it and acts on it with regret, and the vicious has it and acts on it without regret. These desires, however, are not accurately characterizable as "irrational" except in the very special sense that they are counter to normative rationality. As Plato says in *Republic*, a paradigmatic case of the appetitive desire, usually assumed to be irrational, is the love of money, something which is meaningless for any being that is not rational.[89]

Leaving aside the implication of degrees of moral responsibility in the above typology, moral responsibility in general for doing that which we do not will ("no one does wrong willingly") rests with the misuse of reason, not its failure to operate altogether.[90] The misuse of reason consists, I think, in its employment in the service of the appetites while implicitly acknowledging reason's sovereignty. Thus, someone who pursues money immoderately has used her reason to arrive at the self-exhortation to make that pursuit. She has done so by acknowledging the authority of reason to make that determination. But it is incoherent—culpably so, for Plato—to make this acknowledgment at the same time as the rational soul subordinates itself to appetite. Plainly, this admits of degree and there is no doubt an element of mauvaise foi in every such deviant decision or act. Even if the decision or act is not willed because the goal is not really good, it is willed as what appears to be good. And this willing amounts to the delegation of one's true self to its deviant simulacrum, the ephemeral subject of the appetite. Or it is not, when what appears to be good is so in fact. We cannot but bear some moral responsibility for whatever degree of integrative unity we achieve since the achievement is an act of self-reflexive reason. That is, it amounts to self-recognition or self-identification, something that only an intellect can do by and to itself. When I look for the real "I," I cannot circumvent the intellect that is doing the looking. For Plato, the ultimate or real subject of thinking is an intellect.

Here again, we can see the appropriateness of the identification of the Good with the One. For reversions here below are, as Plato repeatedly implies, attempts at integrative unity. When the virtuous person "becomes one out of many," he is engaged in reversion to the One.[91] Integrative unity is

---

89. See *Rep.* 553C5, 580E5, 581A6.

90. *Tim.* 86B–87C is the most important text here. This entire passage can be read as arguing that since no one does wrong willingly, then no one is responsible for doing bad. But Plato says (87 B4–5), that if children are exonerated owing to their bad upbringing, the parents should be held responsible (αἰτιατέον) presumably, even if *they* had bad upbringings. The puzzle is resolved when we realize that Plato is implicitly distinguishing children who have not yet attained the age of reason and everyone else. It is owing to a bad upbringing or to disease, that moral responsibility may be mitigated, though for the most part not entirely eliminated. As Plato says in the next line, "A human being ought to strive, to the extent that he is able, by means of education, practices and studies, to escape from evil and to seize on the contrary."

91. See *Rep.* 443E1. Adam (1921, vol. 1, ad loc.) notes that the phrase "one out of many (εἶς ἐκ πολλῶν)" is a sort of "Platonic motto." Cf. 423D3–6, applying both to the individual and

the criterion of normativity. It can only be such if unity is the source of the beings whose fulfillment normativity is supposed to govern. As we have seen, the source cannot be integrative unity, but rather its principle, unqualified unity, that which is absolutely simple or incomposite. The array of potentially integrated unities is an expression of the eternal possibilities found in the intelligible world. Without the identity of principle and goal, and without their further identification as a uniquely simple activity, Platonic ethics becomes simply question-begging whether this be encapsulated in the Socratic paradoxes or in any other bit of high-minded rhetoric. That is what Naturalists can plainly see. The positing of an absolutely simple first principle of all, variously named "Good" and "One," and the articulation of this metaphysics in terms of remaining, procession, and reversion is no doubt a major stumbling block for anyone who recoils from Naturalism or even questions it. As I have tried to show, however, nothing short of this can provide a coherent alternative to Naturalism.

The structural dynamic of the Platonic system is manifested in the principles of remaining, procession, and reversion. The cornerstone of the structure or system is the One as source; it is the Good as goal. Integrative unity provides the metric for evaluation or normativity. This systematic framework is the source of explanatory adequacy over against the hypotheses of Naturalism. I have been arguing that Plato's explicit rejection of nominalism, materialism, mechanism, relativism, and skepticism can most fruitfully be seen against the background that is this systematic framework. When this systematic framework is ignored or misunderstood, it is hardly surprising that Plato's arguments against the elements of Naturalism will be seen as disjointed, ineffective, or at best inconclusive.

---

to the city, and 462A2–B3, where something is made as good as possible by being made one. See Plotinus, *Enn.* 6.9 [9], 3; Proclus, *In Parm.* 7.74.3ff. Klibansky. In both these extended accounts of ascent to the first principle we see the focus on intellectual activity as essential for the integrative unity of rational animals.

Part 2

The Platonic Project

CHAPTER 7

Aristotle the Platonist

7.1. Introduction

In the first part of this work, I have tried to sketch out the Platonic system, largely as this is found in the dialogues, supplemented by Aristotle's testimony. I have argued that Plato does indeed have a system, the fundamental principle of which is the Idea of the Good or the One. It is this principle that unifies the elements of what I have characterized as Plato's anti-Naturalism, his rejection of nominalism, materialism, mechanism, skepticism, and relativism. Without the first principle of all as the starting point of Plato's explanatory framework, his explicit opposition to the elements of Naturalism may well appear ad hoc at best. The elements of his anti-Naturalism are, as I have tried to show, mutually supporting; in addition, all these elements support and are supported by the postulation of a first principle of all within the explanatory framework.

This description of Platonism no doubt will appear to many as unduly austere. For example, I leave out the immortality of the soul which Cornford once called one of the "pillars" of Platonism. I do this quite deliberately, but not because I think for one moment that Plato did not believe in the immortality of the soul or that he did not put the greatest importance on the truth of this belief. Indeed, it would be hard to find soi-disant Platonists in antiquity who did not share this belief. But whereas the principles of Platonism certainly allow for the possibility of the soul's immortality, they do not logically require it.[1] It is for this reason that, among Platonists, there

---

1. The possibility of ἐπιστήμη entails the immateriality of intellect, but not the immortality of the soul and certainly not personal immortality.

are markedly different accounts of the immortality of the soul and of its moral and epistemological relevance. One reason why readers of ancient philosophy resist the idea that Aristotle was a Platonist in the sense sketched out above is that, whereas Plato believed in the immortality of the soul, Aristotle did not. Yet Aristotle plainly believed in the immortality of intellect. And it is not at all clear that Plato's "immortal part of the soul" in *Timaeus* is anything other than this. Still, we may insist that there are differences between the "immortal part of the soul" in Plato and "immortal intellect" in Aristotle especially with regard to the question of whether soul or intellect is personal or not. Since I maintain that Aristotle was a Platonist, I see these differences, if there be such, as part of a dispute *among* Platonists, a dispute arising precisely because Platonic principles are underdetermining in relation to one account or another of personal immortality. Analogous explanations for differences between Plato and Aristotle and among Platonists generally can be given for matters in moral psychology, politics, art, and so on. And, a fortiori, they can be given for technical questions such as the nature of memory or time.

Platonism dominated Western philosophy more or less from the time of Plato's death until the seventeenth century or, if one is inclined to view revealed theology as muddying of the pure Platonic waters, then at least until the middle of the sixth century. Plato's construction of his systematic philosophy was apparently a project still ongoing at his death. In this chapter and in the following two chapters, I want to focus on what I take to be the stellar contributions of Aristotle, Plato, and Proclus to the completion of the Platonic project. As we shall see, each of these contributed in different ways. In this chapter, I focus on Aristotle. Although it is undeniably true that Aristotle dissented from many claims made by Plato, I am more interested here in the principles he shared with Plato, his arguments for these, and some of the illuminating things he had to say about the application of these principles.[2] Aristotle was as opposed to Naturalism as Plato—as I have characterized it.[3]

7.2. Aristotle on the Subject Matter of Philosophy

Aristotle in *Metaphysics* book E says,

> One might raise the question of whether first philosophy is universal or is concerned merely with some genus and some one nature. In the case of the

---

2. See Owen (1966b, 147–150), who speaks of Aristotle's "[renewed] sympathy with Plato's metaphysical programme" after his initial criticisms. I think that we can express this sympathy more concretely than Owen does: Aristotle rejected Naturalism and embraced a foundational metaphysics focused on an absolutely simple first principle of all.

3. As Richard Rorty insisted, his opposition to Platonism entailed his opposition to Aristotelianism.

mathematical sciences, their objects are not treated in the same manner; geometry and astronomy are concerned with some nature, but universal mathematics is common to all. Accordingly, if there were no substances other than those formed by nature, physics would be the first science; but if there is immovable substance, this would be prior, and the science of it would be first philosophy and would be universal in this manner, in view of the fact that it is first. And it would be the concern of this science, too, to investigate being qua being, both what being is and what belongs to it. (Apostle trans.)[4]

This entire passage is one of the most portentous in the entire Aristotelian corpus, for it seems to be making a programmatic statement about the nature of metaphysics or a science of being qua being.[5] Scholars differ markedly on the question of whether or not this science is to be identified with theology. If it is, then the passage seems to leave unaddressed a truly universal science of being qua being, focusing rather on one specific realm of being, that of the divine or immovable. If the science is not identified with theology, then it is not clear how theology is supposed to be relevant to this science, as this passage clearly asserts it is.

The plain sense of lines 27–29 ("if there were no substances other than . . .") is that if supersensible substance did not exist, then physics would be first science or philosophy. The way this passage is frequently taken is, I maintain, unsupported by the text itself. It is thought that if immaterial or supersensible substances did not exist, then first philosophy, understood as a universal science of being qua being, would still be possible. It is just that the subject matter would be the only things that do exist, namely, sensibles.[6]

---

4. Aristotle, *Meta.* E 1, 1026a23–32: ἀπορήσειε γὰρ ἄν τις πότερόν ποθ' ἡ πρώτη φιλοσοφία καθόλου ἐστὶν ἢ περί τι γένος καὶ φύσιν τινὰ μίαν (οὐ γὰρ ὁ αὐτὸς τρόπος οὐδ' ἐν ταῖς μαθηματικαῖς, ἀλλ' ἡ μὲν γεωμετρία καὶ ἀστρολογία περί τινα φύσιν εἰσίν, ἡ δὲ καθόλου πασῶν κοινή)· εἰ μὲν οὖν μὴ ἔστι τις ἑτέρα οὐσία παρὰ τὰς φύσει συνεστηκυίας, ἡ φυσικὴ ἂν εἴη πρώτη ἐπιστήμη· εἰ δ' ἔστι τις οὐσία ἀκίνητος, αὕτη προτέρα καὶ φιλοσοφία πρώτη, καὶ καθόλου οὕτως ὅτι πρώτη· καὶ περὶ τοῦ ὄντος ᾗ ὂν ταύτης ἂν εἴη θεωρῆσαι, καὶ τί ἐστι καὶ τὰ ὑπάρχοντα ᾗ ὄν. Also see 1026a12–14, which emphatically makes the point that the subject matters of physics and mathematics are not that of being qua being. Cf. K 7, 1064b4–14 which adds the point that the science of being qua being is a different science (ἑτέραν . . . ἐπιστήμην) because there is a different nature for that science to study. Λ 1, 1069a36–b2 is a very difficult and ambiguous text. See Charles and Frede 2000, 70–80. I take the sense of the passage to be that the science of separate substance is different from the science of physics if they do not have a principle in common. But this is so even if it is the case that both sciences do have a principle in common. The common principle, being, is, however, different from the principles of physics itself. So, physics has its own principles but it (like everything else) is included within the science of being qua being though only derivatively.

5. See Berti 2003 and 2015, 115–131, for two concise summaries of most of the modern interpretations of this passage.

6. E.g., Kirwan (1971, 188–189) thinks that Aristotle means that if immovable substances did not exist, then ontology, i.e., the study of being qua being, would be "a *part* of physics" (my italics). There is nothing in the Greek to support this interpretation. Consider the following analogy. If the winner of the race, someone who happens to set a new record, is disqualified,

But Aristotle has just stated in the same chapter what he takes great pains to explain in *Physics*, namely, that physics has as its subject matter a distinct genus, the class of things that have a principle of motion and standstill in themselves.[7] These things all include matter in their definition.[8] Therefore, if immaterial entities did not exist, it is not the case that physics would be metaphysics; rather, the science of nature would be first and there could be no such thing as metaphysics or a science of being qua being. There could only be a science which, as Aristotle says, "cuts off a part of being and studies that" but "does not examine being universally."[9] Primary being excludes matter because it excludes a principle of potency or a principle of change.[10] Accordingly, the next two lines ("but if there is immovable substance . . . And it would be the concern of this science") can only be read to indicate that the science of immovable substances, the science of theology, is identical with the science of being qua being.[11]

This interpretation is resisted on grounds of its supposed implausibility. For if the only being there is is sensible being, how can Aristotle be held to maintain that there can be no science of this, that is, that there can be

---

the runner-up is declared the winner. But the runner-up does not thereby become the new record holder. The ordinality of the sciences (first philosophy, second philosophy) is a question distinct from the cardinality of the number of sciences all, for Aristotle, determined by their distinct subject matter.

7. See *Meta*. E 1, 1025b18–21; K 4, 1061b28–32: τὰ συμβεβηκότα γὰρ ἡ φυσικὴ καὶ τὰς ἀρχὰς θεωρεῖ τὰς τῶν ὄντων ᾗ κινούμενα καὶ οὐχ ᾗ ὄντα (τὴν δὲ πρώτην εἰρήκαμεν ἐπιστήμην τούτων εἶναι καθ' ὅσον ὄντα τὰ ὑποκείμενά ἐστιν, ἀλλ' οὐχ ᾗ ἕτερόν τι) (for physical science investigates the properties and principles of things insofar as they are moving and not insofar as they are beings. But we have said that primary science is concerned with these subjects insofar as they are beings but not insofar as they are something else). Cf. *Phys*. B 1, 192b22 for the definition of nature, the subject of natural science. Also Γ 1, 200b1–3. Aubenque (1972, 37–44) questions the authenticity of book K precisely because it so clearly identifies the primary science, theology, with the science of being qua being. Aubenque (40n4) denies that 1061b28–32 confirms 1026a23–32 because he thinks the latter passage does not identify theology with the science of being qua being, even though theology "touches on" this science.

8. See *Meta*. Z 3, 1029a30–32. Cf. *Phys*. B 2, 194b14–15; and *DA* A 1, 403b15–16.

9. See *Meta*. Γ 1, 1003a21–32. The implication is that no special science studies being qua being. If supersensible substances did not exist, this fact would not change because the nature of each special science would not change. The special science S is determined by its subject matter, not by the existence or nonexistence of something that is precisely not part of that subject matter.

10. See Merlan (1953, 132–165), who provides an extensive argument in support of this interpretation. Merlan was arguing principally against Jaeger (1948, 194–227), who thought that Aristotle had developed away from theology (*metaphysica specialis*) to ontology (*metaphysica generalis*).

11. See the lines above this passage, *Meta*. E 1, 1026a15–19, where the identification of first philosophy with "theological (θεολογική)" science is made explicit. This science is universal because it is first. I suggest that the universality indicates the absolutely unqualified causal scope of the first, just like the unhypothetical first principle in *Republic* which is in a way the cause of all (πάντων) (chap. 5, sec. 5.1, 10). See *Meta*. B 3, 999a20 where καθόλου (universally) is associated with "all" (ἐπὶ πάντων, κατὰ πάντων).

no science distinct from the science of changeable things qua changeable? One way of sharpening this objection is to say that since the proposed universal science of being qua being must, by definition, include sensible being, even if supersensible being did not exist, sensible being would remain to be studied.[12] This objection, however, as we shall see, profoundly misses the point that a universal science of being qua being cannot be universal in the ordinary way, that is, by having as a subject that which is univocally predicable of all the entities that fall under the science. Aristotle argues that the universal science of being qua being is not such a science, that is, it does not study that which all entities falling under it have univocally predicable of them. Therefore, the hypothetical absence of the focus of that science, the primary referent of "being," namely, supersensible substance, leaves what was supposed to be studied in that science as derived from the primary referent without *any* unifying principle. And without a unifying principle, there can be no science at all.[13]

Does the possibility of a science of being qua being really rest on the existence of the Unmoved Mover? Aristotle believes that supersensible or immaterial being exists necessarily, in which case the denial of its existence entails a contradiction. It is precisely because Aristotle identifies the primary referent of "being," the life of the Unmoved Mover, as the subject of first philosophy, that he denies that any other beings could be the subject of first philosophy unless the meaning of "first philosophy" were merely ordinal, so to speak. If being really is what Aristotle says it is, then assuming that this does not exist, the primacy of physics would not turn the science

---

12. See Frede (2000, 8), who argues that what Aristotle means is that since first philosophy is universal, if separate substance did not exist, then physics would be first philosophy and therefore *it* would be universal. In other words, it would deal with everything there is. It is, of course, true that if all there is is sensible substance, then a science that deals with sensible substance deals with everything there is. But a putative science "dealing with everything there is" does not even begin to tell us about the unity of subject matter that this science must have. The unity of the subject matter of physics is clear: it is the changeable qua changeable. Presumably, the unity of a science of being qua being is different. For one thing, a science of being qua being must deal with mathematical objects which are not the subjects of a science of the changeable qua changeable. And how exactly would physics deal with the being of mathematical objects? For another, Aristotle's analysis in book Z of *Metaphysics* results in the conclusion that sensible substances are not the primary referents of "being." This conclusion, along with the previous conclusion that "being" is a πρὸς ἕν equivocal, should lead us to maintain that the unity of the science of being qua being is to be found in the primary referent of "being." Even if separate substance did not exist, the argument for the posteriority of the sensible composite would remain; nothing in that argument requires the assumption of the existence of separate substance.

13. Recall Aristotle's assertion that unity is a principle of knowing, *Meta.* Δ 6, 1016b21–22. Cf. I 1, 1052b31–35, and 1053a31–33. The unity of the subject matter of a science is the unity that is manifested diversely to us in, for example, sensible substances and their accidents which are themselves expressions of species and their commensurately universal properties. The definition or middle term in a first figure syllogism is what unifies the diverse expressions.

of changeable being into the science of being. As we shall see, the Stoics took up the Aristotelian inference and, rejecting the existence of immaterial being, held that physics was first philosophy. But they did not maintain that the science of physics was the science of universal being. Nor, of course, would any Naturalist. That leaves a curious potential no-man's-land for anyone who wants to claim that a science of metaphysics exists but that this science does not have as its object supersensible being for the simple reason that no such thing exists. Aristotle's argument for the subject matter of the science of being qua being supports Plato's identification of the subject matter of philosophy.

The reason why the science of being qua being is identified with theology, a science with a declared specific subject matter, is well known. "Being" is not univocally predicable of all the things that have being. Accordingly, it does not have the univocity required by an ordinary science. Rather, "being" is said neither equivocally nor univocally but with primary and derivative referents, that is, with a primary referent, "one single nature (ἓν καὶ μίαν τινὰ φύσιν)," in relation to which (πρός) all other references are to be made.[14] The subject matter of the sought-for science is that one single nature. Any examples of being other than the first can only be understood in relation to the first. Without the first, there can be no such science, no first philosophy. There is no trace at all in our passage of a science of being qua being which is not πρὸς ἕν. By contrast, a *metaphysica generalis* requires the univocity of "being." That is why such a putative science is undiminished by the addition to or subtraction from its data set of one or another class of beings.

That the primary referent of the science of being qua being is a nature (φύσις) evidently indicates something specific. If this nature does not exist, then there is no object for the science of being qua being. But here one might want to object that if supersensible instances of this nature do not exist, sensible instances still do and so the sought-for science can focus on this nature in the sensible realm. But, again, this is to miss Aristotle's rejection of the univocity of "being," a rejection that implies that it is not the case that suitable subjects for study are indifferently found simply by using one's senses. Of course, these are objects for study both by their proprietary sciences and by the science of being qua being. But the study of the being of sensible substances (as opposed to the study of them as things existing by nature) is the study of *derivative* being.[15] If Aristotle's analysis of the being of sensibles is correct, that being is only available for a science of being qua being if the primary referent of "being" is located.

---

14. See *Meta*. Γ 2, 1003a33–34, b14; K 3, 1060b36–1061a7. That "being" is said in "many ways (πολλαχῶς λεγόμενον)" implies one nature variously instantiated.

15. See W. D. Ross 1924, 1:lxxviii–lxxix, 356; and Owens 2007, 53–54.

Whereas Aristotle implies that physics is "second" philosophy, Plato reserves the term "philosophy" for what Aristotle calls "first" philosophy, declining to designate what Naturalists or philodoxers do as philosophy at all. So, perhaps Naturalists can appeal to Aristotle and accept his inference, asserting that physics is first philosophy without needing to turn it into metaphysics at all. But Aristotle, like Plato, denies the autonomy of physics: "Such, then, is the principle [the Unmoved Mover] upon which depends heaven and nature."[16] So there is no question of physics attaining to ultimate explanations, since physics is not independent of what is in fact the subject matter of metaphysics. It is not merely that heaven and nature depend on the Unmoved Mover for their motion and for their final causality. Since the science of being qua being is the science of the properties of being and these can only be understood when they are understood as derived from the primary referent of "being," namely, the Unmoved Mover, all metaphysics is saturated with the immaterial.

It is true that Aristotle constructs a sort of qualified autonomy for physics that goes beyond what Plato would allow. The starting points for physics are the axioms and definitions of the things that exist by nature. This goes beyond Plato's acceptance of physics as at best a "likely story." Or so it seems. But Aristotle, like Plato, thinks that there is only knowledge of what is universal and necessary.[17] There can be no knowledge of that which can be otherwise, namely, the contingent states of affairs comprised of sensibles. The connection between the Unmoved Mover, the primary referent of "being," and that upon which nature depends, and the necessary and universal truths of a science of nature, is a subject only barely alluded to in the extant Aristotelian material.[18] Whether the Unmoved Mover thinks in some way all these necessary truths as it thinks and thereby guarantees their necessity is not clear. It is the explanation for the necessity and universality of science and the dependence of physics on the primary referent of being that makes it practically impossible to recruit Aristotle to the ranks of Naturalists.[19]

It may be objected that a science of being qua being limited to the natural world is not vitiated by the nonexistence of a supersensible world just

---

16. *Meta.* Λ 7, 1072b13–14: ἐκ τοιαύτης ἄρα ἀρχῆς ἤρτηται ὁ οὐρανὸς καὶ ἡ φύσις.
17. See *An. Post.* 31, 87b28; and 33, 88b30–37. Cf. *Meta.* Z 15, 1039b30–1040a7.
18. See Gerson 2005a, 200–204.
19. Schaffer (2009) proposes a "Neo-Aristotelian metaphysics" presumably not reducible to strict Naturalism. "Metaphysics," says Schaffer (379) "is about what is fundamental and what derives from it." This *sounds* Aristotelian, but what Schaffer thinks is fundamental (376) is "the whole [physical] universe." By contrast, Aristotle thinks that within metaphysics, understood as a science of being qua being, what is fundamental is the nature of being itself. Upon analysis, being turns out not to be identical with the physical universe or any proper part thereof. The fundamentality of the physical, for Aristotle, belongs to physics; the fundamentality sought for in metaphysics belongs to a separate science. Schaffer's view no more captures Aristotle's approach than would a lover of sights and sounds capture Plato's approach by declaring the fundamentality of the empirical.

because perfect instances of being are not found in the former. The perfect is perhaps merely notional, much like an ideal state whose nonexistence does not eliminate political philosophy. But, for Aristotle, there is no science of the merely notional; the object or objects of a science must be real.[20] The merely notional belongs to science fiction, not to science. Furthermore, if supersensible being did not exist, then it would necessarily not exist, that is, it would not be possible for it to exist. There certainly can be no science of the impossible for Aristotle. Therefore, it seems that we should conclude that what Plato calls "philosophy" Aristotle calls "first philosophy" and both identify its subject matter with the intelligible, that is, nonnatural or nonsensible world. What counts as "second philosophy" is the theoretical foundation for a natural science. And precisely because there is no subject matter for second philosophy distinct from the subject matter of the science of nature, what we today call "philosophy of science" or "philosophy of physics" or the like, is not the preserve of anyone other than those who investigate nature. A self-proclaimed philosopher may have something interesting to say about space, time, motion, infinity, and so on, but not because these are subjects other than those available for study to physicists. As much can be said for the social sciences insofar as these are sciences at all.[21]

The objection may be stated in a slightly different way. Aristotle says that the natural scientist needs to include the matter of his subjects of investigation whereas the first philosopher studies ontologically separate form.[22] But if, *ex hypothesi*, there is no such form, then there could still be a science of form that is only separable in thought and this would be first philosophy.[23] Such an objection, however, must ignore Aristotle's argument that "being" is not just said in many ways, but that it is done so with a primary and derivative references. There is no form among the forms inseparable ontologically from matter that could be primary. Hence, a putative

---

20. Taken with the need for a primary referent of "being" that is supersensible, the vacuity of a science of the merely notional may be reflected in the radical diversity of contemporary metaphysics resting upon a Naturalist basis.

21. McDowell (1994) argues for what he calls a "Neo-Aristotelian" conception of nature according to which normativity is part of the intelligible structure of nature. Accordingly, normativity might this way be insinuated into Naturalism and mark off a subject matter for philosophy. If normativity within, say, biological sciences is meant, it is easy to align this view with Aristotle. There is a scientific basis for determining the factors that contribute to the well-being of a plant. As much may be said for normativity within the life of a human being. But the absolutism of normativity is not thereby accounted for and I would suggest that Aristotle believes he needs the theological to do that. See Weinberg (1992, "Against Philosophy"), who draws the appropriate conclusion from a denial of a distinct subject matter for philosophy or metaphysics.

22. See *Phys.* B 2, 193b22–194b15. Cf. *DA* A 1, 403b7–8.

23. See e.g., Wedin (2000, 336), who thinks that the science of being qua being for Aristotle is the science of the forms of sensibles insofar as they are separable in thought.

nonsupersensible science of being qua being would, at least, be something very different from the science that Aristotle envisions, and this is all the more reason for denying the most favored interpretation of the *Metaphysics* passage above. Indeed, without a primary, supersensible referent of "being," all the objections of Naturalism to the very possibility of metaphysics or first philosophy would seem to follow. What would the subject matter of such a science be, supposedly distinguished from the radically equivocal referents of "form?"

Setting aside for the moment the question of how exactly the science of the immovable would be a universal science, our passage clearly expresses the identification of first philosophy with a science other than a science of nature. This is exactly the point insisted on by Plato in *Republic* when he says that what sets philosophers apart from everyone else is their concern with that which is perfectly real, that is, the intelligible world. By calling the science of being qua being "first philosophy," Aristotle implicitly identifies second philosophy with the science of nature.[24] This science is called "philosophy" because it is concerned with principles and causes *within* nature, principles and causes of movables qua movable. Thus, second philosophy is, presumably, the theoretical basis for the mature sciences of Naturalism. Aristotle's point that if the subject matter of first philosophy did not exist, then the science of nature would be first philosophy is, accordingly, not intended to open the door for a metaphysics of the sensible world.[25] For this reason, Aristotle's deeply Platonic point should not be taken to indicate that philosophy, as we understand it, could retain a foothold within a Naturalistic framework because it would focus on the theoretical foundations of the mature sciences.

If, as some would maintain, science needs metaphysics, it is not metaphysics conceived of as focusing on the most general principles and causes within nature.[26] There seems to be no reason why specialists within these

---

24. Cf. *Meta.* Z 11, 1037a15.

25. See *Meta.* Λ 7, 1072b13 which concludes on the basis of his argument from motion that it is unqualifiedly not possible that the Unmoved Mover does not exist. This being the case, the denial of the existence of the Unmoved Mover would entail a contradiction, namely, that that which necessarily exists does not exist. It could not then be Aristotle's claim that if the Unmoved Mover did not exist, metaphysics, the theological science of being qua being, would still be possible. Only if Aristotle were to grant the possibility that a science of being qua being could be detached from theology could this claim be made. But he nowhere does this, as much as many scholars wish that he did. See Reeve (2000, 298–300), who argues that by offering the identification of a science of being qua being with theology as the antecedent of a hypothetical ("if there were no substances other than . . ."), Aristotle "has thereby provided us with a recipe for constructing a naturalistic and Godless primary science on his behalf: it will simply be universal natural science, as he conceives of it."

26. See Lowe (2006), who thinks that the fourfold distinction in Aristotle's *Categories*—substance, individual accidental attribute, species and genera of substances, and species and genera of individual accidental attributes—constitutes the basis for an "ontology" (evidently

sciences are less qualified to investigate the principles of their sciences than are soi-disant philosophers. The principles certainly do not constitute a subject matter different from the things of which they are principles. This claim might seem questionable because what Aristotle considers to be the principles of nature—form, matter, and privation—are introduced by Aristotle in his *Physics* entirely outside of an empirical framework. Thus, matter as a principle is not subject to measurement and is not, as such, even intelligible. The concepts of form and privation have no obvious counterpart within any empirical science. The problem here is an ambiguity underlying the concepts of principle and cause. For Aristotle, the study of principles within a special science is an application of the universal science of principles and causes which is metaphysics.[27] The universal science of these principles and causes is the science of being qua being. It belongs to first philosophy to study form and matter in the most general sense, that is, to study being and its commensurately universal properties. Privation, too, is discussed within first philosophy, but its application belongs exclusively to things that exist by nature.[28] Therefore, if we were to abolish first philosophy, then the study of principles and causes in nature could only be the study of the axioms and definitions belonging to empirical sciences.

The clearest difference between Aristotle's approach to second philosophy from a first philosophy perspective and a Naturalist account of the principles and causes within the mature sciences is with regard to the concept of potency (δύναμις). This is one of Aristotle's greatest contributions to the Platonic project. Aristotle holds that it is literally not possible to attain understanding of any process or event or change or activity in nature without understanding the potency in that which stands at the terminus a quo of the process or event. But potency is not sensible; it is not available for measurement (even by a potentiometer!). Owing to the nonempirical nature of this principle, potentiality has no role to play in Naturalist accounts of the principles of any science. It is not that the concept of potency is missing; it is that, insofar as it is used, it is not a principle.

Insofar as an understanding of potency is not available as the result of sense-experience, it must be understood as a kind of being, the study of which belongs to first philosophy. This is so because potency is necessarily functionally related to form, which is the primary referent of "being" in

---

equivalent to "metaphysics" for Lowe) for the natural sciences. But this is not Aristotle's science of being qua being. For Aristotle, the categories are part of the logical tools for demonstration in any science.

27. See *Meta.* A 2, 982a4–6.
28. See *Meta.* Δ 22. When at *Phys.* A 8, 191a24–25, Aristotle refers to his predecessors speaking about nature in a "philosophical way (κατὰ φιλοσοφίαν)," he seems to mean that they were striving for a "first philosophy" perspective on the study of nature, but they had only a dim idea of what this was.

nature. It is precisely because all sensible substances have potency or matter that they cannot be the primary focus of a science of being qua being.[29] Natural science cannot do without potency; but natural science cannot substitute for primary philosophy because natural science's self-declared preserve is in fact the derivative or dependent.

First philosophy is a search for ultimate principles and causes. The argument in *Metaphysics* book *Alpha elatton* is to the effect that there must be such principles and causes if there are any principles and causes at all. The argument in book *Lambda*, starting from the results attained in books ZHΘ, is that the types of principles and causes converge on or are reduced to one, that is, the Unmoved Mover, the first principle of all. Aristotle agrees with Plato that the subject matter of philosophy or first philosophy is the intelligible world. He agrees, too, that the logic of ultimacy requires that a plurality of principles and causes be reduced to unity. He disagrees with Plato as to the nature of this first unique principle. The disagreement is basically quite simple: Plato holds that the first principle is beyond or above οὐσία whereas Aristotle identifies the first principle with οὐσία.[30] But this disagreement should not overshadow the profound antipathy to Naturalism that Plato and Aristotle share nor their further agreement that the domain of philosophy (or first philosophy) is the intelligible world.

The disagreement between Aristotle and Plato regarding the nature that is the first principle of all should not obscure the fact that Aristotle's denial of the univocity of "being" and his subsequent strategy for constructing a universal science of being qua being are in line with Plato's own procedure. This is so because the first, whether it be οὐσία or beyond οὐσία, must be absolutely simple or incomposite.[31] And, as we have seen, simplicity is

---

29. See *Meta.* Z 3, 1029a30–32: τὴν μὲν τοίνυν ἐξ ἀμφοῖν οὐσίαν, λέγω δὲ τὴν ἔκ τε τῆς ὕλης καὶ τῆς μορφῆς, ἀφετέον, ὑστέρα γὰρ καὶ δήλη· (the substance that is composed of both, I mean form and matter, must be set aside, for it is posterior and clear). It is posterior to whatever the primary referent of "being" turns out to be because it contains matter. Its being is clear to us for it is sensible; but primary being is clearer by nature because it contains no matter. The form of the composite cannot itself be the primary referent since this, while being separable in thought, does not meet the criterion of being unqualifiedly separate. Gill (1989, 16–17) acknowledges that the composite is "posterior," yet she understands this in a way that does not indicate its inferiority to a form unattached to matter.

30. More precisely, Aristotle hypothesizes the identification of being and substance (*Meta.* Z 2, 1028b2–4), then goes on to show that the primary referent of "substance" (Λ 6, 1071b20; 7, 1072a25–26; 8, 1073a30) is the Unmoved Mover. So this is the single nature that anchors a science of being qua being.

31. See *Meta.* Λ 7, 1072a30–34, where Aristotle specifies that "simple (ἁπλοῦν)" indicates a mode of being (πῶς ἔχον), not a measure of quantity. One of his main criticisms of Plato's identification of the Good with the One, is that Plato tends to confuse these. See *EE* A 8, 1218a16–29. Platonists, and presumably Plato, would argue that it is not a confusion to identify the Good with measure (τὸ μέτρον) because being is fundamentally intelligible and intelligibility is fundamentally expressible mathematically, that is, in terms of order. Quantity is only one

uniquely instantiable.[32] Therefore, the primary referent of "being" can only be present, if it is indeed present at all, to whatever else has being in a way that makes the univocity of "being" when applied to each impossible. Plato's Good or One is beyond οὐσία, but it is not nonexistent or nonbeing; being is derived to everything else that has it nonunivocally. While Aristotle is rejecting Plato's claim about the nature that is first, he is at the same time reinforcing his claim that, insofar as everything is explanatorily related to the first, this must occur in a graded or hierarchical manner.

Aristotle and Plato agree that there is an absolutely simple first principle of all. But in reply to the question "What is being (τὸ ὄν)?," Aristotle answers with the hypothesis that this is just the question "What is οὐσία?" Plato gives an answer that separates being as οὐσία from the first principle, whereas Aristotle gives an answer that identifies the primary referent of being with the first principle. It is theoretically open to Plato to agree with Aristotle that being is a πρὸς ἕν equivocal at the same time as he denies that the primary referent of being is the first principle of all because being is identical to οὐσία and the first principle of all transcends οὐσία. If Plato is going to agree that "being" is a πρὸς ἕν equivocal, he can either (1) agree that being is οὐσία, in which case being is not identical with the first principle of all, or (2) deny that being is οὐσία, and maintain that the first principle of all is identical with being.

It seems that Plato does in fact agree that οὐσία is a πρὸς ἕν equivocal since the οὐσία found in the sensible world is derived from the οὐσία found in the intelligible world. But this does not require him to agree that "being" is a πρὸς ἕν equivocal unless he were to agree that being is identical to οὐσία. And yet it seems that he does agree that "being" is a πρός ἕν equivocal, as in his arguments that the being of the temporal is derived from the being of the eternal. As we have already seen, the transcendence of the Good or the One does not mean that it does not have being (chap. 5, sec. 5.1, 15). The Platonic line of thought seems to be that the first principle of all is the primary referent of "being" so long as we refuse to identify being with οὐσία. What, though, could it mean to claim that the first principle of all is being but not οὐσία? What is being *without* οὐσία? Or, stated otherwise, how is the being that transcends οὐσία related to the being that is identical to οὐσία? As we may recall, this is another version of the question left from the second

---

type of order. The conflation of "one" as measure and "one" as a simple mode of being is a feature not a bug of the Platonic system.

32. For Plato, the uniqueness of absolute simplicity is derived from the fact that there can be no more than one entity whose existence and essence are indistinct. If there were more than one, ipso facto, each would have an essence or at least a property that the other did not have: two existents (by hypothesis), two property-instances, entail no absolute simplicity in either case. For Aristotle (*Meta.* Λ 8, 1074a31–38), the absolute simplicity of the first is derived from its having no matter and so being perfect ἐνέργεια or act. So it must be both one in number and in λόγος.

part of *Parmenides*, namely, how is the One of H1 related to the One-Being of H2? There is nothing in the dialogues or in the testimony from Aristotle and the indirect tradition to suggest Plato's answers to these questions. As we shall see in the next chapter, Plotinus does provide an answer that is, perhaps surprisingly, based on an Aristotelian insight.

7.3. The Immateriality of Thought

In his *De Anima*, Aristotle introduces what has been called the active or agent intellect.[33] I do not propose to deal at length with this notoriously difficult passage. I want, though, to point out several striking similarities with the argument in *Phaedo*. In the last sentence of the chapter, Aristotle concludes that without intellect (νοῦς), nothing thinks.[34] We may, I believe, reasonably interpret this conclusion as a transcendental argument to the effect that thinking could not occur without intellect: since thinking obviously does occur, intellect must exist.

But the burden of this chapter is to show that intellect is separable and that it is immortal (ἀθάνατον) and eternal (ἀίδιον). Indeed, from its eternity or everlastingness it follows that it preexists our generation and the only reason we do not remember its activity preembodiment is that it is unaffected (ἀπαθές), whereas the passive (παθητικός) intellect is destructible (φθαρτός). It is not immediately evident how being unaffected is contrasted with being destructible and how this explains the fact that "we do not remember." Minimally, it might seem that the point is that memory requires images (φαντάσματα) which are "percepts without matter (αἰσθήματα ἄνευ ὕλης)."[35] Therefore, we do not remember because intellect, being unaffected, has no images and so no memory. We do not remember the activity of intellect since that would require us to be both the subject of intellection and the subject that remembers the sense-perceptions of intellect. How, then, is intellect supposed to be required for us to think?

Being separate (χωριστός), intellect is in essence actual.[36] This fact alone short-circuits the interpretation according to which the active intellect is a certain sort of ability or potency. For if that were the case, then its actuality would be potency, which is nonsense. Further, if it were a potency, it would be, like all potencies, functionally related to some actual feature of the hylomorphic composite human being. But the composite is mortal,

---

33. *DA* Γ 5, 430a10–25.
34. *DA* Γ 5, 430a25. The words καὶ ἄνευ τούτου οὐθὲν νοεῖ ("and without this nothing thinks" or "without this it thinks nothing") certainly have νοῦς as the referent of τούτου. But it is unclear what the subject of νοεῖ is. In any case, whatever the subject is, thinking (τὸ νοεῖν) cannot occur without νοῦς.
35. See *DA* Γ 8, 432a9. Cf. 7, 431a16–17: διὸ οὐδέποτε νοεῖ ἄνευ φαντάσματος ἡ ψυχή (for this reason, the soul never thinks without images).
36. *DA* Γ 5, 430a17, 22–23.

not immortal, because the soul is the first actuality of a body with organs.[37] What *is* functionally related to the hylomorphic composite is the "so-called intellect (ὁ καλούμενος νοῦς)" which is just the psychical faculty of thinking.[38] We are left with the questions of why an active intellect is needed and how it is related to the cognitive psychical faculty, questions that are not going to be answered until we understand what the active intellect actually does when it is separated from the hylomorphic composite.

The solution to this problem is hampered by a common misunderstanding of an earlier passage. In book B, Aristotle says, "Regarding intellect or the theoretical faculty, nothing is yet clear, but it seems to be a genus different from soul and it is possible for this alone to be separated, just as the eternal is separated from the destructible."[39] The crucial phrase is almost universally translated: "a different kind of soul."[40] This translation does not help us explain why, whereas soul is the first actuality of a body with organs, intellect is said to have no organ.[41] Indeed, the standard translation makes the entire line pointless rather than what it seems to be doing, that is, giving a reason why intellect is separable and eternal. It is true that Aristotle does use the phrase "intellectual soul (ἡ νοητικὴ ψυχή)."[42] But this kind of soul is only its object potentially, not actually. Therefore, it cannot be identified with the separated intellect. The intellectual soul is just the cognitive faculty, set over against the other psychical faculties, including nutritive, reproductive, sensitive, and so on. This just adds to the above puzzle. How is active intellect supposed to be related to the cognitive faculty?

It may appear that the strongest support for what may be called the standard translation is found in the last line which refers to the "remaining parts of the soul" and to the fact that *they* are not separable. Do these words not imply that intellect is itself a part of the soul? I would say yes if we are to take Aristotle as talking about the noetic faculty (the so-called intellect), no if he is talking about intellect itself. But if he is talking about the noetic

---

37. See *DA* B 1, 412a27–28, and 413a3–4.
38. See *DA* Γ 4, 429a22–24. The separable νοῦς cannot be identified with the so-called νοῦς because the latter, being a faculty of soul, is destructible and so not separable.
39. *DA* B 2, 413b24–27: περὶ δὲ τοῦ νοῦ καὶ τῆς θεωρητικῆς δυνάμεως οὐδέν πω φανερόν, ἀλλ' ἔοικε ψυχῆς γένος ἕτερον εἶναι, καὶ τοῦτο μόνον ἐνδέχεσθαι χωρίζεσθαι, καθάπερ τὸ ἀΐδιον τοῦ φθαρτοῦ.
40. English translators are virtually unanimous in rendering the key claim in this passage as if Aristotle is suggesting that intellect is a kind of soul. Thus, the Oxford translation has "it seems to be a different kind of soul . . ."; J. A. Smith has "it seems to be a widely different kind of soul . . ."; Michael Durrant has "it would seem, however, to be a different kind of soul . . ."; D. W. Hamlyn has "it seems to be a different kind of soul . . ."; H. G. Apostle has "this seems to be a different genus of soul . . ."; Polansky has "it seems to be a different kind of soul . . ."; and Christopher Shields has "it seems to be a different genus of soul."
41. See *DA* Γ 4, 429a24–26.
42. *DA* Γ 4, 429a28.

faculty, is it not right to call it a different kind of soul? Aristotle is diffident at best about using the part language to refer to psychical faculties. As we shall see in a moment, he distinguishes intellect from that which is called intellect, namely, the noetic faculty. The connection between the two is of course of the utmost importance and difficulty. But their identity is far from obvious.

In support of the claim that the words "the remaining parts of the soul" presume that intellect is itself another part of the soul are the first words of the passage if the καί is taken in the sense of "or" as I believe it should be. Then, intellect and the theoretical faculty would seem to be one and this would be naturally compared to "the other parts (read: faculties)" of the soul. It makes sense to say that "nothing is yet clear" about this if intellect is a genus different from soul. If intellect is a "different kind of soul" it is not obvious why there is any lack of clarity at all. Indeed, if it is a different kind of soul, there is no reason provided here for why we would even think that it is separable.

In *Nicomachean Ethics*, book K, Aristotle reflects on intellect and its theoretical activity in relation to the composite human being. He says, "Such a life, of course, would be greater than that of a human being, for a human being will live in this manner not insofar as he is a human being, but insofar as he has something divine in him. And the activity of [intellect] is as superior to the activity of the other virtue as [intellect] is superior to the composite. Since the intellect is divine in comparison with the human being, the life according to this is divine in comparison with human life."[43] The "something divine" in the human being is intellect. It is, in a loose sense, a part of him. But it is not a part in the sense of one of the elements that make up a human being. Intellect is a part of the soul, that is, found among the list of psychical faculties, only insofar as it is manifested in embodied thinking which is the actualization of the noetic faculty. But from this it does not follow that "intellect" just stands for that faculty. On the contrary, all the evidence speaks against this identification.

More than a century ago, R. D. Hicks provided the main rationale for the translation more or less followed by everyone. Commenting on this passage Hicks writes,

> Most editors take ψυχῆς as partitive genitive, e.g. Wallace translates:
>
>> "Reason however would seem to constitute a different phase of soul from those we have already noticed." It would be grammatically possible to join ψυχῆς with ἕτερον, "it would seem, however, that intellect is something

---

43. *EN* K 7, 1177b26–31: ὁ δὲ τοιοῦτος ἂν εἴη βίος κρείττων ἢ κατ' ἄνθρωπον· οὐ γὰρ ᾗ ἄνθρωπός ἐστιν οὕτω βιώσεται, ἀλλ' ᾗ θεῖόν τι ἐν αὐτῷ ὑπάρχει· ὅσον δὲ διαφέρει τοῦτο τοῦ συνθέτου, τοσοῦτον καὶ ἡ ἐνέργεια τῆς κατὰ τὴν ἄλλην ἀρετήν. εἰ δὴ θεῖον ὁ νοῦς πρὸς τὸν ἄνθρωπον, καὶ ὁ κατὰ τοῦτον βίος θεῖος πρὸς τὸν ἀνθρώπινον βίον. Cf. K 7, 1177b26–1178a4; I 4, 1166a22–23, and 8, 1169a2.

different from soul." If νοῦς and ψυχή were ἕτερα τῷ γένει, the former might be described as ἕτερον γένος. We should thus avoid making νοῦς a kind of ψυχῆς. But, considering the numerous passages in which νοῦς and νοεῖν are treated as functions of soul and the use of ἡ νοητική [int. ψυχή] 429 a 28, I shrink from this expedient, even though it might remove some superficial difficulties. The fact is that, as pointed out by Zeller and others, the position of νοῦς in the system is anomalous. What is here said of νοῦς agrees exactly with the substance of 408b18–29 of which passage it is a neat summary.[44]

The passage to which Hicks refers in the last line says the following:

> As for intellect, it seems to come to us as a sort of substance, and not to be destructible. For [if it were destructible], it would surely be destructible by the feebleness of old age, whereas in fact what happens is just what happens in the case of our sense-faculties: for if the old man received an eye of a certain kind, he would see like a young man. So, old age is due not to the soul suffering something, but to the body suffering something, as in the case of drunkenness or disease. And, indeed, thinking and speculating are fading when something else in the body is being destroyed. But the intellect is unaffected. Discursive thinking and loving or hating, then, are not states of intellect, but of that in which intellect is, insofar as that has it. For this reason, when it is destroyed, the person neither remembers nor loves; for these belong not to intellect but to the composite which has been destroyed. Intellect, however, is perhaps something more divine and cannot be affected[45]

According to Hicks's understanding of our passage, Aristotle is summarizing a discussion of the noetic faculty, located within the human soul. Aristotle does indeed explicitly refer to a "noetic soul (νοητικὴ ψυχή)" in book Γ.[46] But this, he says, is "the so-called intellect of the soul (ὁ ἄρα καλούμενος τῆς ψυχῆς)."[47] This is the intellect by which the soul engages in discursive thinking (διανοεῖται) and believing (ὑπολαμβάνει). Clearly, this so-called noetic soul is assumed to be different from the intellect which, in the passage to which Hicks refers in interpreting our main passage, is a certain kind of substance and indestructible. The noetic faculty is a faculty of the entire soul, that is, the rational soul of a human being. And as Aristotle has already

---

44. Hicks 1907, 326–327.
45. *DA* A 4, 408b18–29: ὁ δὲ νοῦς ἔοικεν ἐγγίνεσθαι οὐσία τις οὖσα, καὶ οὐ φθείρεσθαι. μάλιστα γὰρ ἐφθείρετ' ἂν ὑπὸ τῆς ἐν τῷ γήρᾳ ἀμαυρώσεως, νῦν δ' ὥσπερ ἐπὶ τῶν αἰσθητηρίων συμβαίνει· εἰ γὰρ λάβοι ὁ πρεσβύτης ὄμμα τοιονδί, βλέποι ἂν ὥσπερ καὶ ὁ νέος. ὥστε τὸ γῆρας οὐ τῷ τὴν ψυχήν τι πεπονθέναι, ἀλλ' ἐν ᾧ, καθάπερ ἐν μέθαις καὶ νόσοις. καὶ τὸ νοεῖν δὴ καὶ τὸ θεωρεῖν μαραίνεται ἄλλου τινὸς ἔσω φθειρομένου, αὐτὸ δὲ ἀπαθές ἐστιν. τὸ δὲ διανοεῖσθαι καὶ φιλεῖν ἢ μισεῖν οὐκ ἔστιν ἐκείνου πάθη, ἀλλὰ τουδὶ τοῦ ἔχοντος ἐκεῖνο, ᾗ ἐκεῖνο ἔχει. διὸ καὶ τούτου φθειρομένου οὔτε μνημονεύει οὔτε φιλεῖ· οὐ γὰρ ἐκείνου ἦν, ἀλλὰ τοῦ κοινοῦ, ὃ ἀπόλωλεν· ὁ δὲ νοῦς ἴσως θειότερόν τι καὶ ἀπαθές ἐστιν.
46. *DA* Γ 4, 429a27–28.
47. *DA* Γ 4, 429a22.

insisted, we should not say that the soul pities or learns or engages in discursive thinking, but that the human being does so, with the soul.[48] Therefore, we can say, incautiously, that the soul thinks or, more accurately, that the human being thinks with the soul. But in neither case is the intellect here mentioned (i.e., "the so-called intellect") said to be a substance or to be indestructible.[49] The substance here is the human being or the essential form of the human being, that is, the noetic soul. Thus, it is at least questionable that 408b18–29 is the passage which explains our main passage given that when Aristotle does refer to a noetic faculty it is not the substantial and indestructible intellect. That is, 408b18–29 does not support the understanding of our passage as reflected in the translation. For that passage is, by Hicks and others, taken to anticipate 429a27–28, which refers to a noetic faculty of the soul that is not a substance and, insofar as it is part of the soul, not indestructible.

One may object, of course, that the claim that our passage summarizes 408b18–29 is not necessary for Hicks's interpretation. We can go directly to 429a27–28 as evidence that "intellect is a different kind of soul" should be understood as referring to a noetic soul.[50] But is it not puzzling that Aristotle would describe a "kind of soul" as γένος rather than εἶδος?[51] Surely, if he meant "species of soul," he would have written εἶδος and not γένος.[52] In addition, one would expect that "a different kind of soul" would either explicitly or implicitly refer to the kind or kinds of soul it is different from. Thus, in book Γ we get a discussion of multiple psychical faculties and how each differs from the others (διαφέρει ἀλλήλων).[53]

One may also object that the words ἕτερον γένος can be used in a loose sense by Aristotle as roughly equivalent to species. Thus, at B 5, 417b7 he refers to the actualization of a potency in a cognitive faculty as either not an alteration (ἀλλοίωσις) or a different sort of alteration (ἕτερον γένος ἀλλοιώσεως). But the two cases are quite different. The question of whether the actualization of a potency is or is not an alteration and if it is what it does and does not share with other species of alteration is a question about the nature of alteration. Nothing follows for our understanding of

---

48. *DA* A 4, 408b13–15.

49. Cf. *DA* Γ 9, 432b26. At A 2, 404b3, Aristotle criticizes Anaxagoras for maintaining that ψυχή and νοῦς are identical. The claim that νοῦς is a γένος different from ψυχή—not the claim that νοῦς is a "different" kind of ψυχή—would seem to be the natural way for Aristotle to express his disagreement with Anaxagoras's view.

50. For example, this is what Shields (2016, 188) does.

51. Cf. Plato, *Tim.* 69C7, ἄλλο εἶδος ψυχῆς, referring to the "mortal" part of the soul over against the "immortal" part.

52. Presumably, the reason some translators avoid "genus" for "kind" is to prevent this embarrassment. Burnyeat translates, "a generically different kind of soul," no doubt sensing the problem, but in fact only succeeding in compounding the obscurity of the traditional translations.

53. *DA* Γ 10, 433b4.

the actualization of the potency from whether the answer to the question is yes or no. But in our passage, from the fact that intellect would seem to be an ἕτερον γένος ψυχῆς, Aristotle claims that it follows that intellect is possibly separable. If Aristotle were merely stating that intellect is a kind of soul unique among kinds of souls or faculties, that in itself would be no reason for inferring that the intellect might be separable. On the contrary, all that Aristotle has hitherto said indicates that the soul and all its faculties are destroyed when the composite is destroyed. There is no possibility of any kind of soul or faculty of soul being separable.

More substantively, it is simply false that intellect is a kind of soul. For intellection or the activity of intellect is life, but not soul.[54] It does not follow if an entity is or has a life that it is ensouled. One of the central points of the entire work is the definition of the soul. Soul is the first actuality of a natural body with organs.[55] But intellect is said to have no organ.[56] If intellect in our passage is just the noetic faculty of the rational soul, and the soul is the actuality of a body with organs, what possible justification would there be for maintaining that intellect, unlike the sensitive faculty, has no organ? Whatever reason there is for maintaining that intellect has no organ is a reason for maintaining that intellect is a genus different from soul, not a faculty of soul.

Further, Aristotle says that with his definition of the soul the question of its immortality is settled in the negative. "It is not unclear, then, that the soul, or parts of it if by its nature it has parts, cannot be separated from the body; for the actualities in some [living things] are those of the parts themselves. But nothing prevents some actualities from being separable, because they are not actualities of any body."[57] Here, the reference is to intellect which is an actuality, but not that of any body. If intellect were just the noetic faculty, then intellect would not be separable.

This point is emphasized in *Generation of Animals* in the well-known account of intellect "on the doorstep." "It remains then for intellect alone so to enter and alone to be divine, for no bodily activity has any connection

---

54. See *Meta.* Λ 7, 1072b26–28, speaking of the Unmoved Mover: γὰρ νοῦ ἐνέργεια ζωή, ἐκεῖνος δὲ ἡ ἐνέργεια· ἐνέργεια δὲ ἡ καθ' αὑτὴν ἐκείνου ζωὴ ἀρίστη καὶ ἀΐδιος (For the actuality of intellect is life, and [the Unmoved Mover] is actuality; and the actuality of that is itself a life which is best and eternal). At *DA B* 2, 413a20–25, Aristotle distinguishes the animate (ἔμψυχον) from the inanimate if there is present (ἐνυπάρχῃ) at least one of the following: intellect, sense-perception, local motion and standstill, or motion with respect to nutrition, deterioration, or growth. Animate life is one kind of life, but not all life is animate. It is of course true that intellect is present to the human being. The question is whether its presence is or is not as a constituent of that human being's nature.

55. *DA* B 1, 412a27–28.

56. *DA* Γ 4, 429a24–27.

57. *DA* B 1, 413a3–7: ὅτι μὲν οὖν οὐκ ἔστιν ἡ ψυχὴ χωριστὴ τοῦ σώματος, ἢ μέρη τινὰ αὐτῆς, εἰ μεριστὴ πέφυκεν, οὐκ ἄδηλον· ἐνίων γὰρ ἡ ἐντελέχεια τῶν μερῶν ἐστὶν αὐτῶν. οὐ μὴν ἀλλ' ἔνιά γε οὐθὲν κωλύει, διὰ τὸ μηθενὸς εἶναι σώματος ἐντελεχείας.

with the activity of intellect."⁵⁸ It would certainly seem that if no bodily activity has any connection with the activity of intellect, then it would be incorrect to say about this intellect, as Aristotle does about the noetic faculty, that the human hylomorphic composite thinks, not the soul. If intellect enters from outside, then how can it be a faculty of the first actuality of a body with organs? A "genus different from soul" is exactly the right way to describe that which is not a part of the first actuality of the body, that which is not a part of the definition of a human being.

Since the active intellect—not the faculty of intellection in the soul or a part of the soul—is essentially in actuality, its natural activity is intellection. That is, it is identical with the objects of intellect.⁵⁹ It seems, then, that the reason why thinking is not possible without this agent intellect is not that it is an eternal power or faculty but that it is an eternal actuality identical with all that is intelligible or knowable. What we do not remember is its activity. Remembering it would, presumably, be equivalent to actualizing the intellection that it has. There is no question of our actualizing it as the agent intellect does, since for we hylomorphic composites there is no thinking without images. Once again, we ask of what use is it to us?

The agent intellect, says Aristotle, operates like light which actualizes potential colors.⁶⁰ This analogy is usually taken to suggest that the agent intellect illuminates content that is already present. And to a certain extent, this must be true. But the content illuminated is contained within images or φαντάσματα. If this were not the case, then images would be irrelevant to thinking. All the content contained within images is particularized form, since the image is just the form of the sensible particular without the matter. Therefore, the illumination by the agent intellect is of a particularized form. And thinking is always and only of form universalized. Without the agent intellect, we could only access cognitively particularized form, which is the condition of animals. The agent intellect makes all form intelligible to us, that is, makes it universalizable. The agent intellect, when it is in us, cognizes universally the particularized form that is present in images. When the hylomorphic composite is gone, this intellect reverts to its essential activity, cognitive identity with all that is intelligible. We could not think at all, much less have knowledge, if we did not have an agent intellect.

The knowledge that the agent intellect has for Aristotle is the same as the knowledge that the preembodied soul has for Plato. Aristotle's remark that intellect is a genus different from soul is intended to clarify the Platonic language. What Plato in *Timaeus* calls the immortal part of the soul, Aristotle

---

58. *GA* B 3, 736b27–29: λείπεται δὴ τὸν νοῦν μόνον θύραθεν ἐπεισιέναι καὶ θεῖον εἶναι μόνον· οὐθὲν γὰρ αὐτοῦ τῇ ἐνεργείᾳ κοινωνεῖ <ἡ> σωματικὴ ἐνέργεια.
59. See *DA* Γ 5, 430a19–20. Cf. 4, 429b9, 430a3–6; 6, 430b25–26; 7, 431a1–2, b17.
60. *DA* Γ 5, 430a15–17.

calls an entity generically different from soul, namely, an intellect.[61] But for both Plato and Aristotle, the immortal part of the soul and the immortal agent intellect must exist if knowledge, and thinking in general, are to be possible.

To summarize the argument in this section so far, we must distinguish intellect from an intellectual faculty which is a kind of soul, indeed, the kind of soul that defines human beings. The former is immortal and the latter is not. But without this immortal or agent intellect, we could not think. The immortal intellect seems to be Aristotle's version of what Plato calls "the immortal part of the soul," that which is separable from the body and capable of knowledge. Plato takes this immortal part of the soul to enter and to leave a body. Aristotle, too, assuming that the agent intellect is separable, takes it to have a status both in and apart from the body. Only in the latter, is it what it is, an actual entity. But at the same time, its embodied status is what makes thinking possible.

The question I would like to address now is why must there be something which is separable from the body for thinking to occur in soul-body composites? No doubt, the answer has something to do with Aristotle's claim that it is absurd to maintain that there is a bodily organ for thinking.[62] The reason for this claim, given in the previous line, is not immediately evident: the soul which is capable of thinking is actually none of the things it thinks prior to thinking. And "for this reason (διό)" it has no bodily organ. Thus, when it thinks it *is* actually these things. Following this line of reasoning, since the objects of thinking are forms,[63] when someone thinks she becomes the forms she thinks. But why is this basic thesis of hylomorphism supposed to lead us to hold that the intellectual soul has no organ and that something which is separable from the composite is needed for thinking to occur? For the mere transference of form from one composite to another certainly does not require that in the latter case the form is not enmattered or embodied. Further, when someone actually thinks, he is identical to that form, but again, why should that identity entail that there be no bodily matter in which the form is instantiated?

Clearly, the identity envisioned here is not the self-identity of the principles of an ordinary hylomorphic composite. This identity is appropriately called "cognitive identity" because it is the one thinking who is identical with the form thought. That is why the intellect itself can be said to be

---

61. See Plato, *Tim.* 69C–D. It may be that if intellect is a genus, its species include the agent intellect and the so-called intellect in the hylomorphic composite.

62. *DA* Γ 4, 429a24–27. Cf. Plato (*Tht.* 184B3–186E10), who argues that ἐπιστήμη is not αἴσθησις. The burden of the argument is to show that the soul attains to being not through any sense organ. There is an interesting argument in support of this view in Rödl 2014.

63. *DA* Γ 4, 429a15–18. This is what Rödl (2018, 75) calls "the original unity of thought and being."

intelligible.[64] The identity is of thinking and the object of thought. And this is to be distinguished from the identity that occurs when the intellect has been informed by the object of thought, but is not actually thinking. Thus, actual thinking is cognitive identity and is self-reflexive.

The difference between the presence of form and the actual thinking of the form present, which is just the actualization of the potency for thinking, is critical. As we have already seen, for both Plato and Aristotle, form is itself neither particular nor universal. It is particular in a hylomorphic composite and is cognized universally in thinking. Self-reflexivity is, then, cognition of the form universally. The universal is the quasi-object of self-thinking. The one thinking becomes the form universally in thinking. There can be no organ for thinking because an organ takes on an individual or particular form, not a form universally. For example, we smell a particular smell or feel a particular texture with our sense-organs. But in actual thinking we become identical with that which, by definition, cannot be exhausted in any sum of particularizations.[65] That is why cognitive identity is unique; in cognition we become the form universally, whereas the presence of form in every other case is a particular presence.

According to Aristotle, the agent intellect that each one of us is is manifested as the rational faculty of a human soul. As such, it has its own hylomorphic composition where the passive intellect is the matter and the agent intellect is the form. It is important to stress that the passive intellect does not have matter; it is matter, but not bodily matter. It is just matter for the reception of all intelligibles, that is, of all forms. Imagination is the faculty for conveying particular forms as perceived to the intellect. Actual thinking is the cognizing of these forms universally. The agent intellect, relieved of the constraints of embodiment, just is cognitively identical with all forms, thinking them universally. But when embodied, it needs the passive intellect to be the matter for the universals being thought. The thinker becomes the intelligibles, that is, we become self-aware agent intellects working under conditions of embodiment.

I take Aristotle's entire epistemological enterprise to be essentially a refinement of Plato's, including his corrections and precisions of Plato's many elusive remarks. His rejection of the view of Naturalists like Empedocles and Democritus that thinking is corporeal just like perceiving, is in line with Plato's argument that belief, including false belief, is not possible

---

64. *DA* 4, 429b9, 430a2–3. In the first passage, I read δὲ αὐτὸν with all the manuscripts rather than δι'αὐτοῦ with Bywater and Ross.

65. See Ross (1992b), who argues along Aristotelian lines that thinking cannot be a "physical process" because thinking is determinate in the way that no physical process can be determinate. Specifically (137), no physical process can have the determinacy of, say, a universal function, e.g., $N \times N = N^2$. The function that is cognized universally cannot be a particular property of a body, specifically, a brain state. Also see Oderberg 2008.

for a body.⁶⁶ It cannot be the state of a body because that state must be particular whereas the belief requires cognition of form universally. The separable immaterial intellect, along with the Unmoved Mover, makes up Aristotle's intelligible world. Indeed, many Aristotle scholars ever since at least Alexander of Aphrodisias, have thought that these are identical.⁶⁷ Aristotle leaves us to wonder whether the ontological foundation for scientific truths, all of which are for him necessary and so eternal, do not also have a place in this intelligible world, even if not as separate Platonic Forms.

I take it that the claim that the intellect is an immaterial entity constitutes a direct attack on Naturalism. Contemporary Naturalists and anti-Naturalists alike admit as much. Aristotle, more than Plato, makes explicit why the immateriality of intellect is so difficult to deny. The conclusion that intellect is immaterial follows ultimately from the hylomorphic composition of sensibles, the fact that in thinking form is separated from matter, and that thinking is of form universally. Since the form of a composite is what the thing is actually, thinking the form is really having the composite in the intellect in its actuality. But the presence of the form in the intellect is not the presence it has in the composite; in the former it is universalized, whereas in the latter it is particularized.⁶⁸ This universalizing of the intellect occurs when thinking actually occurs. If human beings were not conscious thinkers, it could well be the case that the presence of form in the intellect was another particularized version of it, perhaps as a brain state. And indeed, there is considerable puzzlement from an evolutionary point of view as to why actual thinking or the consciousness that is a requirement for it is necessary. Certainly, the presence of form in plants and animals other than human beings (so far as we know) does not require universality. Particularized forms are sufficient to serve as guides for survival, growth, and reproduction.

The denial that we do think universally—however we explain this capacity—seems to efface the distinction between grasping necessary truths and

---

66. See *DA* Γ 3, 427a17–b6. Aristotle acknowledges that the faculty of sense-perception has or is a discriminative capacity, but the sort of discrimination made in sense-perception requires no universality. Even a plant, exercising a tropism, discriminates light from dark or heat from cold. A baby can sense differences and samenesses in sense-properties, but is unable to judge or form the belief that two things are different or the same. To do this requires cognition of form universally. More precisely, it requires cognition that the two sense-properties are instances of the form, a judgment that can only be made if the form is cognized universally. The form is understood universally when it is predicable of many. See *De int.* 6, 17a39. But form cannot be identical with a universal since the form that, as universalized, is predicable of many, can also be particularized. Cf. Plato, *Tht.* 184B–186E.

67. See Alexander of Aphrodisias, *De an.* 89.9–19; and *Mantissa* 2, 112.5–113.6.

68. See Dancy (2004, 309–310), who makes essentially the same point in regard to *Phd.* 102D–103C where the "Forms in us" are just Forms under a certain condition, a condition different from their particularized condition in their instances. Dancy does not add, however, that the Forms in us are thought only universally.

representing them. The universal as a hypostatization of universal thinking is just this representation. I believe that Plato and Aristotle would agree that the representations of necessary truths in language or thought are only intelligible if we understand what the difference is between an accurate and an inaccurate representation. But to understand this is to grasp necessary truth. A similar argument would address the claim that we are deluded when we think we grasp necessary truth. It only makes sense to think of such delusions if we understand at least what it would mean not to be deluded, and that of course is equivalent to grasping the necessary truth that we are supposedly deluded about.

If generalization is at all distinct from universality, then there can be no generalization rooted in Naturalistic assumptions that can achieve universality. Generalizations approach universality asymptotically. But universality—most evident in mathematical thinking—defies Naturalistic reduction since such reduction must revert to the particularization of form, fixed somewhere in a four-dimensional matrix. If Aristotle is right, all thinking is universal, not just mathematical thinking. Our awareness of this should be as evident to us as is our awareness of thinking itself so long as we keep distinct the thinking from our representations of it. A similar line of reasoning pertains to attempts to assimilate universal thinking to rule following. We can follow rules, say, calculations rules, either with or without understanding. The mechanical application of rules is not equivalent to the understanding either in us or in machines which are entirely incapable of understanding the rules they follow. The understanding is the cognitive identity of the intellect and form in the universal mode.

The universality of thinking requires self-reflexivity, that is, the identity of the intellect that is informed and the intellect that thinks the form universally. Thinking the form universally is having as an intentional object that intellect which is informed. If this were not the case, then the intellect that thinks would have to have transferred to it the form from the original informed intellect. And in that case, thinking the form universally would still be the having as an intentional object the newly informed intellect. If this were not the case, that is, if thinking were an activity described along Naturalistic lines, then the thinking would be one part of the brain monitoring another part since the part of the brain that is informed must be distinct from the part that is aware of the information. But the putative transference of the form from the part of the brain informed to the part that is thinking could only amount to a new, particular brain state and universality would not be achieved. Therefore, presence of form and awareness of presence of form must be in the identical subject. And this can only happen if the subject is immaterial and capable of bending back upon itself or overlapping, something that material entities with parts outside of parts cannot do.

The immateriality of the intellect is a focal point of many anti-Naturalistic arguments including those concerning consciousness, intentionality, action, and choice. These arguments depend entirely on thinking as a universal mode of cognition of form, that is, form understood to be a principle of hylomorphic composition. I take Aristotle's extraordinary development and expansion of hylomorphism into all the areas of philosophy to be his thematization of that passage in *Philebus* in which we learn that everything that exists now is composed of limit and unlimited.[69] In addition, it seems clear enough that the thinking of the Unmoved Mover is not universal thinking insofar as this requires images. But all thinking is of form, and involves cognitive identity. Therefore, it would seem that the Unmoved Mover is cognitively identical with whatever form it is thinking. The point is the same whether the form with which it is identical is just the οὐσία that it is or whether it is all form, that is, all that is thinkable. By his analysis of thinking, Aristotle makes explicit what is only implicit in Plato, namely, the cognitive identity of the Demiurge and the Living Animal.

7.4. The Causality of the First Principle

Aristotle, unlike Plato in his written work, provides an argument for a first principle of all. He agrees with Plato that this principle must be unique and absolutely simple. But whatever one might think of Aristotle's Platonic bona fides, it is undoubtedly the case that Aristotle's own account of a first principle of all, the Unmoved Mover, had an enormous effect on how later soi-disant Platonists viewed Plato himself. For although Aristotle explicitly rejects as first principle the superordinate Idea of the Good, along with the rest of Forms, the Demiurge, and also the claim that the One and the Unlimited are the principles out of which the Forms are made, the Unmoved Mover can arguably be held to fulfill the functions of the above. That is, Aristotle collapses or conflates into one the three functions of paradigms of intelligible objects, an eternal intellect cognitively identical with these, and a unique principle of goodness. This conflation encouraged Middle Platonists especially to solve the problems thrown up by Plato's own account of first principles as well as Aristotle's critical supplement to make the first principle of all an intellect and to integrate in one way or another One and Unlimited into this framework.[70]

Aristotle has a distinctive approach for demonstrating that the first principle of all is also the ultimate goal of whatever it causes or explains. "The object of desire and the intelligible object move in this way, i.e., without being moved themselves. Of these, the primary objects are identical. For the object of appetite is what is apparently beautiful, whereas the primary object of rational desire is that which is really beautiful. We desire because it seems [to be beautiful] rather than that it seems to be beautiful because

---

69. See Plato, *Phil.* 23Cff.
70. For the Middle Platonic material, see Boys-Stones 2018, chap. 6.

we desire it; for the starting point is thinking."[71] The argument relies on a distinction made in *De Anima* between the apparent good and the real good.[72] The argument seems to be this: we desire our real good, although we can only desire what appears to us to be good, whether it is the real good or not. But the determination of what is the real good (whether correctly or incorrectly) is the work of thought. Therefore, appetite follows thought, but there is only one place in which they end up, and that is the identical place.[73] I take it that the primary intelligible object is that which is most intelligible, that is, most transparent to the intellect.[74] It is that which lacks matter or potency most of all. That would be the Unmoved Mover, which is pure actuality.

Why, though, should we suppose that what is primarily intelligible is primarily desirable? Why identify the Unmoved Mover with the real good that we desire? Aristotle provides a tentative answer to this question, but it is one that is relativized to the categories. He says that that which is primary is best, or by analogy so.[75] This seems to mean that what is desired in a particular category, for example, the best site for a city, is primary in that category. Determining this is the work of intellect. And this is analogously so across all the categories. But notice that within any category, it is desire that is the starting point, not thinking. One starts with the desire for the best location, and then thinks about what it may be. In the above passage, however, the starting point is thinking, not desire.

---

71. See *Meta.* Λ 7, 1072a26–30: κινεῖ δὲ ὧδε τὸ ὀρεκτὸν καὶ τὸ νοητόν· κινεῖ οὐ κινούμενα. τούτων τὰ πρῶτα τὰ αὐτά. ἐπιθυμητὸν μὲν γὰρ τὸ φαινόμενον καλόν, βουλητὸν δὲ πρῶτον τὸ ὂν καλόν· ὀρεγόμεθα δὲ διότι δοκεῖ μᾶλλον ἢ δοκεῖ διότι ὀρεγόμεθα· ἀρχὴ γὰρ ἡ νόησις. I take it that τὸ καλόν ("the beautiful") is extensionally equivalent to τὸ ἀγαθόν ("the good"). Our appetitive desire is for the former, whereas our rational desire is for the latter. The point of the argument is that these are in fact identical.

72. See *DA* Γ 10, 433a27–28.

73. Laks (2000, 225–226) questions Aristotle's justification for identifying the primary objects of desire and thinking. See the following note.

74. In the lines following our text (30–35), the primacy with respect to intelligibility is assigned to that which is simple and pure actuality. Cf. *Meta.* Z 3, 1029b5–8; and *Phys.* A 1, 184a10–b14. Defilippo (1994, 399–404) thinks that the primary νοητόν is primary for the Unmoved Mover and since it is also the primary object of desire, this is the reason why they are identical. This interpretation is supported by *Meta.* Λ 7, 1072b18–19: δὲ νόησις ἡ καθ' αὑτὴν τοῦ καθ' αὑτὸ ἀρίστου, καὶ ἡ μάλιστα τοῦ μάλιστα (Thinking according to itself is of the best according to itself, and thinking in the highest degree is of the best in the highest degree). However, unless the Unmoved Mover is the primary object of its own desire, this conclusion does not follow. But the Unmoved Mover does not have desire. So the fact that all things that have desire ultimately desire the Unmoved Mover because it is good and the fact that the Unmoved Mover is intelligible to itself does not justify us in concluding that these are identical. The justification comes from the fact that our rational desire and our appetitive desire converge on the identical object owing to our permanent orientation to the good.

75. *Meta.* Λ 7, 1072a35–b1.

In the last chapter of book *Lambda*, Aristotle provides an argument to the effect that the highest good in nature is found both in nature itself and separated (κεχωρισμένον) in the principle of order of nature, namely, that upon which all of nature depends.[76] This highest good is distinct from the goods that belong in each genus or category.[77] Aristotle's point, I take it, is not that the singularity of the primary good negates the goodness in each category or the desire to obtain it in each case, but that achieving it is the way that each thing with desire attains the Good. The Form of the Good is rejected because there is no unity in the categorical goods; the Idea of the Good or absolutely simple first principle of all is affirmed as that which all desire and all achieve insofar as they attain any specific good. The Unmoved Mover is the cause of the order of nature in the way that a general is the cause of the order of the army. Because it is the cause of this order, it is the Good at which all the parts of the order aim. Even though Aristotle disagrees with Plato about the nature of the first principle of all, he agrees with the crucial systematic point that the first principle orders both as explanatorily first and as goal.[78]

There are good grounds for holding that the Unmoved Mover is more than a final cause.[79] There are also good grounds for holding that the Unmoved Mover is not Narcissus-like thinking only of thinking, but rather than it is thinking all that is thinkable.[80] Finally, even insofar as the Unmoved Mover is a final cause, it is, as we have seen, the ultimate object of rational desire, which is that which is really, not apparently, good. Whether or to what extent the ordering of the cosmos by the Unmoved Mover can be cashed out as a mathematical ordering as it is for the Demiurge of *Timaeus*,

---

76. *Meta.* Λ 10, 1075a11–25. Sedley (2000, 335n12) thinks that "separated (κεχωρισμένον)" does not necessarily "mean something transcendent or extracosmic, but simply something over and above the ordering itself." But if something is over an above the cosmic, how does this differ from being extracosmic? See also Fazzo (2018, 368–377), who, too, argues that the separated good of the order is not transcendent. Fazzo's argument, which is based on the admittedly awkward construction καὶ γὰρ ἐν τῇ τάξει τὸ εὖ καὶ ὁ στρατηγός, does not persuade me that we can discount the clear "transcendent" implication of Λ 7, 1072b13–14: "Therefore, heaven and nature depend on such a principle [i.e., the separate Unmoved Mover]."

77. See *Meta.* Λ 7, 1072b18–19: πρὸς μὲν γὰρ ἓν ἅπαντα συντέτακται (everything is ordered in relation to one). Plato's *Symposium* seems to be at the back of Aristotle's mind here. There, Plato goes from the specific object of desire to the Good that is thereby desired. We love beautiful objects because they manifest the Good.

78. See Berti (2018, 261–262), who argues that Aristotle's disagreement with Plato is not with regard to the Good as first principle but with Plato's identification of the Good with the One. Perhaps this insight can be stated otherwise: Plato identifies the Good with the One because the Good must be absolutely simple whereas Aristotle, conceding the absolute simplicity of the Good, identifies it with intellection.

79. See Gerson 2005a, 200–204; and Gerson 2013a, 142n33. Theophrastus (*Meta.* 4b1ff.) considers the inherent difficulties in making an object of desire alone a cause of eternal circular motions.

80. See Gerson 2005a, 195–200.

is difficult to say, although insofar as we are inclined to accept the idea that *all* ordering is essentially mathematical, that the Unmoved Mover should operate in this way is not entirely far-fetched. In any case, motivated both by Aristotle's unqualified acceptance of the existence of an absolutely simple first principle of all, and no doubt by the proof in *Timaeus* that intellect is the cause of the ordering of the cosmos, later Platonists sought to reconfigure the Platonic account into the most defensible structure.

A rather obvious question is why Aristotle's recognition of a first principle of all does not yield a systematic expression of Peripatetic philosophy. The answer suggested by Fritz Wehrli in the final volume of his monumental *Die Schule des Aristoteles*, a *Rücksicht* on the nine volumes of text, translation, and commentary, is that Aristotle did have a systematic philosophy, but that system was Platonism.[81] From the perspective of later Platonists, the problem with Aristotle's version of that system sprang from his identification of the first principle of all, the primary referent of οὐσία, as an intellect. Here, I wish only to emphasize that the consequences of this for the confrontation with Naturalism are considerable, much more so than the mere misidentification of the nature of the unique first principle of all might lead one to believe. For although Aristotle was completely in line with the above five "antis," he has considerable difficulty in articulating his version of their contradictories, to say nothing of his diffidence regarding their underlying logical connections. What I mean is that Aristotle does not clearly set forth the ontological foundation for the universal and necessary scientific truths in which he surely believes. Nor does his graded ontology with a primary and derivative manifestations of being intrude much at all in his anti-Naturalist accounts of nature, particularly the intelligibility of nature. We have only his passing remarks to the effect that all of nature depends on the first principle and all of nature is ordered according to the first principle. Aristotle rejects relativism in ethics, but the ontological grounds for his assertions regarding normativity are elusive. All of these features of the Aristotelian corpus prompted later Platonists to see him as one whose insights could be mined to support and articulate a Platonic systematic framework.

81. See Wehrli 1974, 10:95–97.

CHAPTER 8

Plotinus the Platonist

8.1. The Platonic System

Plotinus eschewed novelty. It is likely that the outline of his systematic Platonic construct was something he received rather than something he invented.[1] It is not entirely implausible that Plotinus got from his honored teacher Ammonius Saccas insights into Platonism that were expressed by Numenius. In fact, we learn from Porphyry that Plotinus was actually accused of "plagiarizing (ὑποβάλλεσθαι)" Numenius.[2]

What is certain, though, is that Plotinus is a sort of watershed in the history of Platonism. When Proclus put him first among exegetes of "the

---

1. Dodds, in his seminal paper of 1928, finds traces of the system in the deeply obscure Moderatus of Gades (first century CE). But he also identifies an important passage in Proclus which indicates that the "Neoplatonic" interpretation of Plato's *Parmenides* can be found in Speusippus. See Halfwassen 1992b, 1993; and Dillon 2003, 57ff. Mention, too, should be made of Eudorus (fl. 25 BCE), who, from the meager fragmentary remains of his works, appears to have acknowledged the systematic foundation consisting of the One and Indefinite Dyad. For Eudorus, Moderatus, and Numenius, Dillon's ([1977] 1996) is most useful. While not endorsing the entirety of his conclusions, Krämer ([1964] 1967, 21–191) provides a wealth of evidence for the doctrinal filiation from Plato to Plotinus. See D'Ancona 2000, 198–212, on the rootedness of Plotinian doctrine in the exegesis of the texts of the Platonic dialogues. It is fashionable now to locate the systematization of Platonism in the early Imperial period. See Bonazzi and Opsomer 2009. The claim I have been trying to substantiate throughout this book is that the origin of the systematization of Platonism is to be found in the Platonic dialogues. But this does not preclude developments within that system or disputes about its development. Many of these did in fact occur in the post-Hellenistic period. See esp. Donini 2011 on systematization in the post-Hellenistic period as inspired by efforts to counter the systematization found in Stoicism. Also see Ferrari 2017, 33–35.

2. See Porphyry, *Life of Plotinus*, 17.1–2. Tarrant (1993, 148–177) sees Moderatus as a source for Numenius. See also Tarrant 2000, chap. 6, for additional information on the Platonic

Platonic revelation (τῆς Πλατωνικῆς ἐποπτείας)," he was, we may assume, endorsing the systematic order into which Plotinus put Plato's philosophy.[3] Plotinus himself regarded his exegesis of Plato as introducing no novelty; indeed, he appeals to Plato to support the claim that neither was Plato.[4] What this must mean is not that Plotinus thought that his arguments regarding detailed philosophical questions or his responses to anti-Platonic attacks were unoriginal, but rather that the lineage of true fundamental philosophical principles extended to well before Plato, although he gave them their stellar expression. These principles are, as I argued in chapter 1, the armature of the positive construct on the basis of Ur-Platonism. In the time between Plato and Plotinus, there were some six hundred years of reflections on the dialogues, Aristotle's testimony, and the indirect tradition. These reflections left multiple seemingly intractable problems and a susceptibility among self-declared Platonists to various charges of inconsistency. In this chapter, I would like to provide a very brief outline of Plotinus's efforts to solve these problems and to introduce consistency into the systematic framework. This task is necessary since all subsequent deviations from Plotinus's account are intentional. That is, despite his stature among later Platonists, his solutions were held to be themselves susceptible to a new batch of problems. If Plotinus's metaphysics is not exactly a Copernican revolution in the history of Platonism, it represents a moment of powerful systematic consolidation analogous to the role of Thomas Aquinas in the history of Christian theology. Plotinus is the touchstone for all Platonists up to the nineteenth century.[5]

The three basic principles or hypostases of Plotinus's system unite the elements of Ur-Platonism and the foundational principle. That is, antinominalism, antimaterialism, antimechanism, antiskepticism, and antirelativism have their theoretical foundation in the hierarchically and causally ordered series One, Intellect, and Soul. What this means, among other things, is that the correct version of what Aristotle calls the science of ultimate principles and causes will arrive at this triad.[6]

---

system in so-called Middle Platonism. Also see Boys-Stones 2018, chap. 3. Krämer ([1964] 1967, 63–92) sees Xenocrates as a primary source for the systematization of Platonism. Numenius, in his work *On the Divergence of Academics from Plato*, fr. 24.5–12, says that Speusippus, Xenocrates, and Polemo, Plato's immediate successors, "maintained for the most part the identical character of Plato's teachings (τὸ ἦθος διετείνετο στῶν δογμάτων σχεδὸν δὴ ταὐτόν)," though he adds that they did "detach themselves from Plato on many issues and tortured the sense of others (εἴς γε τἄλλα πολλαχῇ παραλύοντες, τὰ δὲ στρεβλοῦντες)." See Gerson 2013a, chap. 8, on Numenius's contribution to the systematization of Platonism.

3. Proclus, *PT* 1.1.16ff.

4. See Plotinus, *Enn.* 5.1[10], 8.10–14. See Szlezák 1979, chap. 1; and Chiaradonna 2010.

5. I am not forgetting the enormous influence of Proclus, but he only stands as a substitute for Plotinus in the Christian Platonism of Pseudo-Dionysius and those who came after him.

6. See Aristotle, *Meta*. A 1–2. It is good to keep in mind that when Porphyry, in his *Life of Plotinus*, 14.4, says that Plotinus's *Enneads* are "full of concealed Stoic and Peripatetic

In a relatively early treatise, V 1, Plotinus claims that the hypostases One/Good, Intellect, and Soul are found directly in Plato's dialogues.

> And it is for this reason also that we get Plato's threefold division: the things "around the king of all" (he says, meaning the primary things); "second around the secondary things," and "third around the tertiary things."[7] And he says "father of the cause"[8] meaning by "cause" Intellect.[9] For the Intellect is his Demiurge. And he says that the Demiurge makes the Soul in that "mixing bowl."[10] And since the Intellect is cause, he means by "father" the Good, or that which is beyond Intellect and "beyond essence."[11] Often he calls Being and the Intellect "Idea," which shows that Plato understood that the Intellect comes from the Good, and the Soul comes from the Intellect.[12]

The first principle of all is the Good, based on the *Republic* line quoted. That the Good is the One is affirmed a few lines later when Plotinus says that "Parmenides in [Plato's] work speaks more accurately than does [the historical Parmenides], distinguishing the first One, which is more properly called "One" from the second "One" called "one-many" and the third One, called "one and many."[13] Plotinus will also adduce Aristotle's testimony to support his interpretation, assuming that Aristotle correctly reports the identification of Good and One for Plato but that he misunderstands the correctness of this identification.[14]

Plotinus takes Plato at his word when he says in *Timaeus* that the operations of the Demiurge are the "workings of Intellect."[15] And since the

---

doctrines" what this means concretely for Aristotle's *Metaphysics* is well over 150 direct references to this text. This intense absorption of the argument of *Metaphysics* is literally unprecedented in any known work in the intervening period. As for Stoicism, there are more than two hundred references to Stoic doctrines in the *Enneads*, though no doubt many more are not evident to us owing to the absence of the Stoic or doxographical sources.

7. See Plato [?], *2nd Ep.* 312E1–4.
8. See Plato [?], *6th Ep.* 323D4.
9. See Plato, *Phd.* 97C1–2, quoting Anaxagoras fr. B 12 D–K.
10. See Plato, *Tim.* 34B–35B; and 41D4–5.
11. See Plato, *Rep.* 509B9.
12. Plotinus, *Enn.* 5.1[10], 8.1–10: Καὶ διὰ τοῦτο καὶ τὰ Πλάτωνος τριττὰ τὰ πάντα περὶ τὸν πάντων βασιλέα—φησὶ γὰρ πρῶτα—καὶ δεύτερον περὶ τὰ δεύτερα καὶ περὶ τὰ τρίτα τρίτον. Λέγει δὲ καὶ τοῦ αἰτίου εἶναι πατέρα αἴτιον μὲν τὸν νοῦν λέγων· δημιουργὸς γὰρ ὁ νοῦς αὐτῷ· τοῦτον δέ φησι τὴν ψυχὴν ποιεῖν ἐν τῷ κρατῆρι ἐκείνῳ. Τοῦ αἰτίου δὲ νοῦ ὄντος πατέρα φησὶ τἀγαθὸν καὶ τὸ ἐπέκεινα νοῦ καὶ ἐπέκεινα οὐσίας. Πολλαχοῦ δὲ τὸ ὂν καὶ τὸν νοῦν τὴν ἰδέαν λέγει· ὥστε Πλάτωνα εἰδέναι ἐκ μὲν τἀγαθοῦ τὸν νοῦν, ἐκ δὲ τοῦ νοῦ τὴν ψυχήν.
13. *Enn.* 5.1[10], 8.23–27. 6.9 [9], written just before 5.1, is titled (by Porphyry) "On the Good or the One." See esp. 6.9 [9], 3.16 on the explicit identification. It must be added, though, that "good" and "one" are not descriptive names for the first principle of all. See 6.9 [9], 6. Cf. Proclus, *PT* 3.7, 29.16–25.
14. See chap. 5, sec. 5.6.
15. See Plato, *Tim.* 47E4, referring to what the Demiurge has done as τὰ διὰ νοῦ δεδημιουργημένα.

Demiurge or Intellect is eternally contemplating Forms, where the contemplation is not a representation of Forms, but cognitive identity with them, "Intellect is identical with that which is intelligible; for if they were not identical, there would be no truth."[16] Hence, it is called "one-many."[17] As for the hypostasis Soul, all Plotinus says here is that the Demiurge makes soul "in the mixing bowl" referring to the generation of the world soul or the soul of the universe and then the generation of individual souls. But these souls are "sisters," not it seems, the hypostasis Soul itself.[18] How, then, are these souls together one as well as many? This is an exceedingly difficult question to answer and we will leave it aside for the moment.[19]

By way of introducing Plotinus's account of the causal connections between the One, Intellect, and Soul, I will try to explain first how the Indefinite Dyad comes into the picture. Here is how the Indefinite Dyad is introduced.

> If, then, Intellect itself were that which is generating, that which is generated must be inferior to Intellect, though as close as possible to Intellect and the same as it. But since that which generates is above Intellect, that which is generated is necessarily Intellect. Why is it not Intellect, the actuality of which is thinking? But thinking sees the object of thinking and turns toward this and is in a way completed by this; it is itself indefinite like sight, and made definite by the object of thinking. For this reason, it is said that "from the Indefinite Dyad and from the One" come the Forms and Numbers.[20] For this is Intellect. For this reason, Intellect is not simple, but multiple, revealing itself as a composition, although an intelligible one, and consequently seeing many things. It is, then, itself intelligible, but also thinking. For this

---

16. See *Enn.* 5.3 [49], 5.22–23: καὶ τὸν νοῦν ταὐτὸν εἶναι τῷ νοητῷ· καὶ γάρ, εἰ μὴ ταὐτόν, οὐκ ἀλήθεια ἔσται. Cf. Aristotle, *Meta.* Λ 9, 1075a4–5: ἡ νόησις τῷ νοουμένῳ μία. The "truth" here is ontological, not semantic. It is the relational property of intelligibles of being transparent or available to an intellect. That thinking and the intelligible are one is something Aristotle and Plotinus agree on. But Plotinus thinks that, though thinking and the intelligible are one in reality, they are two in λόγος. If this is so, then Aristotle is wrong to say that the Unmoved Mover is absolutely simple.

17. The subordination of Intellect to the first principle of all is a straightforward inference from Plotinus's reading of *Phil.* 66A–C where within the fivefold classification of "goods," νοῦς ranks third behind two distinct descriptions of the Good or One, the first as measure and the second as commensurability, beauty, perfection, and sufficiency. See Abbate 2010, 115–140, on Intellect as one-many with an illuminating discussion of how this doctrine is cast into systematic format on the basis of a reading and criticism of Parmenides by Plato.

18. See *Enn.* 2.9 [33], 18.16; and 4.3 [27], 6.13 on the souls as sisters.

19. See *Enn.* 4.9 [8] ("If All Souls Are One"); 4.2 [4] ("On the Essence of the Soul," pt. 2); 6.4 [22] and 6.5 [23] ("On the Presence of Being Everywhere," pts. 1 and 2). Also see Proclus, *In Tim.* 303.24–310.2 where we get a valuable survey of ancient views of the Demiurge and its relation to Soul.

20. See Aristotle, *Meta.* A 6, 987b21–22 and M 7, 1081a13–15.

reason, it is already two. But it is also an intelligible other than the One owing to the fact that it comes after the One.[21]

Let us begin with the straightforward exegesis of this highly compressed text. The One generates Intellect which is distinct from the generator.[22] As generated, it must be unformed. Why? Because if it were formed, it would be a complex of structure and that which is structured, in other words, form and matter. And, indeed, Intellect is just this after it is actualized. But because Intellect is analyzable into structure and structured, it is *more* complex than just the latter, that which is called Indefinite Dyad. Therefore, since generation from the One must proceed in the smallest possible increments—otherwise there would be unacceptable gaps in the generative hierarchy—that which is generated first is Intellect considered as the least complex product possible.[23] When Intellect, so generated, seeks its Good, that is, when it turns to the One, it achieves its goal in the only way Intellect can, that is, by thinking. It thinks all possible intelligibles, that is, all the Forms.[24] Thus, the one-many that is actualized Intellect is the product of the One operating on the Indefinite Dyad. But most importantly, the One operates on the Indefinite Dyad by being the object of its desire, because the One is also the Good. The question that is left completely unanswered in Aristotle's account of how the One generates Forms or Numbers from the Indefinite Dyad is thereby given an Aristotelian answer: the One generates the actual or complete Intellect by being its final cause.[25] In addition, another problem left over from Aristotle's testimony is implicitly solved. This is the problem of how the Indefinite Dyad can be both derived from the One and yet a coordinate principle which, with the One, produces everything else. The solution is that, as Aristotle reports, the Indefinite Dyad

---

21. See *Enn.* 5.4 [7], 2.1–12: Εἰ μὲν οὖν αὐτὸ νοῦς ἦν τὸ γεννῶν, νοῦ ἐνδεέστερον, προσεχέστερον δὲ νῷ καὶ ὅμοιον δεῖ εἶναι· ἐπεὶ δὲ ἐπέκεινα νοῦ τὸ γεννῶν, νοῦν εἶναι ἀνάγκη. Διὰ τί δὲ οὐ νοῦς, οὗ ἐνέργειά ἐστι νόησις; Νόησις δὲ τὸ νοητὸν ὁρῶσα καὶ πρὸς τοῦτο ἐπιστραφεῖσα καὶ ἀπ' ἐκείνου οἷον ἀποτελουμένη καὶ τελειουμένη ἀόριστος μὲν αὐτὴ ὥσπερ ὄψις, ὁριζομένη δὲ ὑπὸ τοῦ νοητοῦ. Διὸ καὶ εἴρηται· ἐκ τῆς ἀορίστου δυάδος καὶ τοῦ ἑνὸς τὰ εἴδη καὶ οἱ ἀριθμοί· τοῦτο γὰρ ὁ νοῦς. Διὸ οὐχ ἁπλοῦς, ἀλλὰ πολλά, σύνθεσίν τε ἐμφαίνων, νοητὴν μέντοι, καὶ πολλὰ ὁρῶν ἤδη. Ἔστι μὲν οὖν καὶ αὐτὸς νοητόν, ἀλλὰ καὶ νοῶν· διὸ δύο ἤδη. Ἔστι δὲ καὶ ἄλλο τῷ μετ' αὐτὸ νοητόν.

22. See *Enn.* 2.4 [12] 5, 32–34; 3.8 [11], 1; 5.1 [10], 6.47–48, 7.1–7; 5.2 [11], 1.10–14; 5.3 [49], 11.1–18; 5.4 [7], 2.24–25; and 6.7 [38], 15–17, 37.18–22. See D'Ancona 1996, and Emilsson 2007, chap. 2, on the generation of Intellect from the One.

23. See Proclus (*In Tim.* 1.378.25–26; *PT* 3.4, 15.24–26), who shares the principle of continuity with Plotinus, but who argues that continuity demands more than three hypostases.

24. *Enn.* 5.1[10], 7 is the essential companion text here.

25. The One or Good is eternally desired and the desire is eternally fulfilled analogous to Aristotle's Unmoved Mover which is eternally desired by the soul of the outermost sphere of the heavens. For the latter, the achievement of the object of desire is by circular motion; for the former, it is by contemplation.

has its own unity or oneness.[26] And, leaving aside for the moment how indefinite duality can be a single principle, it was clear to Plotinus that the Indefinite Dyad is (qualifiedly) one, in which case it participates in the One and so is subordinate to it. This clears up the problem of a putative tension between monism and dualism in the Platonic system. There is, indeed, a unique, absolutely first principle of all. Nevertheless, in the production of Being, the One and the Indefinite Dyad are coordinate principles. That is how Being is one-many.

This interpretation seems to leave us with another obvious question, namely, how are the Forms themselves generated? It is clear that Plotinus does not want to say that they are generated by Intellect as Indefinite Dyad. Plotinus consistently maintains the logical priority of being to knowing.[27] It is also clear that they are not generated independently of Intellect which, as Indefinite Dyad, is the first thing generated. The answer to this question takes us to a central feature of Plotinus's systematic account of Platonism: the use of Aristotelian concepts to express Platonic insights.

We recall from *Republic* that the Idea of the Good is "beyond being in rank and power" (chap. 5, sec. 5.1, 8). That the Good should be unlimited in power (δύναμις) does not mean, for Plotinus, that it is something like pure potency. As absolutely simple, the One cannot have any potency whatsoever.[28] In fact, the unlimited δύναμις of the One is synonymous with its perfect activity or actuality (ἐνέργεια).[29] If Forms or intelligibles are already there to be contemplated by Intellect when it aims for the Good, must we

---

26. See Aristotle, *Meta.* N 1, 1087b9–12: καὶ γὰρ ὁ τὸ ἄνισον καὶ ἓν λέγων τὰ στοιχεῖα, τὸ δ᾽ ἄνισον ἐκ μεγάλου καὶ μικροῦ δυάδα, ὡς ἓν ὄντα τὸ ἄνισον καὶ τὸ μέγα καὶ τὸ μικρὸν λέγει, καὶ οὐ διορίζει ὅτι λόγῳ ἀριθμῷ δ᾽ οὔ (For even those who say that the One and the Unequal are the elements, and the Unequal is composed of the Dyad of Great and Small, say that the Unequal or the Great and Small is one, but they do not say definitely that it is one in formula, though not numerically). Aristotle is complaining here that Plato does not definitely assert what would in fact be an inversion of the Aristotelian principle that something can be one in being but multiple in λόγος. If the Indefinite Dyad is one in λόγος, as it must be if it is a single principle, it must be numerically one. It is minimally one, so to speak. That is why the One is not itself one.

27. See esp. *Enn.* 5.9 [5], 7. Also see 6.2 [43], 19.18–21; 6.6 [34], 8.17–18; and 6.7 [38], 8.4–8.

28. See Cohoe 2017 on the argument for the absolute simplicity of a first principle of all.

29. See *Enn.* 6.8 [39], 20.13–15: Εἰ οὖν τελειότερον ἡ ἐνέργεια τῆς οὐσίας, τελειότατον δὲ τὸ πρῶτον, πρῶτον ἂν ἐνέργεια εἴη (If, then, the activity [of the One] is more perfect than substantiality, the first will be most perfect, and activity would be primary). In this passage, Plotinus is considering what it would mean to attribute substantiality to the One. It cannot be, he thinks, that it *has* substantiality for then it and its being would constitute a complex. Plotinus says that its being without οὐσία is "in a way (οἷον)" its "existence (ὑπόστασις)." But if its existence were without ἐνέργεια, it would be defective. That is, it would not be complete or actual. See also 6.8 [39], 16.16. At 6.8, 16.16, Plotinus calls the One a ἐνέργημα. I do not see any real distinction between ἐνέργεια and ἐνέργημα. At 6.7 [38], 17.10, the previous treatise, the One is said not to be ἐνέργεια in the sense in which this implies life (ζωή). That is, it does not have the ἐνέργεια of the Unmoved Mover whose thinking is a paradigm of life. See Lavaud 2018.

say that the Good is or contains these Forms? But the Good is absolutely simple; indeed, it is because the Unmoved Mover is not absolutely simple—since it is thinking all that is intelligible—that it cannot be the first principle of all. If, though the Good does not in some way contain the Forms, and given that the Intellect as Indefinite Dyad does not generate them, and given that they are not independently generated, how do we explain the being of the Forms? This is a major problem since if the Good is not the explanation or cause of the being of the Forms (and all else), then the motive for positing this first principle of all would be at best undermined. The Good or One must be the Forms, but not in the way that they exist for Intellect. That is, the Good cannot be eminently, that is, paradigmatically, all that is intelligible. Rather, it is virtually all that is intelligible in the way, for example, that white light is virtually the color spectrum or a function is virtually its domain and range.[30] It is Intellect, not the One, that is eminently all intelligibles.[31]

The principal support for this interpretation is Plotinus's claim that every ἐνέργεια, including that which is the One, is twofold, that is, there is the ἐνέργεια τῆς οὐσίας and the ἐνέργεια ἐκ τῆς οὐσίας, the first being internal and the second external.[32] The Intellect as actualized is the second or external actuality of the One. As Plotinus puts it, "That which is virtually all things is already all things."[33] The absolute simplicity of the One is thereby

---

30. See *Enn.* 5.1 [10], 7.9–10; 5.3 [49], 15.33, 16.2; 5.4 [7], 1.24–25, 2.38; 5.5 [32], 12.38–39; 6.7 [38], 32.31, 40.13–14; 6.8 [39], 9.45; and 6.9 [9], 5.36–37. The phrase is δύναμις τῶν πάντων or δύναμις πάντων.

31. Plotinus does say (6.8 [39], 14.39) that the One is οἷον παράδειγμα ("in a way a paradigm"). The οἷον is an important qualification. Only Intellect is unqualifiedly the paradigm of the intelligible reality that there is in the sensible world. The One is a paradigm only in the sense that it is the cause of the being of this paradigm. The ἐνέργεια of the One is "in a way" a paradigm of essence. It possesses all intelligibles "indistinctly (μὴ διακεκριμένα)," that is, not as essences but as the ἐνέργεια that it is. See 5.3 [49], 15.30–32. Also 5.2 [11], 1.1–2.

32. See *Enn.* 2.9 [33], 8.22–25; 4.5 [29], 7.15–17, 51–55; 5.1 [10], 6.34; 5.3 [49], 7.23–24; 5.9 [5], 8.13–15; 6.2 [43], 22.24–29; 6.7 [38], 18.5–6, 21.4–6. Here are three passages from the dialogues that provide the Platonic provenance for this doctrine: (1) *Rep.* 509B6–10 on the production of the Forms by the Good; (2) *Tim.* 29E on the ungrudgingness of the Demiurge which flows from its goodness; (3) *Symp.* 206B with 212A, where the beautiful is identified with the Good and the achievement of the Good produces true virtue. See Proclus, *In Parm.* 3.791.9–26, where the internal ἐνέργεια is indicated as causing "by one's own being (αὐτῷ τῷ εἶναι)." Also see *In Tim.* 3.25.1–16.

33. *Enn.* 5.4 [7], 2, 38–39: καὶ ἐκεῖνο μὲν δύναμις πάντων, τὸ δὲ ἤδη τὰ πάντα. Armstrong mistranslates this as "that is the productive power of all things, and its product is already all things" which, I think, misconstrues the ἤδη, making "all things" the subject of the second clause. MacKenna translates, "That transcendent was the potentiality of the All; this secondary is the All made actual." This translation also misconstrues the ἤδη, in this case because MacKenna sees the One as potentiality, thereby also making "the All" the subject of the second clause. Pradeau's translation is more accurate: "Car le Premier est 'au-delà de la réalité', il est puissance de toutes choses, et il est d'emblée toutes les choses." On the extremely important doctrine of the "two actualities," see 2.9 [33], 8.22–25; 4.5 [29], 7.15–17, 51–55; 5.1 [10], 6.34;

preserved at the same time as its causal activity is affirmed. Because the One is virtually all things, there is nothing outside it such that it can be related to anything else.[34] It does not cause anything to be such that as a result of the causality there exists a real relation between cause and effect. To put the argument in a different way, if there were a real relation between the first principle of all and anything else, then the first principle would have to be an οὐσία, since real relations are only between or among οὐσίαι. But since the first principle is not an οὐσία nor does it have one, it cannot be really related to anything.

The identification of the Good or One with ἐνέργεια provides the answer to the pressing question left over from our discussion of *Parmenides* of how the One of H1, which is above οὐσία and is not even one, can generate anything or have any causal role at all. The One's existence is identical with its ἐνέργεια, which is absolutely simple.[35] It will be recalled that in *Parmenides* H1, all the negative conclusions pertaining to the One resulted from rigorously denying any complexity to it, that is, denying that there can be any legitimate predications made of it. From this, it does not follow that the One does not exist at all, just as it does not follow that the Idea of the Good in *Republic* does not exist at all because it transcends being, the being of that which participates in οὐσία.[36] Plotinus finds in Aristotle's analysis of being the possibility of form without matter insofar as form is identified with ἐνέργεια.[37] But a form separate from matter would still be complex insofar as we can distinguish that which it is from the existence it has, as in *Parmenides* H2. Therefore, an absolutely simple first principle of all cannot be something over and above its existence. It is just *actus essendi*. Plotinus believes he is justified in applying the Aristotelian analysis of being in terms of ἐνέργεια to the interpretation of Plato because *actus essendi* is exactly what the first principle of all must be.

5.3 [49], 7, 23–24; 5.9 [5], 8.13–15; 6.2 [43], 22, 24–29; 6.7 [38], 18.5–6, 21.4–6, 40.21–24. See Emilsson 2017, 48–57, for a good exposition of the doctrine within the Platonic context.

34. See *Enn.* 6.8 [39], 8.12–13: Δεῖ δὲ ὅλως πρὸς οὐδὲν αὐτὸν λέγειν (we should say that it [the One] is altogether related to nothing). Also see 11.32. This does not entail that things are not related to it, particularly as the Good. Cf. Proclus, *In Parm.* 7.1135.17–21; *In Tim.* 1.304.6–9. On there being nothing outside the One, see *Enn.* 5.5 [32], 9; 6.4 [22], 2; 6.5 [23], 1.25–26.

35. See *Enn.* 6.8 [39], 16.15–17: τοῦτο δ' ἐστὶν ὑποστήσας αὐτόν (it [the One] has made itself to exist). Plotinus then goes on (lines 17–18, 35) to identify this self-existent with ἐνέργεια.

36. At *Rep.* 534B8–C5, we have the characterization of dialectic as διορίσασθαι τῷ λόγῳ ἀπὸ τῶν ἄλλων πάντων ἀφελὼν τὴν τοῦ ἀγαθοῦ ἰδέαν (separating the Idea of the Good from all the others by distinguishing it in an account). This separation of the Good, which transcends limited being, must involve negative determination, that is, expressing by means of analysis all that the Good is not. See Krämer (1966) 2014 for a fundamental study of this passage. Aristotle, *Meta.* N 4, 1091b14, says that Plato made the One the essence (οὐσία) of the Good. This would explain both the somewhat odd search for a λόγος for that which transcends οὐσία and the equally odd instruction to separate the Good "from all the others." The Forms are all other than that which is unqualifiedly simple.

37. See *Meta.* Θ 8, 1050b2–3.

Owing to this analysis of the One as perfect or unlimited ἐνέργεια, its causal scope cannot be limited in any way.[38] It is not the case that the causal activity of the One stops with Intellect such that a *per accidens* causal series is thereby set up: A causes B, B causes, C, and so on.[39] The One must be implicated in the being of everything there is. The causality of Intellect is instrumental in the being of everything, including itself as actualized.[40] "Since Soul depends on Intellect and Intellect on the Good, in this way all things depend on the Good through intermediaries, some of these being close and some of these being neighbors of those things which are close, and sensibles at the farthest distance being dependent on Soul."[41] Intellect is the principle of the οὐσία of that which has οὐσία. Soul is the principle of life. But the One is the principle of the being of everything with οὐσία, whether it be alive or not. The subordination of Intellect to the One answers the Middle Platonic dalliance with a duality of Intellects. The incorporation of the Aristotelian analysis of οὐσία as ἐνέργεια and the extension of the concept of ἐνέργεια to that which is "above οὐσία" enables Plotinus to explain how the Good or the One can be above οὐσία and have any causal role, indeed, the primary causal role in metaphysics.

Dwelling on the implications for the necessity of an absolutely simple first principle of all, Plotinus claims that this principle must be above οὐσία, and not, as Aristotle holds, identical with it.[42] This allows Plotinus to give the ultimate explanation for the fact that Being, which is identical with Intellect, is not unequivocally one; rather, Being is a one-many.[43] In a way, Aristotle's error is no less, though different from, the error of Parmenides in thinking that Being is one. If the primary referent of "to be" is the Unmoved Mover, this position can be maintained only if the Unmoved Mover is no longer able to be the first principle of everything, that upon

---

38. See D'Ancona 1992b, 75, 104–113.

39. On the metaphor of emanation, originating in the description of the Good in *Republic* (see above, chap. 5, sec. 5.1, 3), and how it differs from a *per accidens* series, see Gerson 1993.

40. On the instrumental causality of Intellect and Soul, see *Enn.* 6.7 [38], 42.21–24; and 6.9 [9], 1.20–26.

41. *Enn.* 6.7 [38], 42.21–24: Ἀνηρτημένης δὲ ψυχῆς εἰς νοῦν καὶ νοῦ εἰς τἀγαθόν, οὕτω πάντα εἰς ἐκεῖνον διὰ μέσων, τῶν μὲν πλησίον, τῶν δὲ τοῖς πλησίον γειτονούντων, ἐσχάτην δ' ἀπόστασιν τῶν αἰσθητῶν ἐχόντων εἰς ψυχὴν ἀνηρτημένων. Cf. 4.3 [27], 12.30–32; 3.2 [47], 2.15–18. Cf. Proclus, *ET* Prop. 57.8–16, which formalizes this claim. Here, Proclus makes the portentous point that even privation of form comes from the Good since Intellect, the locus of Forms, cannot be the cause of privation of form. Thus, the causality of the One or Good extends beyond that of Intellect. In fact, it extends to matter which is unqualified privation. See Menn (1995, chap. 7), who explains the efficient causality of the Demiurge as eternally available for that which is capable of receiving its causal activity. This (instrumental) causality is analogous to the direct causality of the One.

42. See Gerson 2013b, 267–269.

43. See Plato, *Parm.* 144E5–6: Οὐ μόνον ἄρα τὸ ὂν ἓν πολλά ἐστιν . . . ; and Plotinus, *Enn.* 5.3 [49], 15.20–26; 5.8 [31], 9.23–24; 6.2 [43], 15.15–16, 21.6–11; 6.5 [23], 9.36–40; 6.7 [38], 14.11–15.

which everything depends for its being. As for Parmenides, if Being is one, then there can be no multiplicity of intelligible Being. But if this is so, then the intelligible world loses its explanatory role in relation to the sensible world. The explanation for the predicate in "S is f" can no longer be different from the explanation for the predicate in "S is g." It is essential to keep in mind that this does not mean that there are a multitude of beings even though this is true. The materialists in *Sophist* maintain this, but they cannot say what being is. Plotinus's expression of the systematic Platonic point is that Being itself is one-many. This makes no sense unless there is a first principle which transcends Being and which alone is unqualifiedly one.[44] We may state this as: the oneness of Being is just the unity of a multiplicity. This unity is not notional nor the product of an abstraction. It is the unity of that which participates in the first principle. But since the One is uniquely simple, that unity cannot also be simple. It is intrinsically complex or a multiplicity.

In this way, the internal relatedness of all Forms is explained and ontological truth is preserved. Because Being is a one-many, the ascent to the Good in *Republic*, which is necessary for knowledge of Forms, is an ascent to that which explains this internal relatedness or relative identity of all the Forms.[45]

Because the first principle of all is above Being, it is "self-explanatory (αἴτιον ἑαυτοῦ)."[46] This is Plotinus's systematic expression of the τι ἱκανόν of *Phaedo*. Within an explanatory framework, the first principle of all must be, uniquely, self-explanatory. This is only possible if it is absolutely simple. Hence, the explicability and the complexity of all being are necessarily connected. Even that which is minimally complex—what is initially generated from the One—is explicable only by that which is absolutely simple. Self-explicability is entailed by the very idea of adequate explanation. In the first principle of all, there can be no real distinction between what it is and its existence; such a distinction pertains to everything else. It is Plotinus's appeal to the Aristotelian concept of ἐνέργεια that gives sense to the first principle as a genuine explanans.

In addition, the self-explicability of the first principle reveals how anything else is explicable. The being of everything is explained by absolutely simple activity. The analysis of the "essence" of this activity concludes that it is virtually all things. Therefore, the being of everything is a hierarchically arranged series of expressions of this activity. The One or first principle

---

44. See Aubenque 2009.

45. See *Enn.* 6.7 [38], 2, where Plotinus argues that the "why" for any Form is internal to Being; it is not to be transposed to the One. The internal relatedness of all intelligible reality is self-evident to Intellect. And yet the causal priority of the One is not preempted. The One explains the "to be" of Being, which is essentially variegated.

46. See *Enn.* 6.8 [39], 14.41. This appears to be the first time in the history of philosophy that this phrase is used. Cf. 6.9 [9], 6.44–45.

of all is the Good because these expressions are grades of activity that are naturally oriented to the principle on which they depend for their being.

Self-explicability is not equivalent to inexplicability. To say that the One explains itself is not to say that the existence of the One is just a brute fact. The assertion of brute fact is not one type of explanation; rather, it is the abandonment of explanation altogether. If one removes self-explicability from the framework of explanation, then the only possible *explanantia* are *per accidens* causes. But *per accidens* causes are only of pragmatic efficacy. They provide nothing more than the conditions for real explanations as Plato insisted in *Phaedo*. From the Platonic perspective, Naturalism's rejection of the self-explicable amounts to the rejection of explanation altogether in favor of something like empirical adequacy.

I take this drawing out of the implications for the necessary postulate of an absolutely simple first principle of all to be Plotinus's most important contribution to the construction of the Platonic system. This contribution includes the recourse to Aristotle to show that the unhypothetical first principle, because it is absolutely simple, is also unqualifiedly ἐνέργεια. The evidently heartfelt appreciation for Plotinus's achievement in giving systematic expression to Plato's metaphysics did not prevent his successors from expressing intimations of trouble in paradise, as we shall see.

Plotinus's systematic expression of Platonism or, as I prefer to put it, his expression of the Platonic system, is fundamentally a unified account of what is explicitly in the dialogues, with the important additions provided by Aristotle's testimony and, presumably, Platonists of all stripes working over a period of some six hundred years.[47] What stands out as most remarkable is first, his adroit use of Aristotle, especially Aristotle's doctrine of ἐνέργεια, to express the dynamic of the entire system. The internal and external activities of the fundamental principles just are the μονή and πρόοδος of the systematic triad. Since the One is the Good, it follows that the triad is completed by the ἐπιστροφή of everything to the one goal, which is also the source of all being. This is just Plato or Platonism systematically expressed; it is not something usefully called Neoplatonism. Second, Plotinus shows why Aristotle's metaphysics is not to be discarded on behalf of a defense of Plato, but incorporated *within* the Platonic system, mutatis mutandis. Being cannot be absolutely simple, even though there must be an absolutely simple first principle of all. Absolute simplicity is incompatible with being, where "being" means, roughly, an existent with a nature of some sort. So Being is a one-many. The manyness of Being is owing to the eternal activity of Intellect, and its exploration is mainly what dialectic is. The oneness of

---

47. I would not discount the possibility that some of Plotinus's insights were transmitted orally over that period. Ammonius himself, Plotinus's teacher, wrote nothing and urged Plotinus to write nothing. Plotinus only relented on this pledge when he learned that one of his classmates had already put into writing what they both had been taught.

Being is owing to the One, without whose causal activity the entire explanatory edifice on which the possibility of dialectic depends would crumble.

8.2. Critique of Stoicism

Plotinus is a relentless critic of Stoic philosophy. A consideration of some of the facets of that criticism will, I hope, contribute to the understanding of the opposition of Platonism to Naturalism. Stoicism is particularly interesting in this regard because it seems to offer a tertium quid to the stark opposition of Platonism and Naturalism that I have set forth in previous chapters. The Stoics embrace materialism and mechanism, as I have defined these. Somewhat less clearly, they embrace nominalism.[48] But they certainly do not embrace relativism or skepticism. In fact, as we shall see, antirelativism and antiskepticism are essential parts of Stoic philosophy.[49] Take these away and there is little left that would explain their distinctive and pervasive influence on Hellenistic philosophy and after. The question I am primarily concerned with here is whether it is possible for one to be a materialist, mechanist, and nominalist at the same time as one rejects relativism and skepticism. Plotinus's answer to this question is a definite "no." His claim that Stoicism is incoherent does not lead him to dismiss Stoicism altogether in the way that he dismisses Epicureanism.[50] In fact, Plotinus was not the first or last Platonist to express admiration for, among other things, the Stoic way of life. His position is that this way of life is not justifiable by their incoherent philosophy.

Stoicism presents the best example in antiquity and indeed one of the best examples in the history of philosophy of a sophisticated attempt to implicitly deny a stark opposition between Platonism and Naturalism. The attempt to combine elements of each is one form of syncretism.[51] I have argued that this attempt is most likely doomed to failure, at least so long as consistency remains a philosophical desideratum. This is the view of Rorty and others who strive to maintain a consistent and rigorous Naturalism. A Platonist like Plotinus sees that if one recoils from the implications of this position, the only viable alternative is Platonism. Plotinus sees Stoicism as

---

48. See Syrianus (*In Meta.* 104.17–21 [= *SVF* 2.361]), who sees that Stoics maintain that only "particulars (μόνα)" exist. As a result, they abandon the possibility of ἐπιστήμη unless, as Syrianus says, one wishes to call sense-perception knowledge. Syrianus's remark is very much to the point since, as we shall see, it is crucial to the entire Stoic project that ἐπιστήμη be possible.

49. That is why Skeptics took Stoics to be arch dogmatists.

50. See Longo and Taormina 2016 for a collection of essays exploring the facets of Plotinus's rejection of Epicureanism, a position unequivocally Naturalistic according to Plotinus.

51. I am more concerned here with what I take to be the essential syncretism of Stoicism than with the cruder second-order syncretism of someone like Antiochus of Ascalon who evidently aimed to combine Stoicism with Platonism. For some very helpful comments on the syncretism of Antiochus, see Sedley 2012, esp. the essays by Boys-Stones, Brittain, and Bonazzi.

the primary opposition to Platonism still showing some measure of vitality in the middle of the third century. It is the principled materialism and mechanism of Stoicism that Plotinus finds most unsatisfactory.[52] His arguments against the Stoic claims that only bodies and their properties exist and against what Naturalists generally call causal closure give us an opportunity see how Platonism responds to fundamental doctrines of Naturalism more subtle and sophisticated than those of Anaxagoras or of the materialists Plato presents in *Sophist*.

Plotinus's critique is of Stoic physics, not metaphysics as conceived of by Plato and Aristotle. As materialists or corporealists, Stoics reject the existence of an intelligible world or of intelligible objects.[53] Understanding metaphysics as the science of the intelligible world, the Stoics should be content to reject the possibility of such a science.[54] Plotinus, however, attacks Stoic physics as if it were a metaphysics, that is, a putative science of being qua being without the recognition of immaterial being. It will be recalled that Aristotle maintains that if the objects of theology did not exist, then physics would be first philosophy. But Aristotle also maintains that metaphysics is a science of being qua being and a science of causes and principles. Since being is not univocally predicable of everything that has being, if there is to be a science of being qua being, then there must be a primary referent of "being" and all other referents of "being" must be derived from the primary, where "derivation" means somehow causally derived. In other words, the denial of the existence of a primary referent—which could not be a body or something that exists by nature—is the denial of a science of being qua being. The Stoics, it would seem, simply affirm that the object or

---

52. For materialism thus understood see *SVF* 1.88. For mechanism and causal closure see *SVF* 1.89, and 2.336.

53. One may prefer to call the Stoics corporealists rather than materialists because, technically speaking, the Stoics call only the passive principle in bodies "matter." I shall continue to use the terms interchangeably, understanding that a materialist is committed to the existence only of bodies or three-dimensional solids and their properties or, generally, whatever supervenes on bodies. More precisely, the Stoics rejected the possibility of the causal efficacy of immaterial entities. See, e.g., Sextus Empiricus, *M* 8.263 (= *SVF* 2.363). As Long and Sedley (1987, 1:274) note, the Stoic position combines the materialism of the *Sophist*'s Giants with Plato's own criterion for existence, namely, the power to act or to be acted upon (247D8–E4). Plato holds, as we have seen, that the Good is most powerful in this respect. The debate between Platonism and Stoicism, then, is about what it means to act and to be acted on. The Stoic position may be seen as a reaffirmation and sophisticated revision of the Naturalism criticized in *Phaedo*, in Socrates's "autobiography."

54. See Brunschwig ([1988] 1994 and 2003), who argues that the Stoics, while rejecting metaphysics as conceived by Plato and Aristotle, can be said to have a metaphysics in the sense of science of the most general principles of the cosmos and of its parts. For the Stoics, theology is a part of physics. Brunschwig (2003, 209ff.) maintains that this science of the most general principles of the cosmos and its parts can be said to be ontology, that is, a science of being qua being. But Stoic "ontology" is limited to bodies, meaning that being is not a distinct subject matter. Brunschwig seems to recognize this in his references to "ontology" with scare quotes.

objects of Aristotle's theology do not exist, in which case they have no need of metaphysics. But for Plotinus, this means that the Stoics also must eschew a science of being qua being. This, too, need not trouble them at all. But if the rejection of metaphysics as theology and a science of being also means the rejection of ultimate causes and principles, then that is something more serious.

Plotinus sets out to defeat Stoic materialism by borrowing again from Aristotle. This time, he appeals to a principle of potency (δύναμις) to show the insufficiency of any materialist account of nature. As Plotinus argues,

> The most utterly absurd thing is, quite generally, to rank matter, which is in potency, before everything else, and not rank actuality before potency. For it is not possible for that which is in potency ever to progress to actuality, if that which is potency occupies the place of principle among beings. For, indeed, it will not bring itself to actuality; instead, either something in actuality must exist before it, in which case it is no longer the principle, or, if they were to say they are simultaneous, they would place the principles among chance happenings.[55]

A materialist cannot appeal to potency as a principle of change. This is so because both matter (the passive principle) and god (the active principle) are themselves bodies.[56] Neither one can be the principle of potency since a body must be actual. It is true that the Stoics are reported as holding that god is a "power (δύναμις)."[57] But this cannot be a principle of potency since god as power is the putative cause of change and, as Plotinus notes in the above passage, a potency does not cause itself to change. The immediate upshot of this criticism is that the Stoics are unable to give an adequate explanation of a single change.[58] For this reason alone, materialism is thought by Plotinus to be unsatisfactory. The criticism, though, cuts deeper. For the absence of a concept of potency entails the absence of a clear concept of actuality, since these terms are interdefinable.[59] That is, potencies are a function of actualities and actualities are the existence of things other than as potentially existing. Potencies are what actual hylomorphic composites

---

55. *Enn.* 6.1 [42], 26.1–7: Ὅλως δὲ τὸ προτάττειν ἁπάντων τὴν ὕλην, ὃ δυνάμει ἐστίν, ἀλλὰ μὴ ἐνέργειαν πρὸ δυνάμεως τάττειν, παντάπασιν ἀτοπώτατον. Οὐδὲ γὰρ ἔστι τὸ δυνάμει εἰς ἐνέργειαν ἐλθεῖν ποτε τάξεως ἀρχὴν ἔχοντος ἐν τοῖς οὖσι τοῦ δυνάμει· οὐ γὰρ δὴ αὐτὸ ἑαυτὸ ἄξει, ἀλλὰ δεῖ ἢ πρὸ αὐτοῦ εἶναι τὸ ἐνεργείᾳ καὶ οὐκέτι τοῦτο ἀρχή, ἤ, εἰ ἅμα λέγοιεν, ἐν τύχαις θήσονται τὰς ἀρχάς. See Aristotle, *Meta.* Θ 8, 1049b5. Matter is, for Aristotle, a principle; it is the principle of potency. It is not *in* potency (δυνάμει). I take it that Plotinus's words are elliptical for: the composite of form and matter is, owing to its matter, in potency to or has the potency for, change.

56. See *SVF* 1.98; and 2.299, 300. I might add that if the existence of immaterial entities is rejected by the Stoics because they lack causal efficacy, then so, too, should the existence of potentialities and possibilities, neither of which have causal efficacy.

57. See *SVF* 2.311.

58. The identical criticism could be made of the Naturalism of, say, David Hume.

59. See Aristotle, *Meta.* Θ 6, 1048a30–32.

have generally. Therefore, the Stoic's materialist concept of body is itself inadequate, since for them a body is neither potency nor actuality nor a composite of the two.[60]

The Stoics' inability to see the priority of actuality to potency is the reason they eschew metaphysics. According to Plotinus, this is not merely the benign rejection of a particular subject matter for science in favor of another. It is a rejection of any account of being. So, notoriously, when the Stoics posit incorporeals—place, time, void, and "sayables (λέκτα)"—they are asked to explain what corporeals and incorporeals have in common. The answer is the genus "something (τι)."[61] Corporeal entities exist, but incorporeals only "subsist (ὑφίστασθαι)." The demotion of incorporeals from the realm of existents is due to their causal inefficacy. The genus "something" is purely conceptual. This fits nicely into a Naturalist framework, since the incorporeals can easily be imagined to have an essential role in the scientific explanations of Naturalism. This requires no further inquiry into the nature of "something." Nor does it necessarily lead us to identify "something" with being.

Do the Stoics thus avoid the Platonist charge that as materialists they can only provide necessary conditions for the explanation of a change, whereas only a Platonist can provide the true cause? Plotinus thinks that without a distinction between potency and actuality and without a recognition of the ontological priority of the latter to the former, they do not. It seems fair to say that *if* change is the actualization of a potency qua potency as Aristotle stipulates, then, if the Stoics have no concept of potency, they cannot explain change. If they cannot explain change, then the distinction between a change that is explicable and chance collapses. For chance as such is not explicable. But the conflation of change and chance only has purchase on one who wants to insist on the reality of chance. This is something the Stoics do not wish to do.[62] All things happen according to necessity. The causes of whatever happens and whatever exists are then the necessary and sufficient conditions for that happening or existent. However, without a principle of potency, at least, there is no way to distinguish that which is necessarily and sufficiently caused from that which happens by chance. For the putative necessary and sufficient cause must first have the potency for producing its effect and the effect must have the potency to be that effect. If we cannot say that they have this potency, we are not in a position to identify

---

60. Plotinus's attack on Stoic physics with the use of Aristotelian hylomorphism does not prevent him from attacking certain aspects of that hylomorphism.

61. See *SVF* 2.329–332. Brunschwig (2003, 220–227) discusses the Stoic *summum genus*, including Seneca's apparent modification of τι ("something") to *quod est* ("being"). See Aubenque 2009, 327–328, on Plotinus's criticisms of the Stoic *summum genus*.

62. The Stoics held that "chance (τύχη)" referred to things the causes for which we do not know or perhaps even that we could not know. See *SVF* 2.966 (= Aëtius, *Placita* 1.29, 7), where the view of the Stoics on chance is, interestingly, associated with that of Anaxagoras.

the cause or the effect. We are not in a position, say, to attribute the cause of the water boiling to the fire as opposed to some occult power. This is the Humean point about supposedly necessary connections in nature, only from a Platonic perspective. For, of course, Plotinus does not think that if the Stoics were somehow to countenance the concept of potency in their physics, they would thereby be able to give adequate causal explanations for natural events or processes or entities. To allow that potency is, as we saw, requires that we allow actuality. And actuality is the nonmaterial principle of form. Without that, only necessary conditions are available for a Stoic account, just as they were for Anaxagoras. But as soon as one introduces form, then the explanatory priority of Form to form follows.

The canonical reason given by Stoics for their materialism is a commitment to mechanism. Since immaterial entities have no causal relevance to anything that happens in nature, there is no reason to posit their existence. But as we have seen, incorporeals still have a role to play in Stoic physics, albeit a noncausal role. For the Platonist, this amounts to nothing more than an arbitrary limitation on the meaning of "cause." This is a particularly severe limitation since the only causes are in effect necessary conditions. Because Stoics eliminate potency and thereby the distinction between potency and actuality, they thereby eliminate the distinction between matter and form. That is, the work that the concept of form is intended to do for the Platonists is entirely taken over by the active corporeal principle, god or λόγος. But this principle is either itself analyzable into form and matter, in which case it is not a principle and its matter is *another* matter in addition to that of the passive principle. Or else god is form and without matter, which contradicts materialism.[63]

Because the Stoics do not grasp form as a principle, they embrace nominalism. The Stoics hold that matter is itself "without quality (ἄποιος)."[64] A quality is itself corporeal, acting pervasively on the matter.[65] Hence, a quality is primarily unique to its possessor (τὸ ποιὸν ἰδίως).[66] In a secondary sense, a quality is general, in which case it is a "concept (ἐννόημα)."[67] It is the unique quality of an individual that determines its identity throughout time.[68] It is tempting to reject the label "nominalist" for this view, in favor of "conceptualist."[69] This will not do, I think, for two reasons. First, a concept

---

63. See Plotinus, *Enn.* 6.1 [42], 26.12–17. Plutarch (*De comm. not.* 1085b–c [= *SVF* 2.313]) adds the Platonic point that this active principle is supposed to be an "intellectual body (σῶμα νοερόν)." In that case, it is either a property of the underlying matter or else it is a composite of the "intellectual" property and matter.
64. See *SVF* 1.85.
65. See Simplicius, *In Cat.* 217, 20–22 (= *SVF* 2.383).
66. See Stobaeus, *Ecl.* 1.77, 21–79, 17.
67. See Stobaeus, *Ecl.* 1.136, 21, where it is emphasized that a concept is not a quality.
68. See Simplicius, *In De an.* 217, 36–218, 2 (= *SVF* 2.395).
69. See Sedley 1985; Long and Sedley 1987, 1:182; Brunschwig (1988) 1994, 127–128; and Bailey 2014, 298–306.

is corporeal and so particular. Second, even the generality of the concept is expressible as a conditional covering all particulars within its range.[70] The concept is the intentional object of the particular conceptualizing of the rational agent. But this concept or generalization has no ontological import.[71] The Stoics do indeed want to say that a particular man participates in the concept of a man, but this cannot be an ontological claim if the conceptualizing is peculiar to the one who has it. If one supposes that the concept has an existence apart from the conceptualizing, then either this is bodily or else it is immaterial. If the former, then there is no participation; if the latter, then materialism is false.

The close theoretical connections among Stoic materialism, mechanism, and nominalism should be evident. From the Platonic perspective of Plotinus, embracing all three doctrines dooms Stoicism to explanatory inadequacy in relation to the sensible world. The inadequacy is especially glaring in relation to normativity and knowledge. The Stoics were as dogmatic as Platonists regarding the universality of ethical norms. And, perhaps surprisingly, they shared Plato's view that knowledge, the ne plus ultra of cognition, was infallible.[72] This commitment to infallibility was not, as we shall presently see, a mere excrescence of the Stoic worldview. It was essential to the idea of the sage, the embodiment of the ethical ideal. Therefore, we need to consider whether Stoics could coherently combine their anti-Platonism regarding materialism, mechanism, and nominalism with their Platonism regarding universal normativity and knowledge.

8.3. Platonic and Stoic Wisdom

Just as "assimilation to god (ὁμοίωσις θεῷ)" was taken by Platonists to be a sort of slogan expressing the essence of Platonism, so "live in accordance with nature (ὁμολογουμένως τῇ φύσει ζῆν)" was taken to be a comparable slogan for Stoic ethics.[73] Of course, both slogans require considerable expansion, though it should be pointed out that nature for the Stoics has a

---

70. See Sextus Empiricus, *M.* 11.8–11.

71. The Stoics treated concepts as "no-things" representing or standing for nothing besides individuals. See Stobaeus, *Ecl.* 1.146, 21–137, 6 (= *SVF* 1.65).

72. See Stobaeus, *Ecl.* 2.73, 19 (= *SVF* 1.68). I take the words ἀμετάπτωτον ὑπὸ λόγου ("incontrovertible by reason") to indicate the infallibility of a belief state. Also see 2.130; and 3.112.

73. See D.L. 7.87 (= *SVF* 3.4). D.L. 89 adds that Chrysippus held that "following nature" meant nature in general and human nature. Thus, the normativity is inseparable from Naturalism. D.L. also says that living in accordance with nature is equivalent to (ὅπερ ἐστι) living according to virtue. We may recall that we have found reason to argue against those who, like Vlastos and Penner, take virtue as self-justifying because virtue is a good. But this claim requires the superordinate Idea of the Good to avoid begging the question against those who concede that virtue is a good but that this still does not necessarily give one reason to be virtuous. The Stoic denial of the Good pushes them toward prudentialism, while their commitment to impartial rationality pulls them toward absolutism. That is the inconsistency that Plotinus sees.

unity, that is, an intelligible unity, analogous to the unity provided by the Idea of the Good. For this reason, it will not be a Platonic criticism of Stoic ethics that nature is too variegated to serve as an absolutist criterion.[74]

Plotinus treats Stoic philosophy generally in a way analogous to the way that Plato treats the philosophy of Anaxagoras. We recall that what exercised Socrates initially in his "autobiography" was that Anaxagoras had apparently advertised himself as going to show how Νοῦς had arranged all things in the cosmos for the best. As it turned out, his mechanistic explanations did no such thing. Νοῦς became for him a "wheel turning nothing" as Wittgenstein would have put it. Analogously, Plotinus thinks that Stoics want to posit a principle that does Νοῦς-like things, namely, rationally ordering the cosmos or acting providentially.[75] The Stoics' consistent and explicit commitment to divine providence certainly sets them apart from any pre-Platonic philosopher. But Plotinus, like Plato, thinks that a consistent materialist cannot appeal to intellect or to providence. Indeed, one way of looking at Plotinus's argument strategy is to see him trying to show that providence cannot be identified with necessity because whereas the former requires intellect, the latter does not. In fact, within a materialist framework, intellect is not available. Intellect is not available because intellect cognizes form universally and universality is not reducible to generalization or quantification over a class of individuals.

Before considering Plotinus's argument, let us consider for a moment an obvious Stoic objection to such a strategy. Against Plato and Platonists, a Stoic will maintain that the more a putative divine intellect operates rationally, the more it begins to look just like necessity and nothing more. If, for example, Aristotle's Unmoved Mover may be said to be providential, that is only because all nature necessarily obeys its teleological functioning. But that functioning is notoriously not providential in any sense that needs to be distinguished from necessity.

Plato's view is that the Demiurge is provident, meaning that he aims to make the cosmos as perfect as possible.[76] He does this because he is good,

---

74. Annas (2007) argues that Stoic ethics should not be understood as founded on Stoic physics, that is, on their Naturalism. Instead, she argues that the Stoics generally sought an "integrated picture" which included physics and logic as well as ethics as a distinct science. Two particular targets of Annas are Long 1996 and Striker 1996. Annas is surely correct that the Stoics wanted to integrate the parts of philosophy into a comprehensive account of wisdom and that ethics did not dissolve in this integration. Ethics for the Stoics is not straightforwardly derived from physics. Nevertheless, it is Plotinus's claim that Stoic normative claims assume the truth of Naturalism, whereas Naturalism alone does not justify these claims. Perhaps Annas thinks that the Stoics believe that they can derive their normative claims from a source independent of Naturalism, i.e., independent of their anti-Platonism.

75. See *SVF* 1.160, where Zeno is said to have identified providence with fate, the will of Zeus, god, and necessity indifferently. Cf. Stobaeus, *Ecl.* 1.78.18–20 and 1.79.1–12, where it is evident that Chrysippus is following Zeno. Also see D.L. 7.149.

76. See *Tim.* 29D7–30C1.

not the Good, but essentially participating in it. Plato certainly thinks that "good" adds something to "necessity (ἀνάγκη)," for the Demiurge operates over against the impediments thrown up by necessity.[77] What more does it add? Plato does not directly answer this question, but Plotinus does on his behalf. It is that answer that I want to focus on now in considering his argument against the foundations of Stoic ethics.

If living according to nature is the goal, where the goal is the best life, one must either say that anything that lives according to nature has achieved the identical goal or that goals are gradable according to what living according to nature means for each. Therefore, if plants live according to nature, either they have the best life or else the best life for them is, according to some criterion, not the best life overall. A consistent Naturalist should have no trouble saying the former, but that is not the Stoic position. The Stoics hold that rational living is superior to the living of nonrational beings.[78] What is the measure of their superiority? Presumably, it is that rational beings participate in the divinely ordained necessary order of nature in a way that is not available to nonrational beings. Plotinus, of course, agrees with the fact; he denies, however, that the Stoics can explain why rationally participating in the divinely ordained necessity is superior to participating in it in the way that nonrational beings do. Plotinus thinks that the only satisfactory answer to this question, one that is not available to the Stoics, requires the Idea of the Good as a self-conscious goal.[79]

Plotinus's point is that every goal is a good as such. If nonrational beings achieve their goal, they achieve their good as much as do rational beings. But in order to grade the achievements, a superordinate Good is required. Why should we insist on interspecific gradation over and above the intraspecific gradation according to which one rational being might be closer to the goal than another? What humans have that nonhumans do not in relation to living according to nature is reason as an instrument of living. But the superiority of one kind of life in relation to another is not found in the superiority of one instrument over another. Animals by nature possess the relevant instruments for living according to nature. Therefore, if rational living is superior to nonrational living, it is not because of the nature of instrumental rationality.

The way in which rational beings participate in the divine is that they do so self-consciously or with self-awareness. Consider this passage from Epictetus whose version of Stoic philosophy is almost certainly known to

---

77. See *Tim.* 47E3ff.
78. See D.L. 7.94: τὸ τέλειον κατὰ φύσιν λογικοῦ ὡς λογικοῦ (good is the natural perfection of a rational being qua rational). See Seneca, *Ep.* 124.9–13, where the superiority of rational living to the living of nonrational animals is explicit. Seneca says, "the good will never be in an animal which is nonrational." Their goals are only called "good" by extension.
79. See *Enn.* 1.4 [46], 2.31–3.39.

Plotinus.⁸⁰ "Consider who you are. First of all a human being, and this means that you have nothing more authoritative than your power of moral choice (προαίρεσις) and everything else is subordinate to it, but it itself is free and independent. Consider, then, what you are separate from in virtue of your rationality. You are separate from wild beasts and from sheep. And in addition you are a citizen of the cosmos and a part of it—not one of the servile parts but one of its principal parts. For you are able to follow the divine administration and figure out what comes next."⁸¹ Like nonrational beings, we must follow necessity or fate. But unlike nonrational beings, we can participate in this necessity willingly or unwillingly. To do so unwillingly—the standard modus operandi of nonsages—is to fail to distinguish oneself from the way that animals participate in the divine. Our superiority lies in our ability to self-reflexively embrace necessity or rationality.

Plotinus's principal objection to this account of graded goodness or graded happiness is that neither the self-awareness nor the universal standard of goodness are available to materialists.⁸² It is clear enough why the universal trans-specific Good is, for Plotinus, both necessary for normativity and unavailable to the Stoics. It is not so clear why self-awareness is not. For Stoics, the soul is a body and self-awareness takes place there. But a body is an extended magnitude, something with μέγεθος. Therefore, it has parts outside of parts; these parts can only be juxtaposed.⁸³ If a thought is, roughly, a state of one part of that body, then the self-awareness that one is in that state must belong to *another* part. But then the supposed self-awareness is not self-awareness at all. It amounts only to the grasping by one part of the soul of the state or condition of another. Accordingly, the claim to the superiority of rationality is not justified.⁸⁴

---

80. There are at least three places in I 4 alone in which Plotinus is likely thinking of the *Discourses* of Epictetus: 7.21–22, 31–33; 9.1–5; and 11.8.

81. Epictetus, *Disc.* 2.10.1–4. The Aristotelian term προαίρεσις is used in Epictetus to indicate what is "up to us (τὸ εφ' ἡμῖν)" as opposed to what happens by necessity or fate. Plotinus elsewhere (*Enn.* 6.8 [39], 1–6) lays great importance on determining what is up to us or that over which we are authoritative. Wrongdoing is *not* up to us, because no one does wrong willingly; the only thing that is up to us is to do what is good.

82. See Coope (2016), who argues that later Neoplatonists, in particular Ps.-Simplicius, employ a notion of self-reflexivity to criticize the Stoic doctrine of assent. I think this is true, but Coope does not mention the consequence of this for Stoic materialism. For all Platonists, self-reflexivity is possible only for immaterial souls.

83. See *Enn.* 4.7 [2], 8². The Stoics' term for juxtaposition is παράθεσις. Their attempt to manufacture self-awareness within a consistently materialist context by claiming that the parts of a mixture can totally interpenetrate each other is criticized by Plotinus au fond at 2.7 [37].

84. See *Enn.* 5.3 [49] which is an extended analysis of why knowledge is, paradigmatically, self-awareness. See Rödl 2018, passim. At 1.4 [46], 2.25–28, Plotinus argues that for any state deemed superior, the rational awareness of being in that state is superior to the state itself. The argument is directed against Epicureans who think that happiness is being in a pleasurable state, but the argument would apply equally to the Stoics who think that the virtuous state

The resolute Naturalist will not be troubled by this. It is perfectly adequate to maintain that such self-awareness as we have is really something like self-monitoring by one subsystem of another, sort of like the self-checking mechanism of a computer. If the Stoics have trouble defending universal normativity, perhaps the problem is in their thinking that this requires a notion of rationality to which no Naturalist need aspire. Perhaps Stoics should be consistent Naturalists and add relativism to their nominalism, materialism, and mechanism. If they do this, however, then their imperative "live according to nature" must take a relativistic form.[85] Rationality must be construed as the servant of the passions, not the authoritative part of the soul fidelity to which is the mark of the ideal human being. In short, Stoicism cannot retain materialism and universal normativity.

Stoicism, like Epicureanism and other forms of Naturalism, appeals to the efficacy of scientific knowledge as essential to wisdom. For the Stoics, the sage is not just one who has scientific knowledge, but one who is transformed by that knowledge.[86] The transformation entails an elimination in oneself of all that is in tension with fate or necessity. That is why unimpeded rationality must be authoritative. Perhaps surprisingly, the Stoics agree with Plato that knowledge must be infallible. Since, for a materialist, knowledge must be exclusively representational, it seems pointless for the Stoics to insist on infallibility. Yet they clearly do. Why? Perhaps the reason is that without an infallible mental state, having merely true representations of reality could not be sufficiently transformative. "True belief" would be the correct name for such a state, and this is the purview of the fool or anyone but the sage. For example, one may truly believe that the suffering of one's children was inevitable and so providential. But if distress is not eliminated by this true belief, then Stoicism as a form of rational therapy fails. Why, then, is infallible knowledge transformative?

Consider a belief that one has regarding one's own imminent demise. Let us suppose that it is in fact a false belief. Then one discovers that the belief is false, that is, that the true belief is that one's demise is not imminent. We can easily imagine the wave of physical and emotional relief that would pass over one. We could, I think, say with conviction that one was transformed in this by the acquisition of the true belief or, stated otherwise, the realization that one's previous belief was false. The example is of a belief concerning one's own well-being. It is nothing like a belief regarding the well-being of the cosmos. But knowledge, as opposed to belief, is supposed to be about

---

is superior. Also see 1.1 [53], 9.20–22; 4.1 [21], 1.48–53; 4.7 [2], 3.1–5; 5.4 [7], 2.15–20; 5.6 [24], 5.1–8; 6.4 [22], 9.36; and 6.7 [38], 16.19–22, 41.26–27.

85. A Naturalist who is inclined to argue for normativity on the basis of evolution, that is, the survival benefits of, say, cooperation, cannot attain to universality. The simple reason for this is that survival is relative to a particular social or cultural or biological niche.

86. Thus, virtue is identified with the acquisition of knowledge (ἐπιστήμη). See D.L. 7.92 (= *SVF* 3.265); Stobaeus *Ecl.* 2.58, 5 (= *SVF* 3.95); Sextus Empiricus, *M.* 9.153 (= *SVF* 3.274).

oneself only insofar as one is a part of the cosmos. A true belief that the suffering of one's children is inevitable is not transformative even if it arises after a false belief that the suffering is not inevitable because this belief is controvertible by reason. One's concomitant distress is due to one's emotions which are false beliefs. And the true belief is not enough to eliminate the false ones. Only knowledge is like this because only knowledge occurs without the addition of any such false beliefs. To know of the inevitability is to wholeheartedly assent to it. A mere true belief accompanied by the false belief that is an emotion is incapable of being transformational. That is why the Stoics insisted that the sage does not possess representational truths, but that the leading part of the soul is the truth.

Sextus Empiricus reports that the Stoics distinguished between true and truth. The former is an incorporeal sayable and the latter is corporeal and is the leading part of the soul disposed in a certain way.[87] Any fool can say or believe true propositions but only the sage internalizes the rational structure of the cosmos.[88] The rationality that is the active principle in the cosmos transforms the leading part of the soul into a consonant state. It is, so to speak, a formula manifested in a different medium, that of the leading part of the soul. The infallible mental state of the sage seems to be something like a state of grace in which error is impossible.

Plotinus is far from denying the transformative effect of knowledge acquisition. He would go further and agree that the transformation consists in identifying oneself with the objects of knowledge. But, again, the transformative identification is, for him, not possible within a materialist framework. For Plotinus, identification with Intellect is the obverse of separation from the body.[89] For the Stoics, identification with the corporeal leading part of the corporeal soul is the obverse of separation from another part of one's body. In short, the transformation is as implausible as is the self-awareness. The materialist vocabulary does not allow the Stoics to express what the transformation really is, an immaterial identification of the subject of one's appetites with the subject of rational activity. These subjects are both the same and different in precisely the way that any paradigm in the intelligible world is the same as and different from its manifestations in the intelligible world. The kind of transformation Plato and Plotinus both have in mind is not possible in a materialist framework.[90] Indeed, it is also not possible within an entirely intelligible or immaterial framework since any intelligible eternally remains what it is. Rather, the transformation requires a soul that has the ontological structure of an

---

87. See Sextus Empiricus, *PH* 2.81–83. Cf. *M* 7.38 (= *SVF* 1.132).
88. See *SVF* 2.913 where truth, fate, nature, and λόγος are said to be of the same οὐσία.
89. See *Enn.* 1.8 [51], 7.12–13; and 2.9 [33], 6.40.
90. One might speculate that Plotinus's anti-Stoic treatise 2.7 [37], titled "On Complete Blending," is intended to show why, given that two bodies cannot be in the identical place at the identical time, a putative Stoic self-transformation is impossible. Cf. 4.7 [2], 8^2.7–21.

image, that is, it is like its immaterial paradigm but is at the same time manifested in a corporeal substrate.[91]

From the Platonic perspective, Stoics have elevated necessity to the rank of the providential when in fact necessity is in conflict with providence. This does not mean, of course, that providence can overcome necessity. It is just not reducible to it. Whatever the Good or One can do, it does, and it does so freely or without impediment.[92] Providence consists in our being hardwired to the Good, so there is nothing else that we truly desire. To reject providence is to turn in the direction of necessity, the opposite of that desire. For Plotinus, the Stoics' exhortation to embrace necessity is a direct result of their refusal to admit an immaterial first principle of all. Embracing necessity is an option, of course, but not in combination with universal normativity. If Stoics were not half-hearted Naturalists, they would reject universal normativity. But the continued recognition of necessity would provide no basis for their ethics. Nor would it provide a basis for their Platonically inspired recognition of the sovereignty of reason.

Naturalists should agree with Platonists that Stoicism seeks an indefensible tertium quid between Platonism and Naturalism. Stoicism's implicit efforts at rapprochement are particularly instructive since it is in ethics that such efforts are most often found.[93] Plotinus gives short shrift to any effort to isolate ethics from metaphysics, that is, from the supersensible subject matter of philosophy or first philosophy. It is difficult to see how a "Socratic" ethics without metaphysics, as Vlastos and others would have it, can amount to anything other than prudentialism. This is not necessarily a criticism of prudentialism; it is only a criticism of the pretension that ethics without metaphysics names a specific subject matter regarding which philosophers may strive to attain a particular expertise.[94]

---

91. The paradigm is the undescended intellect of each person. See *Enn.* 3.4 [15], 3.24; 4.3 [27], 5.6, 12.3–4; 4.7 [2], 10.32–33, 13.1–3; 4.8 [6], 4.31–35, 8.8; 6.4 [22], 14.16–22; 6.7 [38], 5.26–29, 17.26–27; and 6.8 [39], 6.41–43.

92. See *Enn.* 6.8 [39], 6. The will of the Good makes the will for the Good free.

93. D.L. 7.2 tells us that Zeno, when he came to Athens, studied with Crates but also with Xenocrates, the second successor to Plato in the Academy, and then his successor Polemo for ten years. Simplicius (*In Arist. DC* 12.23) tells us that Xenocrates was Plato's "most authentic (γνησιώτατος)" pupil. So it is hardly surprising that Zeno and his own Stoic successors would have appropriated a great deal of Platonism. It is not so difficult to surmise that they wanted the absolutism of Plato's ethics without the metaphysical baggage that accompanied it. In this, they began a long tradition in Western philosophy that continues to this day.

94. See Putnam (2004, 85), who maintains that ontology (i.e., metaphysics) "has become a stinking corpse, although in Plato and Aristotle it represented the vehicle for conveying many genuine philosophical insights." Putnam's "ethics without ontology," along with his "conceptual pluralism," is one version of prudentialism.

CHAPTER 9

Proclus and Trouble in Paradise

Proclus (412–485), living some two hundred years after Plotinus, extended the systematization of Platonism beyond anything for which we have evidence. And it is Proclus, in part through Pseudo-Dionysius, and in part through the *Liber de Causis*, who served as the gateway to Platonism for the next millennium.[1] Proclus was at once full of admiration for Plotinus as an exegete of Plato and also frequently critical of him. Here, I want to focus on what I take to be a few of Proclus's major contributions to the systematic project. Finally, I want to briefly introduce the analytic prowess Proclus shows in discovering a deep problem in the systematic construction of Platonism. This is a problem that Proclus's student, Damascius, exploits in a remarkable way.

9.1. The Dynamics of the Platonic System

As we saw in both Plato and Plotinus, the fundamental systematic law of Platonism is expressed as "remaining (μονή)," "procession (πρόοδος)," and "reversion (ἐπιστροφή)."[2] The procession, as Proclus says, is *from* the first principle as One and *to* the first principle as Good.[3] In his *Elements*

---

1. See Beierwaltes 1985; Bos and Meijer 1992; Gersh 2014; Adamson and Karfik 2017; and Butorac and Layne 2017 for introductions to the astonishing range of influence that Proclus had on later philosophy.
2. See Plotinus, *Enn.* 5.2 [11], 1.7–21; and *Rep.* 505D5–9, 508B6–7.
3. See Proclus, *ET* Prop. 113; *PT* 2.6, 40.9–17; *In Tim.* 1.285.29–286.4; and *In Parm.* 6.1097.10ff.; 58 Klibansky. The section of the *In Parm.* discovered and edited by Raymond Klibansky is included in translation at the end of Morrow and Dillon 1987.

of Theology, Proclus connects the procession with the distinction between cause (αἰτία) and condition in *Phaedo* and cause and accessory to the cause (συναίτιον) in *Timaeus*.

> Every cause which is said to be a cause in the principal sense transcends its effects. For if such a cause were in its effect, either it would belong to the latter, or else it would be in need of it to exist, in which case it would be inferior to that which is caused. That which is in the effect is more an accessory cause than a real cause, being either a part of that which comes to be or an instrument of the producer. This is so because the part in that which becomes is less perfect than the whole and the instrument serves the producer with respect to the generation, though it is unable by itself to set the limits of production. Therefore, every cause in the principal sense, is really more perfect than that which proceeds from it and itself provides the limit of its production, transcending the instruments, the elements, and everything which is called an accessory to the cause.[4]

Here, the system dynamics is set within the hierarchical explanatory framework. Since every effect as effect is inferior to its cause, and since every cause is also an effect insofar as it is composite, the ultimate cause must be ultimately perfect. Thus, the Forms as paradigms are more perfect than their likenesses, whose intelligibility they serve to explain. But the Forms themselves, being composites, must participate somehow in the One, the ultimate explanation for everything.[5]

What makes an effect related to a cause is its being the same as it, though at the same time inferior, as we have just seen.[6] All reversion depends upon this sameness. For everything desires its own good, and that good is found

---

4. See Proclus, *Elements of Theology* (*ET*), Prop. 75, 70.28–72.4: Πᾶν τὸ κυρίως αἴτιον λεγόμενον ἐξῄρηται τοῦ ἀποτελέσματος. ἐν αὐτῷ γὰρ ὄν, ἢ συμπληρωτικὸν αὐτοῦ ὑπάρχον ἢ δεόμενόν πως αὐτοῦ πρὸς τὸ εἶναι, ἀτελέστερον ἂν εἴη ταύτῃ τοῦ αἰτιατοῦ. τὸ δὲ ἐν τῷ ἀποτελέσματι ὂν συναίτιόν ἐστι μᾶλλον ἢ αἴτιον, ἢ μέρος ὂν τοῦ γινομένου ἢ ὄργανον τοῦ ποιοῦντος· τό τε γὰρ μέρος ἐν τῷ γινομένῳ ἐστίν, ἀτελέστερον ὑπάρχον τοῦ ὅλου, καὶ τὸ ὄργανον τῷ ποιοῦντι πρὸς τὴν γένεσιν δουλεύει, τὰ μέτρα τῆς ποιήσεως ἀφορίζειν ἑαυτῷ μὴ δυνάμενον. ἅπαν ἄρα τὸ κυρίως αἴτιον, εἴ γε καὶ τελειότερόν ἐστι τοῦ ἀπ᾽ αὐτοῦ καὶ τὸ μέτρον αὐτὸ τῇ γενέσει παρέχεται, καὶ τῶν ὀργάνων ἐξῄρηται καὶ τῶν στοιχείων καὶ πάντων ἁπλῶς τῶν καλουμένων συναιτίων. See the stimulating analysis of Lloyd 1990, chaps. 4–5.

5. See *In Parm.* 7.64.1–24 Klibansky, where Proclus argues against those of his predecessors who claim that the One of H1 is nothing or that "One" is an empty name.

6. See *ET* Prop. 29, 34.3–4: Πᾶσα πρόοδος δι᾽ ὁμοιότητος ἀποτελεῖται τῶν δευτέρων πρὸς τὰ πρῶτα (All procession is accomplished through sameness of the secondaries [the effects] to the primaries [the causes]). The sense of "sameness" should be understood according to the following consideration. What makes something an effect of a cause is that the cause is able to produce just that effect. To be the same as a cause is to be a product of the kind of thing that that cause is. It is an analytic truth that a cause cannot produce something that is not the same as it in some respect or at some level of generality. The inferiority of an effect to its cause just follows from the necessary dependence of the effect on the cause. No cause other than the first cause is not inferior to some other cause, that is, it is the effect of some cause.

in the paradigm of the thing's nature.⁷ Thus, all things revert to the Good insofar as they are able or according to kind.⁸ Either they revert merely by existing, or by existing and by living, or by existing, by living, and by cognition.⁹ The limitless fecundity of the first principle of all thus guarantees the maintenance of the system. Since everything depends on the first, along with the instrumentality of Intellect and Soul, for being what each thing is, and since all desire the Good according to kind, the perpetuity of the system is assured.

Procession and reversion are found both in the eternal world and in the temporal world, although the former seems somewhat obscure.¹⁰ If Intellect proceeds from the One and reverts to it, how are these supposed to be distinguished? One part of an answer to this problem is to cast procession and reversion into causal dependence and final causality. That is, B proceeds from A if B is eternally dependent on A. B reverts to A if A is B's good, which it must be since B is the same as A, only inferior to it.

Additionally, understanding procession as a causal relationship requires showing that the idea of stable intellectual motion or activity makes sense.¹¹ Assuming it does, this activity is born out of desire for the Good. At the same time, we know that whatever desires the Good does so because it is produced by the Good as One. The "spiritual circuit" as it is sometimes called, is what an active universe looks like when it is viewed from the top down rather than from the bottom up.¹² Presumably, the way for a Naturalist to stop this line of thinking in its tracks, so to speak, is to deny that everyone and everything desire the one real Good. It seems pointless to deny that all desire and all action based on desire is aimed at a good of some sort. The claim discussed in chapter 6 that desire for the Good should be understood to be desire for integrated unity according to kind deflects the

---

7. See *ET* Prop. 32, 36.3–4: Πᾶσα ἐπιστροφὴ δι' ὁμοιότητος ἀποτελεῖται τῶν ἐπι στρεφομένων πρὸς ὃ ἐπιστρέφεται (All reversion is accomplished through sameness of the things reverting to that to which they revert). As Dodds ([1933] 1963, 219) notes, Proclus no doubt has in mind *Tht.* 176B where the flight to the divine is accomplished through sameness. We should add, though, that the sameness is an achievement requiring "virtue and wisdom." The endowment is the capacity for this achievement, an endowment explained by a cause.

8. See *PT* 1.22, 101.27–102.1. Proclus says that things revert to the Good "some more and some less (τὰ μὲν μᾶλλον, τὰ δὲ ἧττον)." I take this to indicate desire for the Good is according to kind.

9. See *ET* Prop. 39, 40.27–28: Πᾶν τὸ ὂν ἢ οὐσιωδῶς ἐπιστρέφει μόνον, ἢ ζωτικῶς, ἢ καὶ γνωστικῶς (All being reverts either in virtue of being an existent or vitally or cognitionally).

10. See Lloyd (1990, 126–135), who raises the obvious question of how to distinguish reversion from remaining in the intelligible world.

11. See *In Parm.* 7.1152.33ff., 1153.3–6; and *PT* 1.14, 66.8–11. At *PT* 3.6, 26.13–27, Proclus gives a particularly clear exposition of the reason for the claim at *Soph.* 248E6–249A5. Intellect is inseparable from Being. The presence of Intellect entails the presence of motion (and stability) and life (but *not* Soul, which is inferior to Intellect the paradigm of life). See esp. Gersh 1973, 16–24, 115–117.

12. See *ET* Prop. 33, 36.1–6 on the "cyclical activity (κυκλικὴν ἐνέργειαν)."

charge that goods vary. Of course they do, since there are different kinds of things. What the spiritual circuit is taken by Platonists to reveal is that the variety of kinds are not adventitious or accidental and that their explanation as per the argument in *Phaedo* is found only in τι ἱκανόν, the cause of the being of the variety of kinds.[13] That a human being desires the real Good, that is, what is good for a human being, does not seem like a fantastic notion. But why? Why not desire to be a member of a different kind? Why not spiritual linearity rather than spiritual circularity? As Plotinus reasons, to achieve one's own good requires attaining knowledge of one's identity. And this is only possible if one knows where one comes from.[14] "Where one comes from," of course, is to be understood not as a time or place or family, but the paradigmatic cause we instantiate. To understand one's lineage in this sense is inevitably to distance oneself from the desires for anything inferior to oneself. Proclus even more explicitly than Plotinus provides the metaphysical foundation that explains the ascent to the Good in *Symposium* and elsewhere. I think that these Platonists would rest their case on the superiority of their account of the love of the beautiful and the Good to any other, especially the polar opposite of that account that is found in Naturalism.

9.2. A Crack in the System?

Let us begin with a crucial distinction made explicitly by Proclus in his *Elements of Theology*, though probably originally made by Iamblichus. "All that is unparticipated produces from itself the things that participate in it, and all the existents that are participated in are connected in the upward direction to existents not participated."[15] One of the principal problems that the first part of *Parmenides* leaves to be solved by the exercise of the second part is how the Forms can be participated in without them thereby becoming divided. If, on the one hand, the Form is divided, how can it be a one-over-many? If, on the other hand, the Forms are not to be divided, then how can they be participated? The beginning of a solution comes, as we have seen, in *Sophist*, where Plato distinguishes between any one of the μέγιστα

---

13. See *In Parm.* 2.726.2–3, "sameness is a sort of oneness (ἡ ὁμοιότης ἑνότης τις ἐστί)." The overall explanation for reversion is the remaining of that in which everything is one. The sameness of that which processes to that which remains, however, is not reciprocal; it is derivative. See 4.921.5–922.1; Plotinus, *Enn.* 1.2 [19], 2.7.

14. See *Enn.* 5.1 [10], 1.

15. See *ET* Prop. 23, 26.22–24: Πᾶν τὸ ἀμέθεκτον ὑφίστησιν ἀφ' ἑαυτοῦ τὰ μετεχόμενα, καὶ πᾶσαι αἱ μετεχόμεναι ὑποστάσεις εἰς ἀμεθέκτους ὑπάρξεις ἀνατείνονται. Cf. *In Parm.* 1.707.8–18, and 6.1069.23ff. See *In Tim.* 2.240.4–10, 313.15–22, for the attribution of this distinction to Iamblichus. See Dodds ([1933] 1963, 210–211), who notes that this distinction is implicit in Plotinus (see, e.g., 6.2 [43], 12.12–14), though it is only fully thematized by Proclus. The terms ὑπόστασις and ὕπαρξις seem to be used by Proclus synonymously. See Chlup 2012, 99–111, on the uses Proclus makes of this distinction.

γένη and the nature it has. Thus, for example, Identity is self-identical because it participates in its own nature; Difference can participate in the same nature without thereby being identified with Identity.[16] Proclus, citing Iamblichus as a source, applies the threefold distinction between unparticipated, participated, and participant throughout the intelligible world. This distinction is also in line with the distinction implicitly made by Plato between Form and nature, which is repackaged by Aristotle as the distinction between substance or individual and universal.

To distinguish the nature of a Form from the Form itself is to invite the question of whether the nature has its own unity or oneness apart from the oneness that belongs to the composite Form plus nature. For example, if we must distinguish the Form of Circularity from the nature of circularity, the latter being that which is participated in when something is identified as a circle, does this nature have being distinct from the being of the Form? In that case, it would seem to have its own unity.[17] If, though, the nature has its own unity because it has its own being and these are distinct, then an infinite regress obviously threatens to arise.

The distinction is a powerful conceptual tool for articulating the ontological hierarchy and it is an essential corollary to the principle that everything has the nature it has by participation.[18] But were this distinction to be applied to the absolutely simple One, then we would have to distinguish within it the participated element and the unparticipated element.[19] This, however, is impossible for that which is absolutely simple; not even a conceptual distinction can be made in reference to it, for which reason it is truly ineffable.[20] But if this One cannot be participated in, what explanatory role is it supposed to fulfill? Evidently, there is *some* One which can be participated in and which does fulfill *some* explanatory role, although it is not yet clear exactly what this is. But it is precisely because this putatively participatable One cannot be absolutely simple that a superordinate absolutely simple One is needed. The new problem forced on Iamblichus and all his successors is that the necessity of there being an absolutely simple first principle of all along with the above corollary forces us to ask why there must be such a principle at all. Either participation does not require complexity in that which is participated in or else the One cannot be participated in, in which case it is a wheel turning nothing. It is actually worse

---

16. Plato uses the language of participation (τὸ μετέχειν) for the combination or blending of the Kinds, but we need not suppose that this sort of participation is to be characterized in the same way as the participation of the sensible world in the intelligible world.

17. See *PT* 3.3, 13.13–16.

18. See *ET* Prop. 3, 4.1, where the theorem is that "all that becomes one does so by participation in unity (Πᾶν τὸ γινόμενον ἓν μεθέξει τοῦ ἑνὸς γίνεται ἕν)." "One," here, is the generalized predicate standing for any one nature that a thing participates in.

19. See *In Parm.* 7.68.2–4 Klibansky.

20. See *In Parm.* 6.1041.24–26; and 7.1145.26–1146.21, 1149.24–1150.27.

than that. The putative ultimate principle seems no longer to be a goal in any sense, since if it is, we would have to be able to make sense of the idea of being closer or father away from it. But if this is possible, then it would seem to be possible to say what it is; for example, that it is the Idea of the Good. But Iamblichus and Proclus are right to insist that the One of the first hypothesis of *Parmenides* is beyond all determination whatsoever. This denial of determination would presumably include its being virtually all things, as Plotinus maintained.

It will be recalled from the previous chapter that Plotinus identified the first principle of all with ἐνέργεια, but that he denied that this principle is really related to anything.[21] All things are really related to it, primarily in the relation of existential dependence. In addition, all things participate in the One.[22] Plotinus does not address the glaring problem: How can that which is absolutely simple be participated in?

Proclus actually begins the *Elements of Theology* with the sentence: "Every plurality participates in that which is one in some way."[23] It is the small word πῇ ("in some way") that conceals the problem. Proclus specifically denies that the One is ἐνέργεια.[24] Nevertheless, he insists that the One is the cause of everything, that which preserves (σῴζεσθαι) all things in existence.[25] How can it do this without being participated in? How does participating "in some way" solve the problem?

Proclus reasons that, given the absolute simplicity of the first principle of all, the One, it is not possible to derive the multiplicity of intelligibles directly. Therefore, there needs to be posited Henads, paticipatable Ones, one each for every intelligible.[26] The first principle, generally unparticipatable, is participatable "in some way" by participation in the Henads.[27] That is, while each Form is a one, its own unity is participated, and that unity cannot be the first principle. Hence, there must be an intermediary more unified than each Form but less unified that the One itself.[28]

---

21. See *Enn.* 6.8 [39], 17.25–27. Cf. 8.22, 11.32; 1.7 [54], 1.16–17; 6.7 [38], 23.18.
22. See, e.g., *Enn.* 1.7 [54], 2.4; 5.3 [49], 17.8–9; 6.2 [43], 17.18–19.
23. See *ET* Prop. 1, 2.1: Πᾶν πλῆθος μετέχειν πῃ τοῦ ἑνός. Cf. *PT* 2.4, 34.24–35.9; Plotinus, *Enn.* 6.9 [9], 1.1.
24. See *In Parm.* 7.1172.18–19, πρὸ ἐνεργείας ἐστὶ πάσης τὸ ἕν. Also 6.1106.5–6, where Proclus rejects the view of those who place ἐνέργεια prior to οὐσία. Cf. *PT* 2.7, 50.14: μήτε ἐνεργοῦντος; 3.1, 6.1: καὶ πάσης ἐνεργείας κεχωρισμένην [the primary cause, that is, the One].
25. See *In Parm.* 7.1150.13–17; *ET* Prop. 57, 56.14–16; *PT* 2.1, 3.6–8, πρωτίστην αἰτίαν.
26. See *In Tim.* 4.12.22–30. Cf. *In Parm.*1.702.29–34, 5.1032.20–24, 6.1043.9–29; and *PT* 3.3, 13.6–14.3.
27. See *PT* 3.4, 14.11–15.15.
28. See Saffrey 2003, lii–lx; Chlup 2012, chap. 3; and Butler 2014, 1–93. There is undoubtedly a tension in the works of Proclus in regard to how the Henads and the principles of Limit and Unlimited are to be ordered. See D'Ancona 1992a. See *PT* 3.6, 28.18–19; 12, 45.13–46.22; 14, 51.6–7; and 24, 86.7–9, passages which perhaps contain the solution: there is a hierarchy

The Henads are derived from or produced by the One not by any means that implies that these Henads participate in the One.[29] Since procession from the One implies absence of identity, but since there can be no participation in the One as a result of procession, the Henads are said to proceed by way of unity.[30] Whereas Plotinus argued that the uniqueness of the absolutely simple entails that whatever proceeds from the One is different from it, Proclus attempts to infer a sense of "otherness" that is not "difference." If the Henads, as superessential Ones, are not different from each other by essence, their difference from each other may be contrasted with their otherness in relation to the One. If this is the case, then each Henad can provide the unity that participating in an intelligible nature requires without thereby implicating the One itself.

Proclus explicitly justifies this move as necessary to explain his polytheism.[31] Indeed, it is clear that his polytheism is the driving force in the system. For, as he says in the *Parmenides Commentary*, "each of the gods is nothing other than the One as participated."[32] Leaving aside Proclus's religious motivation, the problem remains the same whether there are multiple gods or one god, identified or not identified unqualifiedly with the first principle of all. Insofar as this god must be absolutely simple, it cannot it seems be participated in; but if it cannot be participated in, its causal role seems to be exiguous.

Proclus adds another reason for the positing of Henads either in addition to or instead of the absolutely simple One. Since the One is the Good and the Good is self-diffusive, it cannot proceed by way of a weakening or diminution of itself.[33] But any plurality would represent such a diminution. By contrast, Plotinus insists on the logical point that any procession from the One will be inferior to it but this does not indicate a diminution of the Good itself.

The dispute between Plotinus and Proclus (including those before and after Proclus who noticed the problem about participation) goes to the heart of Platonism. We recall that the motivation for the search for an absolutely simple first principle of all was explanatory adequacy. Only that which was autoexplicable could, finally, explain everything else, that is, everything that is heteroexplicable. Autoexplicability, as Plotinus argued,

---

of Henads, at the apex of which are the Henads identified with the principles of Limit and Unlimited. See Van Riel 2017, 89–94.

29. See *In Parm.* 7.1190.4–1191.7. Here, the Henads are said to be ἄλλα ("other") than the One but not ἕτερα ("different from") it. Cf. *In Tim.* 1.363.26–364.11. Even the Demiurge does not participate in the One.

30. *In Parm.* 2.745.14–747.14. Cf. *PT* 3.3, 12.10–14.

31. See *ET* Prop. 113. See Beierwaltes 1973, 128.

32. See *In Parm.* 6.1069.5–6: καὶ οὐδὲν ἄλλο ἐστὶν ἕκαστος τῶν θεῶν ἢ τὸ μετεχόμενον ἕν. See Butler 2014, 36–38.

33. See *PT* 2.7, 50.12–51.19.

requires, ultimately, absolute simplicity. The explanation was to be for the existence of any composite, anything of which we can say that it is distinct from what it is. The causal dependence of everything on the One is, therefore, another name for its participation in whatever it is that it gets from the One. But what it gets from the One cannot be distinct from the One itself, as would be the case in any other type of participation. In the face of this problem, Proclus posits the Henads, reintroducing at the highest level of metaphysics, the level of superessentiality, plurality of some sort. Even if, as Proclus insists, the Henads are "unified," they are still multiple in some sense and "other" than the One. It is not difficult to see here the metaphysical architecture of polytheism; it is much more difficult to see how this solves the problem.[34] If the problem remains unsolved, the Platonic system is threatened at its core and to the extent that a superordinate and absolutely simple first principle of all supports and is supported by the rejection of Naturalism, the prospects for establishing the subject matter of philosophy become dimmer. This is so because the intelligible world is introduced and serves exclusively as instruments of the first principle in the line of explanation. The Forms of Beauty or Virtue or Triangularity do not, on their own, explain anything that is not already explained by some type of conceptualism.

9.3. Damascius

Damascius (ca. 462–after 538), perhaps a student of members of Proclus's school, particularly Marinus and Isidore, has the sad distinction of being the last head of Plato's Academy, for it was he who was animating the study of Platonism in 529 when Justinian's decree came down closing its operation. Damascius is not just the last head of the Academy but the last of the post-Plotinian Platonists to make an original contribution to the systematic expression of Platonism. That contribution is available to us owing to the preservation of two major works, Ἀπορίαι καὶ Λύσεις περὶ τῶν Πρώτων Ἀρχῶν (known generally as *De principiis*) and a *Commentary on Plato's Parmenides*.[35] The latter work is the only ancient commentary on that dialogue that provides an interpretation of the entire second part.[36] In many respects,

---

34. See Abbate 2008, chap. 1, esp. 14–15, and 185–204, on Proclus's "teologia dell'unità" whereby Platonic metaphysics is deployed to articulate Greek polytheism and to provide the basis for a form of mysticism.

35. These two works are found together in the oldest manuscript, with the last part of the first work and the first part of the second apparently missing. The missing part of the second work seems to be the commentary on H1 since what we have begins with H2. On the structure of both works, see Westerink and Combès 2002a, 1:lvi–lxxii. There are also extant commentaries on *Phaedo* and *Philebus*.

36. Damascius refers repeatedly to Proclus's views on all the hypotheses, thereby evidently proving that his commentary did not end with H1.

Damascius follows Proclus, especially in his correlation of the properties deduced for One-Being in H2 with the Olympian deities. But Damascius is independent minded enough to reject Proclus on numerous points, and occasionally to recur to Iamblichus for support.[37] The *De principiis* probably supplies the substance of the material missing from the manuscript of the *Parmenides* commentary.[38]

In the remarkable beginning of that work, Damascius questions the very idea of the intelligibility of a first principle of all, as this was found by his teachers in *Parmenides* H1 and as Damascius could see for himself in Plato's *Republic* and in Aristotle's testimony. He reasons as follows. If there is a first principle of all, it is either completely disconnected from the totality of things that make up the universe or it is included within this totality. But both alternatives are impossible.[39] For if the first principle is disconnected, then the universe is not really the totality of things. On the other hand, if the first principle is a part of the totality of things, it is not a first principle. For either it is something, in which case it is one of the things in need of a first principle, or else it is nothing. Therefore, the totality of things has no first principle. But this is impossible.[40] Why is Damascius so certain that this is so? Why can we not say that the world is just the totality of whatever there is? Damascius's answer to this question is that, for him, as indeed for all his predecessors, the concept of a principle (ἀρχή) is analytically inseparable from the concept of an explanation (αἰτία). To say that the totality of things has no principle is to be committed to saying that the totality of things has no explanation—it just is. But as Damascius points out, this is as much as to say that the totality is its own principle or explanation. As will be apparent later on, though, this is a highly destructive position to assume. For unless there is a real distinction between that which is explicable and that which is not, then there is no such thing as an explanation. But if there is such a distinction, where does it fall? Damascius's answer is not essentially different from Plotinus's. Explanations answer existential questions; the natures of the things that exist can be analyzed into their components and in their relations, both external and internal, but only the existence of things with these properties requires explanation. Explanations of existence are of two sorts: ultimate and instrumental. For example, the Demiurge or the

---

37. As emphasized by Simplicius, *In Phys.* 795, 15–17.
38. See Cürsgen 2007, 317–458, for a good survey of the doctrines contained in *De principiis* and in the *Commentary*. Also see Westerink and Combès 2002b, 1:ix–lxxi; 2002a, 1:lix.
39. Damascius is perhaps implicitly criticizing Plotinus, 5.4 [7], 2.38–40, where Plotinus reasons that since the products of the One comprise all things, the One must be "beyond all things (ἐπέκεινα τῶν πάντων)."
40. *De princ.* 1.1.4–2.20. Damascius makes the additional point (2.4–6), that however "we conceive of (ἐννοοῦμεν)" this principle, to conceive of a principle of all things is to include it within the concept "all things." For example, a πόλις includes not only all those who are ruled, but the ruler as well.

contents of its intellect is the instrumental explanation for the existence of instances of its paradigmatic nature, but it is only a cause as an instrument of an ultimate explanation. What the ultimate explanation explains is the existence of anything with a nature, that is, anything that has even the minimal compositeness of "one such-and-such." The ultimate explanans must, then, be uniquely simple.[41]

We are left with a profound aporia. There must be an ultimate explanation for everything, but such an explanation can neither be disconnected from everything nor a part of everything. We suppose at this point that the One of H1, under some description, is to be introduced to resolve the dilemma. But it is clear as we proceed that the dilemma is posed precisely to forestall such a resolution. For even the denial of all predicates to the One is to compromise its absolute simplicity by assuming that it is the subject of these denials. Damascius says, "Our soul, therefore, divines that there is a principle of all things, however it is to be conceived, unconnected to all things. Therefore, it should not be called a principle or a cause nor first nor prior to everything, nor beyond everything; it should scarcely be proclaimed at all; it should entirely not be proclaimed at all, nor conceived, nor conjectured."[42] This divination amounts to an argument for a first principle of all that is unintelligible. One would have thought, though, that the conclusion of an argument at least has some sort of intelligibility relative to the premises to which it is logically connected.

This line of reasoning, however, is rejected by Damascius. For he wants to argue that (1) there must be a first principle of all that is not unconnected to that of which it is a principle, and (2) this conclusion takes us to the limit of thought but not to the denial of the need for a first principle that is absolutely unconnected to anything. The One referred to in (1), I will try to show, is in fact Plotinus's One, not really related to anything but nevertheless connected to everything else as principle. That which is "referred to" in (2)—we will presently see the significance of the scare quotes—is the absolutely first ineffable principle of all. Here is how Damascius presents this subtle distinction. He argues first that the One of H1, although it can be referred to by negation and not by affirmation, cannot be cognized, even

---

41. See *De princ.* 1.92.18–21: ἀρκεῖ γὰρ καὶ τὸ μόνον ἓν πρὸς τὸ πάντων αἴτιον· εἰ δὲ καὶ πάντων αἴτιον, οὐκ ἂν εἴη πάντα· εἰ δὲ καὶ πολλὰ τὰ πάντα, τό γε ἓν οὐκ ἂν εἴη πολλά· (for it is also sufficient for the One to be unique for it to be the cause of everything; but if it is the cause of everything, it would not be everything; moreover, if everything is many, the One would not be many).

42. *De princ.* 1.4.13–18: Μαντεύεται ἄρα ἡμῶν ἡ ψυχὴ τῶν ὁπωσοῦν πάντων ἐπινοουμένων εἶναι ἀρχὴν ἐπέκεινα πάντων ἀσύντακτον πρὸς πάντα. Οὐδὲ ἄρα ἀρχήν, οὐδὲ αἴτιον ἐκείνην κλητέον, οὐδὲ πρῶτον, οὐδέ γε πρὸ πάντων, οὐδ' ἐπέκεινα πάντων· σχολῇ γε ἄρα πάντα αὐτὴν ὑμνητέον· οὐδ' ὅλως ὑμνητέον, οὐδ' ἐννοητέον, οὐδὲ ὑπονοητέον· I take it that the words οὐδὲ ὑπονοητέον indicate a refusal even to postulate this as a first principle, that is, the conclusion of an abductive argument.

negatively.⁴³ This is because that would introduce predicative complexity into it. But since this One is relative to that of which it is a principle, namely, the many, it is not absolutely ineffable.⁴⁴ Since there is a residual complexity in that which can be referred to (although not cognizable),

> things that are purified of contraries and prior to mixtures everywhere exist unmixed. For either the superior predicates are in the One existentially, in which case how will their contraries be there at the same time? Or these predicates are there by participation, in which case they will come from elsewhere, that is, from that which is such as to be first. Therefore, prior to the One there will be that which is simply and in every way ineffable, nonreferable, unconnected, and inconceivable in any way. It is to this that the ascent of reasoning itself has hastened by means of the most evident steps, not omitting any intermediaries including the last of all.⁴⁵

The word translated as "nonreferable," ἄθετος, literally means "without position." It is used by Aristotle to describe an indivisible unit, as opposed to a point that is indivisible but does have position.⁴⁶ The context seems to require us to understand Damascius to mean that the ineffable One is "non-positionable" intellectually, that is, not something of which there can be any predicates at all.⁴⁷ The One of H1 is merely relatively ineffable because there can be negative predication of it.

The obvious question to pose to Damascius and to Iamblichus as well, evidently an inspiration here, is why is either the Ineffable or the One of H1 not otiose?⁴⁸ His answer, insofar as we can discern it from the above argument, takes us again to the heart of Platonic metaphysics. The quest to establish an absolutely first principle of all meets conflicting and perhaps irreconcilable exigencies. On the one hand, the first principle must be absolutely simple. On the other, absolute simplicity seems to be impossible for that which is causally connected to anything. The last point is emphasized

---

43. Proclus himself, *In Parm.* 7.76 Klibansky, says that at the end of *Parmenides*, Plato "removes all negations" from the One. Apart from the fact that the text of *Parmenides* does not quite say this, Proclus's One of H1 does, it seems, have to answer to Damascius's objection. Cf. *ET* Prop. 123 on the unknowability of the first principle owing to its being unparticipated.

44. *De princ.* 1.56.1–11.

45. *De princ.* 1.56.11–19: τὰ δὲ καθαρὰ τῶν ἐναντίων καὶ πρὸ τῶν συμμιγῶν ἀμιγῆ προϋπάρχει πανταχοῦ. Ἢ γὰρ καθ' ὕπαρξιν ἐν τῷ ἑνὶ τὰ κρείττω· καὶ πῶς ἔσται ἐκεῖ καὶ τὰ ἐναντία ὁμοῦ; ἢ κατὰ μέθεξιν, καὶ ἑτέρωθεν ἥκει ἀπὸ τοῦ πρώτου τοιούτου· καὶ πρὸ τοῦ ἑνὸς ἄρα τὸ ἁπλῶς καὶ πάντη ἄρρητον, ἄθετον, ἀσύντακτον καὶ ἀνεπινόητον κατὰ πάντα τρόπον· ἐφ' ὃ δὴ καὶ ἔσπευδεν ἡ τοῦ λόγου διὰ τῶν ἐναργεστάτων αὕτη ἀνάβασις, μηδὲν παραλείπουσα τῶν μέσων ἐκείνων τε καὶ τοῦ ἐσχάτου τῶν πάντων· Cf. 2.22.11–23.6.

46. See Aristotle, *Meta.* Δ 6, 1016b25, 30. Westerink and Combès 2002b translate it as "non-posable."

47. Cf. *De princ.* 1.62.9–11.

48. See Simplicius, *In Phys.* 795.11–17, for an indication of Damascius's appreciation of Iamblichus's contribution to the debate over first principles.

by making the reasonable claim that a cause of everything cannot be arbitrarily excluded from a complete inventory of everything. The only way to exempt it from inclusion in the putative inventory is to insist that if it is absolutely simple, it cannot even be referred to. Such a nonreferable principle cannot, of course, have any real causal role to play in the production of any many from it.[49]

Plotinus's subtle solution to this problem, as we have seen, is to argue that the first principle of all is δύναμις τῶν πάντων. As such, it is οἷον ἐνέργεια (actuality), but it is also just ἐνέργεια (activity). Damascius is clear that the One of H1 is neither δύναμις nor ἐνέργεια.[50] These are subordinate principles. The One is pure "existence" or "subsistence (ὕπαρξις)."[51] Then, how does it exercise its explanatory role? Just as the One for Plotinus is already what it produces, so too is the One of Damascius.

> For if it is allowed to provide a definition, the first is the One-All, while the second is the All-One. For it is All because of itself, but somehow is nevertheless One because of the first, while the first, being One because of itself, is nevertheless All insofar as it has produced the second. As for the third, it has oneness from the first, and allness from property of the second, so that it is pluralized in the latter respect and unified in the former, and it is the first to become a composite and to accomplish a unification of all, and to project from itself that which is unified, that which we call "being," the unification of which has the property of being one, just as the principle prior to it has the property of being all, and that which is prior to that has the property of being unqualifiedly prior. There is, therefore, the first One-All prior to everything, and the second All-One and the third All-One, the Unified coming from One and from All.[52]

The Unified is the One-Being of *Parmenides* H2. The One-All is the Limit, as explained by Proclus, and the All-One is Unlimitedness. But what is the

---

49. See Linguitti 1988; Rappe 2000, 208–213; and Abbate 2010, chap. 8, on the consequences for metaphysical discourse of a first principle that is utterly ineffable in the way that Damascius insists.

50. See *De princ.* 1.107.3–8: τὸ δὲ ἓν εἰ καὶ πάντων αἴτιον· ἀλλ᾽ ἓν πάντα ποιεῖ, καὶ οὐδὲ ποιεῖ γε· οὐδὲ γὰρ ἐνεργεῖ· ἡ γὰρ ἐνέργεια διακρίνεταί πως ἀπὸ τοῦ ἐνεργοῦντος· οὔτε γὰρ δύναται. Καὶ γὰρ δύναμις ἐκτένειά ἐστιν, ὥς φασι, τῆς οὐσίας, τὸ δὲ οὐδὲ οὐσία εἶναι βούλεται· τρίτη γὰρ ἀπ᾽ αὐτοῦ ἡ οὐσία κατὰ τὸ μικτόν, ἡ ἑνιαία φημί, καὶ κατὰ τὸ ἑνιαῖον· (Although the One is the explanation for all things, still it makes all things one, and it does not make at all. For it does not act. For activity is somehow distinct from that which is acting; nor does it have potency, for potency is, as they say, an extension of being, and it does not wish to be being. This is so because being is third from it insofar as it is a mixture, that is, unified being, and with respect to its unity).

51. *De princ.* 2.33.10–12, 71.1, 73.19–20; 3.152.13–16. In the last passage (152.25–153.3), this primary ὕπαρξις is identified with the One, prior to οὐσία. The ὕπαρξις of that which has οὐσία is distinct from the ὕπαρξις that is simplicity (ἁπλότης).

52. *De princ.* 2.39.11–25: Ἔστι γάρ, εἰ θέμις ἀφορίσασθαι, ἡ μὲν πρώτη ἓν πάντα, ἡ δὲ δευτέρα πάντα ἕν· αὕτη μὲν γάρ, πάντα οὖσα δι᾽ ἑαυτήν, ὅμως, διὰ τὴν πρώτην, ἕν πώς ἐστιν, ἐκείνη δέ, ἓν δι᾽

cause of the mixture of Limit and Unlimitedness? No tertium quid is needed; the second All-One is the δύναμις of the One-All and the Unified is the ἐνέργεια of it, the actualization of the One-All that makes up the realm of οὐσία.[53] Limit and Unlimitedness and the Unified are aspects of the principles of the intelligible world. Damascius has not exactly collapsed the Ones of H1 and H2 as some suspected Porphyry had done, but he has allowed himself a purely conceptual complexity in the One of H1, evidently justified by affirming the absolute transcendence of the Ineffable. For Plotinus, the initial product of the One, Intellect as Indefinite Dyad, is really distinct from it; for Damascius, it is only conceptually distinct from it. The same is true for the Unified. But at some point, of course, real distinctions will have to enter the picture though it is not at all clear how these are to be explained.

If the One of H1 is relatively ineffable, this is because what it really is is all things. Therefore, we either conceive of it as one, in which case we leave out all the things it is, or we conceive of it as all things, in which case we leave out its absolute simplicity. "For neither "one" nor "all" corresponds to [the One]; for these are opposed and partition our thinking. For if we fix our gaze on the one, we lose the perfect totality of it; if we conceive of all the things that it is together, we cause the one and simple thing to disappear. The reason for this is that we ourselves are divided and we gaze at the divided properties."[54] Is Damascius suggesting here a reductio ad absurdum of the highest principles of Neoplatonic metaphysics? If the true first principle of all is the unqualifiedly Ineffable, then real distinctions, at least at the level of the Henads, either gainsay the reality of this principle, and its simulacrum, the One of H1, or else they have no explanatory principle above them. But since Damascius wants to insist on the cogency of explanation, the only option for him seems to be that the distinctions—for example, the multitude of Proclean Henads—are only conceptual.[55] This sort of reductio

---

ἑαυτὴν οὖσα, ὅμως πάντα ἐστί, καθόσον τὴν δευτέραν προήγαγεν, ἡ δὲ τρίτη τὸ μὲν ἓν ἔχει ἀπὸ τῆς πρώτης, τὰ δὲ πάντα κατὰ τὴν ἰδιότητα τῆς δευτέρας, ὥστε πληθύεσθαι μὲν κατὰ ταύτην, ἑνίζεσθαι δὲ κατ' ἐκείνην, πρώτην δὲ σύνθετον γενέσθαι καὶ ἕνωμα πάντων ἀποτελεσθῆναι, καὶ τοῦτο ἀφ' ἑαυτῆς προβάλλεσθαι τὸ ἡνωμένον, ὃ δὴ καὶ ὂν καλοῦμεν, οὗ καὶ τὸ ἓν ἡνωμένον ἐστὶ τῇ ἰδιότητι, ὥσπερ τῆς πρὸ αὐτοῦ ἀρχῆς τὰ πάντα ἡ ἰδιότης, καὶ τῆς ἔτι προτέρας τὸ πρὸ πάντων. <Ἔστιν ἄρα τὸ πρῶτον ἓν πάντα πρὸ πάντων>, καὶ τὸ δεύτερον πάντα ἓν τὰ πάντα, καὶ τὸ τρίτον πάντα ἕν, τὸ ἐξ ἑνὸς καὶ πάντων τὸ ἡνωμένον. Cf. 2.10.13–23.

53. See *De princ.* 2.71.1–11.

54. *De princ.* 2.80.19–81.2: οὐδὲ γὰρ τὸ ἓν ἁρμόζει, οὐδὲ τὰ πάντα· ἀντίκειται γὰρ καὶ ταῦτα καὶ μερίζει ἡμῶν τὴν ἔννοιαν. Ἐὰν μὲν γὰρ εἰς τὸ ἁπλοῦν ἀποβλέψωμεν, καὶ τὸ ἓν ἀπόλλυμεν τὸ παμμέγα ἐκείνου παντελές· ἐὰν δὲ πάντα ὁμοῦ ἐννοήσωμεν, ἀφανίζομεν τὸ ἓν καὶ ἁπλοῦν· αἴτιον δὲ ὅτι ἡμεῖς διῃρήμεθα καὶ εἰς διῃρημένας ἰδιότητας ἀποβλέπομεν.

55. Cf. *De princ.* 2.73.1–12, where Damascius argues that real distinction requires that the relata have to have or have to be forms. Thus, matter is not distinct from form whereas form is distinct from matter. See 1.77.19–20, 116.4–6. So, although that which proceeds from the Unified is distinct from it, the Unified is not distinct from that which proceeds.

is only a cousin of negative theology, which accepts fully the negative references to the One at the same time as affirming the real distinctness of its products. If Iamblichus is Damascius's inspiration here, he has surely gone beyond anything that Iamblichus would have endorsed.[56]

Damascius takes a tactically different approach to the problem of participating in the absolutely simple from that of Proclus, although the strategy is identical. Whereas Proclus introduces the participatable Henads below the absolutely simple One, Damascius removes the absolutely simple One from being the subject even of the negative predications of *Parmenides* H1. But such a One is evidently causally inert.

Plotinus posed the question "How does a many come from a one?" on numerous occasions.[57] It is a question upon whose answer the possibility of ultimate philosophical explanation depends. The utter generality of the question, as we have seen, includes the "manyness" of any existent, anything whose complexity consists minimally in something with a nature of any kind that exists. The possibility of an adequate answer to this "how" question depends upon their being an absolutely simple explanans. But as Plotinus's successors came to appreciate, there is perhaps an irresolvable tension between the absolute simplicity of the one and its explanatory adequacy for any "many." Damascius's stellar contribution is to bring this tension to the fore. The alternative to Naturalism of any sort, and along with that the possibility of philosophy, depends upon the resolution of this tension.

---

56. Could it be that in Damascius we have an early version of a Kantian argument from antinomies? In this case, the antinomy—either no first principle or a first principle that cannot be a principle—leads to a sort of conceptualism about metaphysics analogous to Kantian a priori principles of knowledge. Combès (Westerink and Combès 2002b, 1:xxv–xxvi), says that, for Damascius, "aporie est méthode," which he identifies with "une méthode spirituelle. C'est en la pratiquant que Damascius se définit, d'une part, philosophe par la radicalisme de sa critique, d'autre part, mystique à force de critique." That is, he follows a method of ascent through successive stages of intellection and criticism of intellection until that which is beyond intellection is reached. See Mettry-Tresson 2012, chap. 7, 435–471, with the arresting title "Naufrage du néoplatonisme?" ("Shipwreck of Neoplatonism?"), which explores the question of whether Damascius has revealed Platonism as a dead end. Her nuanced argument tends rather to support Trabattoni (1985, 199–201), who thinks that it is Damascius who wrests Platonism as metaphysics away from the embrace of Christianity and theurgy. He does this by showing that all forms of conceptual duality are inadequate in relation to the absolutely ineffable first principle of all. Also see O'Meara 2013, chap. 13, on the idea of constructive aporiai in Damascius, attempts to advance in the direction of the truly inexpressible.

57. See *Enn.* 3.8 [30], 10.14–15; 3.9 [13], 4; 5.1 [10], 6.4–5; 5.2 [11], 1.3–4; and 5.3 [49], 15.

CHAPTER 10

Concluding Reflections

In this book, I have tried to set forth an account of Platonism not as *a* systematic philosophy but as systematic philosophy itself. If this is right, it means that all other self-declared systematic philosophers, for example, Spinoza, Hegel, or F. H. Bradley, should be seen as constructing versions of Platonism. I would go further and suggest that insofar as they attempt any accommodation with Naturalism, they should be seen to be deviant forms of Platonism. The hallmarks of Platonism are its rejection of the elements of Naturalism and its derivation of the cosmos and everything in it from a unique absolutely simple first principle of all. The negative and positive sides of Platonism are inseparable and mutually supporting. I think it is a mark of intellectual hygiene to renounce compromises between Platonism and Naturalism. All the compromises on offer in contemporary philosophy known to me have the unmistakable appearance of mauvaise foi.

Platonism insists on the distinctness of its subject matter which is nothing but the subject matter of philosophy. This subject matter is the intelligible world or what is available to thought as opposed to sense-perception. But since there is much that is available to thought that is also available to sense-perception, the subject matter of philosophy includes both what is exclusively available to thought and that which is available to thought but is otherwise accessible. If Platonism is otherworldly, it is also committed to the relevance of the otherworldly to *this* world. The rejection of the elements of Naturalism and the postulation of an absolutely simple first principle of all are underdetermining for the solutions to countless problems that have been traditionally recognized as philosophical. This fact in part accounts for differences among Platonists in their attempts to solve these problems.

For example, even among those who reject materialism, one can find considerable differences in their efforts to explain the relation of the immaterial to the material. Aristotle's explicit hylomorphism constitutes a major contribution to these efforts, but even Aristotle is stymied with regard to exactly how the intellect that comes from outside is connected to the soul-body composite.

The term "Neoplatonism," as I have elsewhere tried to demonstrate, has had a mainly pejorative connotation since its invention in the middle of the eighteenth century.[1] If one insists on giving the term some more or less neutral descriptive content, I would suggest that it be used to refer to the versions of Platonism born out of criticisms of Plotinus by his successors, in particular criticisms both implicit and explicit of his account of first principles. These criticisms for the most part focus on the problem of an absolutely simple first principle of all that is causally efficacious. Plato's answer is to appeal to the metaphor of "flowing" to indicate what the Good does eternally. If, though, the absolutely simple flows, how does the outcome of the flow amount to anything other than absolute simplicity? Plotinus's logical argument is to the effect that if the first principle is unique as well as absolutely simple, then the outcome of the flow must be other than absolutely simple; it must be at least minimally complex. And then continued flow means increasing complexity until maximal complexity, as it were, is achieved. But at the outer limit of complexity—the spatially extended and indefinitely divisible—is lack of unity altogether. The first principle of all flows out to maximal complexity and thereby produces matter, a sort of asymptote of maximal complexity/minimal unity. Among the so-called Neoplatonists, an increasingly more refined account of this flow was sought. But it was recognizably Plotinus's account, and it was rooted both in the dialogues of Plato and in the oral tradition operating between Plato and Plotinus.

This account experienced two waves of attack. The first was from Christian philosophers who wanted to identify the first principle of all with the God of scripture.[2] Their Platonic warrant was, not surprisingly, the creative role of the Demiurge in *Timaeus*.[3] Even if the Demiurge was not exactly

---

1. See Gerson 2013a, 32–33.
2. See Q. Smith 2001 on the unhelpful assimilation of ancient anti-Naturalism to "theistic supernaturalism" in contemporary philosophy.
3. See Rist (1989, 196–205), who cites a number of texts that, according to him, suggest that Plato eventually became inclined to identify the first principle of all with a divine mind. As we have seen, *Tim.* 48C2–6 and 53D4–7 suggest that the first principle of all is not a mind, at least not in the sense in which the Demiurge is. A fragment of Xenocrates, Plato's faithful disciple, is perhaps more promising. Xenocrates apparently held that intellect is a "monad." See fr. 15 Heinze. Rist supposes, wrongly I think, that this monad is the One or the Good. More likely, this monad is the Demiurge, which Xenocrates calls "Zeus" and "father." If, though, Xenocrates is referring to the One or Good, he seems to have also rejected the idea of its absolute simplicity.

comparable to the personal God of scripture, he was considerably closer to that God than was the austere and impersonal Idea of the Good of Plato or the One of Plotinus. It is instructive to see philosophers like Iamblichus and, later, Proclus striving to make Platonism into a pagan religion complete with its own scripture and its own sacramental practices. Among the costs of what I can only call a compromise was the occlusion of eternity and protrusion of everlastingness for the intelligible world. A God who answers prayers cannot easily be said to be eternal. But then a fair response to this complaint would be that a God who is eternal cannot easily be said to be alive. This attack morphed into orthodoxy once pagan philosophy was suppressed in the sixth century. The orthodoxy remains to this day, though its internal divisions mirror those among the pre-Christian Platonists. The upshot of this historical development is that Naturalists tend to assume that the Platonic alternative to Naturalism is a religion, not a philosophical position that in its heyday was entirely innocent of organized or institutional religious pretensions, even in its insistence that "theology" named a subject that was more or less extensionally equivalent to philosophy.[4]

The second wave is related to the first. Roughly in the middle of the seventeenth century, Platonism was so thoroughly mixed up with Christianity that it could not meet the Naturalism of the new physics on philosophical grounds. There is a nice dialectical partnership between, for example, Francis Bacon and John Locke, with the first isolating Platonism with his pronouncement of fideism while the second, inadvertently abandoning the Platonic subject matter of philosophy by an implicit acceptance of this fideism, turning philosophy into the handmaiden of Naturalism. Insofar as Platonists rely on privileged revelations and renounce public reason, it is difficult if not impossible to articulate anti-Naturalistic arguments that are not either question-begging or that do not end in conclusions unacceptable to the religiously ungifted.[5] The result of this parsing of the anti-Naturalist opposition was that the subject matter of philosophy (as opposed to religion) was lost. Accordingly, Platonists cut themselves off from the resources for providing positive alternatives to their opponents.

The very idea of empirical knowledge is a stellar example of philosophical subordination to natural science since the objects of this knowledge are just the objects with which science is concerned. What else could knowledge be knowledge of if the subject matter of philosophy is handed over to religion? The culmination of the concession by Platonists to the supreme cognitive status of empirical knowledge is that epistemology becomes

---

4. Beginning perhaps in the late third century, Platonists began to mirror the institutional and liturgical practices of Christianity. As I have been arguing throughout this book, these are not essential to Platonism.

5. Raymond Sebond, about whom Montaigne wrote so warmly, thought that all the truths of Christianity—save for a few minor details—could be demonstrated strictly by rational argument without any appeal to faith.

a branch of ethology.⁶ Naturalized epistemology is the polar opposite of Platonic epistemology understood as the ne plus ultra of cognition, that is, cognition of τὸ παντελῶς ὄν. The burden of this book has not been primarily a defense of the latter, but a defense of the claim that the former is the only consistent alternative to the latter. If one maintains that cognition is necessarily representational, then it is difficult also to maintain that neuroscience and clinical psychology are not the primary tools for the examination of these representations. The dilemma posed for the antirepresentationalist is stark: either one has to make do with the examination of the representations, in which case it is within natural science that this suitably occurs, or one has to claim that it is what the representations are representations of that should be in focus. But to insist on the latter alternative is to face the inevitable aporia that the putative objects of representation are only accessible via representations. The Platonist's only escape from this dilemma is to deny that knowledge is or is primarily representational. This claim, as we have seen, must be embedded within a larger, antimaterialistic metaphysical framework.

If Richard Rorty and I are right in maintaining that Platonism is philosophy, and if I am also right that Christianity has coopted Platonism to a large extent, then it is hardly surprising that much of what passes for philosophy today is actually work on the theoretical foundations of the natural sciences, in particular the natural sciences that have human beings as their subject matter. From this perspective, it is also hardly surprising to find exiguous the output of work on moral normativity that is not rooted in biology and psychology. Perhaps the simplest way to put the Platonic point here is that ethics without metaphysics may aim for but can never attain universality. Bereft of metaphysics, ethics is bound to be as parochial as those who pursue it. And the only metaphysics that will do, of course, has as its subject matter the intelligible world at the apex of which is the Idea of the Good.

Because Plotinus believed that the sensible world was an image of the intelligible world, he was content to have his auditors focus on any aspect of the former. He was confident that any attempt to explain or account for any phenomenon in the sensible world could not have a satisfactory conclusion elsewhere than in the intelligible world. Ultimately, the first principle of all had to be brought into the explanatory framework. I think it is right for the Platonist to insist on two worlds so long as it is understood that one is subordinate to the other, both in the sense of existentially dependent and in the sense of being explanatorily posterior. If one insists either that there is just one world—the sensible world—or that even if there are two, they are, so to speak, on a par and independent of each other, then solutions to the array of problems that have always faced philosophers are going to appear arbitrary or deeply unsatisfactory. In this regard, I share the amazement

---

6. See, e.g., Kornblith 2002; and Bermúdez 2006.

evinced by Galen Strawson at those who, committed to natural science, feel they must deny the existence of consciousness and attendant mental states. I disagree with him, though, in holding that the correct approach is not to turn to the intelligible world but to take a more capacious attitude toward Naturalism. Anaxagoras provided unsatisfactory accounts of phenomena in the sensible world not because he embraced an outmoded theory of homoiomeres rather than quantum mechanics, molecular biology, and neuroscience, but because he assumed that the satisfactory account must limit itself to the sensible world.

Finally, I would like to suggest that the present work, to the extent that its argument is persuasive at all, implicitly provides a sketch of a new pedagogical approach to the history of philosophy. Instead of the current approach, which is that of stringing together an array of loosely connected vignettes—if it is November, we must be on the Empiricists—we see the history of philosophy as the development of Platonism (with a few interesting outliers), followed in the seventeenth century by the beginning of efforts to find some common ground between Platonism and Naturalism, followed in the eighteenth century and then ever after, by the growing dominance of Naturalism, making sporadic and often arbitrary accommodations with Platonism. If the two poles are well articulated, that is, Platonism and anti-Platonism or Naturalism and anti-Naturalism, the history of philosophy can be seen as comprised of uncompromising defenses of each position along with the much more common attempts of one side to make strategic concessions to the other. At the least, such an approach seems to me to leave the student with a much clearer and more accurate grasp of the terrain called "philosophy" than she would otherwise be expected to have, and also, no doubt, a richer appreciation of what is at stake in this dispute.

Bibliography

I. Editions of Primary Sources

Aëtius. 1879. *De placitis reliquiae.* In *Doxographi Graeci,* edited by H. Diels. Berlin.
Alcinous. 1990. *Alcinoos: Enseigement des doctrines de Platon.* Edited by J. Whittaker. Paris.
Alexander of Aphrodisias. 1887. *De anima liber cum mantissa.* Edited by I. Bruns. *CAG,* supp. 2.1. Berlin.
Aristotle. 1884. *Aristotelis Ethica Eudemia.* Edited by F. Susemihl. Leipzig.
———. 1894. *Aristotelis Ethica Nicomachea.* Edited by I. Bywater. Oxford.
———. 1924. *Aristotle's Metaphysics.* Edited by W. D. Ross. 2 vols. Oxford.
———. 1950. *Aristotelis: Physica.* Edited by W. D. Ross. Oxford.
———. 1955. *Aristotelis: Fragmenta Selecta.* Edited by W. D. Ross. Oxford.
———. 1957. *Aristotelis: Metaphysica.* Edited by W. Jaeger. Oxford.
———. 2017. *Aristotele:. Metafisica.* Edited by E. Berti. Bari.
———. 1958. *Aristotelis Topica et Sophistici Elenchi.* Edited by W. D. Ross. Oxford.
———. 1961. *Aristotle: De Anima.* Edited by W. D. Ross. Oxford.
———. 1964. *Aristotelis Analytica Priora et Posteriora.* Edited by W. D. Ross. Oxford.
———. 1966. *Aristote: De la génération et de la corruption.* Edited by C. Mugler. Paris.
Damascius. 2002. *Traité des Premiers Principes.* Edited by L. Westerink and J. Combès. 3 vols. Paris.
———. 1997–2003. *Commentaire du Parménide de Platon.* Edited by L. Westerink, J. Combès, and A. Ph. Segonds. 4 vols. Paris.
Diogenes Laertius. 1980. *Lives of the Eminent Philosophers.* Edited by R. D. Hicks. 2 vols. Cambridge, MA.
Doxographi Graeci: Collegit recensuit prolegomenis indicibusque instruxit. 1965. Edited by H. Diels. 4th ed. Berlin.
Iamblichus. 1973. *In Platonis dialogos commentariorum fragmenta.* Edited by J. Dillon. Leiden.
Numenius. 1973. *Numénius: Fragments.* Edited by É. Des Places. Paris.
Plato. 1900–1902. *Platonis: Opera.* Edited by J. Burnet. 5 vols. Oxford.

———. 1995. *Platonis Opera. Tome I.* Edited by E. Duke, W. Hicken, W. Nicoll, D. Robinson, and J. Strachan. Oxford.
———. 2003. *Platonis Rempublicam.* Edited by S. Slings. Oxford.
Plotinus. 1964, 1977, 1983. *Opera.* Edited by P. Henry and H.-R. Schwyzer (*editio minor*). 3 vols. Oxford.
Proclus. 1873. *Procli Diadochi in primum euclidis elementorum librum commentarii.* Edited by G. Friedlein. Leipzig.
———. 1899, 1901. *Procli Diadochi in Platonis rem publicam commentarii.* Edited by W. Kroll. 2 vols. Leipzig.
———. 1903–1906. *Procli in Platonis Timaeum commentaria.* Edited by E. Diehl. 3 vols. Leipzig.
———. 1933. *Proclus: The Elements of Theology.* Edited by E. R. Dodds. Oxford.
———. 1954. *Commentary on the "First Alcibiades" of Plato.* Edited by L. G. Westerink. Amsterdam.
———. 1968. *Proclus: Théologie platonicienne.* Edited by D. Saffrey and L. G. Westerink. 5 vols. Paris.
———. 2007–2009. *Procli in Platonis Parmenidem commentaria.* Edited by C. Steel. 3 vols. Oxford.
Prolégomènes à la philosophie de Platon. 2003. Edited and translated by L. Westerink and J. Trouillard. Paris.
Sextus Empiricus. 1914–1958. *Opera.* Edited by H. Mutschmann and J. Mau. 4 vols. Leipzig.
Simplicius. 1882, 1895. *Simplicii in aristotelis physicorum libros commentaria.* Edited by H. Diels. *CAG* 9 and 10. 2 vols. Berlin.
Stobaeus. 1884. *Anthologii libri duo priores qui inscribi solent Eclogae physicae et ethicae.* Edited by K. Wachsmuth. 2 vols. Berlin.
Stoicorum Veterum Fragmenta. 1903–1905. Edited by H. von Arnim. 4 vols. Leipzig.
Syrianus. 1892. *Syriani in metaphysica commentaria.* Edited by H. Rabe. *CAG* 6.1. Berlin.
Xenocrates. 1892. *Xenocrates: Darstellung der Lehre und Sammlung der Fragment.* Edited by R. Heinze. Leipzig.
———. 1982. *Senocrate-Ermodoro: Frammenti.* Edited by M. Isnardi Parente. Naples.

II. Secondary Sources

Abbate, M. 2008. *Il divino tra unità e molteplicità: Saggio sulla Teologia Platonica di Proclo.* Alessandria.
———. 2010. *Parmenide e i neoplatonici: Dal' Essere all'Uno e al di là dell' Uno.* Alessandria.
———. 2014. *Proclo: Commento alla Repubblica di Platone.* Milan.
———. 2016. "Die dynamische und lebendige Natur des intelligiblen Seins bei Platon und in der neuplatonischen Überlieferung. In *Selbstbewegung und Lebendigkeit,* edited by M. Abbate, J. Pfefferkorn, and A. Spinelli, 227–242. Berlin.
Adam, J. A. 1920. *The "Republic" of Plato.* With critical notes, commentary, and appendices. 2 vols. Cambridge.
Adamson, P., and P. Karfik. 2017. "Proclus' Legacy." In *All from One: A Guide to Proclus,* edited by P. d'Hoine and M. Martijn, 290–321. Oxford.
Allen, R. E., ed. 1965. *Studies in Plato's Metaphysics.* London.
———. 1970. *Plato's "Euthyphro" and the Earlier Theory of Forms.* London.
———. 1983. *Plato's "Parmenides."* Minneapolis.
Annas, J. 1981. *An Introduction to Plato's "Republic."* Oxford.
———. 1982. "Aristotle on Inefficient Causes." *Philosophical Quarterly* 32:311–326.

———. 1985. "Self Knowledge in Early Plato." In *Platonic Investigations*, edited by D. O'Meara, 111–138. Washington, DC.
———. 1999. *Platonic Ethics: Old and New*. Ithaca, NY.
———. 2007. "Ethics in Stoic Philosophy." *Phronesis* 52 (1): 58–87.
Apostle, H. G. 1979. *Aristotle's Metaphysics. Translation with Commentary*. Grinnell, IA.
Archer-Hind, R. D. 1888. *The "Timaeus" of Plato*. London.
Armstrong, D. M. 1978. *Universals and Scientific Realism*. 2 vols. Cambridge.
———. 1979. "Naturalism, Materialism and First Philosophy." *Philosophia* 8:261–276.
Aubenque, P. 1972. *Le problème de l'être chez Aristote*. Paris.
———. 2009. "Plotin et le dépassement de l'ontologie grecque classique." In *Problèmes aristotéliciens*, vol. 1: *Philosophie théorique*, 321–330. Paris.
Azzouni, J. 2004. *Deflating Existential Consequence*. Oxford.
Bailey, D. T. J. 2014. "The Structure of Stoic Metaphysics." *Oxford Studies in Ancient Philosophy* 46:253–309.
Baker, S. 2017. "The Metaphysics of Goodness in the Ethics of Aristotle." *Philosophical Studies* 174:1839–1956.
Balaguer, M. 1998. *Platonism and Anti-Platonism in Mathematics*. New York.
Baltes, M. 1997. "Is the Idea of the Good beyond Being?" In *Studies in Plato and the Platonic Tradition*, edited by M. Joyal, 3–23. Aldershot.
Baltzly, D. 1996. "'To an Unhypothetical First Principle' in Plato's *Republic*." *History of Philosophy Quarterly* 13:149–165.
Bealer, G. 1987. "Philosophical Limits of Scientific Essentialism." *Philosophical Perspectives* 1:289–365.
———. 1996. "A Priori Knowledge and the Scope of Philosophy." *Philosophical Studies* 81:121–142.
Bechtle, G. 1999. *The Anonymous Commentary on Plato's "Parmenides."* Bern.
Beierwaltes, W. 1957. *Lux intelligibilis: Untersuchungen zur Lichtmetaphysik der Griechen*. Munich.
———. 1973. "Die Entfaltung der Einheit: Zur Differenz plotinischen und proklischen Denken." *Theta-Pi* 2:126–161.
———. 1985. *Denken des Einem: Studien zur neuplatonischen Philosophie und ihrer Wirkungsgeschichte*. Frankfurt.
———. 2004. "Proklos' Begriff des Guten aus der Perspektive seiner Platon-Deutung." In *Being or Good?: Metamorphoses of Neoplatonism*, edited by A. Kijewska, 97–120. Lublin.
Benitez, E. 1995. "The Good and the Demiurge." *Apeiron* 28:113–140.
Benson, H., ed. 1992. *Essays on the Philosophy of Socrates*. Oxford.
———. 2015. *Clitophon's Challenge: Dialectic in Plato's "Meno," "Phaedo," and "Republic."* Oxford.
Bermúdez, J. 2006. "Knowledge, Naturalism, and Cognitive Ethology: Kornblith's *Knowledge and Its Place in Nature*." *Philosophical Studies* 127:299–316.
Berti, E. 1983. "Il Platone di Krämer e la metafisica classica." *Rivista di filosofia neoscolastica* 75 (3): 313–326.
———. 2001. "Multiplicity and Unity of Being in Aristotle." *Proceedings of the Aristotelian Society* 101:185–207.
———. 2003. "Il dibatto odierno sulla cosidetta 'teologia' di Aristotle." *Paradigmi* 21: 279–297.
———. 2015. *Aristote: Métaphysique Epsilon*. Paris.
———. 2017. *Aristotele: Metafisica*. Bari.
———. 2018. "Bien en soi ou bien humain?: Aristote et Platon." In *XΩPA: Revue d'études anciennes et médiévales* 15–16:257–272.

Beversluis, J. 2006. "A Defense of Dogmatism in the Interpretation of Plato." *Oxford Studies in Ancient Philosophy* 31:85–111.
Blackburn, S. 1984. *Spreading the Word*. Oxford.
Bluck, R. 1955. *Plato's "Phaedo."* London.
Blyth, D. 2000. "Platonic Number in the *Parmenides* and *Metaphysics* XIII." *International Journal of Philosophical Studies* 8 (1): 23–45.
Bobzien, S. 1998. *Determinism and Freedom in Stoic Philosophy*. Oxford.
Bonazzi, M. 2012. "Antiochus and Platonism." In *The Philosophy of Antiochus*, edited by D. Sedley, 307–333. Cambridge.
———. 2015. *Il Platonismo*. Torino.
Bonazzi, M., and J. Opsomer, eds. 2009. *The Origins of the Platonic System: Platonisms of the Early Empire and Their Philosophical Contexts*. Louvain.
Bos, E. P., and P. A. Meijer, eds. 1992. *On Proclus and His Influence in Medieval Philosophy*. Leiden.
Bostock, D. 1986. *Plato's "Phaedo."* Oxford.
Boys-Stones, G. 2012. "Antiochus' Metaphysics." In *The Philosophy of Antiochus*, edited by D. Sedley, 220–236. Cambridge.
———. 2018. *Platonist Philosophy: 80 BC to AD 250*. Cambridge.
Boys-Stones, G., D. El Murr, and C. Gill, eds. 2013. *The Platonic Art of Philosophy*. Cambridge.
Braine, D. 1993. *The Human Person: Animal and Spirit*. London.
Brandom, R. 2000. *Rorty and His Critics*. Oxford.
Brickhouse, T., and N. D. Smith. 1994. *Plato's Socrates*. Oxford.
———. 2010. *Socratic Moral Psychology*. Cambridge.
Brisson, L. 1998. *Le même et l'autre dans la structure ontologique du Timée de Platon*. 3rd ed. Sankt Augustin.
———. 1999. *Platon: Parménide*. 2nd ed. Paris.
———. 2002. "L'approche traditionnelle de Platon par H. F. Cherniss." In *New Images of Plato*, edited by G. Reale and S. Scolnicov, 85–97. Sankt Augustin.
———. 2018. "Sur le Bien de Platon: Métamorphose d'une anecdote." *XΩPA: Revue d'études anciennes et medievales* 15–16:167–180.
Brittain, C. 2001. *Philo of Larissa*. Oxford.
———. 2012. "Antiochus' Epistemology." In *The Philosophy of Antiochus*, edited by D. Sedley. 104–130. Cambridge.
Broadie, S. 2012. *Nature and Divinity in Plato's "Timaeus."* Cambridge.
Brown, J. 2012. *Platonism, Naturalism, and Mathematical Knowledge*. New York.
Brown, L. 1998. "Innovation and Continuity: The Battle of the Gods and Giants, *Sophist* 245–249." In *Method in Ancient Philosophy*, edited by J. Gentzler, 181–207. Oxford.
Brunschwig, J. 1971. "*EE* I 8, 1218a15–32 et le περὶ τἀγαθοῦ." In *Untersuchungen zur Eudemischen Ethik*, edited by P. Moraux and D. Harlfinger, 197–222. Berlin.
———. (1988) 1994. "The Stoic Theory of the Supreme Genus and Platonic Ontology." In *Papers in Hellenistic Philosophy*, 92–157. Cambridge, MA. Originally published as "La théorie stoïcienne du genre suprême et l'ontologie platonicienne," in *Matter and Metaphysics*, Fourth Symposium Hellenisticum, *Elenchos*, edited by J. Barnes and M. Mignucci, 19–127. Naples.
———. 2003. "Stoic Metaphysics." In *The Cambridge Companion to Stoicism*, edited by B. Inwood, 206–232. Cambridge.
Bulmer-Thomas, I. 1983. "Plato's Theory of Number." *Classical Quarterly* 33 (2): 375–384.
Burge, T. 1971. "The Ideas as *Aitiai* in the *Phaedo*." *Phronesis* 16:1–13.
Burgess, J.P., and G. Rosen. 2005. "Nominalism Reconsidered." In *Oxford Handbook of the Philosophy of Mathematics and Logic*, edited by S. Shapiro, 515–536. Oxford.

Burnet, J. 1911. *Platonis Opera: "Phaedo."* Oxford.
Burnyeat, M. 1990. *The "Theaetetus" of Plato.* Indianapolis, IN.
———. 2000. "Plato on Why Mathematics Is Good for the Soul." In *Mathematics and Necessity: Essays in the History of Philosophy*, edited by T. Smiley, 1–81. Proceedings of the British Academy. Oxford.
Butchvarov, P. 1966. *Resemblance and Identity.* Bloomington, IN.
Butler, E. 2014. *Essays on the Metaphysics of Polytheism in Proclus.* New York.
Butorac, D., and D. Layne, eds. 2017. *Proclus and His Legacy.* Berlin.
Cairns, D., F.-G. Hermann, and T. Penner, eds. 2007. *Pursuing the Good: Ethics and Metaphysics in Plato's "Republic."* Edinburgh.
Carnap. R. (1950) 1956. "Empiricism, Semantics, and Ontology." *Revue Internationale de Philosophy* 4 (11): 20–40. Reprinted in Carnap, *Meaning and Necessity: A Study in Semantics and Modal Logic* (Chicago, 1956), 205–221.
Chalmers, D. 2012. *Constructing the World.* Oxford.
Cherniss, H. 1932. "On Plato's *Republic* X 597B." *American Journal of Philology* 53:233–242.
———. 1936. "The Philosophical Economy of Plato's Theory of Ideas." *American Journal of Philology* 57:445–56. Reprinted in Allen, *Studies in Plato's Metaphysics*, 1–12.
———. (1944) 1962. *Aristotle's Criticism of Plato and the Academy.* New York.
———. 1945. *The Riddle of the Early Academy.* New York.
———. 1957. "The Relation of the *Timaeus* to Plato's Later Dialogues." *American Journal of Philology* 78:225–266. Reprinted in Allen, *Studies in Plato's Metaphysics*, 339–378.
Chiaradonna, R. 2010. "Esegesi e sistema in Plotino." In *Argumenta in Dialogos Platonis.* Teil 1: Platoninterpretation und ihre Hermeneutik von der Antike bis zum Beginn des 19. Jahrhunderts, edited by A. Netschke-Hentschke, 101–117. Basel.
Chlup, R. 2012. *Proclus: An Introduction.* Cambridge.
Churchland, Patricia. 1987. "Epistemology in the Age of Neuroscience." *Journal of Philosophy* 84 (10): 544–553.
Churchland, Paul. 2013. *Plato's Camera.* Cambridge, MA.
Cohoe, C. 2017. "Why the One Cannot Have Parts: Plotinus on Divine Simplicity, Ontological Independence, and Perfect Being Theology." *Philosophical Quarterly* 67 (269): 751–771.
Colyvan, M. 2010. "There Is No Easy Road to Nominalism." *Mind* 119:285–306.
Coope, U. 2016. "Rational Assent and Self-Reversion: A Neoplatonist Response to the Stoics." *Oxford Studies in Ancient Philosophy* 50:237–288.
Cooper, J. 1970. "Plato on Sense-Perception and Knowledge: *Theaetetus* 184 to 186." *Phronesis* 15:123–146.
———. 1977a. "Plato's Theory of Human Good in the *Philebus*." *Journal of Philosophy* 74:714–730. Reprinted in Cooper, *Reason and Emotion* (1999), 151–164.
———. 1977b. "The Psychology of Justice in Plato." *American Philosophical Quarterly* 14: 151–157. Reprinted in Cooper, *Reason and Emotion* (1999), 138–149.
———. 1999. *Reason and Emotion.* Princeton, NJ.
Corcilius, K. 2018. "Ideal Intellectual Cognition in *Timaeus* 37A2–C5." *Oxford Studies in Ancient Philosophy* 54:51–105.
Cornford, F. M. 1912. *From Religion to Philosophy.* London.
———. 1934. *Plato's Theory of Knowledge.* London.
———. 1937. *Plato's Cosmology.* London.
———. 1939. *Plato and Parmenides.* London.
———. 1952. *Principium Sapientiae.* Cambridge.
Craig, W. 2016. *God over All: Divine Aseity and the Challenge of Platonism.* Oxford.
Crivelli, P. 2012. *Plato's Account of Falsehood.* Cambridge.

Crombie, I. M. 1963. *An Examination of Plato's Doctrines.* 2 vols. London.
Cürsgen, D. 2007. *Henologie und Ontologie: Die metaphysische Prinzipienlehre des späten Neuplatonismus.* Würzburg.
D'Ancona, C. 1992a. "Proclo: Enadi e ἀρχαί nell'ordine sovrasensibile." *Rivista di storia della filosofia* 47:265–294.
———. 1992b. "ΑΜΟΡΦΟΝ ΚΑΙ ΑΝΕΙΔΕΟΝ: Causalité des formes et causalité de l'un chez Plotin." *Revue de philosophie ancienne* 10:69–113.
———. 1996. "Plotinus and Later Platonic Philosophers on the Causality of the First Principle." In *The Cambridge Companion to Plotinus*, edited by L. Gerson, 356–385. Cambridge.
———. 2000. "La doctrine des principes: Syrianus comme source textuelle et doctrinale de Proclus. 1ère partie: histoire du problème." In *Proclus et la théologie platonicienne*, edited by A. Ph. Segonds and L. G. Westerink, 189–225. Leuven.
Dancy, R. 1999. "The Categories of Being in Plato's *Sophist* 255C–E." *Ancient Philosophy* 19 (1): 45–72.
———. 2004. *Plato's Introduction of Forms.* Cambridge.
Dasgupta, S. 2017. "Normative Non-Naturalism and the Problem of Authority." *Proceedings of the Aristotelian Society* 127:297–319.
Davidson, D. 1984. *Inquires into Truth and Interpretation.* Oxford.
De Caro, M., and D. Volterini, eds. 2010. *Naturalism and Normativity.* New York.
de Vogel, C. 1986. *Rethinking Plato and Platonism.* Leiden.
Des Places, É. 1973. *Numénius: Fragments.* Paris.
Defilippo, J. 1994. "Aristotle's Identification of the Prime Mover as God." *Classical Quarterly* 44 (2): 393–409.
Delcominette, S. 2006. *Le Philèbe de Platon: Introduction à l'agathologie platonicienne.* Leiden.
Dennett, D. C. 2006. *Breaking the Spell: Religion as a Natural Phenomenon.* London.
Denton, M. 2016. *Evolution: Still a Theory in Crisis.* Seattle, WA.
Desjardins, R. 2004. *Plato and the Good.* Leiden.
Deutsch, D. 2011. *The Beginning of Infinity: Explanations That Transform the World.* London.
d'Hoine, P. 2008. "The Intelligent Design of the Demiurge: On an Argument from Design in Proclus." *Études platoniciennes* 5:63–90.
Dillon, J. (1977) 1996. *The Middle Platonists: 80 B.C. to A.D. 200.* 2nd ed. Ithaca, NY.
———. 1987. *Proclus' Commentary on Plato's "Parmenides."* Translated by G. Morrow and J. Dillon. Princeton, NJ.
———. 1993. *Alcinous: The Handbook of Platonism.* Oxford.
———. 2003. *The Heirs of Plato.* Oxford.
Dixsaut, M. 1991. "'Ousia,' 'eidos,' et 'idea,' dans le 'Phédon.'" *Revue Philosophique* 116: 479–500.
———. 2016. *Le naturel philosophe: Essai sur les dialogues de Platon.* Paris.
Dodds, E. R. 1928. "The *Parmenides* of Plato and the Origin of the Neoplatonic 'One.'" *Classical Quarterly* 22 (3/4): 129–142.
———. (1933) 1963. *Proclus: The Elements of Theology.* A Revised Text with Translation. Oxford.
Donini, P. 1994. "Testi e commenti, manuali e insegnamento: La forma sistematica e i metodi della filosofia in età posthellenistica." In *Aufstieg und Niedergang der römischen Welt (ANRW)* II 36.7: 5027–5100. Reprinted in *Commentary and Tradition: Aristotelianism, Platonism, and Post-Hellenistic Philosophy*, edited by M. Bonazzi (Berlin, 2011), 211–282.
———. 2011. *Commentary and Tradition: Aristotelianism, Platonism, and Post-Hellenistic Philosophy.* Edited by M. Bonazzi. Berlin.

Dumoncel, J.-C. 1992. "La théorie platonicienne des idées-nombres." *Revue de philosophie ancienne* 10:3–34.
Duncombe, M. 2016. "Thought as Internal Speech in Plato and Aristotle." *Logical Analysis and History of Philosophy* 19:105–125.
Durrant, M., ed. 1993. *Aristotle's De Anima*. London.
Edelstein, L. 1962. "Platonic Anonymity." *American Journal of Philology* 83:1–22.
Emilsson, E. 2007. *Plotinus on Intellect*. Oxford.
———. 2017. *Plotinus*. London.
Erler, M. 2007. *Platon: Grundriss der Geschichte der Philosophie; Die Philosophie der Antike*. Edited by H. Flashar. Bd. 2/2. Basel.
Fazzo, S. 2018. "L'epilogo del libro *Lambda* della *Metafisica* di Aristotele: Il bene come principio." In *XΩPA: Revue d'études anciennes et medievales* 15–16:359–377.
Ferber, R. 2002. "The Absolute Good and the Human Goods." In *New Images of Plato: Dialogues on the Idea of the Good*, edited by G. Reale and S. Scolnicov, 187–196. Sankt Augustin.
———. 2003. "L'idea del bene è o non è teranscendente?: Ancora su ἐπέκεινα τῆς οὐσίας." In *Platone e la tradizione platonica*, edited by M. Bonazzi and F. Trabattoni, 127–149. Milan.
Ferrari, F. 2003. "L'idea del bene: Collocoazione ontologica e funzione causale." In Vegetti, *La Repubblica*, 5:287–325.
———. 2008. "Intelligenza e intelligibilità nel *Timeo* di Platone." In *Platonism and Forms of Intelligence*, edited by J. Dillon and M. E. Zovko, 81–104. Berlin.
———. 2010. "Dalla verità alla certezza: La fondazione dialettica del sapere nella 'Repubblica' di Platone." In *Giornale critico della filosofia italiana* 6 (3): 601–619.
———. 2017. "Esegesi, sistema e tradizione: La prospettiva filosofica del medioplatonismo." In *Philosophia in der Konkurrenz von Schulen, Wissenschaften und Religionen: Zur Pluralisierung des Philosophiebegriffs in Kaiserzeit und Spätantike*, edited by C. Riedweg, 33–60. Berlin.
———. 2018. "Platone ha effectivamente identificato il demiurgo del *Timeo* e l'idea del bene della *Repubblica*?: Riflessioni intorno a un'antica querelle filosofica." *Χώρα* 15–16:67–91.
Field, H. 1980. *Science without Numbers: A Defense of Nominalism*. Princeton, NJ.
Findlay, J. N. 1974. *Plato: The Written and Unwritten Doctrines*. New York.
Fine, G. 1978. "Knowledge and Belief in *Republic* V." *Archiv für Geschichte der Philosophie* 60:121–139.
———. 1990. "Knowledge and Belief in *Republic* V–VII." In *Companions to Ancient Thought*, edited by S. Everson, 1:85–115. Cambridge.
———. 2016. "The Two-World Theory in the *Phaedo*." *British Journal for the History of Philosophy* 24 (4): 557–572.
Fodor, J. 2002. Review of *Thinking about Consciousness* by D. Papineau. *London Review of Books* 24, no. 17 (September 5):21–22.
Foot, P. 2001. *Natural Goodness*. Oxford.
Forrest, B. 2000. "Methodological Naturalism and Philosophical Naturalism." *Philo* 3 (1): 7–29.
Frede, M. 1967. *Prädikation und Existenzaussage*. Göttingen.
———. 1980. "The Original Notion of Cause." In *Doubt and Dogmatism*, edited by M. Schofield, M. Burnyeat, and J. Barnes, 217–249. Oxford.
———. 1992. "Plato's Argument and the Dialogue Form." In *Methods of Interpreting Plato and His Dialogues. Oxford Studies in Ancient Philosophy*. Supplementary volume, edited by J. Klagge and N. Smith, 201–219. Oxford.
———. 2000. Introduction to Frede and Charles, *Aristotle's Metaphysics Lambda*, 1–52.

Frede, M., and D. Charles, eds. 2000. *Aristotle's Metaphysics Lambda: Symposium Aristotelicum.* Oxford.
Fronterotta, F. 2001. *ΜΕΘΕΞΙΣ: Le teoria platonica delle idee e la partecipazione delle cose empiriche; dai dialoghi giovanili al 'Parmenide.'* Pisa.
———. 2007. "The Development of Plato's Theory of Ideas and the 'Socratic Question.'" *Oxford Studies in Ancient Philosophy* 32:37–62.
Fujisawa, N. 1974. "Ἔχειν, μετέχειν and Idioms of 'Paradigmatism' in Plato's Theory of Forms." *Phronesis* 19:30–58.
Furth, M. 1991. "A 'Philosophical Hero'?: Anaxagoras and the Eleatics." *Oxford Studies in Ancient Philosophy* 9:95–129.
Gaiser, K. (1963) 1968. *Platons ungeschriebene Lehre: Studien zur systematischen und geschichtlichen Begründung der Wissenschaften in der Platonischen Schule.* Stuttgart.
———. 1968. "Quellenkritische Probleme der indirekten Platonüberlieferung." In *Idee und Zahl. Studien zur platonischen Philosophie. Ablandlung der Heidelberger Akademie der Wissenschaften, Phil.-hist. Kl, 2.* Heidelberg: 31–84. Reprinted in *Gesammelte Schriften*, edited by T. Szlezák (Sankt Augustin, 2004), 205–263.
———. 1980. "Plato's Enigmatic Lecture on the Good." In *Gesammelte Schriften*, edited by T. Szlezák, 265–294. Sankt Augustin, 2004.
———. 2004. *Gesammelte Schriften.* Edited by T. Szlezák. Sankt Augustin.
Gallop, D. 1975. *Plato's "Phaedo."* Oxford.
Gersh, S. 1973. ΚΙΝΗΣΙΣ ΑΚΙΝΗΤΟΣ. Leiden.
———. 2014. *Interpreting Proclus: From Antiquity to the Renaissance.* Cambridge.
Gerson, L. 1993. "Plotinus' Metaphysics: Creation or Emanation?" *Review of Metaphysics* 46:559–574.
———. 2003. *Knowing Persons.* Oxford.
———. 2005a. *Aristotle and Other Platonists.* Ithaca, NY.
———. 2005b. "What Is Platonism?" *Journal of the History of Philosophy* 43:253–276.
———. 2006. "The 'Holy Solemnity' of Forms and the Platonic Interpretation of the *Sophist*." *Ancient Philosophy* 26:291–304.
———. 2009. *Ancient Epistemology.* Cambridge.
———. 2013a. *From Plato to Platonism.* Ithaca, NY.
———. 2013b. "Incomposite Being." In *Aristotle on Metaphysics and Method*, edited by E. Feser, 259–276. New York.
———. 2014. "The Myth of Plato's Socratic Period." *Archiv für Geschichte der Philosophie* 96:403–430.
———. 2015. "Ideas of the Good." In Nails and Tarrant, *Second Sailing*, 225–242.
———. 2016. "The Neoplatonic Interpretation of Plato's *Parmenides*." *International Journal of the Platonic Tradition* 10 (1): 65–94.
———. 2018. "Socrates's Autobiography: An Epitome of Platonism." In *Plato's Phaedo: Selected Papers from the Eleventh Symposium Platonicum*, 323–327. Baden-Baden.
Gill, M. L. 1989. *Aristotle on Substance: The Paradox of Unity.* Princeton, NJ.
———. 1996. *Plato: "Parmenides."* Indianapolis, IN.
———. 2012. *Philosophos: Plato's Missing Dialogue.* Oxford.
Gonzalez, F., ed. 1995. *The Third Way: New Directions in Platonic Studies.* Lanham, MD.
Goodman, N. 1978. *Ways of Worldmaking.* Indianapolis, IN.
Gosling, J. C. B. 1973. *Plato: The Arguments of the Philosophers.* London.
Griswold. C. 1999. "E Pluribus Unum?: On the Platonic 'Corpus.'" *Ancient Philosophy* 19:361–397.
Grote, G. 1865. *Plato and the Other Companions of Sokrates.* 3 vols. London.
Guthrie, W. K. C. 1978. *A History of Greek Philosophy.* Vol. 5: *The Later Plato and the Academy.* Cambridge.

Gutiérrez, R. 2012. "Die Stufen der Selbsterkenntnis in Platons *Politeia*." In *Platons Hermeneutik und Prinzipiendenken im Licht der Dialoge und der antiken Tradition*, edited by U. Bruchmüller, 329–344. Hildesheim.
Gutting, G. 2003. "Rorty's Critique of Epistemology." In *Richard Rorty*, edited by. C. Guignon and D. Hiley, 41–60. Cambridge.
Hackforth, R. 1945. *Plato's "Phaedrus."* Cambridge.
Hadot, P. 1995. *Philosophy as a Way of Life*. Edited by A. Davidson. Translated by M. Chase. Chicago.
———. 2002. *What Is Ancient Philosophy*. Translated by M. Chase. Cambridge, MA.
Hale, B. 1987. *Abstract Objects*. Oxford.
Halfwassen, J. 1992a. *Der Aufstieg zum Einen: Untersuchungen zu Platon und Plotin*. Stuttgart.
———. 1992b. "Speusipp und die Unendlichkeit des Einen: Ein neues Speusipp-Testimonium bei Proklos und seine Bedeutung." *Archiv für Geschichte der Philosophie* 74:43–73.
———. 1993. "Speusippus und die metaphysische Deutung von Platons 'Parmenides.'" In *ΕΝ ΚΑΙ ΠΛΗΘΟΣ: Einheit und Vielheit*, edited by L. Hagemann and R. Glei, 339–373. Würzburg.
———. 1997. "Monismus und Dualismus in Platons Prinzipienlehre." *Bochumer Philosophisches Jahrbuch für Antike und Mittelalter* 2:1–21.
———. 2000. "Der Demiurg: Seine Stellung in der Philosophie Platons und seine Deutung im antiken Platonismus." In *La Timée de Platon: Contributions à la histoire de sa réception*, edited by A. Neschke-Hentschke, 39–62. Louvain.
———. 2004. "Platons Metaphysik der Einen." In *Platon verstehen: Themen und Perspektiven*, edited M. van Ackern, 263–278. Darmstadt.
Hamlyn, D. W. 1993. *Aristotle: De Anima. Books II and III*. Oxford.
Harte, V. 2017. "Knowing and Believing in *Republic* 5." In *Rereading Ancient Philosophy: Old Chestnuts and Sacred Cows*, edited by V. Harte and R. Woolf, 141–162. Cambridge.
Hermann, F.-G. 2005. "Plato's Answer to Democritean Determinism." In *La catena delle cause*, edited by C. Natali and S. Maso, 37–55. Amsterdam.
Hicks, R. D. 1907. *Aristotle: De anima*. Cambridge.
Hitchcock, D. 1985. "The Good in Plato's *Republic*." *Apeiron* 19 (2): 65–92.
Horn, C. 1995. "Kritik der bisherigen Naturforschung und die Ideentheorie." In *Phaidon*, edited by J. Müller, 127–142. Berlin.
Hösle, V. 1984. *Wahrheit und Geschichte: Studien zur Struktur der Philosophiegeschichte unter paradigmatischer Analyse der Entwicklung von "Parmenides" bis Plato*. Stuttgart.
Huffman, C. 1993. *Philolaus of Croton: Pythagorean and Presocratic*. Cambridge.
Hursthouse, R. 1999. *On Virtue Ethics*. Oxford.
Irwin, T. 1995. *Plato's Ethics*. Oxford.
———. 1999. "The Theory of Forms." In *Plato I: Metaphysics and Epistemology*, edited by G. Fine, 143–170. Oxford.
———. 2007. *The Development of Ethics*. Vol. 1. Oxford.
Jaeger, W. 1948. *Aristotle: Fundamentals of the History of His Development*. Translated by R. Robinson. London.
Johansen, T. 2004. *Plato's Natural Philosophy: A Study of the "Timaeus-Critias."* Cambridge.
———. 2013. "Timaeus in the Cave." In *The Platonic Art of Philosophy*, edited by G. Boys-Stones, D. El Murr, and C. Gill, 90–109. Cambridge.
Kahn, C. (1976) 2009. "Why Existence Does Not Emerge as a Distinct Concept in Greek Philosophy." In *Essays on Being*, 62–74. Oxford.
———. 1996. *Plato and the Socratic Dialogue: The Philosophical Use of a Literary Form*. Cambridge.

———. 2002. "On Platonic Chronology." In *New Perspectives on Plato, Modern and Ancient*, edited by J. Annas and C. Rowe, 93–127. Cambridge, MA.
———. 2013. *Plato and the Post-Socratic Dialogue: The Return to the Philosophy of Nature.* Cambridge.
Kamtekar, R. 2017. *Plato's Moral Psychology.* Oxford.
Karfik, P. 2004. *Die Beseelung des Kosmos: Untersuchungen zur Kosmologie, Seelenlehre und Theologie in Platons Phaidon und Timaeus.* Munich.
Kelsey, S. 2004. "Causation in the *Phaedo.*" *Pacific Philosophical Quarterly* 85:21–43.
Kirwan, C. 1971. *Aristotle's "Metaphysics" Books Γ, Δ, E.* Translated with Notes. Oxford.
Kitcher, P. 1988. "Mathematical Naturalism." In *The History and Philosophy of Modern Mathematics*, edited by P. Aspray and P. Kitcher, 11:293–325. Minnesota Studies in the Philosophy of Science. Minneapolis.
———. 1992. "The Naturalist Returns." *Philosophical Review* 101:55–114.
Kornblith, H. 1994. "Naturalism: Both Metaphysical and Epistemological." In *Naturalism*, edited by P. French, T. Uehling, and H. Wettstein, 19:39–52. *Midwest Studies in Philosophy.* South Bend, IN.
———. 2002. *Knowledge and Its Place in Nature.* Oxford.
Korsgaard, C. 2008. *The Constitution of Agency.* Oxford.
Krämer, H. J. 1959. *Arete bei Platon und Aristoteles: Zum Wesen und zur Geschichte der platonischen Ontologie.* Heidelberg.
———. (1964) 1967. *Der Ursprung der Geistmetaphysik.* 2nd ed. Amsterdam.
———. (1966) 2014. "Über den Zusammenhang von Prinzipienlehre und Dialektik bei Platon: Zur Definition des Dialektikers, Politeia 534B–C." *Philologus* 110:35–70. Reprinted in *Gesammelte Aufsätze zu Platon*, ed. D. Mirbach, 33–71. Berlin.
———. (1969) 2014. "ΕΠΕΚΕΙΝΑ ΤΗΣ ΟΥΣΙΑΣ: Zu Platon, Politeia 509B." *Archiv für Geschichte der Philosophie* 51:1–30. Reprinted in *Gesammelte Aufsätze zu Platon*, ed. D. Mirbach. Berlin.
———. 1990. *Plato and the Foundation of Metaphysics.* Albany, NY. See also the 6th edition of the Italian version, *Platone e i fondamenti della metafisica* (2001, Milan).
———. (1997) 2014. "Die Idee des Guten. Sonnen- und Liniengleichnis (Buch VI 504a–511e)." In *Platon: Politeia*, edited by O. Höffe, 179–203. Berlin.
———. (2001) 2014. "Ist die Noesis bei Platon fallibel?" In *Sein und Werden im Lichte Platons*, edited by E. Jain and S. Grätzel, 111–121. Freiburg.
———. 2014. *Gesammelte Aufsätze zu Platon.* Edited by D. Mirbach. Berlin.
Kremer, K. 1987. "Bonum est diffusivum sui: Ein Beitrag zum Verhältnis von Neuplatonismus und Christentum." In *Aufstieg und Niedergang der römischen Welt (ANRW)*, vol. 36/2, edited by W. Haase and H. Temporini, 994–1032. New York.
Kuhn. T. 1970. "Reflections on My Critics." In *Criticism and the Growth of Knowledge*, edited by I. Lakatos and A. Musgrave, 231–278. Cambridge.
Ladyman, J., and D. Ross. 2007. *Everything Must Go: Metaphysics Naturalized.* Oxford.
Laks, A. 2000. "*Metaphysics* Λ 7." In Frede and Charles, *Aristotle's Metaphysics Lambda*, 207–243.
Lavaud, L. 2018. "Y-a-t-il, selon Plotin, une *energeia* du Bien?" Χώρα. *Revue d'études anciennes et médiévales* 15–16:515–544.
Lavecchia, S. 2006. *Una via che conduce al divino: La "homoiosis theo" nella filosofia di Platone.* Milan.
———. 2010. *Oltre l'uno ed i molti.* Milan.
———. 2012. "Agathologie oder Henologie?: Platons Prinzipienphilosophie jenseits von Monismus und Dualismus." In *Platons Hermeneutik und Prinzipiendenken im Licht der Dialoge und der antiken Tradition*, edited by U. Bruchmüller, 363–382. Hildesheim.
Ledger, G. R. 1989. *Re-Counting Plato: A Computer Analysis of Plato's Style.* Oxford.

Leiter, B. 2015. "Normativity for Naturalists." *Philosophical Issues* 25 (1): 64–79.
Leng, M. 2010. *Mathematics and Reality.* Oxford.
Lennox, J. 1985. "Plato's Unnatural Teleology." In *Platonic Investigations*, edited by D. J. O'Meara, 196–218. Washington, DC.
Linguitti, A. 1988. "Giamblico, Proclo e Damascio sul principio anteriore all' Uno." *Elenchos* 1:95–106.
Lloyd, A. C. 1990. *The Anatomy of Neoplatonism.* Oxford.
Long, A. 1996. "Stoic Eudaimonism." In *Stoic Studies*, 179–201. Cambridge.
Long, A., and D. Sedley, eds. 1987. *The Hellenistic Philosophers.* 2 vols. Cambridge.
Longo, A., and P. Taormina, eds. 2016. *Plotinus and Epicurus.* Cambridge.
Lott, M. 2014. "Why Be a Good Human Being?: Natural Goodness, Reason, and the Authority of Human Nature." *Philosophia* 42:761–777.
Lowe, E. J. 2006. *The Four-Category Ontology: A Metaphysical Foundation for Natural Science.* Oxford.
Luchetti, C. 2014. *Tempo ed Eternità in Platone.* Milan.
MacArthur, D. 2004. "Naturalizing the Human or Humanizing Nature: Science, Nature, and the Supernatural." *Erkenntnis* 61:29–51.
MacKenna, S. 1962. *Plotinus: The Enneads.* 3rd ed. Revised by B. S. Page. London.
McDowell, J. 1994. *Mind and World.* Cambridge, MA.
———. 2000. "Towards Rehabilitating Objectivity." In Brandom, *Rorty and His Critics*, 109–124.
McEvoy, M. 2018. "Apriority, Necessity, and the Subordinate Role of Empirical Warrant in Mathematical Knowledge." *Theoria* 84:157–178.
Meinwald, C. 1991. *Plato's "Parmenides."* Oxford.
Meixner, U. 2009a. "From Plato to Frege: Paradigms of Predication in the History of Ideas." *Metaphysica* 10:199–214.
———. 2009b. "Three Indications for the Existence of God in Causal Metaphysics." *International Journal for the Philosophy of Religion* 66:33–46.
Menn, S. 1995. *Plato on God as Nous.* Carbondale, IL.
Merlan, P. 1953. *From Platonism to Neoplatonism.* The Hague.
———. 1967. "Greek Philosophy from Plato to Plotinus." In *The Cambridge History of Later Greek and Early Medieval Philosophy*, edited by H. Armstrong, 14–132. Cambridge.
Mesch, W. 2003. *Reflektierte Gegenwart: Eine Studie über Zeit und Ewigkeit bei Platon, Aristoteles, Plotin und Augustinus.* Heidelberg.
Mettry-Tresson, C. 2012. *L'aporie ou l'expérience des limites de la pensée dans le Péri Archôn de Damaskios.* Leiden.
Migliori, M. 1990. *Dialettica e Verità: Commentario filosofico al 'Parmenide' di Platone.* Milan.
Miller, M. (1980) 2004. *The Philosopher in Plato's "Statesman."* Including "Dialectical Education and Unwritten Teachings in Plato's *Statesman*." 2nd ed. Las Vegas, NV.
———. 1986. *Plato's "Parmenides."* Princeton, NJ.
———. 1995. "'Unwritten Teachings' in the *Parmenides*." *Review of Metaphysics* 48: 591–633.
Mohr, R. 2005. *God and Forms in Plato.* Las Vegas, NV.
Moore, C. 2015. *Socrates and Self-Knowledge.* Cambridge.
Moore, G. E. 1903. *Principia Ethica.* Cambridge.
Morel, P.-M. 2016. "Plotinus, Epicurus and the Problem of Intellectual Evidence." In *Plotinus and Epicurus: Matter, Perception, and Pleasure*, edited by A. Longo and D. Taormina, 96–112. Cambridge.
Morris, S. 2018. "Carnap and Quine: Analyticity, Naturalism, and the Elimination of Metaphysics." *Monist* 101:394–416.
Morrow, G., and J. Dillon. 1987. *Proclus' Commentary on Plato's "Parmenides."* Princeton, NJ.

Mueller, I. 1989. "Platonism and the Study of Nature." In *Method in Ancient Philosophy*, edited by J. Gentzler, 76–89. Oxford.
Murphy, N. R. 1951. *The Interpretation of Plato's "Republic."* Oxford.
Nagel, T. 2012. *Mind and Cosmos*. Oxford.
Nails, D. 1995. *Agora, Academy, and the Conduct of Philosophy*. Dordrecht.
———. 2013. "Two Dogmas of Platonism." *Boston Area Colloquium on Ancient Philosophy* 28 (1): 77–101.
Nails, D., and H. Tarrant, eds. 2015. *Second Sailing: Alternative Perspectives on Plato*. Helsinki.
Nef, F. 2012. "Platon et la métaphysique actuelle." *Études platoniciennes* 9:13–46.
Nehemas, A. 1975. "Plato on the Imperfection of the Sensible World." *American Philosophical Quarterly* 12:105–117.
Neurath, O. 1931. "Physicalism: The Philosophy of the Vienna Circle." *Monist* 41 (4): 618–623.
Nightingale, A. 1995. *Genres in Dialogue: Plato and the Construct of Philosophy*. Cambridge.
Nikulin, D., ed. 2012. *The Other Plato: The Tübingen Interpretation of Plato's Inner-Academic Teachings*. Albany, NY.
Nussbaum, M., ed. 1986. *Logic, Science and Dialectic*. Collected Papers in Greek Philosophy. G. E. L. Owen. Ithaca, NY, 1986.
O'Brien, D. 2005. "Einai copulatif et existential dans le *Parménide* de Platon." *Revue des Études Grecques* 118:229–245.
———. 2006. "Un problème de syntaxe dans le *Parménide* de Platon." *Revue des Études Grecques* 119:421–435.
———. 2013. "Forms and Concepts." In *Plato, Poet and Philosopher*, edited by E. Moutsopoulos and M. Protopapas-Marnelli, 193–244. Athens.
O'Brien, M. 1967. *The Socratic Paradoxes and the Greek Mind*. Chapel Hill, NC.
O'Conaill, D. 2018. "Grounding, Physicalism, and Necessity." *Inquiry* 61 (7): 713–730.
O'Meara, D. 2013. *Sur les traces de l'Absolu: Études de philosophie antique*. Fribourg.
O'Rourke, F. 1992. *Pseudo-Dionysius and the Metaphysics of Aquinas*. South Bend, IN.
Oderberg, D. 2008. "Concepts, Dualism, and the Human Intellect." In *Psycho-Physical Dualism Today: An Interdisciplinary Approach*, edited by A. Antonietti, A. Coradini, and E. J. Lowe, 211–233. Lanham, MD.
———. 2014. "Being and Goodness." *American Philosophical Quarterly* 51:345–356.
Owen, G. E. L. 1953. "The Place of the *Timaeus* in Plato's Dialogues." *Classical Quarterly* 3:79–95. Reprinted in Nussbaum, *Logic, Science and Dialectic*, 65–84.
———. 1966a. "Plato and *Parmenides* on the Timeless Present." *Monist* 50:317–340. Reprinted in Nussbaum, *Logic, Science and Dialectic*, 27–44.
———. 1966b. "The Platonism of Aristotle." *Proceedings of the British Academy* 51:125–150. Reprinted in Nussbaum, *Logic, Science and Dialectic*, 200–220.
Owens, J. 2007. *The Gradations of Being in Metaphysics E-Z*. Edited by L. Gerson. South Bend, IN.
Palmer, J. 1999. *Plato's Reception of Parmenides*. Oxford.
Papineau, D. 1993. *Philosophical Naturalism*. London.
Patterson, R. 1985a, "On the Eternality of the Platonic Forms." *Archiv für Geschichte der Philosophie* 67:27–46.
———. 1985b. *Image and Reality in Plato's Metaphysics*. Indianapolis, IN.
Penner, T. 1971. "Thought and Desire in Plato." In *Plato II*, edited by G. Vlastos, 96–118. New York.
———. 1973. "Socrates on Virtue and Motivation." In *Exegesis and Argument: Studies in Greek Philosophy Presented to Gregory Vlastos*, edited by E. Lee, A. Mourelatos, and R. Rorty, 133–151. *Phronesis*. Supplementary volume 1.
———. 1991. "Desire and Power in Socrates: The Argument of *Gorgias* 466A–468E That Orators and Tyrants Have No Power in the City." *Apeiron* 24:147–202.

———. 1992. "Socrates and the Early Dialogues." In *The Cambridge Companion to Plato*, edited by R. Kraut, 121–169. Cambridge.
———. 2003. "The Forms, the Form of the Good, and the Desire for the Good in Plato's *Republic*." *Modern Schoolman* 80:191–233.
———. 2007a. "Introduction: The Good and the Form of the Good in Plato's *Republic*." In Cairns, Hermann, and Penner, *Pursuing the Good*, 1–13.
———. 2007b. "What the Form of the Good Is the Form of?: A Question about the Plot of the *Republic*." In Cairns, Hermann, and Penner, *Pursuing the Good*, 15–41.
Penner, T., and C. Rowe. 2005. *Plato's "Lysis."* Cambridge.
Perl, E. 1998. "The Demiurge and the Forms: A Return to the Ancient Interpretation of Plato's *Timaeus*." *Ancient Philosophy* 18:81–92.
———. 1999. "The Presence of the Paradigm: Immanence and Transcendence in Plato's Theory of Forms." *Review of Metaphysics* 53 (2): 339–362.
———. 2011. "*Esse Tantum* and the One." *Quaestiones Disputatae* 2 (1–2): 185–200.
———. 2014. "The Motion of Intellect: On the Neoplatonic Reading of *Sophist* 248E–249D." *International Journal of the Platonic Tradition* 8:135–160.
Peterson, S. 2011. *Socrates and Philosophy in the Dialogues of Plato*. Cambridge.
Pigler, A. 2002. *Plotin: Une métaphysique de l'amour*. Paris.
Plantinga, A. 2006. "Against Materialism." *Faith and Philosophy* 23:3–32.
Plass, P. 1964. "Philosophical Anonymity and Irony in the Platonic Dialogues." *American Journal of Philology* 85:254–278.
Polansky, R. 2007. *Aristotle's De Anima*. Cambridge.
Politis, V. 2010. "Explanation and Essence in Plato's *Phaedo*." In *Definition in Greek Philosophy*, edited by D. Charles, 62–114. Oxford.
Pradeau, J.-F. 1997. *Platon et la cité*. Paris.
Press, G., ed. 1993. *Plato's Dialogues: New Studies and Interpretations*. Lanham, MD.
———, ed. 2000. *Who Speaks for Plato?* Lanham, MD.
Price, H. 2008. "One Cheer for Representationalism." In *The Philosophy of Richard Rorty*, edited by R. Auxier, 304–322. Lasalle, IL.
———. 2011. *Naturalism without Mirrors*. Oxford.
Primavesi, O. 2012. "Text of *Metaphysics* A." In *Aristotle's "Metaphysics" Alpha*, edited by C. Steel with edition of Greek text by O. Primavesi, 465–516. Oxford.
Prior, W. 1997. "Why Did Plato Write Socratic Dialogues." *Apeiron* 30:109–123.
———. 2004. "Socrates Metaphysician." *Oxford Studies in Ancient Philosophy* 27:1–14.
Pritchard, P. 1995. *Plato's Philosophy of Mathematics*. Sankt Augustin.
Putnam, H. 2000. "Richard Rorty on Reality and Justification." In Brandom, *Rorty and His Critics*, 81–87.
———. 2004. *Ethics without Ontology*. Cambridge, MA.
Quine, W. V. O. (1948) 1980. "On What There Is." *Review of Metaphysics* 2 (5): 21–38. Reprinted in Quine, *From a Logical Point of View*, 1–19.
———. (1951) 1980. "Two Dogmas of Empiricism." *Philosophical Review* 60 (1): 20–43. Reprinted in Quine, *From a Logical Point of View*, 20–46.
———. 1953. "Mr. Strawson on Logical Theory." *Mind* 62:433–451.
———. 1969. "Epistemology Naturalized." In *Ontological Relativity and Other Essays*, 69–90. New York.
———. 1980. *From a Logical Point of View: Nine Logico-Philosophical Essays*. 2nd ed. Cambridge, MA.
———. 1981. *Theories and Things*. Cambridge, MA.
Rappe, S. 2000. *Reading Neoplatonism: Non-Discursive Thinking in the Texts of Plotinus, Proclus, and Damascius*. Cambridge.
Rea, M. 1998. "Sameness without Identity: An Aristotelian Solution for the Problem of Material Constitution." *Ratio* 11 (3): 316–328.

———. 2002. *World without Design*. Oxford.
Reale, G. 1997. *Towards a New Interpretation of Plato*. Translated by J. Catan. Washington, DC. Translation is from *Per una nuova interpretazione di Platone: Rilettura della metafisica dei grandi dialoghi alla luce delle "Dotrine non scritte,"* 10th ed., 1991. Milan.
———. 2008. *Autotestimonianze e rimandi dei dialoghi di Platone alle "dottrine non scritte."* Milan.
Reeve, C. D. C. 2000. *Substantial Knowledge*. Indianapolis, IN.
Resnik, M. 1981. "Mathematics as a Science of Patterns: Ontology and Reference." *Nous* 15 (4): 529–550.
———. 1982. "Mathematics as a Science of Patterns: Epistemology." *Nous* 16 (1): 95–105.
Richard, M.-D. (1986) 2005. *L'enseignement oral de Platon*. 2nd ed. Paris.
———. 2012. "Un débat toujours d'actualité dans le domaine de l'histoire de la philosophie: Le débat autour de l'enseignement oral de Platon." In *Platons Hermeneutik und Prinzipiendenken im Licht der Dialogen und der antiken Tradition*, edited by U. Bruchmüller, 41–79. Hildesheim.
Rist, J. 1989. *The Mind of Aristotle: A Study in Philosophical Growth*. Toronto.
———. 2002. *Real Ethics: Rethinking the Foundations of Morality*. Cambridge.
Ritchie, J. 2017. *Understanding Naturalism*. Stocksfield.
Robin, L. 1908. *La théorie platonicienne des idées et des nombres d'après Aristote*. Paris.
Robinson, T. M. 1979. "The Argument of *Timaeus* 27Dff." *Phronesis* 24:105–109.
Rodier, G. 1902. "Les mathématiques et la dialectique dans le système de Platon." *Archiv für Geschichte der Philosophie* 15:479–490.
Rödl, S. 2014. Review of *Transcendental Philosophy and Naturalism*, edited by J. Smith and P. Sullivan. *European Journal of Philosophy* 22:483–504.
———. 2018. *Self-Consciousness and Objectivity*. Cambridge, MA.
Rodriguez-Pereyra, G. 2002. *Resemblance Nominalism*. Oxford.
Rorty, R. 1979. *Philosophy and the Mirror of Nature*. Princeton, NJ.
———. 1982. *Consequences of Pragmatism: Essays, 1972–1980*. Minneapolis, MN.
———. 1995. "Is Truth a Goal of Inquiry?: Davidson vs. Wright." *Philosophical Quarterly* 45:281–300.
———. 2000. *Philosophy and Social Hope*. London.
———. 2001. *Objectivity Relativism and Truth. Philosophical Papers*. Vol. 1. Cambridge.
Rosenberg, A. 2015. "Disenchanted Naturalism." http://intertheory.org/rosenberg.htm.
———. 2017. "Darwinianism as Philosophy: Can the Universal Acid be Contained?" In *How Biology Shapes Philosophy: New Foundations for Naturalism*, edited by D. L. Smith, 23–50. Cambridge.
———. 2018. "Making Mechanism Interesting." *Synthese* 195:11–33.
Ross, J. 1992a. *Thought and World: The Hidden Necessities*. South Bend, IN.
———. 1992b. "Immaterial Aspects of Thought." *Journal of Philosophy* 89:136–150.
Ross, W. D. 1924. *Aristotle: Metaphysics*. 2 vols. Oxford.
———. 1951. *Plato's Theory of Ideas*. Oxford.
Rowe, C. 2007. *Plato and the Art of Philosophical Writing*. Cambridge.
Russell, B. 1935. *Religion and Science*. Oxford.
Saffrey, H. D. 2003. Introduction to *Proclus: Théologie platonicienne*, livre 3, edited and translated by H. D. Saffrey and L. Westerink, ix–ci. Paris.
Saffrey, H. D., and L. Westerink, eds. 1968. *Proclus: Théologie platonicienne*, livre 1. Paris.
Santas, G. 1979. *Socrates: Philosophy in Plato's Early Dialogues*. London.
———. 1980. "The Form of the Good in Plato's *Republic*." *Philosophical Inquiry* 2:374–403.
Sayre, K. 1983. *Plato's Later Ontology: A Riddle Resolved*. Princeton, NJ.
———. 1995. *Plato's Literary Garden: How to Read a Platonic Dialogue*. Princeton, NJ.

———. 1996. *Parmenides' Lesson.* South Bend, IN.
———. 2006. *Metaphysics and Method in Plato's "Statesman."* Cambridge.
Scanlon, T. 2010. "Metaphysics and Morals." In *Naturalism and Normativity*, edited by M. De Carlo and D. Volterini, 7–22. New York.
Schaffer, J. 2009. "On What Grounds What." In *Metametaphysics: New Essays on the Foundation of Ontology*, edited by D. Manley, D. Chalmers, and R. Wasserman, 347–383. Oxford.
———. 2010a. "The Internal Relatedness of All Things." *Mind* 119:341–376.
———. 2010b. "Monism: The Priority of the Whole." *Philosophical Review* 119 (1): 31–76.
Schur, B. 2013. *Von hier nach dort: Der Philosophiebegriff bei Platon.* Göttingen.
Scolnicov, S. 2003. *Plato's "Parmenides."* Berkeley, CA.
———. 2017. "Atemporal Teleology in Plato." In *Teleology in the Ancient World*, edited by J. Rocca, 45–57. Cambridge.
Sedley, D. 1985. "The Stoic Theory of Universals." *Southern Journal of Philosophy.* Supplementary volume 23:87–90.
———. 1990. "Teleology and Myth in the *Phaedo.*" *Proceedings of the Boston Area Colloquium on Ancient Philosophy* 11, edited by J. Cleary and D. Shartin, 359–384. Lanham, MD.
———. 1995. "The Dramatis Personae of Plato's *Phaedo.*" *Proceedings of the British Academy* 85:3–26.
———. 2000. "*Metaphysics* Lambda 10." In Frede and Charles, *Aristotle's Metaphysics Lambda*, 327–350.
———. 2002. "The Origin of Stoic God." In *Philosophia Antiqua: Studies in Hellenistic Theology; Its Background and Aftermath*, edited by D. Frede and A. Laks, 41–81. Leiden.
———, ed. 2012. *The Philosophy of Antiochus.* Cambridge.
———. 2013. "Socratic Intellectualism in the *Republic*'s Central Digression." In *The Platonic Art of Philosophy*, edited by G. Boys-Stones, D. El Murr, and C. Gill, 70–89. Cambridge.
Sellars, W. (1956) 1997. *Empiricism and the Philosophy of Mind.* Cambridge, MA.
———. (1963) 1991. *Science, Perception, and Reality.* 2nd ed. London.
———. 1980. *Naturalism and Ontology.* Reseda, CA.
Shapiro, S. 1997. *Philosophy of Mathematics: Structure and Ontology.* Oxford.
———. 2000. *Thinking about Mathematics.* Oxford.
Sharma, R. 2009. "Socrates's New *Aitia*: Causal and Metaphysical Explanations in Plato's *Phaedo. Oxford Studies in Ancient Philosophy* 36:137–177.
———. 2015. "*Phaedo* 100B3–9." *Mnemosyne* 68 (3): 393–412.
Shields, C. 2011. "Plato and Aristotle in the Academy." In *The Oxford Handbook of Plato*, edited by G. Fine, 504–525. Oxford.
———. 2016. *Aristotle: De Anima.* Oxford.
Shorey, P. 1933. *What Plato Said.* Chicago.
Sillitti, G. 2005. "L'idea del bene tra geometria e dialettica nei libri VI e VII della *Repubblica* platonica." In *Eidos-Idea: Platone, Aristotele e la tradizione platonica*, edited by F. Fronterotta and W. Leszl, 91–101. Sankt Augustin.
Silverman, A. 2002. *The Dialectic of Essence.* Princeton, NJ.
Skrbina, D. 2005. *Panpsychism in the West.* Boston, MA.
Smith, J. A. 1931. *Aristotle's De Anima.* Oxford.
Smith, N. D. 2000. "Plato on Knowledge as Power." *Journal of the History of Philosophy* 38 (2): 145–168.
———. 2014. "Socratic Metaphysics?" *Apeiron* 47 (2): 419–434.
———. 2018. "Aristotle on Socrates." In *Socrates and the Socratic Dialogue*, edited by A. Stavru and C. Moore, 602–622. Leiden.
Smith, Q. 2001. "The Metaphilosophy of Naturalism." *Philo* 4 (2): 195–215.

Sorabji, R. 1982. "Myths about Non-Propositional Thought." In *Language and Logos: Studies in Ancient Greek Philosophy Presented to G. E. L. Owen*, edited by M. Schofield and M. Nussbaum, 295–314. Cambridge.

———. 2000. "Is the True Self an Individual in the Platonist Tradition?" In *Le Commentaire: Entre tradition et innovation*, edited by M.-O. Goulet-Caze, 293–299. Paris.

Steel, C. 2012. "Plato as Seen by Aristotle (*Metaphysics* A 6)." In *Aristotle's "Metaphysics" Alpha*, edited by C. Steel, 167–200. Oxford.

Steinthal, H. 1998. "L'Enseignement oral dispensé par Platon." *Les Études philosophiques* 1:57–68.

Stenzel, J. (1924) 1933. *Zahl und Gestalt bei Platon und Aristoteles*. Leipzig.

Strahler, A. 1992. *Understanding Science*. Buffalo, NY.

Strawson, G. 2006. *Consciousness and Its Place in Nature: Does Consciousness Entail Panpsychism?* Edited by A. Freeman. Exeter.

———. 2012. "Real Naturalism." *Proceedings and Addresses of the American Philosophical Association* 86 (2): 125–154.

Strawson, P. 1985. *Scepticism and Naturalism: Some Varieties*. London.

Striker, G. 1996. "Following Nature." In *Essays in Hellenistic Epistemology and Ethics*, 221–280. Cambridge.

Svavarsson, S. 2009. "Plato on Forms and Conflicting Appearances: *Phaedo* 74A9–C6." *Classical Quarterly* 59 (1): 60–74.

Szaif, J. (1996) 1998. *Platons Begriffe der Wahrheit*. Munich.

———. 2007. "Doxa and Epistémé as Modes of Acquaintance in *Republic* V." *Études platoniciennes* 4:253–272.

Szlezák, T. 1979. *Platon und Aristoteles in der Nuslehre Plotins*. Basel.

———. 1985. *Platon und die Schriftlichkeit der Philosophie*. Berlin.

———. 1994. "Tre lezioni su Platone e la scrittura della filosofia." *Rivista di filosofia neoscholastica* 86:3–43.

———. 1997a. "Schleiermachers 'Einleitung' zur Platon-Übersetzung: Ein Vergleich mit Tiedemann und Tennemann." *Antike und Abendland* 43:46–62.

———. 1997b. "Über die Art und Weise der Erörterung der Prinzipien im *Timaios*." In *Interpreting the "Timaeus-Critias." Proceedings of the IV Symposium Platonicum*, edited by T. Calvo and L. Brisson, 195–203. Sankt Augustin.

———. 1998. "Notes sur le débat autour de la philosophie orale de Platon." *Les Études philosophiques* 1:69–90.

———. 2000. "οὓς μόνους ἄν τις ὀρθῶς προσείποι φιλοσόφους. Zu Platons Gebrauch des Namens φιλόσοφος." *Museum Helveticum* 57:67–75.

———. 2003. *Die Idee des Guten in Platons Politeia*. Sankt Augustin.

———. 2004. "Friedrich Schleiermacher und das Platonbild des 19. und 20. Jahrhunderts." In *Protestantismus und deutsche Lieartur*, 2:223–246. Göttingen.

———. 2010. "Von Brucker über Tennemann zu Schleiermacher: Ein folgenreiche Umwalzüng in der Geschichte der neuzeitlichen Platondeutung." In *Argumenta in dialogos Platonis*. Teil 1: Plataoninterpretation und ihre Hermeneutik von der Antike bis zum Beginn des 19. Jahrhunderts, 411–433. Edited by A. Neschke-Hentschke. Basel.

———. 2011. "Platon und die Pythagoreer: Das Zeugnis des Aristoteles." *Perspektiven der Philosophie*, 9–32.

———. 2015. "Are There Deliberately Left Gaps in Plato's Dialogues." In Nails and Tarrant, *Second Sailing*, 243–256.

Tait, W. W. 1986. "Plato's Second Best Method." *Review of Metaphysics* 39 (3): 455–482.

Tarán, L. 1979. "Perpetual Duration and Atemporal Eternity in Parmenides and Plato." *Monist* 62:43–53.

Tarrant, H. 1979. "Numenius fr. 13 and Plato's *Timaeus*." *Antichthon* 13:19–29.

———. 1985. "Albinus, Nigrinus, Alcinous." *Antichthon* 19:87–95.
———. 1993. *Thrasyllan Platonism.* Ithaca, NY.
———. 2000. *Plato's First Interpreters.* Ithaca, NY.
Taylor, A. E. 1926. "Forms and Numbers: A Study in Platonic Metaphysics I." *Mind* 35:419–440.
———. 1927. "Forms and Numbers: A Study in Platonic Metaphysics II." *Mind* 36:12–33.
———. 1928. *A Commentary on Plato's "Timaeus."* Oxford.
Taylor, C. C. W. 1969. "Forms as Causes in the *Phaedo.*" *Mind* 78:45–59.
Teloh, H. 1981. *The Development of Plato's Metaphysics.* University Park, PA.
Tempesta, S. 2003. "Sul significato di δεύτερος πλοῦς in *Fedone* di Platone." In *Platone e la tradizione platonica,* edited by M. Bonazzi and F. Trabattoni, 89–125. Milan.
Thompson, D. 1945. *On Growth and Form.* 2nd ed. Cambridge.
Trabattoni, F. 1985. "Per una biografia di Damascio." In *Rivista di storia della filosofia* 40:179–201.
Turnbull, R. 1988. "Becoming and Intelligibility." *Oxford Studies in Ancient Philosophy.* Supplementary volume, edited by J. Annas and R. Grimm, 1–14. Oxford.
van Inwagen, P. 2006. "What Is Naturalism? What Is Analytic Philosophy?" In *Analytic Philosophy without Naturalism,* edited by A. Corradini, S. Galvan, and E. J. Lowe, 90–104. London.
———. 2014. *Existence: Essays in Ontology.* Cambridge.
Van Riel, G. 1997. "The Transcendent Cause: Iamblichus and the *Philebus* of Plato." *Syllecta Classica* 2:31–46.
———. 1999. "Beauté, proportion et verité comme 'vestibule' du bien dans le *Philèbe.*" *Revue philosophique de Louvain* 97:253–267.
———. 2017. "The One, the Henads, and the Principles." In *All from One: A Guide to Proclus,* edited by P. d'Hoine and M. Martijn, 73–97. Oxford.
Vasilakis, D. 2017. "Platonic Eros, Moral Egoism, and Proclus." In *Proclus and His Legacy,* edited by D. Butorac and D. Layne, 45–52. Berlin.
Vasiliou, I. 2008. *Aiming at Virtue in Plato.* Cambridge.
———. 2015. "Plato, Forms, and Moral Motivation." *Oxford Studies in Ancient Philosophy* 49:37–70.
Vegetti, M. 1992. "Megiston mathēma. L'idea del 'buono' e le sue funzioni." In Vegetti, *La Repubblica,* 253–286.
Vegetti, M., trans. and ed. 2003. *La Repubblica.* Vol. 5. Naples.
Vlastos, G. 1969. "Reasons and Causes in the *Phaedo.*" *Philosophical Review* 78:291–325.
———. 1971. "Introduction: The Paradox of Socrates." In *The Philosophy of Socrates,* edited by G. Vlastos, 1–21. Garden City, NY.
———. 1973. *Platonic Studies.* Princeton, NJ.
———. 1991. *Socrates: Ironist and Moral Philosopher.* Ithaca, NY.
Vuillemin, J. 2001. *Mathématiques pythagoriciennes et platoniciennes.* Paris.
Wagner, A. 2017. *The Arrival of the Fittest.* London.
Wedin, M. 2000. *Aristotle's Theory of Substance.* Oxford.
Wehrli, F. 1967. *Die Schule des Aristoteles.* 9 vols. Basel.
———. 1974. *Die Schule des Aristoteles.* Supplementary volume 10. Basel.
Weinberg, S. 1992. *Dreams of a Final Theory.* New York.
Westerink, L., and J. Combès, eds. 2002a. *Damascius: Commentaire du Parménide de Platon.* 4 vols. Paris.
———, eds. 2002b. *Damascius: Traité des premiers principes.* 3 vols. Paris.
White, N. 1979. *A Companion to Plato's "Republic."* Indianapolis, IN.
Whittaker, J. 1967. "Moses Atticizing." *Phoenix* 21:196–201.
———. 1968. "The 'Eternity' of the Platonic Forms." *Phronesis* 13:131–144.

Williams, B. 2008. "Plato's Construction of Intrinsic Goodness." In *The Sense of the Past*, edited by M. Burnyeat, 118–137. Princeton, NJ.

Williams, M. 2000. "Epistemology and the Mirror of Nature." In Brandom, *Rorty and His Critics*, 191–213.

Winzenrieth, J. 2018. "Après les nombres, après les idées: Le statut des grandeurs au sein du platonisme." *Les Études philosophiques* 1:57–68.

Wittgenstein, L. 1922. *Tractatus Logico-Philosophicus*. London.

Wreen, M. 2018. "What Is Moral Relativism?" *Philosophy* 93:337–354.

Yount, D. 2014. *Plotinus the Platonist*. London.

General Index

Abbate, M., 140n, 227n
abductive inferences, 31, 134
absolute simplicity, 133–35, 139, 159, 208, 222, 229–30, 234, 252, 254, 256–57, 259–60, 262
Academic Sceptics, 67
Academy, 12, 15, 20, 40–42, 64, 80, 140, 157, 246, 254, 271, 274, 278, 281
actuality, activity (ἐνέργεια), 24, 209, 214–15, 218, 221, 227, 229, 237–39, 252, 258
actus essendi, 231
ἀλήθεια (truth), 72, 107, 121
Anaxagoras, 9, 13, 20, 23, 47–49, 51–55, 57–59, 61, 64–65, 68, 70, 213, 236, 238–39, 241
anti-materialism, 13–14, 21, 25, 62, 118, 162, 225
anti-mechanism, 21, 25, 62, 162, 225
anti-Naturalism, 13, 23, 33, 50, 197, 218, 265
anti-nominalism, 13–14, 25, 62, 76, 162, 225
anti-philosophy, 8, 12
anti-Platonism, 4, 8–9, 21, 23, 65, 155, 240–41, 264–65
Antisthenes, 139, 143
aporia, 65, 256
ἀρχή (principle), 55–58, 157, 237, 255
Archer-Hind, R. D., 89n, 190n
Aristotelianism, 17, 198, 272
Aristotle's testimony, 19–20, 39, 42–44, 48, 60–61, 64–65, 120, 127, 150, 155, 157, 161–62, 225–26, 228, 234
Armstrong, D., 14n, 27n, 48n

assimilation to god, 50, 72, 150, 184, 189, 240, 243
Atomism, 23
Aubenque, P., 200n, 238n
autoexplicability, 253
αἴσθησις, 100, 107, 111, 130, 216
αἴτιον, 48–49, 248, 259
  αἴτιον ἑαυτοῦ, 233
αἰτίαι, 49
αἰών, 90
αἰώνιος, 89–90

Balaguer, M., 84n, 88n
Baltes, M., 125n
Baltzly, D., 122n
Bealer, G., 92n
beauty, 52–53, 57, 60, 62, 66, 68, 76–77, 82, 85–86, 90–91, 131, 149–51, 172, 176–80, 187
becoming one out of many, 178, 192
becoming, 58, 90–91, 100, 102–3, 107, 109, 122, 131, 142
being
  complexity of, 142, 147
  created by the Good, 121
  cognitional representations of, 147
Benitez, E., 154n
Benson, H, 39n, 54n
Berti, E., 156n, 199n, 222n
biology, 7, 25–26, 36, 86, 98, 264
  molecular, 265
Bluck, R., 56n

Blyth, D., 62n
Bonazzi, M., 16n, 224n, 235n
Bos, A., 247n
Boys-Stones, G. R., 220n, 235n
brain states, 70, 114–15, 117, 217–18
Brickhouse, T., 40n, 167n, 174n
Brisson, L., 90n, 121n, 134n, 159n, 164n
Brittain, C., 109n, 235n
Broadie, S., 190n
Brunschwig, J., 157n
Burnyeat, M., 213n
Butorac, D., 247n

Carnap, R., 23n, 27n
Caro, R., 32n
Cartesian dualism, 22
causal closure, 19, 32, 36, 48–49, 70, 236
causality, 31, 48–50, 52, 98, 122, 133–35, 220, 231–32, 272
causes
  accessory, 248
  auxiliary, 49
  efficient, 133
  father of the, 226
  final, 53, 121, 222, 228
  formal, 49, 53, 63
  instrumental, 31–32, 49, 58
  necessary, 134
  paradigmatic, 250
  primary, 62, 252
  real, 49, 248
  sufficient, 238
  supernatural, 29, 52
  ultimate, 248
  unifying, 151
Cherniss, H., 40n, 89n, 131n, 148n, 164n
Chlup, R., 190n, 250n
Christianity, 17, 260, 263–64
Churchland, P., 27n
cognition
  direct, 114
  disembodied, 113
  embodied, 113, 116
  fallible, 67, 109
  higher, 189
  inerrant, 109
  non-perceptual, 78
  non-representational, 112
  universalizing, 119
  unmediated, 113
cognition of form, 105, 115, 218
cognitive identity, 96, 151–52, 185, 189, 215–17, 219–20, 227
  eternal, 96
cognitive state, 118
  complex, 116
Cohoe, C., 229n

Colyvan, M., 88n
Combès, J., 254n, 257n, 260n
commensurability, 60, 123, 149–51, 176–80, 187, 227
common nature, 86
complexity, 92, 95, 116, 129, 131, 133–34, 141, 145, 160–61, 231, 233, 251, 260, 262
  conceptual, 259
  internal, 147
  maximal, 262
  minimal, 141
  predicative, 257
  structural, 129
contradictions, 16, 56, 65, 80, 84, 201, 205, 223
Coope, U., 243n
Cooper, J., 106n, 150n, 167n
Cornford, F. M., 10n, 90n, 96n, 129n, 133n, 134, 197n
Cradle Argument, so-called, 24
Craig, W. L., 17n, 65n
Crombie, I. M., 53n, 57n, 112n

d'Hoine, P., 154n, 268, 272, 283
Damascius, 12, 17, 127, 247, 254–60, 267, 279, 283
Dancy, R., 57n, 145n, 218n
Darwin, C., 28
Dasgupta, S., 166n
defining criteria, 108
Delcomminette, S., 149n
Demiurge, 59–61, 78–79, 85–86, 92–94, 96–97, 113, 146–47, 151–55, 188, 190, 220, 226–27, 230, 241–42, 262
Democritus, 9, 23, 102, 139, 217
Dennett, D., 87n
Denton, M., 98n
Descartes, R., 62
Desjardins, R., 127n, 189n
developmentalism, 38–39, 40, 44
Dillon, J., 120n, 130n, 136n, 224n
Dixsaut, M., 66n, 125n
Dodds, E. R., 224n, 249–50n
dogmatism, 24, 67, 270, 273
Donini, P., 224n
dualisms, 5, 10, 160, 229, 278
Dumoncel, J.-C., 161n
δόξα, 66–71, 74, 117, 130
δύναμις, 124, 126, 139–40, 206, 229, 237, 258–59
  unlimited, 229
δύναμις πάντων, 230

early dialogues, 39–40, 61, 279
Edelstein, L., 42n
Eleaticism, 48

GENERAL INDEX   287

Eleatics, 274
embodiment, 20, 62, 177, 183, 217, 240
    pre-exists, 113
Empedocles, 55, 61, 77, 102, 217
empiricism, 22, 24, 27, 33–34, 47, 263
epistemology, 5, 9, 13, 124, 263, 271, 275,
    280, 284
essence (οὐσία)
    beyond, 121, 124, 226
    eternal non-sensible, 154
    scattered, 131–32
    variegated, 99
eternal intellect, 81, 85–86, 97, 142, 145–46,
    154, 161, 190, 220
eternity, 17, 70, 88–90, 92, 97–98, 209, 263,
    283
existence and essence, 57, 63–64, 121–22,
    124–25, 135, 137, 147, 153, 161, 175,
    208
existents, 88, 133, 135–36, 208, 234, 238,
    249–50, 260
    necessary, 87
explanation
    adequate, 53, 57, 69, 75, 86, 99, 233, 237
    alternative, 55
    assimilating, 50
    causal, 19, 24, 29–30, 97
    comprehensive, 61
    formal, 51, 54
    nominal, 57
    real, 36, 49, 52, 58, 86, 98, 234
    scientific, 48, 54, 238
    sufficient, 27
    teleological, 54, 56–57
    true, 30, 48, 50, 55, 58, 68, 87
explanatory adequacy, 27, 55, 62, 86–88,
    119, 145, 193, 253, 260
εἶναι, 95, 124–25, 136, 142, 157, 177

Fazzo, S, 222n
Findlay, J. N., 43n, 62n
first philosophy, 7, 12, 14, 24, 46, 198–99,
    201–7, 236, 246, 269
Fodor, J., 13n
form
    generic, 55, 63, 144, 168–69, 173
    immutable, 108
    individual, 143
    intelligible, 116, 173
    particularized, 107, 215, 217, 218
Frede, M., 41n, 48n, 145n, 201n
Frege, G., 23n
Fronterotta, F., 120n
Furth, M., 48n

Gaiser, K., 121n, 159n
Gallop, D., 54n

Gersh, S., 247n, 249n
Gerson, L., 11n, 17n, 43–44n, 63n, 80n,
    106n, 130n, 140n, 146n, 156n, 222n,
    225n, 232n
Gill, M. L., 134n, 142n, 207n
Gonzalez, F., 41n
Gosling, J., 125n
Greatest Kinds, 138, 144–45
Grote, G., 41n
grounding, 18, 30, 278
Guthrie, W. K. C., 162n
Gutiérrez, R., 178n

Hackforth, R., 53n, 56n, 186n
Hadot, P., 45n
Hale, B., 21n
Halfwassen, J., 96n, 121n, 125n, 132n, 152n,
    160n, 165n, 189n, 224n
Hamlyn, D. W., 210n
happiness, 24, 27, 135, 141, 159, 176, 180–83,
    243
Harte, V., 67–68n, 71n
Henads, 252–54, 259, 283
    participatable, 260
    posited, 252
Hermann, F.-G., 23n
Hicks, R. D., 211–13n
historical Socrates, 39, 44, 155, 179
    real, 20
Hitchcock, D., 125n, 127n, 135n, 178n
Hösle, V., 132n
Huffman, C., 61n
Hursthouse, R., 168n
hylomorphism, 209–10, 215–18, 220, 237
hypostatization (universalizing), 80–81, 105

Idea of the Good, 19, 163, 263
    One identical with, 127, 159–60
    Good-like, 123, 126, 151, 170–71, 174,
        178–79, 183
immaterial entities, 18, 22–23, 32, 52, 998,
    114, 117–18, 175, 200, 209, 218–19,
    236–37, 239
Indefinite Dyad, 59–60, 62, 64, 132, 135,
    145, 150, 154, 157–61, 224, 227–30,
    259
    coordinate Form of Good, 160
individuals, 78, 80, 84, 123, 147, 184,
    240–41
infallible cognition, 19, 24, 45, 67–68, 112–13,
    240, 244
    possibility of, 19, 24
instrumental causality, 30–31, 57, 232
integrative unity, 122, 126, 150–51, 153,
    171–73, 176–80, 183–87, 192–93
    optimal, 184, 186
    principle of, 126–27, 178, 186

intellect
    active (agent), 209–10, 215, 217
    actualized, 228
    complete, 228
    embodied, 99, 146
    immaterial human, 36
    immortal, 198, 216
    indestructible, 213
    passive, 217
    self-aware agent, 217
    undescended, 246
intellect and forms, 96, 219
intellect-intelligibles, 153
intellection, 95, 121, 146, 152, 209, 214–15, 222, 260
intelligible entities, 30, 45, 142
intelligible objects, 67, 131, 179, 220, 236
intelligible reality, 59, 96, 141, 146, 154, 230, 233
Irwin, T., 22n, 39n, 51n, 125n, 167n, 179n, 181n

Jaeger, W., 156n, 200n
Johansen, T., 49n, 122n
judgments, diachronic, 103
judgments of identity and difference, 100, 102

Kahn, C., 40–41n, 78n, 125n
Kamtekar, R., 179n
Karfik, J., 247n
Kelsey, S., 49n
Kitcher, P., 23n, 97n
knowability, 122, 158, 161
knowledge (ἐπιστήμη)
    definition of, 72, 102, 109
    embodied, 96
    objects of, 68, 72, 116, 155, 245
    occurrent, 115
    possibility of, 67, 106, 108
    propositional, 116
    scientific, 158–59, 244
knowledge of forms, 68, 70, 72, 112, 124, 154, 233
κοινωνία τῶν εἰδῶν, 95, 143, 177
κοινός, 102, 104, 107, 180
Kornblith, H., 29n, 46n, 264n
Korsgaard, C., 166n
Krämer, H. J., 19n, 45n, 120–21n, 123–25n, 149n, 161n, 224n, 231n
Kuhn, T., 26n
κίνησις, 93–94, 144

Ladyman, J., 46n
Lavecchia, S., 135n, 142n, 178n, 189n
Layne, M., 247n
Ledger, G. R., 40n

Leiter. B., 28n, 32n
Lennox, J., 52n
limit and unlimitedness, 150, 259
Linguitti, A., 258n
Living Animal, 59, 89, 91, 93–94, 96, 152–53, 190, 220
    intelligibility of, 153
Longo, A., 235n
Lott, M., 168–69n
Lowe, E. J., 205–6n
Luchetti, C., 92n

MacArthur, D., 35n
MacKenna, S., 230n
materialism, 13–14, 18, 21, 24, 27, 33, 35, 48, 52–53, 114, 118, 193, 236–37, 239–40, 244, 255, 262
    eliminative, 117
    first philosophy and, 269
materialists, 13, 18, 20, 56, 63, 136, 139–40, 233, 235–38, 243–44
    moderate, 139
    reformed, 141
mathematical objects, 67, 161, 201
    posited, 156
mathematical truth, 27, 35, 97–99, 199
McDowell, J., 5n, 32n, 204n
mechanism, 18–19, 24, 32–33, 48, 52, 62, 77, 115, 118–19, 133, 197, 235–36, 239–40, 244
Meijer, P. A., 247n
Meinwald, C., 134n
Meixner, U., 49n, 84n
Menn, S., 49n, 140n, 232n
Meno's paradox, 190
mental states, 28, 69–70, 265
    infallible, 244–45
Merlan, P., 161n, 200n
metaphysica generalis, 200, 202
metaphysica specialis, 200
metaphysics
    foundational, 198
    rejection of, 236
    systematic, 183
    two-world, 44, 60–61
Mettry-Tresson, C., 260n
μετέχειν, 109, 142, 274
Middle Platonism, 25, 154, 220, 232
Migliori, M., 127n
Miller, M., 127n, 134n, 151n, 155n, 187n
Moderatus, 224
monism, 160, 229, 281
Moore, G. E., 169n
moral normativity, 25, 28, 34, 264
Morel, P.-M., 24n
Morris, S., 6n

motion (κίνησις), 31, 36, 89, 93–94, 97, 129, 139–40, 142–44, 165, 200, 203–5, 214, 249
Murphy, N., 53n

Nagel, T., 60n, 112n, 166n
Nails, D., 40n, 122n
Naturalism
  capacious, 27
  consistent, 25
  contemporary, 17
  elements of, 75, 193, 197, 261
  framework of, 19, 32, 46, 76, 119, 205
  just enough, 14
  liberal, 32, 35
  metaphysical, 27
  methodological, 14, 29, 31, 88, 273
  object of, 4, 26
  pragmatic, 11
  principles of, 35
  soft, 32
  strict, 203
  theological, 27
Naturalists
  consistent, 28, 242, 244
  half-hearted, 8, 246
  normativity for, 277
  representationalist, 9
natural kinds, 30, 84, 151, 177, 179, 184
Neoplatonic interpretation of Parmenides, 134
Neoplatonic metaphysics, 259
Neoplatonism, 127, 234, 262, 269, 277
Nikulin, D., 121n
nominalism, 13–14, 18, 27, 33–34, 61–62, 77, 80, 99, 102, 106–8, 118–19, 193, 197, 240, 244
  defense of, 14, 273
  psychological, 6
  resemblance, 33, 280
normativity, 19, 28, 32, 169, 177–79, 186, 193, 204, 240, 243–44, 272, 281
νοῦς, 48–49, 52–53, 59, 72, 121, 148–49, 151, 153, 209, 212–13, 228, 241
νόησις, 221, 227

O'Brien, D., 128n, 180n
O'Conaill, D., 30n
Oderberg, D., 170n
Old Academy, 12, 19–20, 42, 120, 131
O'Meara, D., 260n
one and many, 226
One-Being, 132, 158, 161, 165, 209, 255, 258
oneness
  absolute, 149
  derivative, 129

one over many, 79, 128, 130, 250
ontological foundations, 85–86, 120, 143–45, 218, 223
ontology, 27, 199–200, 205, 236, 246, 279–81, 283
  ethics without, 246
Opsomer, J., 224n
order, 16, 31, 46, 78, 89, 93, 143, 154, 172, 185, 207–8, 222
  mathematical, 78, 152, 161, 186
  systematic, 225
ordinals, 92, 201
O'Rourke, F., 17n
Owen, G. E. L., 88n, 131n, 198n
οὐσία, 57, 85, 121, 123–27, 130–32, 134, 138–39, 145–48, 153, 164, 166, 169–70, 177, 207–8, 231–32, 258
  above, 96, 125, 141, 149–50, 153, 207, 232
οὐσίαι, 107, 123, 164–65, 170, 177, 231
  participatable, 61

Palmer, J., 129n
panpsychism, 14, 35, 281
  detaching, 146
Papineau, D., 35n, 47–48n, 109n, 172n
paradoxes, 58, 134, 154, 161, 181–82
Parmenides, 79, 81, 88, 102, 127–30, 133–36, 138, 140, 160–61, 226–27, 232–33, 257, 270–71, 274–75, 277–78
Participation (μέθεξις), 58–59, 62, 77–78, 82, 91, 98, 127, 138, 143–45, 156, 160, 240, 251–54, 257
particularity, 79, 81, 104, 113, 115–16
Patterson, R., 80n, 91n
Penner, T., 166–67n, 171n, 174n, 180n, 182n, 240n
Perl, E., 86n, 94n, 140n, 152n
persons, 12, 39, 118, 130, 159, 169–71, 176, 178, 181, 184, 187–88, 246
  disembodied, 113
philodoxers, 66, 68, 70–71, 78, 203
philosophy
  derived, 70
  edifying, 5, 8
  ethical, 155
  history of, 16, 22, 32, 42, 80, 233, 235, 265, 271, 273–74, 281
  incoherent, 235
  pagan, 263
  possibility of, 9, 14, 36, 46–47, 260
  second, 7, 46, 203–6
  subject matter for, 5–6, 9, 11, 13, 23, 44–45, 60, 66, 68, 71, 74, 92, 141, 198, 202, 204, 261, 263
  systematic, 8, 12, 14, 41, 43, 59, 123, 198, 223, 261

physicalism, 26, 278
Plass, P., 42n
Platonic system, 21, 43, 124, 132, 147, 163, 193, 197, 208, 224, 229, 234, 247, 254, 270
Platonism, 3–5, 8–9, 13–25, 27, 32–34, 36–38, 40–43, 65–67, 162–64, 197–98, 234–36, 246–47, 260–65, 269–74, 277–78
   elements of, 15, 22, 75
   history of, 12, 16, 224–25
Platonism vs. Naturalism, 12–13, 16, 21, 28, 32, 35–37, 43, 76, 86, 88, 141, 147, 235, 261, 265
pluralism, 35, 137
   conceptual, 246
   epistemological, 25
   ontological, 35
Polansky, R., 210n
Polemo, 225
   successor, 246
polytheism, 253–54, 271
potency (δύναμις), principle of, 200, 237–38
predication, 3, 77, 82–85, 109, 142–43, 145, 277
Price, H., 4n, 26n, 112, 114n
Primavesi, O., 156n
Prime Mover, 272
principles of limit, 127, 132, 186, 252–53
Pritchard, P., 62n
privation, 156, 206
Proclus, 126–27, 130, 164–65, 190–91, 193, 224–25, 227–28, 230–31, 247–50, 252–55, 257–58, 260
prudentialism, 167–68, 176, 179, 240, 246
Pythagoreans, 20, 61, 156–57, 160, 170, 275

Quine, W. v. O., 6n, 11n, 26n, 29n, 46n, 101n, 105n

radical Heracliteanism, 59, 103
Rappe, S., 258n
rationality, 24–25, 183, 185, 243–45
Rea, M., 29n, 82n
real distinctions, 81, 96, 131, 138, 141–43, 145, 229, 233, 255, 259
recollection argument, 33, 99–100, 111–12
Reeve, C. D. C., 205n
representationalism, 4–6, 8–11, 19, 26–27, 71, 112–13, 244
representations, 4–6, 8–11, 19, 27, 74, 89, 112–13, 116–18, 146–47, 219, 227, 264
resemblance, 33–34, 271
Richard, M.-D., 42n, 148n, 156n, 161n
Rist, J., 262n
Ritchie, J., 88n
Robin, L., 61n
Robinson, T. M., 90n

Rodier, G., 62n
Rödl, S., 216n, 243n
Rodriguez-Pereyra, G., 33n
Rorty, R.
   anti-representationalism of, 3–11, 13, 17, 27, 112, 114, 147, 198, 235
   division of philosophy, 8
   pragmatism of, 9, 11
   rejection of Platonism, 8
Rosenberg, A., 26–28n, 32n
Ross, W. D., 46n, 48n, 61n, 80n, 156n, 159n, 217n
Rowe, C., 39n, 180n

Saffrey, H. D., 127n, 252n
sameness (ὁμοιότης), 18, 23, 58, 71, 79–81, 83–84, 96, 98–99, 101–3, 128, 142, 144, 218, 248–50, 279
   deficient, 113
   judgments of, 100
Santas, G., 122n, 174n, 180n
Sayre, K., 122n, 134n, 150n
Scanlon, T., 32n
scepticism, 282
Schaffer, J., 27n, 93n, 203n
science of being, 7–8, 199–207, 236–37
Scolnicov, S., 94n
Sedley, D., 20n, 54n, 235–36n, 239n
self
   empirical, 178
   true, 175, 182, 192, 282
self-awareness, 115, 242–45
Sellars, W., 6n, 58n, 105n
Shapiro, S., 92n
Sharma, R., 53n
Shields, C., 80n, 210n, 213n
Shorey, P., 41n
sights and sounds, lovers of, 7, 44, 65–66, 69, 72, 117, 203
Sillitti, G., 122n
Silverman, A., 134n, 145n
simple first principle, 135, 137, 147, 151, 160, 163, 186, 193, 198, 222–23, 231–32, 234, 251, 253–54, 261–62
Smith, N. D., 38n, 40n, 44n, 68n, 167n, 174n, 210n
Socratic definitions, 108
Socratic dialogues, 40, 44, 174, 275, 281
   elenchus, 181
   ethics, 39, 179, 246
   so-called, 18, 38
Sorabji, R., 112n
soul
   embodied, 186, 190
   immaterial, 243
   immortal, 146, 184

immortal part of the, 198
incarnated, 147
intellectual, 210, 216
pre-embodied, 215
rational, 212, 214
temporalized, 190
soul-body, 262
soul-care, 175–76, 182
  desirability of, 182–83
Steel, C., 44n
Steinthal, H., 157n
Stenzel, J., 57n, 61–62n
Stoicism, 7–8, 22, 24, 162, 191, 224, 226, 235–36, 240, 244, 246
  ethics of, 269
  materialism of, 25, 236, 240, 243
  metaphysics of, 7, 269–70
  physics of, 8, 236, 238–39, 241
  summum genus, 238
Strahler, A., 30
Strawson, G., 14n, 35n
Strawson, P., 32n
Striker, G., 241n
substance
  sensible, 201–2, 207
  supersensible, 199–201
sufficient conditions, 32, 49–52, 55, 68, 70, 238
supernaturalism, 22, 32
superordinate Idea, 22, 28, 53, 61, 63, 67, 75, 124–25, 158, 163–65, 167–68, 171, 179–81, 183, 185
supervenience, 35
Svavarsson, S., 81n
syncretism, 235
Szaif, J., 67n
Szlezák, T., 61n, 66n, 120–21n, 123n, 157n

Tait, W. W., 54n
Taormina, D., 235n
Tarán, L., 88n
Tarrant, H., 224n
Taylor, A. E., 57n, 62n, 93n, 152n, 190n
Teloh, H., 121n
testimony, oral, 19, 42, 64–65, 127, 155, 157, 159, 209
  Aristotle's, 11, 43, 123
time, 13–16, 18, 26–27, 77, 79–81, 88–94, 97–98, 109, 130, 132, 153–54, 176, 198, 237–39, 248–50
transcendent, 132, 166, 172, 187, 222, 230
truth
  analytic, 174, 248
  contingent, 72, 144, 153
  eternal, 88, 97–98, 133
  necessary, 72, 92, 144, 153, 189, 203, 218–19
  ontological, 107, 149, 151, 169, 233
  representational, 245
  universal, 23, 203
Turnbull, R., 92n

ultimacy, ontological, 31, 50, 58, 60, 88, 91, 97, 126, 132, 155, 192, 237, 255
ultimate explanations, 36, 62, 76, 89, 92, 126, 173, 203, 232, 248, 256
  true, 87
understanding, 7, 12, 23–24, 68–70, 99, 150, 159, 172, 175, 181, 184, 206, 213, 219, 235–36
unhypothetical first principle, 19–21, 23, 31, 47, 54, 56–58, 60–62, 118, 120, 122–24, 128, 134–35, 161, 200, 234
unification, 112, 178, 258
  integrative, 178
  sub-optimal, 184
unificatory process, 21, 112, 159, 189
  dynamic integrative, 189
  integrative, 189
unified functionality, 151
unity
  absolute, 96
  complex, 21, 96
  explanatory, 126
  generic, 50
  integrated, 60, 172, 184–85, 189, 193, 249
  intelligible, 241
  interspecific, 184
  intraspecific, 184
  principle of, 127, 150, 155
  reductive, 145
unity of being, 153, 269
universals, 14, 44, 79–81, 101, 168, 217, 269, 281
  commutative, 80
  immanent, 27
univocity, 130, 202, 207–8
unlimitedness, 126, 148–50, 258–59
  principle of, 132, 186
Unmoved Mover, 46, 97, 201, 203, 205, 207, 214, 218, 220–23, 227–30, 232, 241
  separate, 222
unwritten doctrines, 121, 187
Ur-Platonism, 76, 225

van Fraassen, B., 9n
van Inwagen, P., 21n, 154n
Van Riel, G., 149n, 253n
Vasilakis, D., 189n
Vasiliou, I., 167n
Vegetti, M., 122n, 135n

virtue
  knowledge of, 167, 181
  ordinary, 181–82
  part of, 142
  political, 181, 188
  purificatory, 181
  the sovereignty of, 183
  species, 174
  wisdom and, 249
virtue ethics, 275
Vlastos, G., 38n, 53n, 60n, 64n, 174n, 180n, 182–83n, 188n, 240n, 246n
Vogel, C. J. de, 123n
Vuillemin, J., 62n

Wedin, M., 204n
Wehrli, F., 223n
Weinberg, S., 204n

Westerink, L., 127n, 254n, 257n
Wittgenstein, L., 23n, 33n, 241n
world
  corporeal, 77
  empirical, 47
  eternal, 52, 72, 249
  eternal intelligible, 103, 145
  immaterial, 118
  intelligible, 47
  non-sensible, 154, 204
  physical, 35
  supersensible, 203
  temporal, 249
world soul, 116, 227

Xenocrates, 15, 42, 157, 159, 225, 246, 262, 268
φιλοσοφία, 44–45, 66
φύσις, 37, 63, 202–3

Index Locorum

ALEXANDER OF APHRODISIAS

Commentary on Aristotle's Metaphysics (In Meta.) (Hayduck)

55.20–35   156n.118

De anima (De an.) (Hayduck)

89.9–19   218n.67

Mantissa

2, 112.5–113.6   218n.67

De fato (Bruns)

169.13–15   191n.86
181.2–14   191n.86
199.8–9   191n.86
211.21–23   191n.86

ANONYMOUS PROLEGOMENA TO PLATO'S PHILOSOPHY (WESTERINK/TROUILLARD)

26   136n.52

ARISTOTLE

De anima (DA)

A 1, 403b7–8   204n.22
A 1, 403b15–16   200n.8
A 2, 404b3   213n.49
A 4, 408b13–15   213n.48
A 4, 408b18–29   212n.45
B 1, 412a27–28   210n.37, 214n.55
B 1, 413a3–7   210n.37, 214n.57
B 2, 413a20–25   214n.54
B 2, 413b24–27   210n.39
Γ 2, 426b14–15   101n.71
Γ 3, 427a17–b6   77n.2, 218n.66
Γ 3, 427a18–428a14   102n.76
Γ 4, 429a15–18   216n.63
Γ 4, 429a22   212n.47
Γ 4, 429a22–24   210n.38
Γ 4, 429a24–26   210n.41
Γ 4, 429a24–27   214n.56, 216n.62
Γ 4, 429a27–28   210n.42, 212n.46
Γ 4, 429b9   215n.59, 217n.64
Γ 4, 430a2–3   217n.64
Γ 4, 430a3–6   215n.59
Γ 5, 430a10–25   209n.33, 215n.60
Γ 5, 430a17   209n.36
Γ 5, 430a19–20   215n.59
Γ 5, 430a22–23   209n.36
Γ 5, 430a25   209n.34
Γ 6, 430b25–26   215n.59
Γ 7, 431a1–2   215n.59
Γ 7, 431a16–17   209n.35
Γ 7, 439b17   215n.59
Γ 8, 432a9   209n.35
Γ 9, 432b26   191n.87, 213n.49
Γ 10, 433a27–28   191n.87, 221n.72
Γ 10, 433b4   213n.53

De caelo (DC)

A 9, 279a18–22   90n.30

De generatione animalium (De gen. an.)

B 3, 736b27–29   215n.58

De generatione et corruptione (GC)

B 9, 335b9–16   48n.37

Eudemian Ethics (EE)

A 8, 1218a15–32   157n.122
A 8, 1218a16–29   184n.58, 207n.31
A 8, 1218a25–30   177n.41

Magna Moralia (MM)

A 1, 1182a27–30   159n.129

Metaphysics (Meta.)

A 2, 982a4–6	206n.27
A 5, 987a13–19	20n.16
A 6, 987a14–18	156n.117
A 6, 987a29–988a17	19n.13
A 6, 987a29–b7	44n.19
A 6, 987a29ff	39n.6
A 6, 987a32–b10	20n.14
A 6, 987b19–20	20n.16, 154n.112
A 6, 987b20–21	177n.41
A 6, 987b21–22	227n.20
A 6, 988a8–14	60n.83, 157n.121
A 6, 988a14–17	55n.64
A 8, 990a29–32	20n.16, 156n.119
A 9, 991a8–b1	52n.49
A 9, 991b3–9	47n.37
A 9, 992a20–22	160n.135
B 1, 995b15ff	156n.117
B 3, 999a20	200n.11
Γ 1, 1003a21–32	200n.9
Γ 2, 1003a33–34	202n.14
Γ 2, 1003b14	202n.14
Γ 5, 1009b12–28	102n.76
Γ 5, 1010a1–4	47n.32
Δ 1, 1013a7–8	157n.123
Δ 3, 1014a26–27	157n.123
Δ 5, 1015a20–21	49n.42
Δ 6, 1016b20–21	158n.128
Δ 6, 1016b21–22	201n.13
Δ 6, 1016b25	257n.46
Δ 11, 1019a1–4	6n.7
E 1, 1025b18–21	200n.7
E 1, 1026a15–22	7n.9, 200n.11
E 1, 1026a23–32	199n.4
Z 2, 1028b2–4	207n.30
Z 2, 1028b19–21	156n.117
Z 3, 1029a30–32	200n.8, 207n.29
Z 3, 1029b5–8	221n.74
Z 4, 1029b13	128n.26
Z 11, 1036b13–25	20n.16, 156n.119
Z 11, 1037a15	205n.24
Z 15, 1039b30–1040a7	203n.17
H 4, 1044a23–25	75n.126
Θ 6, 1048a30–32	237n.59
Θ 8, 1049b5	237n.55
Θ 8, 1050b2–3	231n.37
I 1, 1052b31–35, 158n.128,	201n.13
I 1, 1053a31–33	201n.13
K 1, 1059b2	156n.117
K 3, 1060b36–1061a7	202n.14
K 4, 1061b28–32	200n.7
K 7, 1064b4–14	199n.4
Λ 1, 1069a27–28	128n.26
Λ 1, 1069a30–b2	46n.27, 199n.4
Λ 1, 1069a33ff	156n.117
Λ 6, 1071b20	207n.29, 207n.30
Λ 7, 1072a25–26	189n.79, 207n.30
Λ 7, 1072a26–30	221n.71
Λ 7, 1072a30–34	207n.31
Λ 7, 1072a35–b1	221n.75
Λ 7, 1072b13–14	37n.51, 203n.16, 205n.75, 222n.76
Λ 7, 1072b18–19	221n.74, 222n.77
Λ 7, 1072b26–27	97n.60, 214n.54
Λ 8, 1073a18–19	20n.16, 156n.119
Λ 8, 1073a30	207n.30
Λ 8, 1074a31–38	208n.32
Λ 9, 1075a4–5	227n.16
Λ 10, 1075a11–25	222n.76
Λ 10, 1075b18–20	160n.133
M 1, 1076a19ff	156n.117
M 4, 1078b9–12	20n.16, 156n.119
M 5, 1080a2–8	47n.37
M 6, 1080b11–14	20n.16, 156n.119
M 7, 1081a5–7	20n.16, 156n.119
M 7, 1081a13–15	227n.20
M 8, 1083a18	20n.16, 156n.119
M 8, 1084a37–b2	160n.135
M 8, 1084a7–8	20n.16, 156n.119
M 9, 1086a11–13	20n.16, 156n.117, 156n.119
M 9, 1086a32–b11	79n.6
N 1, 1087b9–12	160n.132, 229n.26
N 1, 1087b21	128n.26
N 2, 1090a4–6	20n.16, 156n.119
N 3, 1090a16	20n.16, 156n.119
N 3, 1090a35–36	156n.117
N 4, 1091b13–15	19n.13, 55n.64, 60n.83, 157n.122, 177n.41, 231n.36
N 5, 1092a14	125n.16
N 7, 1081a22	157n.124

Nicomachean Ethics (EN)

A 6, 1096b5–7	158n.127
Γ 3, 1112b23–24	75n.126
K 7, 1177b26–31	211n.43
I 4, 1166a22–23	211n.43
I 8, 1169a2	211n.43

Physics (Phys.)

A 1, 184a10–b14	221n.74
A 4, 187a16–20	156n.118
A 8, 191a24–25	206n.28
A 9, 192a3–12	156n.118
A 9, 192a30–192b1	37n.51
B 1, 192b22	200n.7
B 2, 193b22–194b15	200n.8, 204n.22
B 3, 195a23–36	191n.87
Γ 1, 200b1–3	200n.7
Γ 3, 202b16–22	95n.48
Γ 5, 204a34ff	128n.26

Posterior Analytics (An. Post.)

A 31, 87b28	203n.17
A 33, 88b30–37	203n.17

Index Locorum

Rhetoric (Rhet.)
A 10, 1369a2–4   191n.87

Topics (Top.)
Z 8, 146b36–
  147a11   191n.87

ARISTOXENUS

Harmonic Elements
2.30–31 (=Aristotle, *On the Good*, p.111 Ross) 98n.2, 159n.129, 204n.97

DAMASCIUS

De principiis (*De princ.*)
  (Westerink/Combès)

1.1.4–2.20	255n.40
1.107.3–8	258n.50
1.116.4–6	259n.55
1.4.13–18	256n.42
1.56.1–11	257n.44
1.56.11–19	257n.45
1.62.9–11	257n.47
1.77.19–20	259n.55
1.92.18–21	256n.41
2.10.13–33	259n.52
2.22.11–23.6	257n.45
2.33.10–12	258n.51
2.39.11–25	258n.52
2.71.1	258n.51
2.71.1–11	259n.53, 259n.55
2.73.19–20	258n.51
2.80.19–81.2	259n.54
3.152.13–16	258n.51

DIOGENES LAERTIUS (D.L.)

Lives and Opinions of the Philosophers

3.58	136n.52
7.149	241n.75
7.92	244n.86
7.94	242n.78
10.132	166n.14

EPICTETUS

Discourses (Oldfather)

2.10.1–4	243n.80
7.21–22	243n.80
7.31–33	243n.80
9.1–5	243n.80
11.8	243n.80

IAMBLICHUS

Fragments (Dillon)
1   136n.52

NUMENIUS

Fragments (Des Places)
24.5–12   225n.2

PARMENIDES

Fragments (Diels/Kranz)
B3   85n.19
B8   85n.19

PLATO

(?) 2nd Epistle
312E1–4   226n.7

(?) 6th Epistle
323D4   226n.8

(?) 7th Epistle

341C5–6	121n.3
342D1–2	149n.92
344A8–B2	65n.94

Alcibiades I (Alc.)
133B   174n.34

Apology (Ap.)

28B5–6	183n.56
28B5–9	166n.15, 183n.56
28D6–9	166n.15
28E5–6	45n.22
29B–30D	175n.37
29E1–2	65n.94
30C6–D5	181n.52
31D–32A	170n.23
37A5	173n,31
38A5–6	45n.22
40A–C	170n.23
41C8–D2	181n.52

Charmides (Charm.)

173D3–5	181n.52
174B11–C3	181n.52

Cratylus (Crat.)

386E1	164n.4
440B4–C1	95n.52

Crito (Cr.)
47C8–48A1   65n.94

48B8–9	181n.52
48C6–D5	166n.15, 183n.56

Definitions (Pseudo–Platonic)

414B10	69n.109
414C3–4	69n.109

Epinomis (Epin.)
978B3–4   63n.91, 164n.3

Euthydemus (Euthyd.)
303C3   125n.15

Euthyphro (Eu.)
11A7   164n.4

Gorgias (Gorg.)

457B–C	175n.37
466A4–467C4	174n.32
479C5–6	159n.128
483B4–C6	168n.17
484C4–E3	183n.57
488A3	173n.31
498E10	159n.128
503E–504A2	172n.29

Hippias Minor (Hip. Mi.)

Laches (La.)
187D–188C   175n.37

Laws (Lg.)

731C–D	173n.31
897D3	97n.58

Meno (Men.)

77C1–2	173n.30
81C9–D1	20n.17
82B	109n.91

Parmenides (Parm.)

128A8–B1	129n.29
130B7–9	63n.91, 164n.3
131A–E	54n.58
132A1–4	79n.5, 103n.77, 14n.68
132B2	16n.134
132B2–C11	81n.10, 110n.93, 153n.107
132D1–2	22n.20
133C4	164n.4

135B5–C3	71n.113, 128n.25	66D8–E4	72n.118	98E2–99A4	48n.39
135C9–D1	128n.26, 129n.31	66E1–2	65n.94, 66n.101	99A4–5	49n.42
135D6	65n.94, 128n.27	67D7–8	66n.101	99A8–B1	49n.41
136C5	65n.94	72A3–78B3	33n.46	99B3–4	49n.42, 49n.40
136E1–3	65n.94	72E3–78B3	100n.68, 109n.91	99C5–6	49n.42, 123, 151n.101, 178n.44
136E5ff	128n.28	73C4–D1	111n.94		
137C4–D3	129n.32, 137n.55	74A6	81n.9	99D1	53n.54
		74B2–3	112n.95	99E1–4	48n.36
140A1–3	160n.131	74B7–9	51n.48	99E6	65n.94
141E7–8	142n.71	74D6	81n.9	100A2–7	50n.45
141E11	142n.71	74E4	81n.9	100D5	81D9
142B3	130n.33	74E9–75B2	172n.27	101C2–5	54n.58
142B5–143A1	96n.57	75C10–D2	63n.91, 164n.3	101D5–7	55n.59
142B5–6	130n.34, 131n.37, 158n.125	76D7–9	83n.91, 164n.3	101E1–3	55n.62, 55n.62
		76E5–7	95n.52	102D6–8	81n.9
142B8–C2	142n.71	77A2	164n.4	105B5–C7	51n.47, 55n.60
142C4–5	133n.46, 142n.71	78B4–84B4	99n.65		
		78D1–3	90n.30, 95n.51, 164b.4	106B6	53n.52
143A6–7	142n.71			107A8–B10	55n.63
143B3	142n.71			107B4–9	56n.65
144A6	160n.134	78D5	89n.27		
144E5–6	232n.43	79A6	6n.7	*Phaedrus* (*Phdr.*)	
149C5	160n.134	79A6–11	90n.27	245C5–246A2	189n.81
150B8	160n.134	79A6–7	45n.23	246A–253C	33n.46
151D3	160n.134	79B16–17	112n.98	247E1–2	95n.52
152A2–3	142n.71	79D1–7	140n.67	248B–C	171n.23
155D5–6	131n.40	80B1–2	90n.30	248D2–3	66n.101
156A1–2	142n.71	80B1–7	140n.67	249B5–C8	65n.94
156A4–5	142n.71	81A5	140n.67	249C	109n.91
158C4	160n.134	81C5	125n.15	249C4–5	66n.101
159B–160B	135n.50	81E–86C	33n.46	264C	172n.29
162A6–B2	142n.71	82D2–3	175n.36	268D	172n.29
162C2	93n.43	83A7–B2	178n.44	270D2–7	139n.63
164E–165E	132n.42	84A8–9	65n.94	274B6–278E3	41n.10
165E–166C	135n.50	87A11–B3	175n.36		
		95E8–96A1	49n.42, 55n.64	*Philebus* (*Phil.*)	
Phaedo (*Phd.*)		96A8–10	49n.42, 55n.64	14B1–2	125n.16
61C2–9	66n.101			15A4–7	63n.91, 164n.3
64E8–65A2	72n.117	96B8–12	112n.95	15B1–2	177n.42, 186n.66
65A1–3	123	96C4	48n.36		
65A9–C1	72n.118	97B3–7	49n.42, 55n.64	15B1–8	131n.38
65C11–D2	72n.117	97B8–C5	53n.54	16C1–17A5	148n.89, 157n.124
65D4–7	63n.91, 164n.3	97C1–2	226n.9		
65D9–10	77n.2	97C7	49n.42, 55n.64	16C7–10	148n.90, 186n.64
65D11ff	72n.117	97D1	54n.56	16C9–D7	96n.53, 184n.60
65D13	164n.4	97E5–98A8	49n.42		
65E2	65n.94	98C1–2	48n.37	16D7	160n.134
66A1–2	66n.101	98C2–E1	48n.38	17E6–7	128n.25
66A6	72n.118				
66D7	65n.94				

Index Locorum   297

19C	54n.54	476A9–D6	45n.23,	505E1–506A2	170n.23
20D1–10	149n.92,		65n.94,	506D8–E3	121n.3
	169n.20		68n.106,	506E3	121,
23C–27C	157n.124,		66n.98		188n.73
	220n.69	476C7–D2	7n.9	507B4–6	63n.91,
23C4–D8	148n.90	476D7–478E5	66n.95		164n.3,
23C4–D8	150n.101,	477A2–4	45n.24,		164n.6
	186.63		66n.97,	507B9–10	77n.2
25A6–B3	150n.97		90n.29,	508A9–B7	121
26B10	186n.65		141n.70	508B13	121
26C6–8	149n.91,	477A7	141n.70	508B6–7	121,
	160n.134	477A9–B1	66n.99		188n.73,
28D5–9	148n.88	477B9–10	108n.88		247n.2
29C2	160n.134	477D1–3	126n.18	508C1	6n.7
30C5	186n.65	477E6–7	45n.25,	508C10	60n.82
30D1–4	149n.91		108n.88	508D4–7	125n.15
41C9	159n.128	478A11–13	67n.104	508D10–E2	107n.85
58A2	90n.30	478B1–2	66n.100	508E1–4	121,
58B9–D1	72n.118	478D5–6	47n.32,		122
58C3	159n.129		66n.99,	509A6	123
59C2–D6	90n.30,		117n.106,	509A7	121n.3
	72n.118		141n.70	509B1–3	19n.13,
64A1–3	170n.21		66m.96		122n.8
65A1–5	60n.80,	478E7–480A13	68n.105,	509B6	121
	149n.94,	479A1–7	90n.30	509B8	164n.5
	150n.101		125n.15	509B9–10	121,
67A1–8	149n.92	479C7	141n.70		188n.72,
		479D5	66n.98		226n.11
		479D10–E4	45n.24	509D1–3	6n.7
Protagoras (*Protag.*)		479E6–7	90n.30	510B6–7	56n.65,
313B	174n.34	479E7–9	68n.105		122
345D8	173n.31	480A4	45n.24	511A4–C2	47n.33
358C7	173n.31	481B5	65n.94	511B2–C2	11n.19,
		484B3–6	45n.23,		57n.69,
Republic (*Rep.*)		484B4–7	66n.98		57n.71,
357B5	165n.11	484C9	65n.94		122n.9,
357C6	165n.11	485C3–D5	65n.94		162n.137
367C6–D3	164n.12,	486A10–B3	45n.23	511B5–6	122
	180n.50	487A7–8	66n.98	511B5–C2	122
422E–423B	178n.44,	490B5–6	65n.94	511D1–2	47n.33
	184n.58	498C3	123	516B10	121
423B9–10	184n.59	500B8–C7	72n.118	516C1–2	122,
423D3–6	184n.59,	504C1–4	123		188n.70
	192n.91	504D2–5	121	517B3	6n.7
439B–C	117n.107	504E2–3	123	517B8–C1	57n.68,
443E1–2	178n.44,	504E8	121n.3		122
	192n.91	505A1–4	121n.3,	517C1	123
462A2–B3	184n.58,		180n.50	517C1–2	121
	193n.91	505A6–7	121	517C2–3	121
474C1–3	66n.98	505D11–E1	121	517C3	121
475E2–4	60n.82,	505D5–506A2	188n.70	517C3–4	123
	65n.94	505D5–9	126n.20,	518C9	123
476A–480B	6n.7		169n.20,	518D11	175n.37
476A5–8	79n.5,		190n.84,	523B1ff	69n.108
	177n.43		247n.2	524C6–8	112n.97

524C13	77n.2	245B7–C3	95n.47,	166C4	100n.69
525A2	112n.97		138n.58	172C3–177C2	71n.114
526E4–5	123	246A7–B8	139n.62	174B4–5	71n.115
527D8–E3	112n.97	246B1	139n.65	175C2–3	71n.115
529D8–E3	152n.106	247A5–7	81n.9	176A5–9	72n.116
530A5–8	57n.68	247A9–10	139n.64	176B1	189n.80
531C9–D4	95n.51	247D8–E4	139n.63,	181B–183C	59n.73
532A1–D4	95n.51		236n.53	182A4–E12	82n.12
532B1	122	248E6–249A2	94n.46	184B3–186E10	216n.62,
532C6–7	123	248E6–249A5	140n.67,		218n.66
532E2–3	123		140n.69,	184E8–185A2	101n.70
533A8–9	122		152n.105	185A4–12	101n.72
533B5–C6	47n.33	249D4	125n.15	185E1	101n.73
533C7	128n.25	250B8–C4	143n.73	186A6–B9	48n.36,
533C7–D4	122	251A5–C7	84n.17,		63n.91,
533C8–534A1	68n.104		143n.75		164n.3
533C9	57n.67	251D5–252A4	143n.74	186B2–4	104n.79
534A3	125n.17	254A8–10	6n.7,	186B6–8	106n.82
534B3–D1	122,		73n.124,	186B11–C10	102n.75
	126n.20,		145n.84	186C7–D5	106n.83
	231n.36	254B8–255E6	138n.61,	196D–199C	114n.101
537C7	159n.128		144n.78,	197B–D	114n.102
540A7–B1	123,		147n.87	201D–E	143n.75
	186n.63	254D12	95n.47,		
540B6–C2	123		143n.76	*Timaeus* (*Tim.*)	
551D5–7	184n.59	255B11–C4	144n.79	27D5–28A4	45n.23,
553C5	192n.89	255C13–14	145n.82		77n.2,
554E4–6	178n.44	255D3–E1	145n.80		89n.27,
580E5	192n.89	255E2–6	138n.61,		90n.28,
581A6	192n.89		145n.81		131n.39
589A7–B1	178n.45	263B6–D4	83n.14	29A3	153n.111
589C6	173n.30			29D7–30C1	241n.76
597D2	141n.70	*Statesman* (*Sts.*)		29E1–3	152n.104,
606A7–8	175n.36	262D–E	84n.15		188n.76
608E6–609A4	63n.91,	269D	151n.102	30A6–7	59n.76
	164n.3	270A	151n.102	30B1	94n.45
610E10–611A2	89n.27	273B–C	151n.102	30B4–5	94n.45
611E1–612A4	65n.94	278D8–E2	72n.118	30C2–31A1	59n.77,
611E2–3	90n.27	281E1–5	47n.42		93n.40,
613B1	189n.80	283D8–9	131n.39		152n.105,
617E5	191n.88	283E8	164n.4		153n.110
619B7–D1	72n.118,	300C	54n.55	31B4–8	178n.44
	175n.36			32A7–B2	178n.44
		Symposium (*Symp.*)		34B–35B	226n.10
Sophist (*Soph.*)		192C–D	172n.26	35A1–8	90n.32,
216C2–D2	135n.51	204D–206B	60n.81,		95n.51,
242D6	129n.29		188n.70		99n.64,
243D8–E2	136n.53	211A1	90n.27		147n.85
244B6–10	129n.29,	211B1–2	90n.27	37A2–B3	90n.32,
	137n.57	211D1–3	66n.101		99n.65,
244B6–245E5	137n.55	212A1–2	66n.101,		131n.39,
244B6–7	137n.54		188n.74		132n.44
244C1–2	137n.55			37C6–D7	89n.25,
244C8–E13	137n.56	*Theaetetus* (*Tht.*)			90n.27
245A1–3	138n.60	152C5–6	100n.68	37D2	90n.27
245A8–9	137n.55,	153B	174n.34	37D6	90n.27,
	138n.59	156A5	47n.32		96n.57

INDEX LOCORUM   299

37E1–38B5	91n.34,	1.2.2.7	250n.13	5.3	243n.84
	132n.43	1.4.2.25–28	243n.84	5.3.11.1–18	228n.22
38A2	89n.27,	1.4.2.31–3.39	242n.79	5.3.15	260n.57
	90n.30,	1.7.1.16–17	91n.36,	5.3.15.20–26	232n.43
	91n.33,		252n.21	5.3.15.30–32	230n.31
	93n.43	1.7.2.4	252n.22	5.3.15.33	230n.30
38A4–5	90n.31	1.8.7.12–13	245n.89	5.3.16.2	230n.30
38B6–7	90n.31			5.3.17.8–9	252n.22
38C3–5	90n.31	2.4.5.32–34	228n.22	5.3.5.22–23	227n.16
38E–39E	91n.35	2.7	243n.84	5.3.7.23–24	230n.32,
40B5	90n.27	2.9.18.16	227n.18		231n.33
40D–41D	154n.115	2.9.6.40	245n.89		
41D4–42A3	147n.86,	2.9.8.22–25	230n.32,	5.4.1.24–25	230n.30
	226n.10		230n.33	5.4.1.34–36	188n.76
42D5	90n.31	3.1.9.4–16	191n.85	5.4.2.1–12	228n.21
42E5–6	188n.76,	3.4.3.24	246n.91	5.4.2.15–20	244n.84
	190n.83	3.8.1	228n.22	5.4.2.24–25	228n.22
46C7	49n.42	3.8.10.5–10	190n.83	5.4.2.38	230n.30
46D1	49n.42	3.8.10.14–15	260n.57	5.4.2.38–39	230n.33
46E3–5	49n.42	3.9.4	260n.57	5.4.12.28–29	230n.30
46E7–47C4	54n.55			5.5.9	231n.34
47A4–B1	70n.111	4.1.1.48–53	244n.84	5.5.12.40–49	190n.83
47E3–48B2	49n.42,	4.3.5.6	246n.91	5.6.5.1–8	244n.84
	59n.75,	4.3.6.13	227n.18	5.8.9.23–24	232n.43
	153n.109,	4.3.12.3–4	246n.91	5.8.13.20	184n.58
	226n.15,	4.3.12.30–32	232n.41	5.9.7	229n.27
	242n.77	4.5.7.15–17	230n.32,	5.9.8.13–15	230n.32,
48C2–6	59n.79,		230n.33		231n.22
	154n.112	4.5.7.51–55	230n.32,		
51D3–52A4	49n.42,		230n.33	6.1.26.1–7	237n.55
	77n.2	4.7.3.1–5	244n.84	6.1.26.12–17	239n.63
52B2	107n.86	4.7.8²	243n.83	6.2.12.12–14	250n.15
52B3–5	47n.32	4.7.8².7–21	245n.90	6.2.15.15–16	232n.43
52D–53C	97n.61	4.7.10.32–33	246n.91	6.2.17.18–19	252n.22
53B4–5	59n.78,	4.7.13.1–3	246n.91	6.2.19.18–21	229n.2
	93n.41,	4.8.4.31–35	246n.91	6.2.21.6–11	232n.43
	152n.106,	4.8.6.1–18	188n.76,	6.2.22.24–29	230n.32,
	153n.109,		190n.83		231n.33
	154n.112	4.8.8.8	246n.91	6.4.14.16–22	246n.91
53D4–7	159n.79,			6.4.2	231n.34
	54n.112	5.1.1	250n.14	6.4.9.36	244n.84
68E4–7	49n.42	5.1.3.11–15	190n.83	6.5.1.25–26	231n.34
69C–D	216n.61	5.1.6.4–5	260n.57	6.5.9.36–40	232n.43
69D7	213n.51	5.1.6.27–30	190n.83	6.6.1.1–14	184n.58
76D6	49n.42	5.1.6.34	230n.32	6.6.8.17–18	229n.27
86C7–D1	173n.31	5.1.6.47–48	228n.22	6.7.5.26–29	246n.91
87C4–6	150n.98	5.1.7	228n.24	6.7.8.4–8	229n.27
88A9–B2	183n.57	5.1.7.1–7	228n.22	6.7.14.11–15	232n.43
90B6–C4	65n.94,	5.1.7.9–10	230n.30	6.7.15–17	228n.22
	171n.23,	5.1.8.1–10	226n.12	6.7.16.19–22	244n.84
	189n.80	5.1.8.10–14	225n.4	6.7.17.10	229n.29
		5.1.8.23–27	226n.13	6.7.18.5–6	230n.32,
		5.2.1.1–2	230n.31		231n.33
PLOTINUS		5.2.1.3–4	260n.57	6.7.21.4–6	230n.32,
		5.2.1.7–21	190n.83,		231n.33
Enneads (Enn.)			246n.2	6.7.22.8–9	187n.69
				6.7.23.18	252n.21
1.1.9.20–22	244n.84	5.2.1.10–14	228n.22	6.7.25.1–16	165n.8

300   INDEX LOCORUM

6.7.32.31	230n.30	6.1051.34–		57, p.56.14–16	252n.25
6.7.37.18–22	228n.22	1064.12	127n.23	75, p.70.28–	
6.7.40.13–14	230n.30	6.1069.5–6	253n.32	p.72.4	248n.4
6.7.41.26–27	244n.84	6.1069.23ff	250n.15	113	247n.3
6.7.42.21–24	232n.40,	6.1097.10ff	247n.3		
	232n.41	7.1135.17–21	231n.34	*Platonic Theology* (*PT*)	
6.8.6.41–43	246n.91	7.1145.26–		(Saffrey/Westerink)	
6.8.8.12–13	231n.34	1146.21	251n.20	1.14, p.66.8–11	249n.11
6.8.8.22	252n.21	7.1149.24–		1.22, p.101.27–	
6.8.8.22	91n.36	1150.27	251n.20	p.102.1	249n.8
6.8.9.45	230n.30	7.1150.13–17	252n.25	2.1, p.3.6–8	252n.25
6.8.11.32	91n.36,	7.1152.33ff	249n.11	2.4, p.34.24–	
	252n.21	7.1153.3–6	249n.11	p.35.9	252n.23
6.8.14.39	230n.31	7.1172.18–19	252n.24	2.6.p.40.9–17	247n.3
6.8.14.41	233n.46	7.1190.4–1191.7	253n.29	2.7.p.46.13–20	165n.8
6.8.15.1–2	172n.26,	7.58 (Klibansky)	247n.3	2.7.p.49.14	127n.21
	187n.69	7.64.1–24		2.7, p.50.12–	
6.8.16.13	187n.69	(Klibansky)	248n.5	p.51.19	252n.33
6.8.16.15–17	229n.29,	7.68.2–4		3.7, p.29.16–25	226n.13
	231n.35	(Klibansky)	251n.19	3.3, p.13.13–16	251n.17
6.8.17.25–27	91n.36,	7.74.3ff		3.4, p.14.11–	
	252n.21	(Klibanksy)	193n.91	p.15.15	252n.27
6.8.20.13–15	229n.29	7.76 (Klibansky)	257n.43	3.4, p.15.24–26	228n.23
6.9.1.20–26	232n.40			3.6, p.26.13–27	249n.11
6.9.3	193n.91	*Commentary on Plato's*		3.6, p.28.18–19	252n.28
6.9.3.16	226n.13	*Republic* (*In Remp.*) (Kroll)		3.12,	
6.9.6	226n.13	1.269.19–270.20	165n.9	p.45.13–p.46.22	252n.28
6.9.6.36–37	230n.30	1.270.20–24	165n.10	3.14, p.51.6–7	252n.28
6.9.6.44–45	233n.46	1.271.20–26	165n.12	3.24, p.86.7–9	252n.28
6.9.9.11-1–3	184n58	1.273.11	165n.12		
		1.278. 22–279.2	165n.8	**SEXTUS EMPIRICUS**	

PORPHYRY

Life of Plotinus

17.1–2	224n.2

PROCLUS

Commentary on Plato's Alcibiades (*In Alc.*) (Westerink)

30.16–17	189n.77

Commentary on Plato's Parmenides (*In Parm.*) (Steel)

1.630–645	16n.4
1.702.29–34	252n.26
1.707.8–10	250n.15
2.726.2–3	250n.13
4.921.5–922.1	250n.13
5.1032.20–24	252n.26
6.1041.1–20	130n.35
6.1041.24–26	251n.20
6.1043.9–29	252n.26

Commentary on Plato's Timaeus (*In Tim.*) (Diehl)

1.285.29–286.4	247n.3
1.303.24–310.2	227n.19
1.304.6–9	231n.34
1.313.15–22	250n.15
1.363.26–364.11	253n.29
1.378.25–26	228n.23
2.240.4–10	250n.15
4.12.22–30	252n.26

Elements of Theology (*ET*) (Dodds)

Props.

1, p.2.1	252n.23
3, p.4.1	251n.18
13	127n.21
23, p.26.22–24	250n.15
25–39	190n.82
29, p.34.3–4	248n.6
32, p.36.3–4	249n.7
33, p.36.1–6	249n.12
39, p.40.27–28	249n.9

Against the Dogmatists (*M.*) (Mutschmann/Mau)

7.38	245n.87
9.13–14	67n.103
9.153	244n.86
10.276–277	156n.117
11.8–11	240n.70

Outlines of Pyrrhonism (*PH*) (Mutschmann/Mau)

1.79–91	16n.5
2.81–83	245n.87

SIMPLICIUS

Commentary on Aristotle's Physics (*In Phys.*) (Diels)

151, 6–19	159n.129
453, 22–30	159n.129
454, 28–455, 3	156n.117
454, 809	160n.132
545, 23–25	159n.129
795, 11–17	257n.48
795, 15–17	255n.37

Index Locorum

SPEUSIPPUS

Fragments (Isnardi Parente)

STOBAEUS

Eclogues (Ecl.) (Wachsmuth/Hense)

1.77.21–79.17	239n.66
1.78.18–20	241n.75
1.79.1–12	241n.75

STOICORUM VETERUM FRAGMENTA (SVF) (VON ARNIM)

1.160	241n.75
1.65	240n.71
1.68	240n.72
1.85	239n.64
1.89	236n.52
1.98	237n.56
2.299	237n.56
2.300	237n.56
2.311	237n.57
2.313	239n.63
2.329–332	238n.61
2.336	236n.52
2.361	235n.48
2.383	239n.65
2.395	239n.68
2.966	238n.62
3.265	244n.86
3.4	240n.73
3.95	244n.86
3.274	244n.86

Commentary on Aristotle's Metaphysics (In Meta.) (Rabe)

THEOPHRASTUS

Fragments (Wimmer)

48	197n.69
	245n.87

Metaphysics (Laks/Most)

4b1ff	222n.79

XENOCRATES

Fragments (Isnardi Parente)

213	153n.109

XENOPHON

Memorabilia (Mem.)

1.2.35	44n.20

www.ingramcontent.com/pod-product-compliance
Ingram Content Group UK Ltd.
Pitfield, Milton Keynes, MK11 3LW, UK
UKHW022030200825
462079UK00006B/243